Imitation in Infancy

This is the first book to bring together the extensive modern evidence for innate imitation in babies. Contemporary research has shown imitation to be a natural mechanism of learning and communication which deserves to be at centre stage in developmental psychology. Yet, the very possibility of imitation in newborn humans has had a controversial history. Defining imitation has proved to be far from straightforward, and scientific evidence for its existence in neonates is only now becoming accepted, despite more than a century of inquiry. In this book, some of the world's foremost researchers on imitation and intellectual development review evidence for imitation in newborn babies. They discuss the development of imitation in infancy, in both normal and atypical populations and in comparison with other primate species, stressing the fundamental importance of imitation in human development, as a foundation of communication and a precursor to symbolic processes.

JACQUELINE NADEL is Research Director in the Laboratoire de Psychobiologie du Développement, at the CNRS, Paris. She has published widely on imitation and communication in infants and is the editor of the French journal *ENFANCE*.

GEORGE BUTTERWORTH is Professor of Psychology in the School of Cognitive and Computing Sciences at the University of Sussex, England. His research has spanned perception and cognitive development in infancy and early childhood, including recent extensive studies on manual pointing in babies. He is currently editor of the journal *Developmental Science* and is General Editor of the book series *Cambridge Studies in Cognitive and Perceptual Development*.

Cambridge Studies in Cognitive Perceptual Development

Series Editors
George Butterworth (General Editor), University of Sussex, UK
Giyoo Hatano, Keio University, Tokyo, Japan
Kurt W. Fischer, Harvard University, USA

Advisory Board
Patricia M. Greenfield, University of California, Los Angeles, USA
Paul Harris, University of Oxford, UK
Daniel Stern, University of Geneva, Switzerland
Esther Thelen, Indiana University, USA

The aim of this series is to provide a scholarly forum for current theoretical and empirical issues in cognitive and perceptual development. As the twentieth century draws to a close, the field is no longer dominated by monolithic theories. Contemporary explanations build on the combined influences of biological, cultural, contextual and ecological factors in well-defined research domains. In the field of cognitive development, cultural and situational factors are widely recognised as influencing the emergence and forms of reasoning in children. In perceptual development, the field has moved beyond the opposition of 'innate' and 'acquired' to suggest a continuous role for perception in the acquisition of knowledge. These approaches and issues will all be reflected in the series which will also address such important research themes as the indissociable link between perception and action in the developing motor system, the relationship between perceptual and cognitive development to modern ideas on the development of the brain, the significance of developmental processes themselves, dynamic systems theory and contemporary work in the psychodynamic tradition, especially as it relates to the foundations of self-knowledge.

Forthcoming titles include

Margaret Harris and Giyoo Hatano (eds.)
Learning to Read and Spell: A cross-linguistic perspective

Paul Light and Karen Littleton
Social Processes in Children's Learning

Michael Siegal and Candida Peterson (eds.)
Children's Understanding of Biology and Health

Nobuo Masataka
The Onset of Language

Imitation in Infancy

Edited by

Jacqueline Nadel

and

George Butterworth

CAMBRIDGE
UNIVERSITY PRESS

PUBLISHED BY THE PRESS SYNDICATE OF THE UNIVERSITY OF CAMBRIDGE
The Pitt Building, Trumpington Street, Cambridge CB2 1RP, United Kingdom

CAMBRIDGE UNIVERSITY PRESS
The Edinburgh Building, Cambridge, CB2 2RU, UK   http://www.cup.cam.ac.uk
40 West 20th Street, New York, NY 10011–4211, USA   http://www.cup.org
10 Stamford Road, Oakleigh, Melbourne 3166, Australia

© Cambridge University Press 1999

First published 1999

Printed in the United Kingdom at the University Press, Cambridge

Typeset in 10/12pt Monotype Plantin in QuarkXPress™ [SE]

A catalogue record for this book is available from the British Library

Library of Congress cataloguing in publication data

ISBN 0 521 58033 1 hardback

Contents

Notes on contributors

DR KIM A. BARD is at the Yerkes Regional Primate Research Center, Emory University, Atlanta, Georgia, USA

PROFESSOR GEORGE BUTTERWORTH is at the Psychology Department in the School of Cognitive and Computing Sciences, University of Sussex, England

DR GERALDO A. FIAMENGHI JR. is at the Instituto de Psicologia, PUC-Campinas, Brazil

DR CAROLINE GUÉRINI is at the Laboratoire Psycho-Biologie du Développement, Paris, France

PROFESSOR MIKAEL HEIMANN is at the Department of Special Education and Department of Psychology, Göteborg University, Sweden

THEANO KOKKINAKI is at the Department of Psychology, University of Edinburgh, Scotland

PROFESSOR GIANNIS KUGIUMUTZAKIS is in the Department of Psychology, University of Crete, Greece

PROFESSOR ANDREW N. MELTZOFF is Head of Developmental Psychology at the University of Washington, Seattle, Washington, USA

M. KEITH MOORE is a Research Scientist at the Center on Human Development and Disability, University of Washington, Seattle, Washington, USA

DR JACQUELINE NADEL is Research Director at the Laboratoire de Psycho-Biologie du Développement, CNRS, Paris, France

ANN PEZÉ is at the Laboratoire de Psycho-Biologie du Développement, CNRS, Paris, France

CHRISTINE RIVET is at the Foyer pour Adultes Sourds-Aveugles, La Varenne, APSA, Poitiers, France

DR SALLY J. ROGERS is at the University of Colorado Health Sciences Center, Denver, Colorado, USA

DR CONNIE L. RUSSELL is at the Yerkes Regional Primate Research Center, Emory University, Atlanta, Georgia, USA

EMERITUS PROFESSOR COLWYN TREVARTHEN is at the Department of Child Psychology and Psychobiology at the University of Edinburgh, Scotland

DR EVA ULLSTADIUS is at the Department of Education and Department of Psychology, Göteborg University, Sweden

The late PROFESSOR INA Č. UŽGIRIS was with the Department of Psychology at Clark University, Worcester, Massachusetts, USA

It was with great regret that we learned of the death of Ina Užgiris, just before this book reached completion. We thank Vytautas I. Užgiris for his assistance with the proofs.

Jacqueline Nadel and George Butterworth
September 1998

Introduction
Immediate imitation rehabilitated at last

Jacqueline Nadel and George Butterworth

This collection of papers offers a timely summary of the 'state of the art' in contemporary research on imitation in human infants. The book brings together, for the first time, the foremost researchers on imitation in babies, and it addresses the topic in normal, comparative and psychopathological perspectives.

Until the 1970s the term 'imitation' did not even appear as a keyword in reference bases such as Psychological Abstracts. The word was simply taken to be synonymous with observational learning, which, as Bandura (1971) defined it, occurs without incentives, without trial and error and does not require reinforcement. The development of imitation was most readily captured under the keyword 'symbolic play' and referred in particular to the ability to imitate after a delay and without the model being present (so called deferred imitation). The existence of immediate imitation in development was hardly suspected and its role was ignored.

Valentine (1930) quite early on noted the chaotic state of research on imitation and proposed that the ambiguous definition of imitation might explain this disagreement in results. Forty years later Aronfreed (1969) made the same statement, although by then three systematic approaches to imitation could be distinguished in current research. The first approach considered imitation to be a particular case of instrumental learning. A second approach viewed imitation as allowing the acquisition of new responses on the basis of social experience, and a third approach explained imitation as a form of cognitive development (Piaget 1945). In their review of research on imitation, Hartup and Coates (1970) summarised results obtained within a learning theory perspective and emphasised how meagre was the number of studies. When defined in terms of comparisons of imitation ability at different ages, only ten studies were available in 1970. Eight years later, Yando, Seitz and Zigler (1978) identified seventy-six new studies but this hardly amounted to a dramatic increase in interest in the field.

How can we explain this neglect? Yando, Seitz and Zigler (1978) attributed it to the long-lasting imperialism of learning theories in the United

1

States. Learning theories as a group tend to assimilate microgenesis and ontogenesis into a single explanatory system, thus offering learning as an explanation for development. Within this framework, developmental studies are not necessary, since learning accounts for development. However convincing this explanation may be, it does not explain why immediate imitation was neglected in countries where developmental theories were strong, as in Europe, and, especially, Francophone Europe. In the European case, there are at least two explanations for this neglect, the first related to the Platonic tradition in philosophy and the second to the influence of Piaget in developmental psychology.

An insidious influence on imitation research had been established for centuries in the Platonic tradition. Girard, Oughourlian and Lefort (1978), in their book *Des choses cachées depuis la fondation du monde,* analysed the negative influence of Plato on the study of imitation. Plato characterised imitation as holding danger for individual identity and for self-consciousness. Mimesis was seen to limit intelligence, destroy identity and even to lead to murder or suicide! This mythic fear was so universal that in some cultures it resulted in forbidding similarity as, for example, in the compulsory disappearance of one of a pair of identical twins, or when the son was too much like the father. Even today, conformism, lack of initiative and submissiveness are associated with imitation. In developmental psychopathology, immediate echolalia in children with autism is still considered by some psychiatrists as a negative symptom, rather than as a positive basis for the development of communication.

This led to generations of psychologists following Guillaume's (1925) definition which implies that imitation requires at least an elementary level of representation. For instance, the famous French psychologist Wallon (1942) adopted this restrictive definition, claiming that imitation does not occur prior to eighteen months. Wallon used the term 'mimetism' in the case of immediate matching of emotional models, and in the case of partial imitations, 'echopraxis' or 'echolalia'. He did not make any direct theoretical link between these 'pseudo-imitations' and 'real' that is to say, deferred imitation. By contrast, in the same period Piaget criticised Guillaume's definition. He proposed to define imitation as an action by which a model is reproduced, whether the process depends on perception or representation. Step by step Piaget noted any matching behaviour that occurred during sensorimotor development, including reflex-like matching. The systematic follow-up of his three children led Piaget to consider immediate imitation as separate from the process of intelligent adaptation. In intelligent acts there is a kind of equilibrium between accommodation and assimilation, whereas in immediate (or direct) imitation it is conceived exclusively as a mechanism of accommodation, whereby the organism 'bends' to the demands of the environment.

References to imitation are found in several places in Piaget's work, and there is one book devoted to the topic (Piaget, 1945). In this work, the development of imitation is described in parallel with that of sensorimotor intelligence. Piaget found no evidence of immediate hetero-imitation in the first two stages of development (0–6 months). During stage I (0–1 month), some reflex-like behaviours were noted followed by sporadic imitation during stage II (1–5 months), if the experimenter modelled behaviours which had just been displayed by the baby. At this stage, imitation is still governed by circular reactions. During stage III (6–9 months), Piaget noted that babies will now imitate sounds and gestures which are part of their repertoire. For Piaget, imitation only becomes interestingly intelligent between 9 and 12 months (from stage IV to stage VI) as the capacity for deferred action arises. The first indices of this capacity emerge during stage IV, when the infant becomes able to imitate movements, such as facial movements, of parts of the body which she cannot see. This implies a kind of representation in action, in its proper meaning of a second presentation. This capacity increases during stage V when new movements can be imitated. Piaget argued that deferred imitation available at stage VI marks the beginning of representation and is a key aspect of the symbolic process. This is revealed by the concomitant development of symbolic play, words and drawing from 18 to 24 months. Until the 1970s, the exciting question of the emergence of the semiotic function as framed by Piaget led Francophone studies to focus almost exclusively on the role of deferred imitation in the acquisition of symbolic processes.

Developmental studies carried out since the 1970s have progressively changed this climate of opinion. Notice, for instance, that Piaget had regarded imitation as a single ability, an assumption questioned by later researchers who found that gestural and vocal imitation develop differently (Užgiris and Hunt, 1987). Many important discoveries have been made and these have completely altered the theoretical basis for understanding the contribution of imitation to development. This book addresses the major issues arising from recent research with contributions by the foremost researchers in the area.

The chapters in the first section of the book reassess the Piagetian tradition especially concerning the relation between immediate imitation, deferred imitation and mental representation. We begin with the seminal work of Meltzoff and Moore who make particular reference to the innate origins of a theory of mind, to the precocious appearance of both immediate and deferred imitation in human development and to the mechanisms which may serve the innate ability to imitate. The importance of imitation as a precocious index of preference for human stimulation and communication is also stressed by Kugiumutzakis in his chapter.

The second section moves on to theoretical issues concerned with the ontogeny and phylogeny of imitation. Butterworth considers the history of research on neonatal imitation, problems of definition and theoretical issues concerning the mechanisms and motives for imitation in ontogeny and evolution. The comparative study of imitation is further discussed by Bard and Russell with particular reference to chimpanzees, our closest primate relatives, animals who are often considered to be the prototypical mimics.

In the third section, which focuses on the social and emotional motives for imitation, Trevarthen, Kokkinaki and Fiamenghi stress especially the role of primary intersubjectivity or the meeting of minds in early imitative interaction sequences. In her chapter, Užgiris considers imitation in the context of activity theory, as a form of interpersonal goal-directed action.

The final section of the book explores the value of imitation as a marker for normal and atypical communicative development. Nadel, Guérini and Rivat propose that spontaneous imitation is an evolving format which first allows mutual attention and exchanges and later scaffolds intentional aspects of communication, such as turn taking and topic sharing. Children with autism showed spontaneous imitative behaviour and answered to being imitated. The prevalent cognitive models of autism disagree on the question whether imitation is a primary deficit. The predictive value of neonatal imitation for subsequent social development is addressed by Heimann and Ullstadius with particular reference to differences in social competence between autistic and Down's syndrome children. The link between impairments in immediate imitation and impairments in communication in autistic children is addressed by Rogers. She is the co-author of a theory which proposes that a central deficit (executive function impairment) hinders the development of immediate imitation in autism. In her chapter, she develops the hypothesis that a praxic deficit causes disruption in social co-ordination.

We hope this book will serve as a positive testimony to the importance of imitation in human development and re-establish immediate imitation as a fundamental mechanism of communication in humans.

REFERENCES

Aronfreed, J. (1969). The problem of imitation. In L. P. Lipsitt and H. W. Reese (eds.), *Advances in child development and behavior.* New York: Academic Press.
Bandura, A. (1971). *Psychological modeling: Conflicting theories.* Chicago Aldine.

Girard, R., Oughourlian, J-M. and Lefort, G. (1978). *Des choses cachees depuis la fondation du monde.* Paris: Grasset.

Guillaume, P. (1925). *L'imitation chez l'enfant.* Paris: Alcan.

Hartup, W. W. and Coates, B. (1970). The role of imitation in childhood socialisation. In R. A. Hope, G. A. Milton and E. Simmel (eds.), *Early experiences and the processes of socialisation.* New York: Academic Press.

Piaget, J. (1945). *La formation du symbole chez l'enfant.* Neuchatel-Paris: Delachaux et Niestle. English translation: *Play dreams and imitation in childhood* (1952). New York: Norton.

Valentine, C. W. (1930). The psychology of imitation with special reference to early childhood. *British Journal of Psychology*, 21, 105–32.

Wallon, H. (1942). *De l'acte à la pensée.* Paris: Flammarion.

Yando, R., Seitz, V. and Zigler, E. (1978). *Imitation: a developmental perspective.* Hillsdale: Lawrence Erlbaum.

Užgiris, I. Č. and Hunt, J. McV. (1987). *Infant performance and experience: New findings with the ordinal scales.* Urbana: University of Illinois Press.

Part I

Imitation in human infancy

1   Persons and representation: why infant imitation is important for theories of human development

Andrew N. Meltzoff and M. Keith Moore

A complete theory of early development will have to account for infants' understanding of both people and things. There has been a plethora of research on infants' perception and understanding of the physical world. A distinguishing feature of research on infant imitation is that it informs us about infants' understanding of *persons*. Just as inanimate objects and their movements in space are presented to infants in studying their understanding of the physical world, people and dynamic human acts are presented to infants in studies of imitation. Imitation is one of the most sensitive tools available for investigating the foundations of infants' understanding of people.

There are also other means of investigating early notions of persons – for example, the perception and discrimination of human faces and biological motion. Research on imitation complements this work and enriches it in two ways. First, infant imitation not only tells us about perception (events must be perceived to be imitated), but about linkages between perception and action. Second, imitation provides information about infants' notions of self, other and the mapping between the two. By the very act of imitating, infants show us that they relate their hands to our hands, their faces to our faces, and their specific acts to similar ones of ours. We will argue that infants' apprehension that adults are at some level 'like me' and that seen acts are 'like the ones I do' are equivalence classes that have some of the most far-reaching implications of infancy, ones foundational for later developments in intersubjectivity, communication and social cognition.

In the modern era, infant imitation has been underutilised as a source of information for theories of human development.[1] This can be traced to two misconceptions. One wide-spread misconception is that infants learn to imitate – either by reinforcement of matching behaviour, acculturation, or through Piagetian stage-like mechanisms. It has now been shown that newborns only a few minutes old can imitate human acts (e.g., Meltzoff and Moore, 1983). Imitation is an innate capacity in the human species.[2] Imitation is something infants bring to their very first interactions with other people. It is not the product of learning, but rather a species-typical mechanism for social learning and the transmission of acquired characteristics from one generation to the next.

A second misconception is that early imitation is rote, mindless and automatic. Because imitating motor movements is so easily accomplished by adults, it is assumed to be so in infancy. But surely this is mistaken reasoning. Even if adult imitation does not require focal attention, this may be the result of age and practice rather than the initial state of infants. We will argue that infant imitation consists of effortful, intentional acts. This view is buttressed by new empirical evidence showing that when infants make mistakes imitating, they correct their behaviour to match the seen behaviour of others. What is crucial about infant imitation, then, is not so much *that* infants imitate, but the manner in which they do so, which provides clues to the psychological mechanisms which mediate it and the functions it serves.

Janus-like character of imitation: social and cognitive perspectives

The Roman god Janus was depicted as having two heads that enabled him to look in two directions at once. Imitation has the Janus-like quality of providing perspectives on both cognitive and social domains.

Cognitive perspective

Infant imitation bears on questions of perception and the control of action. This is a straightforward theoretical connection, inasmuch as infants see a modelled act and spontaneously produce an action based on this perception. Described in this way, imitation bears resemblance to a host of other phenomena showing early perceptual-motor coupling. For example, young infants can catch moving objects (Van der Meer, Van der Weel and Lee, 1994; Von Hofsten, 1983), make postural compensations to shifts in the visual framework (Bertenthal, 1996; Butterworth and Hicks, 1977; Jouen, 1990) and act to protect against looming objects (Bower, Broughton and Moore, 1970). Gibson (1966, 1979) argued that such cases show a tight coupling (he called it 'resonance') between visual perception and distally appropriate output without requiring learning to associate the stimulus with the adaptive response. Imitation might be a similar case, one that reveals an *interpersonal coupling*. Infants are regulating their actions to bring them in line with a dynamically changing animate display, rather than an inanimate object or visual framework, but many of the same issues about perceptuomotor regulation arise.

Imitation also informs us about preverbal representation. The key evidence derives from discoveries about deferred imitation, in which infants are imitating a person or action that has disappeared from view. In deferred imitation, infants are not calibrating their actions to what is before their eyes, but according to their memory of a now-absent event. In certain cases of deferred imitation to be discussed, the target act may have disappeared a day or week previously. In other cases, we will show that infants *override* their current perception and are motivated to imitate an action from the past even though presently seeing a contradictory act.

Facial imitation raises issues of representation and invisibility in a different way. In facial imitation, infants see the adult's facial expression but cannot see their own face. If facial imitation is performed after the model has disappeared, there is a kind of double invisibility. Infants must match a gesture they no longer see with an act of their own that they cannot see. Such distancing from the here-and-now world was thought to be impossible for young infants as classically conceived. New evidence suggests that even very young infants can successfully perform deferred facial imitation (Meltzoff and Moore, 1994, 1997). Once again, it is not just *that* infants imitate but the conditions under which they do so that provides insights for theory construction.

Taken together – the phenomena of immediate, deferred and facial imitation – provide a rich evidentiary basis for describing the origins, mechanisms and development of imitation within a cognitive perspective.

Social perspective

According to everyday folk psychology (sometimes called 'theory of mind'), people are special entities in the world of moving objects. People are viewed as sentient beings who wilfully pursue their intentions and deserve special moral status. Even the most intelligent machines are not treated in the same way. Where does this construal of people come from?

We think that infants are launched in their career as folk psychologists with the primary perceptual judgment, 'Here is something like me.' The apprehension that others are *like me* is the foundation on which our more mature folk psychology is constructed. Even our moral sense is anchored here. We 'do unto others' in a special way because there is a deeply felt equivalence between self and other. Without a sense of like-me-ness, we do not think our folk psychology and moral judgments would take the form they do.

Theories of development from Freud to Piaget explicitly denied that young infants could apprehend equivalences between self and other. Among the experiments that changed this view are those showing that newborns imitate facial and manual movements. These findings suggest that young infants can, at some level of processing, recognise equivalences between body-transformations as felt in the self and body-transformations as seen in others. This has profound implications for the origins of understanding persons.

These findings bolster nativist claims. Modern nativists sometimes pit the existence of initial structure against development, however, as if these are either/or propositions. In fact, a powerful original state does not preclude developmental change. For example, we think that developmental change is prompted by social interactions in which parents imitate infants, mirroring their actions and emotional expressions back to them. The experience of being imitated has special significance for infants not only because of the temporal contingencies in the mutual behaviour, but because infants recognise the adult's acts as structurally similar to their own. Many things in the world can move contingently on my action, but only other humans can generatively act like infants, whatever they choose to do. We will argue that reciprocal imitation games serve as private tutorials in folk psychology, giving infants input about interpersonal mutuality that allows them to transcend their initial state.

Looking in two directions at once

Imitation is fundamentally an act of social cognition, and so any assignment of imitation into 'cognitive' or 'social' camps, however tempting for theorising, does not occur for the baby. In this essay, we will try to bring both perspectives to bear (see also Užgiris, 1981). First, deferred imitation will be examined, with the aim of uncovering what this tells us about early memory and representation. The way deferred imitation is used in the real world for acquiring culturally relevant adult behaviour patterns will also be considered. Second, facial imitation will be examined, with special emphasis on the psychological mechanisms which mediate it. We will argue that facial imitation is based on a cross-modal matching between self and other and consider the social implications of such intercorporeal correspondences. Third, we examine what prompts young infants to imitate in the first place and the adaptive functions subserved by such behaviour. Fourth, we examine the role of reciprocal imitation games in extending interpersonal understanding beyond the initial state. In each of the four sections, we first pose the problem we plan to address before marshalling the relevant empirical evidence.

Deferred imitation and infant representation

Posing the problem

In deferred imitation, infants are re-enacting behaviour on the basis of their representation of the past. An important question to be asked is: what is their representation the representation of? Two alternatives can be distinguished that have very different impacts on theory, and indeed are central to whether one wants to invoke the notion of 'infant representation' at all. One alternative is that infants represent the past visual event. Another is that they are remembering and repeating their own past actions.

This distinction is relevant both to modern cognitive-neuroscience and to classical Piagetian theory. Cognitive-neuroscience has shown that different types of memory are functionally dissociable and mediated by different neural systems. An amnesic patient can see a person or object and subsequently have no recall of this event. The intriguing point is that not all types of memory are damaged. If such a patient learns a skill over a series of days (e.g., mirror writing) he or she will retain the skill level between sessions. Thus, a distinction has been drawn between 'procedural' versus 'declarative' memory. The former is spared in amnesia, the latter is not. The former consists of memory for skills learned gradually over a series of trials, and the latter of memories for objects or events after one-time exposure with no motor involvement. Insult to the medial temporal lobe causes such deficits in declarative but not in procedural memory (Squire, 1987; Squire, Knowlton and Musen, 1993).

This procedural–declarative distinction is reminiscent of one made in developmental psychology 50 years earlier. In classical theory, there is a difference between a 'sensorimotor' and a 'representational' stage of development (e.g., Piaget, 1952, 1962). Young infants were said to live in a rich here-and-now perceptual world and their relation to the past was highly constrained. They could retain their motor habits (circular reactions) but could not recall actions or events that had been seen but not practised. In classical developmental theory, the shift beyond sensorimotor functioning occurred at 18 months of age.

Modern findings have challenged the idea of a shift from purely sensorimotor to representational functioning at 18 months of age (e.g., Baillargeon, 1993; Bertenthal, 1996; Gopnik and Meltzoff, 1997; Mandler, 1988; Meltzoff, 1990b, 1995b; Meltzoff and Moore, 1998; Spelke, Breinlinger, Macomber and Jacobson, 1992). A pressing question for developmental science is whether a declarative-like memory system is in place from the earliest phases of infancy or whether it emerges from the procedural system. Our view is that both co-exist in the young infant, rather than one preceding the other.

The 'observation-only' design

Debates about infant representation cannot be decided simply by results showing that the past influences the present. As the foregoing makes clear, virtually every theory of infancy, including Piaget's, accommodates that. What is crucial is to devise recall tests that force infants to use the past while distinguishing: (a) repeating their own behaviour or motor habits enacted during the initial event, from (b) accessing a representation of the initial event formed without acting at Time $t1$.

Deferred imitation can be used to distinguish between these alternatives. In the 'observation-only' design developed by Meltzoff (1985, 1988c, 1988d), infants are shown a target act but not allowed to respond at Time $t1$. For example, the adult performs the target act on a novel object and does not allow the infant to handle the object. The infant is confined purely to observation. A delay is imposed, and infants are subsequently tested for deferred imitation. In this design, infants could not be retaining a habit or motor procedure, because the objects were unavailable to touch in the first place. There was no opportunity to develop the motor procedure to begin with.

Another way of testing imitation from memory is the 'observation + practice' design. In this procedure, infants are allowed to handle the objects and perform immediate imitation before the delay is imposed (e.g., Bauer and Mandler, 1992; Bauer and Hertsgaard, 1993). This still tests memory after the delay, but could be explained as remembering one's own acts rather than representing the event. In fact, in a direct comparison of procedures, Meltzoff (1990a) found that under certain circumstances practising the target act through immediate imitation at $t1$ elevates performance after the delay. We will limit the subsequent discussion to three studies that used the observation-only design to illuminate the nature and scope of early representation.

Age of onset and length of delay

The initial challenge to the view that deferred imitation marked a 'stage change' at 18 months was the discovery that 14-month-olds could imitate after a 1-day delay with impressive facility, and in fact were no worse than 24-month-olds (Meltzoff, 1985). The research has now been extended to far younger ages and longer delays. Klein and Meltzoff (in press) reported that 12-month-old infants can succeed over a 1-month delay. Deferred imitation effects have also been reported in 9-month-olds (Heimann & Meltzoff, 1996; Meltzoff, 1988d), 6-month-olds (Barr, Dowden and Hayne, 1996), and even 6-week-olds (Meltzoff and Moore, 1994) over a 24-hour delay.

A striking discovery is the length of the retention interval over which the target acts can be recalled. A recent study demonstrated that 14-month-olds can imitate with fidelity after delays as long as 4 months (Meltzoff, 1995b). This is not to say there is no forgetting. There was a rapid drop off in retention over the first 2 months, and then a more gradual decline in forgetting from 2 to 4 months. Work has also begun to trace individual differences in memory and deferred imitation. One study showed that individual infants who were poor at deferred imitation at 9 months were poor on an independent test of deferred imitation using new materials a half-year later (Heimann and Meltzoff, 1996), suggesting that deferred imitation might tap stable cognitive traits.

Apparently, deferred imitation does not mark a 'stage transition' in development, certainly not one at 18 months. We believe that the ability to act on a stored representation of perceptually absent events is the starting-point of cognitive development in infancy and not its culmination. An analysis of the preverbal representation we think supports early deferred imitation is provided elsewhere (Meltzoff, 1990b; Meltzoff and Moore, 1994, 1997, 1998).

Novel acts can be imitated

Can young infants set up a representation of a completely novel act? In one study, toddlers were shown the act of an adult leaning forward and using his forehead to touch a yellow panel (Meltzoff, 1988c; also Rast and Meltzoff, 1995). This activated a microswitch, and the panel lit up. Infants were not given a chance for immediate imitation or even a chance to explore the panel during the demonstration session. A 1-week delay was imposed. At that point infants returned to the laboratory and the panel was put out on the table. The results showed that 67% of the infants imitated the head-touch behaviour when they saw the panel. An example of the head-touch response is shown in Figure 1.1.

Such novel use of the forehead was exhibited by 0% of the controls who had not seen this act on their first visit. Successful imitation in this case must be based on observation of the adult's act, because perception of the panel itself did not elicit the target behaviour in the naive infants. Moreover, the findings tell us something about what is represented. If the only thing they remembered from *t1* is that 'the panel lit up' (an object property), they would have returned and used their hands to press it.

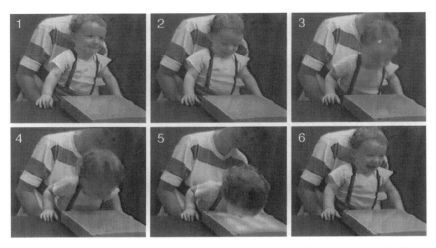

Figure 1.1. A 14-month-old infant imitating the head-touch act. Infants often mark successful imitation with a smile, as shown in photo 6.

Instead, they re-enacted the same unusual act as used by the adult. The absent act had to have been represented and used to generate the behaviour at *t2*.

Generality of deferred imitation

Infant memory and representation may differ from more mature forms by being highly context bound. For example, Rovee-Collier (1990) found that infants trained to move a mobile by footkicks could do so on the next day with no further training. However, they did not respond with foot-kicks if the pattern on the crib liner was changed from one day to the next. Everything had to remain identical between the training and test phase for this effect to be manifest.

In all of the studies of deferred imitation discussed so far, context was held constant. Perhaps constancy of context between learning and test is necessary to support early deferred imitation. If so, Piaget was right all along, not so much about the raw ability, but about an inability to use it flexibly across contexts. Such rigidity would undercut its use in the real world as a mechanism for social learning.

To test this point, infants were shown the target actions in one setting and subsequently given the objects in a changed setting. In one series of studies, 1-year-olds were shown target actions on objects in a room with the walls covered in garish polka-dot fabric. In effect, they were surrounded by a bizarre tent. After a delay ranging from 10 minutes

(Barnat, Klein and Meltzoff, 1996) to 1 month (Klein and Meltzoff, in press, Experiment 3), they were subsequently tested in a normal, white-walled laboratory room. The results showed successful deferred imitation.

It is conceivable that two university rooms, no matter how visually distinct, are both treated as the same by babies, since they are both in the category of 'not home'. Further studies investigated deferred imitation in and out of the infants' homes. In one study, an experimenter drove to the infant's house and demonstrated target actions while the infant sat at the living-room table or in the backyard in the sunshine. After a 1-week delay, infants were brought to the windowless laboratory and tested by a different adult. Even under these conditions the 12-month-olds produced deferred imitation (Klein and Meltzoff, in press, Experiment 2).

The utility of deferred imitation in 'real world' situations has also been demonstrated. It is well established that infants imitate their peers during ongoing play episodes (e.g., Eckerman, 1993; Nadel, 1986; Nadel-Brulfert and Baudonnière, 1982). We have also found deferred imitation of peer behaviour. In one study, 16-month-olds at a day-care centre watched peers play with toys in unique ways. The next day, an adult went to the infants' house (change of context) and put the toys on the floor. The result showed that infants played with the toys in the particular ways that they had seen peers play 24 hours earlier (Hanna and Meltzoff, 1993). In another study, 14-month-olds saw a person on television demonstrate target acts. When they returned to the laboratory the next day, they were handed the 3-D toys for the first time. Infants re-enacted the events they saw on TV the previous day (Meltzoff, 1988a).

Taken together, this research indicates that deferred imitation is robust across a variety of contextual changes. For imitation to be useful in cultural learning (Meltzoff, 1988b: Tomasello, Kruger and Ratner, 1993), it would have to function with just such flexibility. Infants could learn from observing at grandma's house and apply this knowledge in the home.

Facial imitation, crossmodal mapping, and the AIM model

Posing the problem

Infants can see the adult's face but cannot see their own faces. They can feel their own faces move, but have no access to the feelings of movement in the other. The holy grail for theories of facial imitation is to elucidate the mechanism by which infants can connect the felt but unseen movements of the self with the seen but unfelt movements of the other.

Innateness

On the standard view, newborns should have no intrinsic link between a facial act of another and their own unseen facial movements. Such links were thought to be forged through experience, for example with mirrors (which made the unseen visible) or by manual exploration of faces (which rendered both self and other in tangible terms). To eliminate these learning experiences we tested imitation in newborn babies in a hospital setting (Meltzoff and Moore, 1983, 1989) the youngest being 42 minutes old. A large sample of newborns was tested ($N = 80$). The results demonstrated successful facial imitation. This finding of imitation in the first hours after birth has been replicated by several investigators (e.g., Field, Woodson, Greenberg and Cohen, 1982; Kaitz, Meschulach-Sarfaty, Auerbach and Eidelman, 1988; Kugiumutzakis, 1985; Reissland, 1988; Vinter, 1986). Apparently, the capacity for facial imitation is innate.

Flexibility and scope

Some form of nativism is called for, but we cannot stop there. The spectrum of choices ranges from reflexive, wholly stimulus-driven behaviour on the one end, to a more intentional cross-modal matching of human acts on the other end. Adults can act intentionally; can newborns? The boundary between a reflex and an intentional act may be fuzzy, but one can sharpen the issue. It makes a difference to our theories of mind to determine whether the newborn is best described as a collection of reflexes and no more, or as an intentional organism.

One relevant finding concerns the range of gestures that can be imitated, the generativity of the phenomenon. Adults can imitate a wide range of acts because they can use the other's body as a target, or guide, against which to fashion a matching response. We need to know about the range of gestures that can be differentially imitated in infancy. In Meltzoff and Moore (1977), 12- to 21-day-olds were shown to imitate four different gestures, including facial and manual movements. Infants did not confuse either actions or organs. They differentially responded to tongue protrusion with tongue protrusion and not lip protrusion, showing that the specific *body part* could be identified. They also differentially responded to lip protrusion versus lip opening, showing that differential *movement patterns* could be duplicated using the same body part.

Numerous independent studies have found imitation of tongue-protrusion and mouth-opening in infants less than 2 months old (Abravanel and Sigafoos, 1984; Fontaine, 1984; Heimann, 1989; Heimann, Nelson and Schaller, 1989; Heimann and Schaller, 1985;

Jacobson, 1979; Kaitz, Meschulach-Sarfaty, Auerbach and Eidelman, 1988; Legerstee, 1991; Kugiumutzakis, 1985; Maratos, 1982; Reissland, 1988; Vinter, 1986). Imitation has also been reported for components of emotional expressions (Field et al., 1983; Field, Goldstein, Vaga-Lahr and Porter, 1986; Field et al., 1982) and a variety of other gestures, including head movements, eye blinking, cheek movements and hand gestures (Fontaine, 1984; Meltzoff and Moore, 1989; Vinter, 1986). The fact that tongue protrusion may be the researchers' favourite choice (it is easiest to code) is sometimes misinterpreted as indicating that it is the only one that can be imitated. The evidence across laboratories has established that a range of adult displays can be imitated.

Other research has sought to investigate whether early imitation is rigidly time-bound and stimulus-driven. In an early study, imitation was reported even if infants had a pacifier in their mouth so they could not imitate during the stimulus-presentation itself (Meltzoff and Moore, 1977). The pacifier was then withdrawn. The results were that infants initiated their imitative response in the subsequent 2.5-minute response period while looking at a passive face. Classical reflexes (Moro, Babinski, pupilary, etc.) are not *initiated* after the stimulus has disappeared, as was observed in this case. In a more dramatic example along these lines, 6-week-olds were found to perform deferred imitation across a 24-hour delay (Meltzoff and Moore, 1994). Infants saw a gesture on one day and returned the next day to see the adult with a passive-face pose. Infants stared at the face and then imitated from long-term memory. It makes little sense to say that infants have a 'reflex' that fires 1 day after the target act has disappeared.

A concern that shows up in textbooks is that early facial imitation 'drops out' at about 2 to 3 months of age. Infants were said to lose their ability to imitate, just as they lose other neonatal reflexes. However, research has demonstrated that this is not the correct interpretation of the data. It is now known that the observed decline is due to simple motivational changes not a change in competence. Two- to 3-month-olds have learned that adults in an *en face* situation typically play interactive games (tummy tickling, head bobbing, cooing, etc.). This may interfere with eliciting imitation unless the study is designed to take these social expectancies into account. For example, in one experiment investigating this issue, 2- to 3-month-old infants did not imitate early in the social encounter. However, after the infants tried to solicit familiar games (but failed due to the experimental design), the infants began to imitate (Meltzoff and Moore, 1992). This suggests that there is not a fundamental drop out of competence; instead, it is masked by a growth in social expectancies. When the conditions are arranged properly, 2- to 3-month-old infants imitate facial gestures as well or better than younger infants (Field et al., 1986; Kugiumutzakis, 1985; Meltzoff and Moore, 1992).

Goal directedness

A characteristic of goal-directed action is that it converges toward the goal and does so along flexible routes. Such goal-directedness has been demonstrated in the kind of imitative errors infants make, and how they correct their responses. In one study, 6-week-old infants were shown the unusual gesture of a large-tongue-protrusion-to-the-side. A microanalysis showed that the initial response was not an exact copy of the adult. Infants gradually corrected their imitative attempts to achieve a more faithful matching of the target (Meltzoff and Moore, 1994, 1997). Their early attempts were to focus on the lateral components: the tongue either went into the cheek, or was thrust slightly forward and then slid laterally during retraction. These approximations were corrected and their behaviour converged to the target gesture. Approximations have also been noted by other investigators (e.g., Abravanel and Sigafoos, 1984; Heimann et al., 1989; Kuhl and Meltzoff, 1996; Maratos, 1982).

Some infants responded in an even more revealing way to the tongue-to-the-side display. They poked out their tongues and simultaneously turned their heads to the side creating a new version of tongue-to-the-side (Meltzoff and Moore, 1997). Although the literal movements differed, the goals of the acts are similar. In our view, tongue protrusion + head turn is a creative error, not the work of a mindless reflex.

The correction of imitative responses and creative errors both suggest that the stimulus did not simply release or spark a fixed response. In the former, infants made repeated attempts and their intention was not satisfied by the initial motor performance stemming from it. This suggests that there is a differentiation between the representation of the target act that was derived from the external world and the representation of the infant's own body acts. The intention is apparently to bring these two into congruence. The creative errors suggest that the response was not prewired and released, but was actively constructed by infants; they responded with their best interpretation of what they saw.

A theoretical model of mechanism

Meltzoff and Moore (1997) offered a theoretical model of the mechanism underlying early facial imitation. We believe that infant imitation depends on a process of active intermodal mapping (AIM). The crux of the AIM hypothesis is that imitation, even early imitation, is a matching-to-target

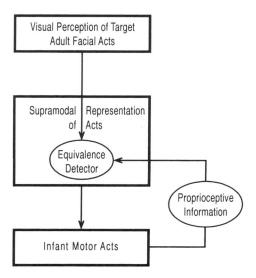

Figure 1.2. A schematic of the AIM hypothesis offered to account for the mechanism underlying early facial imitation. According to AIM, imitation is a matching-to-target process. Infants can correct imitative errors by using proprioceptive feedback to compare their own actions to a visually specified target. (From Meltzoff and Moore, 1997)

process. The goal or behavioural target is specified visually. Infants' self-produced movements provide proprioceptive feedback that can be compared to the visually specified target. AIM proposes that such comparison is possible because both perceived and performed human acts are represented within a common supramodal framework (see Figure 1.2).

Our account also specifies the metric infants use to detect cross-modal equivalence in human acts. The key insight is that an imitative act is not one indissociable unit. It can be differentiated into the *body part* used and the *movement* performed. Regarding the former, the evidence suggest that neonates select what body part to use before they have determined what to do with it. For example, when they see tongue protrusion, there is often a quieting of the movements of other body parts and an activation of the tongue. They do not necessarily protrude the tongue during this initial phase, but may elevate it, wiggle it or move it slightly in the oral cavity. The important point is that the tongue, rather than the lips or fingers, is energised before the movement is isolated. We call this *organ identification.*

Regarding the movement component, we do not think it is innately specified as to which muscle movements yield which particular body configurations. This could be the result of experience. Infants' self-generated prenatal movements, which we term body babbling, provide experience linking muscle movements to resulting body configurations. Neonates acquire a rich store of information through such body babbling. With sufficient practice, they map out an 'act space' enabling new body configurations to be interpolated within this space.

We argue that infants can appreciate the equivalence between the adult 'tongue to lips' (a seen *organ relation*) and their own felt tongue to lips because they express the same configuration of body parts. When infants observe an adult act, they can imitate because body babbling has identified the movements that will result in that configuration of body parts.

Infants use imitation to determine the numerical identity of people

We have marshalled evidence implying an innate foundation for treating people as special. None the less, there are fundamental aspects of person-hood that neonates do not grasp. One of the most surprising immaturities about young infants' notions of people concerns the *identity* of people. The problem of numerical identity is most often discussed in relation to inanimate objects (e.g., Bower, 1982; Meltzoff and Moore, 1998; Moore, Borton and Darby, 1978; Moore and Meltzoff, 1978; Spelke, Kestenbaum, Simons and Wein, 1995; Xu and Carey, 1996).[3] However, we argue that the same problem arises with regard to people.

Posing the problem

In the real world, people do not sit still in front of an infant. They come and go, causing breaks in perceptual contact, and they look different in the morning than they do at night, causing featural changes. Young infants can become confused by such transformations. What criteria could infants use to determine person identity besides spatiotemporal and featural parameters? We propose that infants also use *functional criteria* to help determine the identity of human individuals. In particular they use a person's distinctive behaviours, which we call 'gestural signatures'. For infants, adults are identified (in part) by the games we play.

Identifying people

Several studies have illuminated the relation between numerical identity and imitation. In one study, 6-week-olds saw two different people coming and going, the mother and a male stranger (Meltzoff and Moore, 1992). The mother showed one gesture (e.g., tongue-protrusion gesture) and then exited, and the stranger showed a different gesture (e.g., mouth opening).

The findings surprised us. Instead of differentially imitating the two actors, many infants stared at the second adult . . . paused . . . and then intently produced the previous person's gesture (whether it was mother or stranger). After videotape review, we discovered that a determinant of what infants did was whether they saw the adults as they disappeared and reappeared. Infants who had *not* maintained continuous visual tracking of the people as they entered and exited re-enacted the gesture of the first person. Infants who had continuously tracked the exchange of persons switched and imitated the new person.

We therefore conducted a new experiment in which everything remained the same save for one factor. The procedure was modified to ensure that all infants continuously tracked the adults as they entered and left on opposite paths. This small procedural change yielded a large change in results. Infants now readily switched from imitating person-1 to imitating person-2 without a problem (Meltzoff and Moore, 1992).

Such a reaction is understandable in terms of numerical identity. Infants in the first months of life are hypothesised to use simple place and trajectory rules to trace the identity of objects as they move through space (e.g., Bower, 1982; Meltzoff and Moore, 1998; Moore et al., 1978; Moore and Meltzoff, 1978; Xu and Carey, 1996). Moving objects need to be on different trajectories to be unambiguously understood as numerically distinct individuals. People may be special to infants, but, whatever else they are, they certainly are 3-D objects moving through space. Infants who had not tracked well enough to establish a person's trajectory would have no definitive spatiotemporal means for tracing numerical identity. Perhaps they were using deferred imitation as a kind of behavioural probe, to test whether the person before them was the original person or a new one.

Another study is also compatible with this conceptualisation. Recall the study in which 6-week-olds saw a person show a gesture on one day and then returned to the laboratory the next day to see the person with a passive-face pose (Meltzoff and Moore, 1994). In this case, the self-same person was not acting in the same way as he had earlier. The results showed that infants who had seen the person demonstrate tongue protrusion looked at the (now passive) adult and produced tongue protrusions. Infants who had seen the person demonstrate mouth openings, looked at the (now passive) adult and produced that gesture. It is as if the infants were probing the adult, 'Are you the one who did *x*? Don't we play this game?'

A function of imitation is to verify the identity of individuals

We thus have two studies in which infants confront people after a break in perceptual contact, a break that throws the spatiotemporal criteria for identity into doubt. Infants must turn to something besides spatiotemporal criteria to test the identity of the person. We hypothesised that infants use functional criteria to determine the identity of human individuals. In this sense, early imitation serves a *social identity function* (Meltzoff and Moore, 1992, 1994, 1995)

On this view, distinctive behaviour and interactive games of people serve as markers of their identity. If infants are ambiguous about the identity of a person who is perceptually present, they will be motivated to test whether this person has the same behavioural properties as the old one, whether she acts the same, because the body-actions and expressive behaviour of people are identifiers of who they are. The special value of human acts as functional criteria for identity is that they allow the infant to initiate as well as observe, enabling them to probe and test who this is. In our view, one reason infants re-enact a person's past gestures is to help determine whether this is the same person that they previously encountered.

Reciprocal imitation games prompt development in notions of self and other

Posing the problem

Many parent–infant games and even infant–infant games involve reciprocal imitation (e.g., Nadel 1986). Does being imitated have any psychosocial value? Why is being imitated so attention-getting to infants? What do the actors learn from reciprocal imitation?

There has been a lot of discussion of the turn-taking aspect of games (Brazelton and Tronick, 1980; Bruner, 1975, 1983; Stern, 1985; Trevarthen, 1979). We do not dispute that timing and contingencies are important, but think that the uniqueness of such interaction lies in the equivalence of the *form* of the participants' behaviour, the fact that the experienced self and the seen other are performing identical acts. Physical objects may come under temporal control. Only people, indeed only people who are paying attention to you and acting intentionally, can systematically match the form of your behaviour in a generative fashion. It is well known that infants are sensitive contingency detectors. Is there any evidence that they recognise that the form of their behaviour is being matched?

Mechanisms by which infants recognise being imitated

We designed a series of studies for infants between 6-weeks and 14-months old to test whether they could recognise being imitated themselves, and what value they placed on it. Let's start with the 14-month-olds. The infants in this study sat across a table from two adults. There were two TV monitors behind the infant and in view of the adults. One displayed the actions of the current infant, live; the other displayed the video record of a previous subject. One adult imitated the current infant and the other imitated the previous subject. Although both adults were continuously imitating infant behaviours and thus were good controls for one another, they were reacted to in very different ways. Infants looked longer at the person who was imitating them and also smiled more often at that person (Meltzoff, 1990a).

Infants could have identified the imitating adult on either of two bases. First, they could have used temporal contingency information. According to this alternative, infants only need to detect that when they do X, the adult does X′. Infants need not recognize that X and X′ are identical. The second alternative is that infants can do more than this, that they can recognise that the acts of the self and other share a commonality at a deeper level – they have the same form. Infants may recognise that the adult is acting 'just like me', not 'just when I act'.

Another study was devised in which purely temporal aspects of the contingency were controlled by having both experimenters act at the same time (Meltzoff, 1990a). Both experimenters sat passively until the infant performed one of the target actions on a preset list. If and only if the infant exhibited one of these target actions, both experimenters began to act in unison. One of the adults matched the infant; the other performed the predetermined mismatching response. This achieves the goal of having both of the adults' actions contingent on the infant's. The results showed that the infants looked significantly longer and smiled more at the matching rather than the mismatching adult.

An additional aspect of infants' responses suggests infants are reacting to the adult as an actor, not just the acts themselves. There is a constellation of behaviours that we call 'testing behaviour'. By testing we mean that infants modulated their acts by performing sudden and unexpected movements while staring at the adult, as if to check whether the adult was intentionally mimicking. For example, the infant might slide the toy across the table as she checks the adult's face, then modulate her act by going faster and faster as if to check if the experimenter is shadowing him . . . or suddenly freeze to see if the experimenter freezes. Infants directed significantly more of this testing behavior to the imitating adult.

We found this pattern of looking, smiling and testing at all the ages tested down to about 9 months of age. However, this is not an innate reaction. There are significant developmental differences. Our recent work has shown that infants in the first months of life are attentive to being imitated, but they do not switch to mismatching gestures to test if they will be copied. For example, if a young infant's mouth-opening is being copied, her attention is attracted and she generates more of this behaviour, but does not switch to tongue protrusion to test this relationship. In a situation where adults are imitating them, younger infants seem to regard the adult's immediate imitation of them as a direct consequence of their own actions. The older infants go beyond this and treat the interaction as a generative matching game. That is, the older infants seem to abstract the notion that the game is 'you will do what I do' where the particular behaviours are infinitely substitutable. It is not the notion of a behaviour to behaviour link (e.g., mouth opening causes mouth opening) as per the neonate, but a more abstract notion of 'matching game' generalised across particular instances.

Changes in self and steps towards 'other minds'

There are at least two developmental consequences of engaging in reciprocal imitation games. First, although the initial supramodal framework relates self to other, it has limitations. Because early imitation is mediated by supramodal equivalence, modality-specific information need not be preserved. Neonates can successfully imitate without yet knowing what their acts look like in a purely visual sense, from the outside looking in. Classical developmental theory has supposed that mirrors are the chief avenue for such development. However, not all cultures at all times in history used mirrors, and one would not want to speculate that their notion of self was therefore deviant. Another mechanism that is more culturally universal, is being copied by human caretakers or peers in reciprocally imitative games. In such cases of biological mirroring, infants would gain a sense of what his or her felt acts look like. There are aspects of self that can only be known by seeing reflections of yourself as others see you.

Second, imitation games provide occasions for infants to go beyond surface behaviours to the *intentions* that generate behaviour. Consider the richness of the interaction. At first, infants perform their own actions without concern for their effects on the adult (because they do not know they are in a mutual imitation encounter). When the infants notice the adult movement, they shift their attention and begin to vary their own behaviour. If the adult continues to match, infants produce novel 'testing probes' and smile as the adult follows suit. This everyday interactive game carries a host of information: (a) the adult's behaviour matches the infant's, (b) it is not a random congruence but is systematic, (c) the specific behaviours do not matter, because the invariant in this situation is 'to match', and (d) from the infant's viewpoint, the infant's own novel behaviours were intended acts.

Taken together, these four components provide fertile ground for infants to make an interpersonal inference: 'I intend my acts, the other systematically performs matching acts, perhaps the other also intends his or her acts.' This inference expands interpersonal understanding beyond the neonates'. On the one hand, the infant now ascribes more to the other; he or she is an intending other. On the other hand, the inference allows infants to render self and other as equivalent agents, bearers of commensurate psychological properties not just common body movements. Seen in this way, reciprocal games provide infants with opportunities to see both self and other as producers of intended acts, instead merely of equivalent surface behaviours.

Summary and conclusions

In this section, we highlight the broader theoretical implications of the imitation for four classic topics in infancy: (a) cross-modal functioning, (b) preverbal representation, (c) understanding persons and (d) mechanisms of interpersonal development.

Cross-modal functioning

A view that is compatible with early imitation is that humans register information in a form that is not specific to the modality in which it was originally perceived. This idea was forcefully put forward by Gibson (1966, 1979) with regard to adults, and many researchers have been active in extending it to infant perception (e.g., Bower, 1982; Butterworth, 1990, 1993; Kuhl and Meltzoff, 1982; Meltzoff, 1990b; Meltzoff and Borton, 1979; Spelke, 1987). On this view, infants are not confined to the sense-specific impressions classically ascribed to them. Instead, they use a 'supramodal' code that allows them to unite information from separate perceptual modalities in one framework. The ability of young infants to imitate, and especially the goal-directed nature of error correction, demonstrate that cross-modal organisation is an intrinsic aspect of the human perceptual system in play right from birth.

Infant representation

The second point goes beyond perception. The results from deferred imitation indicate that infants can form representations from observation alone, without simultaneous action. These representations persist, and infants can subsequently access and use them as a basis for action even after substantial delays.

It is perhaps useful to compare deferred imitation with another representationally mediated phenomenon, the search for occluded objects (object permanence). In the permanence case, an object is seen and then made to disappear. Infants must respond on the basis of a representation of the invisible entity. Object permanence is viewed as a prototypical case of infant cognition because current perceptual information alone cannot determine or guide the response of manual searching. In deferred imitation there is a parallel. Infants see a human act. The person performing the act then disappears from view. After a delay, the infant is tested to see if they can produce the imitative act on the basis of a stored representation of what is now invisible. Of course there are differences. In the permanence case, the representation is about a particular absent object at a location in space; in the deferred case, the representation is about an absent act. The point here is that deferred imitation taps representation just as surely as object permanence does (Meltzoff and Moore, 1998).

Deferred imitation also provides leverage for understanding representation not available in tests of object permanence (whether assessed by looking–time measures or manual search). It does so in two ways. (a) In the permanence case, delays are typically on the order of a few seconds, but, in the deferred case, delays of days and weeks have been investigated. (b) In the permanence case, there is typically no change between the hiding and test, but in studies of deferred imitation the surround has been transformed, showing that infant representations can be decontextualised and accessed even without unchanging contextual support. One can argue that object permanence has been overused and deferred imitation underused as means for investigating infant representation. Both perspectives taken together will provide a richer view (Meltzoff and Moore, 1995, 1998).

Origins of folk psychology and understanding 'other minds'

If one wants to find the earliest roots of the child's understanding of mind, a good place to look is infants' initial understanding of persons. We have suggested that the most elementary foundation on which our folk psychology is constructed is the apprehension that others are similar to the self. Infants are launched on their careers of interpersonal under-standing with their first judgment of: Here is something *like me*.

Our argument extends beyond the claims made about infant face per-ception. It is sometimes held that infants are endowed with a special attentiveness to other human beings, in particular to the human facial pattern. For example, Morton and Johnson (1991) have proposed an innate pattern detector for a facial Gestalt. This may be so, but this is not the sole or even the most basic grounding for the 'like me' judgment. Although such a pattern detector might direct visual attention, it would not provide a link between the self and other. Infants might treat faces as attention-getting entities, yet, because they cannot see their own facial features, why should they think of themselves as connected to this entity?

One answer to this question comes from the AIM model proposed to account for early imitation. According to AIM, human acts are a metric by which self and other can be rendered in commensurate terms. We define a human act as an organ transformation, and the goal of an act as the end-state of the transformation. A human act is not simply a vector of move-ment nor an isolated body part, but rather a goal-directed organ transformation. In our view, infants' first 'like-me' experiences are based on the correspondence of human acts. Human acts are especially relevant to infants because they look like the infant feels himself to be and because human acts are things that the infant can intend. We are thus suggesting that one reason infants find people so engaging is the apprehension that those entities are like me because our acts are alike.

Early imitation thus becomes relevant to folk psychology because it provides a first opportunity for infants to make a connection between the visible world of others and the infants' own internal states, the way they 'feel' themselves to be. The human act may be the earliest parsing of the world into things that have bearing on 'self' and those that do not. The bearers of human acts become a class of objects that are given special meaning not accorded to mere things.

Interpersonal experience in developmental change

Imitation is not only an index or measure of primitive self–other mapping, but also provides a means for elaborating it. The same cognitive machinery that enables infants to imitate, makes them sensitive to inter-personal exchanges in which they are imitated by others. In this case, infants are *recognising* a cross-modal match between themselves and others instead of *producing* one.

Parents reflect infants' behaviour back to them as well as the reverse, creating a reciprocal imitation game. When parents mirror certain actions back to the infant, this has significance not only because of the temporal contingencies involved, but because infants can recognise the structural similarity between the adult's acts and their own. Imitative play thus offers a special channel for early communication, in which the timing and the form of the behaviour give both partners an opportunity to share in the exchange. Mutual imitation produces a powerful impression in both the infant and caretaker that they have psychologically made contact, that they are in relationship.

We think that infants' ability to detect that something out there in the world is like me and can do what I do, has cascading developmental effects. The reciprocal imitation games between parents and infants serve a didactic function prompting infants to elaborate a sense of self and self–other correspondences beyond the neonatal level. The developmental progression would be from seeing another as an entity who behaves like me, to someone who shares other deeper equivalences as well – a being who has goals, desires and intentions just like the self, and, farther along the developmental pathway, moral rights equivalent to one's own (Meltzoff, 1995a; Meltzoff and Moore, 1997).

We have come full circle. Infant imitation is a channel through which we can learn about the infants' mind, but more importantly, it is an avenue by which they come to understand ours. Imitation and the interpersonal experiences it generates play a role in the genesis of the notion of self, other and the relation between the two. The development of imitation from birth to 2 years of age illuminates how infants come to treat others as sentient beings, just like the self. This is why imitation is so important for theories of human development – imitation is not just a behaviour, but a means for learning about who we are.

ACKNOWLEDGMENTS

We are indebted to Pat Kuhl for helpful comments on an earlier draft of this chapter and Craig Harris and Calle Fisher for assistance on the research. George Butterworth and Jacqueline Nadel proved to be excellent editors; suggestions from them have improved this essay. Work on this chapter was supported by a grant from NIH (HD–22514). Correspondence should be sent to Andrew N. Meltzoff, Department of Psychology, University of Washington (Box 357920), Seattle, WA 98195.

NOTES

1 In earlier times imitation played a more central role in theories of human development, especially in the work of Baldwin (1894, 1899), Wallon (1942), and Piaget (1962). Other turn-of-the-century theorists also featured discus-

sions of imitation (e.g., Guillaume, 1926/1968; James, 1890; Mead, 1934; Preyer, 1890; Stern 1930). These early theorists did not anticipate that newborns imitate or the scope of deferred imitation in the first year of life, and, consequently, the course charted for development often veered from the mark. None the less, these early essays are beautifully argued and still raise fundamental issues in developmental psychology.

2 We are aware of the diverse meanings and connotations of 'innate'. It is here used as a code word to indicate: present at birth and prior to the experience of learning a particular association between a stimulus (in this case, the adult's facial movement) and a response (the infants' matching facial movement).

3 Numerical identity refers to an object being a particular individual. Numerical identity is a different concept from featural identity. Two coffee mugs can be featurally identical but are numerically distinct individuals.

REFERENCES

Abravanel, E. and Sigafoos, A. D. (1984). Exploring the presence of imitation during early infancy. *Child Development*, 55, 381–92.

Baillargeon, R. (1993). The object concept revisited: New directions in the investigation of infants' physical knowledge. In C. Granrud (ed.), *Visual perception and cognition in infancy* (pp. 265–315). Hillsdale, NJ: Erlbaum.

Baldwin, J. M. (1894). *Mental development in the child and the race*. New York: Macmillan.

(1899). *Social and ethical interpretations in mental development*. (2nd edn). New York: Macmillan.

Barnat, S. B., Klein, P. J. and Meltzoff, A. N. (1996). Deferred imitation across changes in context and object: Memory and generalization in 14-month-old infants. *Infant Behavior and Development*, 19, 241–51.

Barr, R., Dowden, A. and Hayne, H. (1996). Developmental changes in deferred imitation by 6- to 24-month-old infants. *Infant Behavior and Development*, 19, 159–70.

Bauer, P. J. and Hertsgaard, L. A. (1993). Increasing steps in recall of events: Factors facilitating immediate and long-term memory in 13.5- and 16.5-month-old children. *Child Development*, 64, 1204–23.

Bauer, P. J. and Mandler, J. M. (1992). Putting the horse before the cart: The use of temporal order in recall of events by one-year-old children. *Developmental Psychology*, 28, 441–52.

Bertenthal, B. I. (1996). Origins and early development of perception, action, and representation. *Annual Review of Psychology*, 47, 431–59.

Bower, T. G. R. (1982). *Development in infancy*. (2nd edn). San Francisco: W. H. Freeman.

Bower, T. G. R., Broughton, J. M. and Moore, M. K. (1970). The coordination of visual and tactual input in infants. *Perception & Psychophysics*, 8, 51–3.

Brazelton, T. B. and Tronick, E. (1980). Preverbal communication between mothers and infants. In D. R. Olson (ed.), *The social foundations of language and thought* (pp. 299–315). New York: Norton.

Bruner, J. S. (1975). From communication to language – A psychological perspective. *Cognition*, 3, 255–87.

(1983). *Child's talk: Learning to use language.* New York: Norton.

Butterworth, G. (1990). On reconceptualizing sensori-motor development in dynamic systems terms. In H. Bloch and B. I. Bertenthal (eds.), *Sensory-motor organizations and development in infancy and early childhood* (pp. 57–73). The Netherlands: Kluwer Academic Publishers.

(1993). Dynamic approaches to infant perception and action: Old and new theories about the origins of knowledge. In L. B. Smith and E. Thelen (eds.), *A dynamic systems approach to development: Applications* (pp. 171–87). Cambridge, MA: MIT Press.

Butterworth, G. and Hicks, L. (1977). Visual proprioception and postural stability in infancy: A developmental study. *Perception,* 6, 255–62.

Eckerman, C. O. (1993). Imitation and toddlers' achievement of co-ordinated action with others. In J. Nadel and L. Camaioni (eds.), *New perspectives in early communicative development* (pp. 116–38). New York: Routledge.

Field, T., Goldstein, S., Vaga-Lahr, N. and Porter, K. (1986). Changes in imitative behavior during early infancy. *Infant Behavior and Development,* 9, 415–21.

Field, T. M., Woodson, R., Cohen, D., Greenberg, R., Garcia, R. and Collins, E. (1983). Discrimination and imitation of facial expressions by term and preterm neonates. *Infant Behavior and Development,* 6, 485–9.

Field, T. M., Woodson, R., Greenberg, R. and Cohen, D. (1982). Discrimination and imitation of facial expressions by neonates. *Science,* 218, 179–81.

Fontaine, R. (1984). Imitative skills between birth and six months. *Infant Behavior and Development,* 7, 323–33.

Gibson, J. J. (1966). *The senses considered as perceptual systems.* Boston: Houghton Mifflin.

(1979). *The ecological approach to visual perception.* Boston: Houghton Mifflin.

Gopnik, A. and Meltzoff, A. N. (1997). *Words, thoughts, and theories.* Cambridge, MA: MIT Press.

Guillaume, P. (1968). *Imitation in children* (Elaine P. Halperin, trans.). University of Chicago Press (originally published, 1926).

Hanna, E. and Meltzoff, A. N. (1993). Peer imitation by toddlers in laboratory, home, and day-care contexts: Implications for social learning and memory. *Developmental Psychology,* 29, 701–10.

Heimann, M. (1989). Neonatal imitation, gaze aversion, and mother–infant interaction. *Infant Behavior and Development,* 12, 495–505.

Heimann, M. and Meltzoff, A. N. (1996). Deferred imitation in 9- and 14-month-old infants: A longitudinal study of a Swedish sample. *British Journal of Developmental Psychology,* 14, 55–64.

Heimann, M., Nelson, K. E. and Schaller, J. (1989). Neonatal imitation of tongue protrusion and mouth opening: Methodological aspects and evidence of early individual differences. *Scandinavian Journal of Psychology,* 30, 90–101.

Heimann, M. and Schaller, J. (1985). Imitative reactions among 14–21 day old infants. *Infant Mental Health Journal,* 6, 31–9.

Jacobson, S. W. (1979). Matching behavior in the young infant. *Child Development,* 50, 425–30.

James, W. (1890). *Principles of psychology.* New York: Holt, Rinehart & Winston.

Jouen, F. (1990). Early visual-vestibular interactions and postural development.

In H. Bloch and B. I. Bertenthal (eds.), *Sensory-motor organizations and development in infancy and early childhood* (pp. 199–215). Dordrecht: Kluwer.

Kaitz, M., Meschulach-Sarfaty, O., Auerbach, J. and Eidelman, A. (1988). A reexamination of newborn's ability to imitate facial expressions. *Developmental Psychology*, 24, 3–7.

Klein, P. J. and Meltzoff, A. N. (In press). Deferred imitation across changes in context: Memory and forgetting in 12-month-old infants. *Developmental Science*.

Kugiumutzakis, J. (1985). *Development of imitation during the first six months of life* (Uppsala Psychological Reports No. 377): Uppsala, Sweden: Uppsala University.

Kuhl, P. K. and Meltzoff, A. N. (1982). The bimodal perception of speech in infancy. *Science*, 218, 1138–41.

(1996), Infant vocalizations in response to speech: Vocal imitation and developmental change. *Journal of the Acoustical Society of America*, 100, 2425–38.

Legerstee, M. (1991). The role of person and object in eliciting early imitation. *Journal of Experimental Child Psychology*, 51, 423–33.

Mandler, J. M. (1988). How to build a baby: On the development of an accessible representational system. *Cognitive Development*, 3, 113–36.

Maratos, O. (1982). Trends in the development of imitation in early infancy. In T. G. Bever (ed.), *Regressions in mental development: Basic phenomena and theories* (pp. 81–101). Hillsdale, NJ: Erlbaum.

Mead, G. H. (1934). *Mind, self, and society from the standpoint of a social behaviorist.* University of Chicago Press.

Meltzoff, A. N. (1985). Immediate and deferred imitation in fourteen- and twenty-four-month-old infants. *Child Development*, 56, 62–72.

(1988a). Imitation of televised models by infants. *Child Development*, 59, 1221–9.

(1988b). Imitation, objects, tools, and the rudiments of language in human ontogeny. *Human Evolution*, 3, 45–64.

(1988c). Infant imitation after a 1-week delay: Long-term memory for novel acts and multiple stimuli. *Developmental Psychology*, 24, 470–6.

(1988d). Infant imitation and memory: Nine-month-olds in immediate and deferred tests. *Child Development*, 59, 217–25.

(1990a). Foundations for developing a concept of self: The role of imitation in relating self to other and the value of social mirroring, social modeling, and self practice in infancy. In D. Cicchetti and M. Beeghly (eds.), *The self in transition: Infancy to childhood* (pp. 139–64). University of Chicago Press.

(1990b). Towards a developmental cognitive science: The implications of cross-modal matching and imitation for the development of representation and memory in infancy. In A. Diamond (ed.), *Annals of the New York Academy of Sciences. Vol. 608: The development and neural bases of higher cognitive functions* (pp. 1–31). New York Academy of Sciences.

(1995a). Understanding the intentions of others: Re-enactment of intended acts by 18-month-old children. *Developmental Psychology*, 31, 838–50.

(1995b). What infant memory tells us about infantile amnesia: Long-term recall and deferred imitation. *Journal of Experimental Child Psychology*, 59, 497–515.

Meltzoff, A. N. and Borton, R. W. (1979). Intermodal matching by human neonates. *Nature*, 282, 403–4.

Meltzoff, A. N. and Moore, M. K. (1977). Imitation of facial and manual gestures by human neonates. *Science*, 198, 75–8.

(1983). Newborn infants imitate adult facial gestures. *Child Development*, 54, 702–9.

(1989). Imitation in newborn infants: Exploring the range of gestures imitated and the underlying mechanisms. *Developmental Psychology*, 25, 954–62.

(1992). Early imitation within a functional framework: The importance of person identity, movement, and development. *Infant Behavior and Development*, 15, 479–505.

(1994). Imitation, memory, and the representation of persons. *Infant Behavior and Development*, 17, 83–99.

(1995). Infants' understanding of people and things: From body imitation to folk psychology. In J. Bermúdez, A. J. Marcel and N. Eilan (eds.), *The body and the self* (pp. 43–69). Cambridge, MA: MIT Press.

(1997). Explaining facial imitation: A theoretical model. *Early Development and Parenting*, 6, 179–92.

(1998). Object representation, identity, and the paradox of early permanence: Steps toward a new framework. *Infant Behaviour and Development*, 21, 201–35.

Moore, M. K., Borton, R. and Darby, B. L. (1978). Visual tracking in young infants: Evidence for object identity or object permanence? *Journal of Experimental Child Psychology*, 25, 183–98.

Moore, M. K. and Meltzoff, A. N. (1978). Object permanence, imitation, and language development in infancy: Toward a neo-Piagetian perspective on communicative and cognitive development. In F. D. Minifie and L. L. Lloyd (eds.), *Communicative and cognitive abilities – Early behavioral assessment* (pp. 151–84). Baltimore: University Park Press.

Morton, J. and Johnson, M. H. (1991). CONSPEC and CONLERN: A two-process theory of infant face recognition. *Psychological Review*, 98, 164–81.

Nadel, J. (1986). *Imitation et communication entre jeunes enfants*. Paris: PUF.

Nadel-Brulfert, J. and Baudonnière, P. M. (1982). The social function of reciprocal imitation in 2-year-old peers. *International Journal of Behavioral Development*, 5, 95–109.

Piaget, J. (1952). *The origins of intelligence in children*. New York: International Universities Press.

(1962). *Play, dreams and imitation in childhood*. New York: Norton.

Preyer, W. T. (1890). *The mind of the child (Part I). The senses and the will* (H. W. Brown, trans.). New York: Appelton.

Rast, M. and Meltzoff, A. N. (1995). Memory and representation in young children with Down syndrome: Exploring deferred imitation and object permanence. *Development and Psychopathology*, 7, 393–407.

Reissland, N. (1988). Neonatal imitation in the first hour of life: Observations in rural Nepal. *Developmental Psychology*, 24, 464–9.

Rovee-Collier, C. (1990). The 'memory system' of prelinguistic infants. In A. Diamond (ed.). *The development and neural bases of higher cognitive functions. New York: Annals of the New York Academy of Sciences*, 608, 517–42.

Spelke, E. S. (1987). The development of intermodal perception. In P. Salapatek and L. Cohen (eds.), *Handbook of infant perception: Vol. 2. From perception to cognition* (Vol. 2, pp. 233–73). New York: Academic Press.

Spelke, E. S., Breinlinger, K., Macomber, J. and Jacobson, K. (1992). Origins of knowledge. *Psychological Review*, 99, 605–32.

Spelke, E. S., Kestenbaum, R., Simons, D. J. and Wein, D. (1995). Spatiotemporal continuity, smoothness of motion and object identity in infancy. *British Journal of Developmental Psychology*, 13, 113–42.

Squire, L. R. (1987). *Memory and brain.* New York: Oxford University Press.

Squire, L. R., Knowlton, B. and Musen, G. (1993). The structure and organization of memory. *Annual Review of Psychology*, 44, 453–95.

Stern, D. N. (1985). *The interpersonal world of the infant.* New York: Basic Books.

Stern, W. (1930). *Psychology of early childhood up to the sixth year* (Anna Barwell, trans.). London: George Allen.

Tomasello, M., Kruger, A. C. and Ratner, H. H. (1993). Cultural learning. *Behavioral and Brain Sciences*, 16, 495–552.

Trevarthen, C. (1979). Communication and cooperation in early infancy: A description of primary intersubjectivity. In M. Bullowa (ed.), *Before speech* (pp. 321–47). New York: Cambridge University Press.

Užgiris, I. Č. (1981). Two functions of imitation during infancy. *International Journal of Behavioral Development*, 4, 1–12.

Van der Meer, A. L. H., Van der Weel, F. and Lee, D. N. (1994). Prospective control in catching in infants. Perception, 23, 287–302.

Vinter, A. (1986). The role of movement in eliciting early imitations. *Child Development*, 57, 66–71.

Von Hofsten, C. (1983). Catching skills in infancy. *Journal of Experimental Psychology: Human Perception and Performance*, 9, 75–85.

Wallon, H. (1942). *De l'acte à la pensée.* Paris: Flammarion.

Xu, F. and Carey, S. (1996). Infants' metaphysics: The case of numerical identity. *Cognitive Psychology*, 30, 111–53.

2 Genesis and development of early infant mimesis to facial and vocal models

Giannis Kugiumutzakis

Introduction

This chapter describes a longitudinal study, starting from when babies were less than 1 hour old, undertaken to investigate the origins and development of facial and vocal imitation during the first 6 months of life (Kugiumutzakis, 1985, Study V). The longitudinal design allows study not only of what happens during the newborn period, but also of whether imitation disappears, as certain reflexes do (Abravanel and Sigafoos, 1984; Jacobson, 1979); whether imitative responses to different models follow a nonlinear course (Maratos 1973, 1982) and whether infant imitation develops in the way Piaget (1962) described.

Piaget (1962) argued that development progresses from absence of imitation (1st month), to sporadic imitation of vocal, head-and-hand models (1–4 months), systematic imitation of known sounds and of visible gestures (i.e. that babies can see themselves make, 4–8 months), and, finally, imitation of non-visible facial models (8–12 months). Thus, Piaget assumes a developmental course from non-imitation to imitation, and also that self-imitation precedes and leads to hetero-imitation. This means that Piaget considers imitation to be, at first, an intrapersonal phenomenon, which gradually becomes an interpersonal phenomenon in infancy, until at 2 years of age it becomes again intrapersonal as interiorised imitation. For Piaget, imitation during the first 8 months of life is not essentially different from circular reaction because the infant considers the actions modelled by another person as a kind of continuation of her own activity. True, spontaneous imitation, based upon active, spontaneous assimilation appears later in development, while 'pseudo-imitation' of a facial model does not last, says Piaget, except under the influence of continual stimulation. True imitation, however, lasts, that is, it does not disappear 'even when it is only sporadic' (1962, p. 18). After the eighth month (stage IV, 8–12 months) Piaget relies on the passive process of association for the further development of imitation, because the active processes of assimilation and accommodation cannot explain the appearance of facial imitation. Piaget notes that 'training in imitation is necessary, especially when it is a case of imitation of movements which the child cannot see himself make' (p. 41).The basis for facial imitation is the co-ordination of secondary circular reactions, parental training and the constitution of a system of 'mobile indices' which function as mediators between the facial model and the infant's own behaviour. Piaget excludes by definition rather than by observation (see Kugiumutzakis, 1993, p. 24) the possibility of neonatal imitation, the contribution of intermodal co-ordination and the contribution of representation in the development of early infant imitation (see also Kugiumutzakis, 1985, 1988, 1993,1998; Maratos, 1973, 1982, 1998; Meltzoff and Moore 1977, 1983, 1989, 1992).

We know today that both Piaget's theory and his observations during the neonatal period are inadequate to explain the origin of human imitation. The fact of neonatal imitation indicates that human imitation is, from the start, an interpersonal phenomenon in which newborns actually imitate facial models 8 to 12 months earlier than Piaget had proposed (Bard, 1994; Field, Woodson, Cohen, Greenberg, Garcia and Collins, 1983; Field, Woodson, Greenberg and Cohen, 1982; Fontaine, 1984; Heimann and Schaller, 1985; Kugiumutzakis 1985, 1998, 1993; Legerstee, 1991; Maratos, 1973, 1982, 1998; Meltzoff and Moore 1977, 1983, 1989, 1992; Reissland, 1988; Vinter, 1986). This fact creates serious problems for Piaget's theory that imitation develops in six invariably ordered stages.

Bain (1855, cited in Miller and Dollard, 1941) observed 'disappearance' of imitation in early infancy. Piaget also made an observation in this respect, but he did not try to interpret this interesting phenomenon (1962, pp. 9–10, obs. 2, 3). Maratos (1973) observed a decline in imitative behaviour towards different models at different age levels. Various hypotheses have been offered for the decrease in early infant imitative behaviour. It may occur because the babies' capacity for processing incoming information is momentarily lost (Maratos, 1982), or because after the second month the 'matching' ability disappears, as is the case with certain neonatal reflexes (Jacobson, 1979), or because the mother does not reinforce certain socially unacceptable behaviours such as tongue protrusion (Dunkeld, 1978), or because there is a relationship between the decline in infant attentiveness and the decrease in imitation of facial models (Field, Goldstein, Vega-Lahr and Porter, 1986; Fontaine, 1984; Heimann, 1989), or because each imitative response reaches its zenith and declines as the child seeks 'fresh stimuli' (Guillaume, 1925/1971). Given the interesting results and stimulating disagreements obtained in previous studies, the development of infant imitation during the first 6 months invites further investigation.

Methods of studying the development of imitation in the first six months of life

Since there has been much controversy over the existence of neonatal imitation, the methods adopted by the author for its study will first be described in some detail. The procedure is sensitive to the newborn and young infants' interests, needs, individual differences and communicative readiness at the moment of the test. The method was based on two pilot studies, one carried out with 40 babies less than 45 minutes old in a maternity hospital in Iraklion, Crete, and another by Olga Maratos, with 18 infants, 2 to 8 months old, in the Metera Babies' Center in Athens (see Kugiumutzakis, 1985).

The procedure during the first examination in the maternity hospital and the visits to the infants' homes was as follows. With the permission of the doctors and the parents-to-be, the writer was present at the births of the infants. In the delivery room, the mother and the pediatrician were asked for permission to test the baby. The time of birth and the Apgar scores were noted and the experimenter attended the baby's first pediatric examination and first bath conducted by the midwife. About 10 to15 minutes after the birth, the infant met the father, grandparents and other relatives in a room close to the lying-in room. There, with the help of the clinic's staff, the permission of the father and grandparents to test the baby was obtained. This granted, the father, or more often he and the grand-mother(s), took the newborn to the laboratory and placed the infant gently on the baby bed. Relatives and the pediatrician observed the testing on a soundless TV screen located at the corner of the room, behind a black screen out of sight of the baby.

The laboratory was an isolated and warm room, where other crying babies were out of earshot. The baby bed was set at about 10 degrees to the horizontal. Behind and above the bed a large vertical mirror reflected the experimenter's face and hands. Beside the bed there was a dimmer control, to regulate the lighting. The bed, the mirror, a small table and the experimenter's seat were surrounded by a black screen ($2.0 \times 2.0 \times 2.0$ m) ensuring that the experimenter's face would be the brightest object in the baby's visual field. For the same reason, the experimenter wore a black shirt during the test. A video camera with high light sensitivity was located behind the black screen, directed to the baby's face and the mirror, recording simultaneously the movements of experimenter and the baby (Kugiumutzakis, 1985, 1988; see also Meltzoff and Moore, 1977, 1983). At the babies' homes, the camera-person was situated at a distance of 2.0–2.5 m from the baby and she attracted very little attention from the infants. Four babies, during the second and the third month, looked at the camera rather than at the experimenter. In those cases the test was stopped and the babies were visited again on the next day. During the test the parents were out of the visual field of the baby.

Since the baby's state depended to some extent on the posture, a flexible approach was adopted since it was necessary that the baby be calm for the presentation of the facial models. It was observed in the delivery room that a change of posture of a whimpering baby often stimulated a calm state and it was natural for the midwives to change the baby's posture in an effort to calm the baby. This is a practice also adopted intuitively by parents during the neonatal period (see Ronnqvist, 1993; Stratton, 1982).

The first test, with facial models, was with the newborn baby either lying down on the baby bed or, if the baby did not like this posture (as judged from whimpering or a facial expression of uneasiness), the experimenter held the baby upright with the head in one hand and torso in the other. At home, the posture of the infant on each visit was regulated following the mother's advice. The babies were examined either lying down on a sofa with a pillow under the head or in an inclined infant seat. In cases where the infants did not tolerate the seat, the session was conducted with the baby held upright by the experimenter, with the head supported in one hand and torso in the other. In this way, the procedure was adapted to the infants' postural needs at the moment of the test.

The lighting conditions were also carefully modified during the test of the newborns to allow for the difficulties of many babies for visual adaptation to the new environment immediately after birth. The experimenter either lowered or turned off the light, put his hands around the baby's face or stood between the baby's eyes and the source of the light. If helped in one of the above ways, the neonates in the delivery room were observed to open their eyes in less than 40 seconds. It was decided that if the eyes of the baby were closed when they entered the laboratory, the experimenter would lower or turn off the light with the dimmer control in an effort to help the infant's visual adaptation. Again the design was adapted to the babies' visual functioning and responsivity at the moment of the test (see also Attkinson and Braddick, 1982; Prechtl, 1982; Stratton, 1982; Trevarthen, 1986).

Testing, in the first examination, began with an adaptation period of 40 to 100 seconds with the baby alone on the baby bed and the experimenter out of sight. Until this moment, the baby had no opportunity to observe the experimenter's face. This adaptation period was introduced to help the babies to adapt to the room's lighting, or to adapt the room's lighting with the dimmer control to the baby's visual system and to determine whether the facial models could be presented with the baby lying down or with the baby held upright.

Masters (1979) proposed that responses of the newborn during presentation of the standard model should be ignored, because the experimenter might actually be imitating the baby. In the pilot study, each model was presented five times and then the experimenter waited for the baby's response. The majority of the babies (77%) reacted after the fifth presentation of the model while the remainder reacted (imitatively or not) after either the first, second, third or fourth model presentation. Masters' advice was not followed here because (a) each model was presented as soon as the baby was entirely motionless and silent, (b) the digital timer on the video recording makes it easy to decide who influences whom, and (c) Masters' criterion ignores entirely the individual differences in communicative readiness of neonates and young infants in early interactions.

It was clearly necessary to choose a maximum number of presentations of the models (say five times), but some babies did not need all five model presentations – some needed four, and some only one. Thus, it was decided that when the baby started reproducing the model (for instance tongue protrusion) or emitted other scored responses (mouth opening, blinking, etc.), the modelling stopped regardless of the number of presentations already made. In natural mother–infant interactions, co-actions are the exception rather than the rule. Again, the design was suited to the babies' communicative readiness at the moment of the test (Kugiumutzakis, 1985, 1988, 1993, 1998, Stratton, 1982).

Longitudinal study of the origin and development of imitation.

Kugiumutzakis (1985) studied fourteen infants who were examined for facial and vocal imitation from just after delivery until the sixth month. The first examination took place in the maternity hospital with the newborns less than 40 minutes old. The average age of the babies was 32 minutes (range 19–40 min). The infants (7 girls and 7 boys) were full-term babies ($\bar{x} = 39.2$ gestational weeks), of normal birth weight ($\bar{x} = 3570$ g) and of normal Apgar scores (1-min Apgar: $\bar{x} = 7$; 5-min Apgar: $\bar{x} = 9.2$). Eight out of the 14 babies were first-born and 6 were second-born. The study took place in Iraklion, Crete.

In the subsequent examinations, the infants were visited in their houses every two weeks from the time they were 15 days old until they were 180 days old. Thus a total of 13 examinations were made of each infant. All sessions both in the hospital and at the babies' homes were video-recorded. The home environment was prefered to a standard laboratory setting since this avoided having to familiarise the infant to anything more than the experimenter. Since it is difficult to control the reinforcing behaviour of the mother during the test, the experimenter rather than the mother administered the models. To avoid practice of the modelled actions between the sessions, the parents were told that the aim of the study was to observe the reflex behaviour of the babies. Despite this precaution, one cannot, of course, be sure that all parents refrained from practicing the models and from playing imitative games in parent–infant interaction (Kugiumutzakis, 1993; Pawlby, 1977; Trevarthen, 1977, see also Trevarthen, this volume). The visits to the infants' homes took place during the half hour immediately following feeding because this is an optimal time for social games and there are few spontaneous oral movements.

Facial models presented for imitation were mouth opening (MO), tongue protrusion (TP) and eye movements/blinking (EM). Vocal models were rhythmical emissions of the sounds /m/, /a/ and /ang/. There were three criteria for admission to the study: (a) The infants were not 'at risk' babies, (b) they should be less than 40-minutes old on the first examination and (c) at each age level each baby would be exposed to all the models once. The experimental design of a series of five studies of babies less than 45-minutes old is described fully in Kugiumutzakis ,1985, 1988, 1998.

Each model was presented up to five times for a duration of 15 seconds. Given individual differences in infant visual and auditory functioning, and in responsivity and communicative readiness, the actual stimulus time depended on when the baby looked at the experimenter (for facial models). The average stimulus time was 10 seconds and, as noted above, the frequency of model presentation and the reaction time was controlled by the baby, with an upper limit of 15 seconds. The facial models were presented at a distance of 20–23 cm from the infant's face, when the infant was entirely calm with open eyes, regular respiration and lack of gross movements or vocalisation. The vocal models were presented when the baby was silent, but whether the infant looked at the experimenter or not was not taken into account. The models were presented in random order with a different order for each baby.

Two judges scored the six facial and vocal responses in the following way. Mouth Opening: the lips of the baby must be widely separated and form an O. Yawning was not scored. Tongue Protrusion: the tongue must be seen to leave the mouth and then to re-enter the buccal cavity, a clear forward thrust of the tongue beyond the lips. Eye Movements: the two eyelids must be seen to close and open making a clear observable blink. Sounds /m/ (consonant), /a/ (vowel) and /ang/ (vowel–consonant combination): any vocal response containing clearly the sounds /m/, /a/ and /ang/ respectively. To assess the intrascorer reliability, the judges

Table 2.1. *Cochran test's Q values for each infant response at each age level (months, except the first one)*

Responses	AGE												
	32 min	0.5	1	1.5	2	2.5	3	3.5	4	4.5	5	5.5	6
Tongue Protrusion	+++ 10.36	++ 9.14	+++ 13.50	++++ 14.60	+++ 10.36	1.55	1.00	0.00	0.25	0.54	++ 8.90	+++ 12.92	++++ 15.85
Mouth Opening	+++ 9.84	+++ 11.23	+++ 10.66	+++ 12.16	+ 7.16	3.25	1.50	2.33	0.28	1.00	1.00	4.00	2.36
Eye Movement	++ 8.90	+++ 11.23	+++ 9.50	+++ 10.36	++ 8.90	+ 8.60	+ 6.20	+ 7.16	+++ 9.33	++ 4.66	1.55	0.40	0.40
Sound M	2.88	0.00	0.25	0.88	3.71	+ 7.53	++++ 14.72	+++ 13.50	++ 8.76	++ 7.82	3.25	4.00	2.80
Sound A	+++ 10.36	0.25	1.75	2.36	3.71	+++ 11.23	++++ 16.54	+++ 10.36	+++ 10.42	+++ 10.40	2.25	4.33	3.25
Sound ANG	0.36	0.00	1.20	1.00	3.00	++ 8.60	+++ 11.16	+++ 11.63	+++ 11.40	+ 7.16	2.18	3.60	1.00

Notes:
$++++ < 0.0005$; $+++ \ p < 0.005$; $++ \ p < 0.01$; $+ \ p < 0.025$

scored the data again 15 days later. The first judge's intrascorer reliability ranged from 0.91 to 0.97, and that of the second scorer ranged from 0.93 to 0.98. To assess interscorer reliability the Φ correlation was computed between the scores of the pair of the judges. These correlations were 1.0 in all cases. During the analysis of the infant facial responses, the scorers could see only the baby's image on the screen, while the experimenter's image was hidden by a black cloth.

A general problem with the analysis of this kind of data is that because some responses may occur spontaneously they may be miscounted as imitative. That is, the response frequency after the presentation of the corresponding model (e.g. TP responses to the TP model) should be adjusted to reflect a certain base rate (BR). That is, tongue protrusion (TP) to tongue protrusion models should be decreased by the rate of TP responses to the mouth-opening (MO) and eye-movement (EM) models. Categorical treatment of the data was preferred since there were large individual differences in the frequencies of the infant responses at different age levels. Zero signified the absence of a response and one signified the presence of a response whatever the frequency. For each facial and vocal response at each age level, Cochran's Q test was used to compare the probability of a response after the presentation of the corresponding model with the BR (Siegel, 1956). True imitation can be said to occur only if the babies produce significantly more TP responses after the presentation of the TP model than after the presentation of the other models (MO and EM).

Table 2.1 gives Q values for each response at each age level.

From the first examination in the maternity hospital, the results demonstrate that imitative responses are given significantly more often in the presence of the corresponding model than in its absence, even though these responses also occur in spontaneous neonatal behaviour. On this criterion, neonates, less than 40 minutes old, imitated the facial models of TP, MO and EM. Also, they clearly tried to imitate the sound /a/, but not the sounds /m/ and /ang/. The imitative responses to the sound /a/ were strained. The baby tried hard to emit the sound, and the result was usually an intense explosion of a prolonged and unstructured /a/ sound. The response was sometimes accompanied by stretching hand movements and closed eyes.

Further analysis of the imitators' behaviour during the presentation of the facial models and the sound /a/ showed that neonates used two strategies of attention: the first strategy shown by a majority of the neonates is to try, with a real, observable effort, to direct their attention to the moving part of the experimenter's face. The attention intensifies from a relatively fixed gaze to selective visual exploration. During the presentation of the

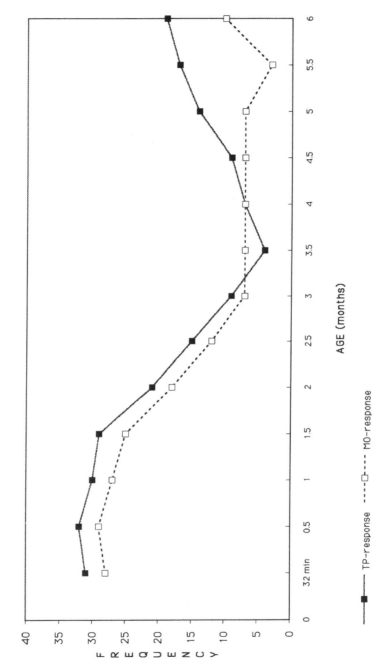

Figure 2.1. TP responses to TP model and MO responses to MO model at each age (in months, except the first one).

sound /a/ model, in the majority of the imitators there was observed a gradual localisation of the sound by head-turning and eye-widening while the brows were held high, a movement which occurs in attentive listening (Rinn, 1984). A second strategy was observed in only a minority of the imitators. In the case of the facial models, the infant looks at the modelled movement hastily, and, as far as one can see from the slow-motion video recordings, it is as if the baby observes only the first presentation and starts reproducing the model immediately. A minority of neonates responded immediately after the first or the second presentation of the sound /a/. Examining the recordings in slow motion, showed eye-widening only during the model presentation time (see Kugiumutzakis, 1985, 1988, 1998).

Three forms of reproductive behaviour were observed in imitation of the facial models: (i) immediate or direct imitation: the neonates reproduce the models once and the similarity of their reaction to the model's action is precise. The EM model was reproduced by the majority of the imitators once. (ii) Successive, improving imitation: the newborns reproduce the model a number of times, and in every additional effort they converge towards a more precise matching. This observation confirms findings reported by Maratos (1973) and Meltzoff and Moore (1977, 1983). The babies follow this pattern mostly when imitating TP and MO models. Sometimes their efforts start with preparatory movements of the tongue inside the buccal cavity. (iii) Successive deteriorating imitation: the first imitative effort is a satisfactory reproduction of the model, and as they continue, neonates do not produce better results. In every additional 'effort' they depart more and more from the result of their first successful effort. It is as if they lose interest in imitation (Kugiumutzakis, 1985). These two strategies of attention and the three forms of reproductive behaviour are not typical either of automatic reflexes or of fixed action patterns.

Figures 2.1, 2.2 and 2.3 represent the frequencies of responses to the corresponding models at each age level.

The development of the imitative responses to the six models as shown by the results (see also Table 2.1) indicate that the infant's ability to imitate remains constant during the first 6 months, but what will or will not be imitated changes. Imitation of TP and MO develops according to a U-shaped curve, imitation of the vocal models in an inversely U-shaped manner and imitation of EM in a negative linear fashion. There was no effect of birth order or gender on imitation.

Smiling, undetermined vocalisations, dinstinct phonemes, tongue protrusions inside the mouth, silent lip and mouth movements, imitation of the rhythm of the vocal models, efforts to grab the experimenter's moving

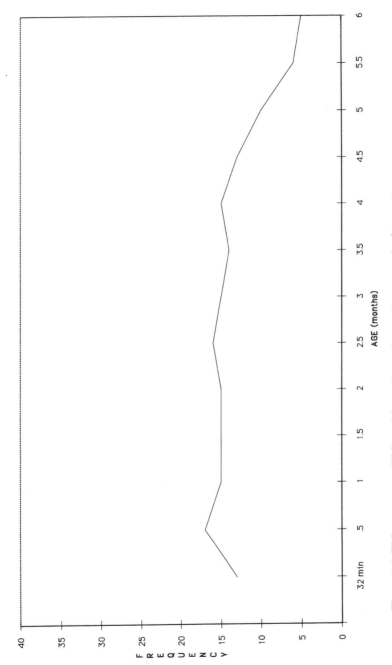

Figure 2.2. EM responses to EM model at each age (in months, except the first one).

facial parts and avoidance responses were observed both when there were imitative responses and when there was no imitation. The first appearance of a smile as a response to the models was observed at 15 days of age. Recently, Kugiumutzakis (1994) observed a smile after the presentation of the models in one infant of two days. The smile appears at all age levels in the longitudinal study, except the first examination in the maternity hospital. Many babies smiled after the presentation of the model and before its imitation, or during and after the presentation of the model, or during the periods of decrease of the different imitative responses.

In addition to the smile, the babies reacted to the models in the periods of decrease of facial imitative responses by cooing, clear vocalisations, inside the mouth TP to the TP model and by yawning to the MO model. Moreover, during the periods of non-imitation and decrease of responses to the vocal models, cooing, silent lip and mouth movements and imitation of the rhythm of emission of the vocal models were observed. Imitation of the rhythm was observed sporadically even immediately after birth, and it appears also during the periods of increase of vocal imitation when the infants imitate both the phonological characteristics of the model and its rhythm. At 5.5 months reaching clearly makes its appearance in imitative interaction. In addition to the accompanying responses, clear avoidance reactions were observed in the infants. They moved their heads or their eyes intentionally away from the experimenter's face. The experimenter then had either to wait a few minutes until the baby decided to return to interact, or to try the examination the next day.

The interconnection between the origin and development of imitation.

The problems of the origin and early development of human imitation have many interconnected aspects. Here, a few of them will be discussed.The longitudinal study confirmed the findings of other writers adding the finding that facial and vocal imitation can occur at even the first 40 minutes after birth (Field et al., 1983; Field et al., 1982; Fontaine, 1984; Heimann and Schaller,1985; Kugiumutzakis, 1985, 1993, 1998; Legerstee, 1991; Maratos, 1973; Meltzoff & Moore, 1977, 1983, 1989, 1992; Reissland, 1988; Vinter, 1986). The results also confirmed Aristotle's notion that human beings imitate by nature, but not his hypothesis that infants are not able to imitate at birth (see Kugiumutzakis, 1998). The present study and four other experimental studies with subjects less than 45 minutes old (Kugiumutzakis, 1985, Studies I – V; 1988; 1998) indicate that the ability of imitation is innate in our species. Given the many functions served by human imitation, its

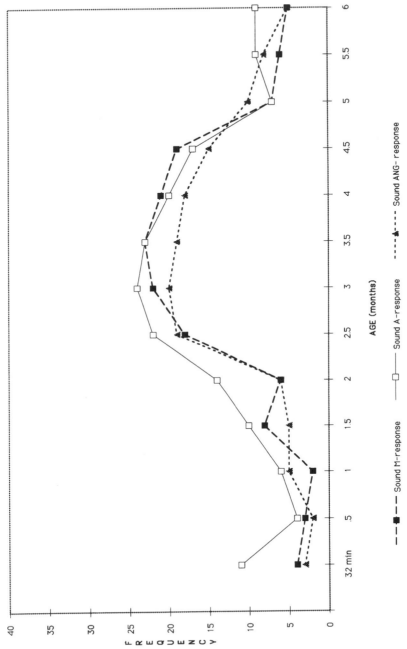

Figure 2.3. Vocal /m-/, /a-/, and /ang-/ responses to /m-/, /a-/, and /ang-/ model, respectively, at each age (in months, except the first one).

innate origin is not surprising. This fact does not exclude either the individual differences in the ability *per se* or the influence of experience in the development of imitation during the lifespan. The contribution of maturation and experience in the development of imitation invites more specific planned, cross-cultural, longitudinal studies, (see Trevarthen, this volume).

In the experimental setting, neonatal imitation is more easily observed under very specific internal states. Namely, a high level of communicative readiness with the baby in a state of quiet alertness (open eyes, regular respiration and lack of gross movements and vocalisation, state 3 in Prechtl and O'Brien, 1982). Secondly, imitation is more readily observed under flexible, experimental conditions. That is, when the modelled movements and sounds belong to the baby's spontaneous repertoire and when the infant regulates the duration and frequency of the stimulus presentation as well as the onset of the response. Similarly, it is observed when the lighting of the experimental room and the posture of the neonate are regulated by the baby's needs and with the facial models presented at a distance of 20–23 cm from the infant's face. The relatively slow accommodation of some quiet, alert newborns to experimental stimuli, flexible adaptation of the presentation of the models to fit the newborns' environmental preferences, changes of alertness and interest and individual differences can greatly improve the predictability and differentiation of responses.

In the present study, as in four other studies with newborns (Kugiumutzakis, 1985, Studies I–IV) two forms of attention were observed during the presentation of the models, three kinds of reproductive behaviour, individual differences in communicative readiness for imitation and active participation of the imitators' whole body. Some alert neonates did not imitate any of the models. This polymorphic emergence undermines the ethological and reflexological interpretations of neonatal imitation. The age of the newborns, the fact that they had no experience that would enable them to learn the correspondences existing in their own face and the face of the experimenter, the fact that they never had seen a mirror, that 75% of the imitators reproduced the models correctly in their first imitative effort and that imitative responses, although present in spontaneous neonatal behaviour, are given significantly more often in the presence than in the absence of the corresponding model, undermine the behaviouristic and Piagetian interpretations on the origin of human imitation (see also Kugiumutzakis, 1985, 1988, 1993, 1998; Maratos, 1973, 1982; Meltzoff and Moore, 1977, 1983, 1989).

Both in the first examination in the maternity hospital and later in the infants' houses, the babies imitated TP and MO models more easily and more often than EM models which were imitated only once and with clear difficulty by the great majority of the infants. One possible reason is that the oral region is controlled by many agile, small muscles that permit movement in many directions while the upper part of the face is controlled by fewer less differentiated muscles that do not permit movement in many directions. In addition, the muscles that move the mouth and especially the tongue have more proprioceptive receptors than the muscles that move the eyes (Rinn, 1984). Moreover, there are differences in how parts of the face are represented in the so called topographic map of the body's muscles, located in the anterior lip of the central sulcus of the cerebral cortex. The size of the 'representation' of each face part reflects the corresponding degree of fine motor control (Rinn, 1984). The 'representation' of the oral area is much larger than that of the upper face area. Also, in the brainstem there is a column of cell bodies making up the facial nerve nucleus. Specific cell groups in this nucleus map specific peripheral parts of the facial nerve. Those cell groups that innervate the muscles of the mouth are larger than the ones that innervate the upper face (Rinn, 1984). These data suggest that the control of the oral region develops earlier, which may explain why the baby is able to imitate oral models so much better, and why neonates make immediate or direct imitation when they reproduce the EM model.

Also, in the first examination, the neonates imitated (or better, tried to imitate) the sound /a/, but not the sounds /m/ and /ang/. According to Ferguson (1978, pp. 278–9), the progression of myelinisation in the primary motor cortex goes from the back of the mouth to the front. The emission of the sound /m/ requires neuromuscular control of the front part of the mouth and the neonate's vocal system is less mature for such an achievement. The vocal model of /ang/ may, likewise, be too difficult for imitation by babies less than 40 minutes old. The emission of the sound /a/, which is a non-front vowel (see Kugiumutzakis, 1985), is evidently easier for them; the sound appears in crying and in other vocal emissions observed during the first hour of life. Two months later, the babies are able to imitate all three sounds much better, as we have found in the present longitudinal study and in another, naturalistic, longitudinal study (Kugiumutzakis, 1993).

In an effort to offer one possible explanation of this complex, social phenomenon of neonatal imitation, it can be assumed that, after the presentation of the model and before the first, correct, imitative response, the neonate has to try to perceive the models clearly. These observable efforts can be considered as a conscious neonatal activity, seeking and regulating experience. The neonate must also discriminate the self and the other as two separate persons coexisting in the same 3-D space, both involved within an interacting unit. This is evidenced by the fact that 77% of the neonates in the present study (see also Kugiumutzakis, 1985, Studies I – IV, 1988, 1998) reacted after the fifth presentation of the models, although they had the opportunity to inter-rupt the experimenters' actions and that 75% of the imitators repro-duced the models correctly in their first imitative effort. This initial dualism (see Butterworth, 1981; Kugiumutzakis, 1988, 1998; Neisser, 1993; Trevarthen, 1977, 1993) means that neonates have some aware-ness of their body parts and of themselves in relation to others as evi-denced in turn taking as a core characteristic of the human ability for dialogue. Furthermore, the infant must recognise that his own unseen, unmoving mouth corresponds to the experimenter's moving mouth. This crucial recognition must happen before the start of the reproductive movements, for otherwise one cannot explain the correctness of the first imitative movement. The majority of the imitators made a TP response to the TP model from the start. Whatever this mechanism is called (see Kugiumutzakis, 1985, 1998; Maratos, 1982, 1998; Meltzoff and Moore, 1977, 1983, 1989) it is, by logical and psychological necessity, recogni-tion of face isomorphism, a part of the initial dualism, a pre-condition of neonatal imitation, which supports the idea of a non-reflex intermodal co-ordination functioning at birth (see also Butterworth and Hopkins, 1988). The infant must also detect the experimenter's intention and motivation for communication through imitation, when the model is being presented. It is proposed that the neonate may detect the defining invariants of the experimenter's motivation for communication, which lie behind the kinematic and acoustical surface of the models (Kugiumutzakis, 1985; see also Gibson, 1979; Michotte, 1946/1963; Runeson and Frykholm, 1983; Trevarthen, 1986; Vedeler, 1991). One may speculate that the neonate detects that the modelled movements and sounds are incomplete and that it is the baby's turn and task to act and feel in a complementary way in the form of an imitation (Kugiumutzakis, 1992, 1994, 1998). Direct perception of this psycho-logical invariant may answer the fundamental question: how does the neonate detect that the modelled movements and sounds are presented in order to be imitated ?

Finally, the infant, during the imitative interaction, may feel two emo-tions: pleasure and interest. The recognition of the modelled movements and sounds as incomplete may evoke the emotion of interest. This requires the infant to be in possession of tools of communication in the behavioural repertoire, while the recognition of the other as a partner for intersubjective games may evoke the pleasure of being together. Both pleasure and interest may motivate the complementary, co-operative, social, imitative game (see Kugiumutzakis, 1998; Bråten, 1988, 1992, 1994; Maratos, 1998; Nadel, 1980; Trevarthen, 1993).

The longitudinal study also shows that the ability to imitate remains constant during the first 6 months of life despite the fact that what will be imitated changes. Selective imitation never disappears during the first 6 months. When, at 2 months, infants' imitative behaviour to the TP and MO models declined (in a U-shaped curve), the babies continued to imitate the EM model (on a negative linear developmental course), and, at the same age, they began to imitate the vocal models systematically (on an inverse U-shaped developmental curve, Figures 1, 2 and 3). Clearly, one cannot draw general conclusions about the early development of imitation from measurements of just one kind of response. Both linear and non-linear development can be observed, depending on which response is selected. Thus, Jacobson's (1979) hypothesis, that imitative ability declines as certain reflexes do, is not supported because the imitative ability *per se* never declines or disappears. For the same reasons, Dunkeld's (1978) hypothesis that imitation declines because the mothers do not reinforce certain unacceptable behaviours, is not supported. In fact, the infants continued to imitate another model (EM) and they started to imitate systematically new vocal models, while after the fifth month the imitation of the TP model again increases. Field et al.s (1986) hypothesis, that the decrease in imitation of facial models is related to a decline in infant attentiveness, is not supported because the infants continued to imitate the EM model and also continued attending to the TP and MO models, despite the fact that they did not imitate them.

Piaget's (1962) theory of imitative development in six invariably ordered stages is not supported by this (and other) studies, because, contrary to his assertion that sporadic imitation appears after the first month, the present study shows that systematic imitation occurs from the first 40 minutes. Also, he claims that infants imitate first the visible parts of the body (hand models), while the present study shows that they imitate the non-visible parts earlier. Where Piaget asserts that training is necessary for facial imitation at the end of the first year, the infants in the present study imitated the facial models without the aid of training. Where Piaget says that vocal imitation precedes facial imitation the present results show the opposite, and, finally, where Piaget asserts that self-imitation precedes and leads to hetero-imitation, the present data show that imitation of other people occurs immediately after birth. Thus, imitation may develop in stages, but the stages are not the ones Piaget proposed, at least during the first 6 months. Despite Piaget's tremendous work in developmental psychology and his meticulous observation during infancy, his theory of infant imitation needs some fundamendal revision.

The results are in agreement with Maratos' (1973) findings concerning the non-linear course of the MO and TP imitative responses. However, the negative linear course of the EM imitative responses indicates that linear and non-linear developmental changes coexist throughout the 6-month period. Maratos' hypothesis that the decrease in early imitation occurs because the infant's capacity for processing incoming information is momentarily lost, is not supported by the present data. After the decrease of the imitative responses to the TP and MO models, the assumed capacity for processing incoming information is still functional for imitation of the vocal and EM models. However, the longitudinal study is in agreement with Maratos' thesis that the decline of the oral imitative responses coincides with an increase in vocal imitative responses because vocalisation is a more powerful form of communication in mother–infant interaction (see Kugiumutzakis, 1985; Maratos, 1973, 1982; Trevarthen, 1977, 1986). It is also interesting that the pattern of development of the vocal imitative responses is almost the mirror-image of that for the oral responses (Figures 2.1 and 2.3). It is as if the imitation of the oral models (tongue protrusion and mouth opening) is replaced by vocal imitation, that is, by another more productive form of imitation, emanating from the same facial part, the oral cavity. The change of locus of imitation from visual to auditory modality may reflect the onset of maturational changes at the sensory level, a temporary sensory substitution given that imitation of TP starts to increase again after the fifth month and the selective character of early infant imitation is to serve intersubjective communication with the best available means. Despite the stability of imitation during the 6-month period, the ups and downs (linear, non-linear and negative developmental courses) may occur because of periodic reorganisations in the infant's motivational system, a type of development presumably related to anatomical changes in the brain, which are known to be extensive at this early age (Trevarthen, 1982, 1986; Kugiumutzakis, 1993). These reorganisations lead to motor, perceptual, emotional and cognitive changes, motivating the infants to seek 'fresh stimuli' in their imitative games, as Guillaume (1925) proposed many years ago (for alternative hypotheses see Butterworth, 1989).

Recently Maratos (1998, see also Maratos, 1973) described in detail the differences of the imitative response to the TP model during the neonatal period and at around 8 to 9 months. For example, she describes differences in the latency of the TP response, and its accuracy. The present study adds the information that imitation to the TP model appears systematically during the first 2 months, then it decreases to reappear systematically again at 5–6 months (Table 2.1 and Figure 2.1) and then it probably decreases to re-appear systematically at 8 or 9 months. At 5 months, the infant looks at the model carefully, usually smiles and then, after a very short latency, imitates once and perfectly. Despite the differences in motor and perceptual activity observed in the imitative responses across the three time intervals, these infant reproductions can be regarded as being governed by the same motives and emotions. However, after the second month, imitation serves in a more amusing and teasing way in the smart, free games of confirmation and disconfirmation of the other's expectations, which are characteristic of *homo ludens* (Reddy, 1991).

Neonatal and early infant imitation as a basic means of human interaction does not occur in a communicative vacuum. As noted earlier, smiling, cooing, clear and undetermined vocalisations, distinct phonemes, inside mouth TPs to the TP model, silent lip and mouth movements, imitation of the rhythm of the vocal models, efforts to grab the experimenter's moving facial parts (after the 5.5 month) and avoidance responses were observed in the present study when there were imitative responses as well as when there was no imitation or decrease of imitation. This finding invited further investigation, but experimental studies, even with a flexible design, are not planned to investigate the communicative frame of early imitation (see Trevarthen, 1986). In another naturalistic, longitudinal study we tried to investigate spontaneous vocal imitation in 21 mother–infant pairs from the fifteenth day after delivery to the sixth month, every 15 days, in the home environment, during their free-play interactions (Kugiumutzakis, 1993). The analysis showed that: mothers imitated the vocal sounds of their infants more frequently than vice versa (73% maternal and 27% infant vocal imitative responses); the mean number of vocal imitations was relatively low (one vocal imitation in 3 minutes); vocal imitations were extraordinarily fast (mean 3.2, SD 3.5 sec, a median of 2.2 sec and modes in the area of 1.0 to 1.4 sec). Turn taking was the rule (only 7.3% of the corpus was overlapping imitation); the mothers imitated both sexes to the same extent, no significant differences were found between the vocal imitations of girls and boys while both groups followed the same pattern of significant change in the number of imitations with age. The majority of vocal imitations took place in simple sequences (64% two turns/one round); imitation of speech sounds was significantly more frequent than imitation of non-speech sounds. The temporal pattern remained stable throughout the period of study, with the exception of an interesting increase in the duration of the infant's imitations after the third month, while the number of the vocal imitative episodes changes with age, following approximately a third-degree polynomial curve. The latter finding confirms the present study concerning the inversely U-shaped curve of the vocal imitative responses. The vocal imitations analysed in this naturalistic, longitudinal study (Kugiumutzakis, 1993) showed the same temporal pattern, the same turn-taking nature, a less relaxed quality and the same pattern of developmental change as has been described for maternal speech to infants in conversational play during the first 6 months (Fernald, 1989; Trevarthen and Marwick, 1986). These social, mirroring, exchanges may be described as a part of the mother–infant intersubjective communication. They were clear, selective vocal games, in which the reproduction of the sound was probably the result of mutual regulation of their central states of motivation. During the early months, the most basic function of imitation (and the first to appear) in mother–infant (and, in part, in stranger–infant) interactions is an interpersonal sense of communicative sharing. But what kind of sharing?

In neonatal and early infant imitation, parents and infants appear to share the same 3-D space, the same companion space, the same tendency to act and interact in turns, the same temporal pattern, the same ability for self–other discrimination, the same ability for recognition of face and voice isomorphism, the same code of communication, the same ability to read each other's motives and intentions, the same transient emotions, the same innate ability to imitate each other's actions and the same developmental changes in early infancy. Certainly they do not share many things, but what they do share is enough for the first emotional contacts (Bråten, 1988, 1992, 1994; Kugiumutzakis, 1985, 1988, 1993, 1998; Trevarthen, 1986, 1993). Developmentally, imitation first serves communication, and then, at around the fifth month in the frame of communication, it begins to serve learning and novelty.

In enunciating the above hypotheses the concept of mutuality is intentionally avoided although it is a basic characteristic of intersubjective communication (Nadel, 1980; Trevarthen, 1980, 1986; Užgiris, 1981). The reason is obvious. The experimenter, even with the flexible experimental design, did not reciprocate by imitating the neonatal and early infant behaviour, as happens in natural parent–infant interactions. Infant imitation in experimental conditions have helped us to reconsider our conceptions about the cognitive, social, perceptual, emotional and motor abilities of neonates and young infants (see also Hobson, 1993; Nadel and Pezé, 1993). At the same time, the lack of spontaneous, mutual imitative behaviour on the part of the adult in all the experimental studies does not permit the babies to experience the mutuality reported from naturalistic studies (Kugiumutzakis, 1993). Experimental neonatal and early infant imitation is a semi-natural kind of interaction that may both release some infant abilities and block others, and for that reason the experimental studies of infant imitation require completion by naturalistic studies.

REFERENCES

Abravanel, E. and Sigafoos, A. D. (1984). Exploring the presence of imitation in early infancy. *Child Development*, 55, 381–92.

Attkinson, J. and Braddick, O.(1982). Sensory and perceptual capacities of the neonate. In P. Stratton (ed.), *Psychobiology of the Human Newborn* (pp. 191–220). New York: Wiley.

Bard, K. A. (1994). *Social-experiental contributions to imitation and emotional expression in chimpanzies.* Paper presented at the Symposium on Intersubjective Communication and Emotion in Ontogeny, in The Norwegian Academy of Science and Letters, Oslo, 25–30 August.

Bråten, S. (1988). Between dialogic mind and monologic reason: postulating the virtual other. In M. Campanella (ed.), *Between rationality and cognition* (pp. 205–35). Torino: Meynie.

(1992). The virtual other in infant's minds and social feelings. In A. H. Wold (ed.), *The dialogical alternative* (pp. 77–97). Oslo: Scandinavian University Press.

(1994). *Self–other connections in the imitating infant and in the dyad: The companion space theorem.* Paper presented at the Symposium on Intersubjective Communication and Emotion in Ontogeny, in The Norwegian Academy of Science and Letters, Oslo, 25–30 August.

Butterworth, G. (1981). Object permanence and identity in Piaget's theory of infant cognition. In G. Butterworth (ed.), *Infancy and epistemology. An evaluation of Piaget's theory* (pp. 137–169). Brighton: The Harvester Press,.

(1989). On U shaped and other transitions in sensori-motor development. In *Proceedings of the European Science Foundation Workshop on Transition Mechanisms in Cognitive-Emotional Development: The Longitudinal Approach.* Grachen, Switzerland, March 1987.

Butterworth, G. and Hopkins, B. (1988). Hand–mouth coordination in the newborn baby. *British Journal of Developmental Psychology*, 6, 303–14.

Dunkeld, J. (1978). The function of imitation in infancy. Doctoral dissertation. Department of Psychology, University of Edinburgh.

Ferguson, C. A. (1978). Learning to pronounce: the earliest stages of phonological development in the child. In F. D. Minifie and L. L. Lloyd (eds). *Communicative and Cognitive Abilities-Early Behavioral Assessment* (pp. 273–97). Baltimore: University Park Press.

Fernald, A. (1989). Intonation and communicative intent in mothers' speech to infants and adults. *Child Development*, 60, 1497–510.

Field, T. M., Goldstein, S., Vega-Lahr, N. and Porter, K. (1986). Changes in imitative behavior during early infancy. *Infant Behavior and Development*, 9, 415–21.

Field, T. M., Woodson, R., Cohen, D., Greenberg, R., Garcia, R. and Collins, K. (1983). Discrimination and imitation of facial expressions by term and preterm neonates. *Infant Behavior and Development*, 6, 485–490.

Field, T. M., Woodson, R., Greenberg, R. and Cohen, D. (1982). Discrimination and imitation of facial expressions by neonates. *Science*, 218, 179–81.

Fontaine, R. (1984). Imitative skills between birth and six months. *Infant Behavior and Development*, 7, 323–33.

Gibson, J. J. (1979). *The ecological approach to visual perception.* Boston: Houghton-Mifflin.

Guillaume, P. (1925). *Imitation in children.* University of Chicago Press (1971).

Heimann, M. (1989). Neonatal imitation, gaze aversion and mother–infant interaction. *Infant Behavior and Development,* 12, 495–505.

Heimann, M. and Schaller, J. (1985). Imitative reactions among 14–21 day old infants. *Infant Mental Health Journal,* 6(1), 31–9.

Hobson, P. R. (1993). *Autism and the development of mind.* Hove: Erlbaum.

Jacobson, S. W. (1979). Matching behavior in young infants. *Child Development,* 50, 425–30.

Kokkinaki, N. (1998). The contribution of imitation in infant–father and infant–mother interaction in two cultures. Ph.D. thesis, Department of Psychology, University of Edinburgh (in preparation).

Kugiumutzakis, G. (1985). The origin, development and function of early infant imitation. Ph.D. thesis, Department of Psychology, University of Uppsala.

(1988). I genesis tis anthropinis mimesis. (The origin of human imitation.) *Psychologica Themata,* 1(1), 5–21.

(1992). *Self-recognition as pre-condition of the infant imitative communication.* Paper presented at the XIVth Congress of the International Primatological Society, Strasburg, 15–21 August.

(1993). Intersubjective vocal imitation in early mother–infant interaction. In J. Nadel and L. Camaioni (eds). *New perspectives in early communicative development* (pp. 23–47). London: Routledge.

(1994). *Is early human imitation an emotional phenomenon?* Paper presented at the Symposium on Intersubjective Communication and Emotion in Ontogeny in The Norwegian Academy of Science and Letters, Oslo, 25–30 August.

(1998). Neonatal imitation in the inter-subjective companion space. In S. Bråten (ed.), *Inter-subjective communication and emotion in ontogeny.* Cambridge University Press.

Legerstee, M. (1991). The role of person and object in eliciting early imitation. *Journal of Experimental Child Psychology,* 51, 423–33.

Maratos, O. (1973). The origin and development of imitation in the first six months of life. Ph.D. thesis. Department of Psychology, Geneva University.

(1982). Trends in the development of imitation in early infancy. In T. G. Bever (ed.), *Regressions in mental development: Basic phenomena and theories* (pp. 81–101). Hillsdale, NJ: Erlbaum.

(1998). Neonatal and later imitation: Same order phenomena?. In F. Simion and G. Butterworth (eds.), *The development of sensory, motor and cognitive capacities in early infancy. From perception to cognition* (pp. 145–60). Hove: Psychology Press.

Masters, J. C. (1979). Interpreting 'imitative' response in early infancy. *Science,* 205, 215.

Meltzoff, A. N. and Moore, M. K. (1977). Imitation of facial and manual gestures by human neonates. *Science,* 178, 75–8.

(1983). Newborn infants imitate adult facial gestures. *Child Development,* 54, 702–9.

(1989). Imitation in newborn infants: Exploring the range of gestures imitated and the underlying mechanisms. *Developmental Psychology*, 25(6), 954–62.

(1992). Early imitation within a functional framework: The importance of person identity, movement and development. *Infant Behavior and Development*, 15, 479–505.

Michotte, A. (1946/1967). *The perception of causality*. London: Methuen.

Miller, N. E. and Dollard, J. (1941). *Social learning and imitation*. New Haven: Yale University Press.

Nadel, J. (1980). The functional role of imitation in personality development: Wallon's contribution. *French-Language Psychology*, 1, 169–77.

Nadel, J. and Pezé, A. (1993). What makes immmediate imitation communicative in toddlers and autistic children. In J. Nadel and L. Camaioni (eds.), *New perspectives in early communicative development* (pp. 139–56). London: Routledge.

Neisser, U. (1993). *The self perceived*. In U. Neisser (ed.), *The perceived self: Ecological and interpersonal sources of self-knowledge* (pp. 3–21). Cambridge, MA: Cambridge University Press.

Pawlby, S. J. (1977). Imitative interaction. In H. R. Schaffer (ed.), *Studies in mother–infant interaction* (pp. 203–24). London: Academic Press.

Piaget, J. (1945/1962). *Play, dreams and imitation*. London: Routledge and Kegan Paul.

Prechtl, H. F. R. (1982). Assessment methods for the newborn infant: A critical evaluation. In P. Stratton (ed.), *Psychobiology of the human newborn* (pp. 21–52). New York: Wiley.

Prechtl, H. F. R. and O'Brien, M. J. (1982). Behavioral states of the fullterm newborn: The emergence of a concept. In P. Stratton (ed.), *Psychobiology of the human newborn* (pp. 53–73). New York: Wiley.

Reddy, V. (1991). Playing with others' expectations, teasing and mucking about in the first year. In A. Whiten (ed.), *Natural theories of mind* (pp. 143–158). Oxford, Blackwell.

Reissland, N. (1988). Neonatal imitation in the first hour of life: Observations in rural Nepal. *Developmental Psychology*, 24, 464–9.

Rinn, W. E. (1984). The neuropsychology of facial expression: A review of the neurological and psychological mechanisms for producing facial expressions. *Psychological Bulletin*, 1, 52–77.

Ronnqvist, L. (1993). Arm and hand movements in neonates and young infants. Ph. D. thesis, Department of Psychology, University of Umea, Sweden.

Runeson, S. and Frykholm, G. (1983). Kinematic specification of dynamics as an information basis for person-and-action perception: Expectation, gender, recognition, and deceptive intention. *Journal of Experimental Psychology: General*, 112(4), 585–615.

Siegel, S. (1956). *Nonparametric methods for the behavioral sciences*. New York: McGraw-Hill.

Stratton, P. (1982). Rhythmic functions in the newborn. In P. Stratton (ed.), *Psychobiology of the human newborn* (pp. 119–45). New York: Wiley.

Trevarthen, C. (1977). *Descriptive analyses of infant communicative behavior*. In H. R. Schaffer (ed.), *Studies in mother–infant interaction* (pp. 227–70). London: Academic Press.

(1982). Basic patterns of psychogenetic change in infancy. In T. T. Bever (ed.), *Regressions in mental development: basic phenomena and theories* (pp. 7–46). Hillsdale, NJ: Erlbaum.

(1986). Development of intersubjective motor control in infants. In M. G. Wade and H. T. A. Whiting (eds.), *Motor development in children: Aspects of coordination and control* (pp. 209–61). Dordrecht: Marthinus Nijhof.

(1993). The function of emotions in early infant communication and development. In J. Nadel and L. Camaioni (eds.), *New perspectives in early communicative development* (pp. 48–81). London: Routledge.

Trevarthen, C. and Marwick, H. (1986). Signs of motivation for speech in infants and the nature of a mother's support for development of language. In B. Lindblom and R. Zetterstrom (eds.), *Precursors of early speech* (pp. 279–308). Basingstoke: Macmillan.

Užgiris, I. Č. (1981). Two functions of imitation during infancy. *International Journal of Behavioral Development*, 4, 1–12.

Vedeler, (1991). Infant intentionality as object directedness: an alternative to representationalism. *Journal for the Theory of Social Behavior*, 21(2), 431–48.

Vinter, A. (1986). The role of movement in eliciting early imitations. *Child Development*, 57, 66–71.

Part II

Imitation: theoretical issues in phylogeny and ontogeny

3   Neonatal imitation: existence, mechanisms and motives

George Butterworth

Introduction

Modern research has shown imitation to be a natural mechanism of learning and communication which deserves to be at centre stage in developmental psychology. Yet, the very possibility of imitation in newborn humans has been deeply controversial. Defining imitation has proved to be far from straightforward and scientific evidence for its existence in neonates is only now becoming accepted, despite more than a century of inquiry. This chapter will concentrate on imitation in the neonatal period, in an attempt to make further progress. It will be necessary to differentiate imitation from other processes which can give rise to similarities in behaviour between individuals in order to establish that imitation is a means of learning in its own right. The question of the evolutionary significance of imitation will also be addressed. Mimesis occurs in various forms in nature: from protective colouration, to vocal imitation, to the imitation of complex sequences of action. How does imitation in humans fit into such a naturalistic perspective? Imitation as a means of transmission of culture also needs to be brought into consideration. Developmental analysis, or the genetic method, as it was called by Baldwin (1902), will be adopted here. The chapter will begin by defining imitation, then it will review evidence for imitation in nature and its existence in human newborns, and conclude by considering possible mechanisms and motives for the abilities revealed.

Defining imitation

Baldwin (1894, 1903) considered imitation simultaneously to be a biological and social phenomenon. In his theory of imitation, he was influenced by the sociologist Gabriel Tarde (1895), on the role of suggestion as a means of diffusion of social behaviour, and by Spencer (1870) and Romanes (1884, 1889), who were speculating on possible biological mechanisms whereby characteristics acquired in ontogeny might become heritable (Richards, 1988).

Tarde (1895) had defined imitation as a form of copying 'every impression of an inter-psychical photography, so to speak, willed or not willed, passive or active' (p. xiv). Baldwin (1894) was critical of this rather vague formulation and substituted his own definitions. He defined imitation in three related ways (Baldwin, 1901). First, interpersonally as 'performance in movement, thought or both movement and thought, of what comes through the senses or by suggestion, as belonging to another individual' (p. 519). On this criterion, another person serves to set the copy to be imitated. A second, intrapersonal definition suggests a link between imitation and memory: 'Any repetition in thought, action or both which reinstates a copy' (p. 519). A third definition specified a potential developmental mechanism both for imitation and memory: 'An organic reaction of the stimulus repeating or self sustaining type [which is] synonymous with the physiological conception of a circular reaction' (p. 519).

Baldwin hit upon the simple fact that imitation involves repetition. He said 'The effect of imitation, it is clear, is to make the brain a repeating organ, and the muscular system is, as far as this function goes, the expression and evidence of this fact' (Baldwin, 1894, p. 26). On this rather unusual definition, repetition of an action is imitative of the act of which it is a repetition. Lloyd-Morgan (1896) criticised Baldwin for abandoning the accepted definition of imitation as 'the repetition by one individual of the behaviour of another individual' (p. 168). In so doing, however, Baldwin was seeking to trace the origins of imitation, which, through development, give rise to hetero-imitation. Thus, for Baldwin, whose broad sketch was subsequently elaborated by Piaget (1962) with reference to development in infancy, imitation originates in intrapersonal phenomena. Only with development does imitation become interpersonal. This, in turn, paves the way for symbolic processes, the acquisition of speech and verbal transmission of culture.

Mimetism

Baldwin (1901) further distinguished between imitation, mimetism and mimicry. Mimetism is a pathological form of imitation in which adults with brain damage express themselves in slavish, obligatory copying or pantomime. Such phenomena have recently been studied by Lhermitte, Pillon and Serdaru (1986) who found that patients with rather specific, focal lesions in the lower half of either the left, right or both frontal lobes engaged in involuntary imitation. A distinction was made between imitating the examiner's gestures (imitation behaviour) and imitating the examiner's use of objects (utilisation behaviour). Gestures made by the medical examiner, such as a threatening movement of the finger, or putting on spectacles, or combing the hair, or kneeling in prayer were slavishly repeated. Lhermitte et al. (1986) suggest that the sight of the movement is taken by the patient as an order to imitate. They postulate that frontal-lobe lesions release inhibition on the parietal lobes, with the consequence that the patient becomes 'enslaved' by the immediate social environment.

As patients recovered, they first became able to suppress utilisation behaviour and, later, to suppress the tendency to imitate gestures. The sequence of recovery suggests that imitation of gestures and of instrumental actions may be distinctly organised processes. The order is the inverse of the acquisition process generally observed in development (e.g., Piaget, 1962). The effect of brain damage in adults is of interest because, in the absence of strong frontal lobe influence, newborn babies may actually be particularly prone to imitate. Furthermore, evidence from Lhermitte et al. (1986) tends to support Trevarthen's contention (this volume) that the hands serve two distinct modes of purposeful operation, (i) for intentions of the self directed to objects and (ii) for communication with others, of which the latter is the more basic in development.

However, imitation in newborns should not be considered as somehow equivalent to pathological mimetism. Neonatal imitation does not have the same quality of compulsion observed by Lhermitte et al. (1986). Attempts to imitate have been reported in newborns which may better be considered as sustained, intentional efforts to match observed behaviour (Meltzoff, 1994; see also Kugiumutzakis, Meltzoff and Moore, Trevarthen, this volume).

To summarise, the prototypical case of imitation is when one individual voluntarily reproduces behaviour observed in another who acts as the model for the form of a behaviour.

Evolution, mimicry, imitation and mimesis

Baldwin (1902) linked imitation and evolution in proposing the principle of 'organic selection'. According to Baldwin, imitation as a mechanism of individual adaptation serves as an auxiliary means to evolution by natural selection (Voneche, 1982). An objection to Darwin's (1859) theory of evolution by natural selection is that small variations between organisms may not provide a sufficient basis for natural selection to operate upon. Baldwin (1902) realised that small, inborn variations may be very much amplified if they are linked with environmentally determined sources of variation. Natural selection of a small inborn variation may therefore be based primarily on the amplifying characteristics of the linked, acquired variation (he called these processes ontogenetic adaptation and organic selection). Thus, imitation offers a biological mechanism which can screen developing organisms from the effects of natural selection and does so sufficiently to allow nascent, adaptive variations to become widespread in the population. He said mimicry 'prevents the incidence of natural selection . . . and so keeps alive the creatures which have no instincts for the performance of the actions required' (Baldwin, 1902, p. 78). Organic selection over succeeding generations has the effect of stabilising population variability more closely around the mean. This contribution to evolutionary theory has become known as the 'Baldwin effect' (see Gottlieb, 1992). For Baldwin, imitation is important in biology because it acts as a contributory factor to evolution, and in psychology because the new generation thereby functions within the social framework created by the previous generation.

The term mimicry in biology is in use generically to denote organism–environment similarities as in camouflage, as well as resemblances between and within species (McFarland, 1981). Baldwin (1901) defined mimicry as 'a resemblance between certain species inhabiting the same country independent of their affinity' (p. 79). Examples include both protective and aggressive mimicry, where mimicry of body colouration between different species is closely linked to advantages in predation or protection from predation. Such mimicry does not require the individual to be endowed with a specific ability to imitate, nor is it socially transmitted.

However, there are examples of mimicry in nature which clearly are socially transmitted, as when birds copy the songs of those around them. This form of mimicry may be entirely intraspecific, as in robins and chaffinches, or partially interspecific, as in starlings and mocking birds, who will incorporate into their song sounds from other species in the vicinity (Slater, 1990). Davis (1981) reports that up to 80% of the vocalisation of a species of lyre bird comprises calls borrowed from other species (including the sound of barking dogs, musical instruments and other noises such as the blows of an axe). Vocal mimicry serves to promote individual recognition of one songbird by another; it contributes to learning at the individual level and there may be considerable individual variation in ability.

Donald (1991) further distinguishes between mimicry as a literal copy, as in protective colouration, imitation which is an approximative copy and mimesis. Mimesis, according to Donald (1991), develops out of mimicry and imitation, in that it adds a representational dimension. Mimesis involves intentional re-enaction of an event or relationship. It may involve an audience and serve to communicate, or it may serve simply to represent an event to oneself. Mimesis is particularly useful in modelling social roles, communicating emotions and in transmitting rudimentary tool-using skills. In considering human evolution, Donald (1991) proposed that *Homo erectus* (1.8 to 0.3 million years BP), may have lived in a mimetic culture. Mimetic culture on this view was a successful adaptation strategy for a million years, before human cultural transmission became primarily dependent on language.

In summary, an evolved capacity for intraspecific mimicry may be expected to confer developmental benefits. Xitco (1988) has listed some general advantages: (a) imitation provides an alternative to expensive trial-and-error learning; (b) it facilitates the rapid acquisition of adaptive behaviour in the young by providing a head start; (c) it allows direct incorporation of the learned repertoire of the society; and (d) in large-brained social animals it facilitates the formation of social and affective relationships necessary for survival. To this list we may add some more specifically human benefits; (e) it serves communication, role taking and language (Kugiumutzakis, 1985; Trevarthen, this volume); (f) it serves individual identification (Meltzoff and Moore, this volume); (g) an innate capacity for imitation in humans might be expected to contribute to the social transmission of culturally accumulated characteristics (Donald, 1991).

Imitation and novelty

Another issue of definition concerns the criterion that to be truly imitative a behaviour must be novel and not already in the repertoire. Imitation is defined by Thorpe (1963) as 'the copying of a novel or otherwise improbable act or utterance for which there is clearly no instinctive tendency'. Such a definition assists in determining whether complex sequences of action involving tool use are truly imitative, in the sense that a new behaviour has been learned through observation. However, it presents problems in interpreting neonatal imitation. Novelty requires that the target behaviour should not already be in the repertoire, yet in newborns the phenomena of interest can occur only because some behaviours are already in the repertoire.

Visalberghi and Fragaszy (1990) emphasise that whether a behaviour is considered novel or not depends on a number of factors (e.g., where it is carried out, exactly how it is performed). An action may be in the repertoire, but, if the circumstances of testing make it unlikely that it will ever have been carried out before, then, in principle, imitation can be accepted. On this criterion, innate imitation would amount to selecting from a wider repertoire, a modelled improbable behaviour, in order to match it.

Other mechanisms ensuring behavioural convergence

Of course, non-imitative mechanisms can also ensure convergence of behaviour between organisms, but there is no reason to suppose that all evidence of imitation in newborn humans can be explained away by alternative processes of social learning. Figure 3.1 is a taxonomy of social learning mechanisms, adopted from Whiten and Ham (1992), which is sufficient to explain many anecdotal reports of imitation in animals. Behavioural conformity may be brought about through social facilitation, where an individual may become motivated to carry out an action by observing a conspecific behaving similarly, or through stimulus enhancement, where the conspecific directs attention to a salient aspect of the environment which promotes similar behaviour in the observer (see also Zentall, 1996 and Galef, 1988). However, imitation is not simply about establishing behavioural conformity. Mere conformity lacks the hallmark of true imitation, which is the 'transfer' of an action from one individual to another.

Taking all these factors into consideration leads to the following defining characteristics of imitation. (i) The prototypical case of imitation is when one individual voluntarily reproduces behaviour observed in another who acts as the model for the form of a behaviour. (ii) It involves an essential quality of transfer of information which forms the basis for establishing behavioural correspondence. (iii) Imitation in humans may be related to mimicry in its broader biological sense in ensuring that infants come to 'blend' with their social surroundings.

Imitation in non-human primates and other animals

The etymological root of the verb 'to imitate' in many languages designates monkeys, apes and primates (Visalberghi and Fragaszy, 1990). Despite the fact that monkeys were long considered to be the foremost imitators in nature, contemporary evidence suggests that humans by far exceed their capacities (as do apes and dolphins, see Andrew, 1962; Byrne, 1995). Much of the evidence for imitation in monkeys and apes comes from cross-species tests which use humans as models. There is evidence that a chimpanzee, reared by humans, imitated mouth-opening and tongue-protrusion movements at 5 weeks (Myowa, 1996) and Bard (this volume) reports various types of facial imitation in chimpanzees aged 11 days or less. The question whether imitation among the apes

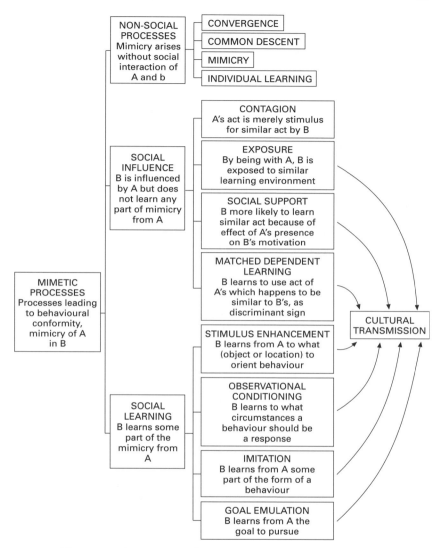

Figure 3.1. A taxonomy of mimetic processes.

depends on human contact is important and remains to be fully resolved (Tomasello, 1996). However, most comparative studies have not been concerned with innate imitation, nor even with development, but simply to find out whether imitation exists at all.

Adult great apes are certainly capable of imitating complex sequences of actions, including using petrol to start a fire! (Russon and Galdikas, 1993). In monkeys there is little evidence for imitation in tasks which require tool use (Visalberghi and Fragaszy, 1990) but monkeys can imitate actions in which the task incorporates elements similar to those that occur in the wild, such as peeling fruit (Whiten and Custance, 1996). In general, therefore, a capacity for imitation exists among primates, although whether this ability is actually used in the wild is not well established. Despite the methodological problems involved in studying other organisms, Whiten (1998) notes that carefully controlled studies have recently shown visual imitation of simple actions in rats, pigeons and parrots (Heyes, Dawson and Nokes, 1992; Moore, 1992; Zentall, Sutton and Sherburne, 1998). Bugnyar and Huber (1997) also report rather precise visual imitation in 3 out of 5 marmosets who had observed a conspecific retrieving food using a simple bimanual action. Thus, visual imitation of actions does not appear to be restricted to higher primates. Of course, the representational ability available to model different actions may vary considerably between species (and even between individuals).

Few scientists would dispute that learning song dialects in some species of birds occurs through imitation (Andrew, 1962). According to Slater (1990) song learning, at least in some species, depends on the juvenile coming into contact with an adult (usually male) bird from whose song the fledgling incorporates heard elements, to give rise to the eventual adult form. The song form varies in when it becomes fixed, depending on species and on its function. If the function is mate attainment, it becomes fixed by reproductive age, but if it is territorial defence, copying new songs may extend into adult life. Davis (1981) suggests that song learning occurs even in the absence of reward, which supports the view that bird song is elaborated on an innate base by imitation.

Whiten and Ham (1992) argue that the discrepancy of incidence between vocal and visual imitation in nature may occur because visual imitation is more computationally demanding. It may involve a greater number of steps between seeing the model and imitating, than between hearing the model and matching the vocalisation. Thus, visual imitation may require greater brain size. Andrew (1998), on the other hand, argues that it is misleading to discuss a general ability to mimic which is dependent on brain size. Rather, he suggests that, once an ability has evolved sufficiently to be controlled by feedback, whether auditory or visual, the by-product of that form of motor control is the ability to copy the sounds or visual movements of a conspecific. Mimicry can evolve in the absence of a high level of intelligence, if there is a need during development to acquire species, group or individually specific patterns of vocalisation.

In summary, there may be several types of imitation, each dependent on feedback control, which may have evolved independently in different species. Advanced forms of imitation, such as those involving tool use, may depend on representing the intentions of the model (Tomasello, 1996). However, advanced representational abilities need not be postulated for other forms of imitation, for which perception may be sufficient (see also Heyes and Galef, 1996).

Human neonatal imitation: existence

That hetero-imitation may be possible early in human development was long suspected. For example, Tiedemann (1787) speculated that imitation may be instinctive in humans, McDougall (1931) described his nephew imitating tongue movements at 3 months and Preyer (1892) described his daughter imitating at 4 months. Such anecdotal observations of tongue-protrusion imitation did not carry much weight. Zazzo (1957) reports that he had filmed imitation of tongue protrusion in his 25-day-old son as long ago as 1945, but his observations were met with scepticism by Henri Wallon. Zazzo eventually followed this up with a diary study of 23 babies aged between 7 and 15 days, using parents as trained observers, who also reported that their babies imitated tongue protrusion (Zazzo, 1988).

One of the major methodological refinements of recent times has been controlling for the possibility that imitation in young humans may be an artefact of the conditions of testing. Meltzoff and Moore (1977) pioneered a cross-target procedure in which the infant observes one of several behaviours being modelled. Judges who are blind to the actual model, categorise the infant's video-recorded behaviour according to a range of alternatives. It is unlikely that the statistically reliable correspondence which raters find between infant behaviour and that of the model can be due to non-imitative mechanisms of social learning, such as inadvertent shaping by the experimenter, by contagion, or as a sign-released stimulus (e.g., criticisms by Hayes and Watson, 1981; Masters, 1979). Together with sensitive procedures for exploring the range of imitative abilities in babies, some less than 45 minutes old, it now seems safe to say that newborn humans can imitate both in the visual and auditory modality (Kugiumutzakis, 1985; Maratos 1973; Meltzoff and Moore, this volume).

There have been many replications of newborn imitation in the visual modality which include not only mouth, tongue and other facial movements, but also eye blinking and sequential finger movements (e.g., Fontaine, 1984; Kugiumutzakis, 1985; Reissland, 1988; Vinter, 1986). The newborn baby often takes time to respond to the stimulus and, in the case of tongue protrusion, appears to make 'searching' movements, which suggest that the imitative response is rather effortful and not automatically released (Meltzoff and Moore, 1994; Meltzoff and Moore, this volume). Kugiumutzakis (1985, this volume) reports that three types of response were observed in his studies of newborns: (i) immediate imitation in which the model is reproduced once in a relatively precise fashion; (ii) successive improving imitation in which the model is reproduced by the newborn a number of times, converging toward a more precise matching; (iii) successive deteriorating imitation in which the first imitative effort is satisfactory but additional efforts are less so. The newborn makes observable efforts to direct attention to the moving parts of the experimenter's face, sometimes frowning during the effort. Maratos (1998) reports (for 1-month-old infants) 'Mouth opening is . . . imitated after a long latency, often during presentation of the model with hesitant and almost constant movements in the area of the mouth, including swallowing, until one sees the final response with the mouth open wide (p. 146). All this suggests that early imitation is effortful and voluntary. Even so, one isolated critic acknowledges only the case of tongue protrusion and he considers this to be a triggered response (Anisfeld, 1996). In the auditory modality there is evidence for neonatal imitation of the vowel sound 'aah' (Kugiumutzakis, 1993, this volume). In describing the imitative responses of 15-day-old babies to auditory stimuli, Kugiumutzakis (1993, p. 35) states that the sounds emitted were not vegetative or emotional reactions. The baby gradually localises the sound as it is being presented, with a facial expression consistent with attentive listening, and the imitative attempt was usually an approximate vocal response, accompanied by stretching hand movements and closed eyes characteristic of effort.

There is also evidence for innate imitation of emotional expressions in 2-day-old humans (Field, Woodson, Greenberg and Cohen, 1982). It has been argued that Field et al.'s (1982) findings may be explained by contagion (Kaitz, Meschulach-Sarfaty and Auerbach, 1988, see Table 1). On this view, the infant's matching responses to the modelled emotional expressions of happiness, sadness and surprise were 'triggered' rather than imitated. Contagion is 'the performance of a more or less instinctive pattern of behaviour by one (which) will tend to act as a releaser for the same behaviour in others' (Thorpe, 1963, p. 133).

Set against this, it is known that empathic responses occur in adults which cannot have been triggered by merely observing a particular behaviour. For example, observers may duck to avoid a danger threatening the model, even though the model does not duck (Bavelas, Black, Lemery, MacInnis and Mullett, 1986). By the same token, imitation of emotional expressions in newborns may be a primary, empathic response. Tiedemann (1787) puts it nicely in discussing his 26-day-old son: 'And herein lies the first source of sympathy; for by looking upon others, who are stirred by some emotion, the soul projects itself into the same situation, wherein it has once experienced that feeling . . . thus the boy who had already formed some idea of pleasant and unpleasant sensations, might not yet have known or conceived of their expression in the human physiognomy, yet he was moved to smiles by a cheerful and pleasant look . . . for between expression and emotion there is a natural connection' (p. 17).

According to Wallon (1934), human infants are fundamentally sociable, and emotions, through their facial and bodily expressions (gestures), allow a first level of communication. Nadel (1994) points out, however, that Wallon believed that such affective sharing does not begin until 3 months. Trevarthen (1993, this volume) argues that emotional expression is an innate means of early communication and the basis for primary intersubjectivity. Imitation and being imitated carry strong affiliative signals. The emotions serve to communicate a subjective evaluation with respect to one's own body, other persons and other things. If affiliation is one of the social functions of imitation, it seems quite possible that newborn babies do indeed imitate emotional expressions. It is misdirected parsimony to dismiss such evidence as merely due to contagion. In fact, contagion itself may serve the purpose of social coupling, and, even if contagion is not imitation, it may set the stage for imitation in the emotional arena (Provine, 1997).

In summary, the question whether there is an innate ability (or abilities) for imitation in humans nowadays usually receives an affirmative answer. The discussion can move on to consider possible mechanisms: how can the newborn baby imitate visible and invisible movements as well as auditory targets?

Mechanisms of imitation

Classical theories, under Baldwin's influence, served to restrict possible mechanisms at the origins of imitation to reflexes and the simple circular reactions (e.g., Guillaume, 1926; Piaget 1962; Wallon, 1942). Circular reactions are pleasurable, which maintains their repetitive cycle, and they are inherently variable, which offers a mechanism for adaptive change. As theorised by Piaget (1962), circular reactions are constructed from co-ordinated reflexes, which progressively accommodate to a greater variety of sensory experiences. Sensory stimuli, in turn, re-elicit the actions in circular fashion, to give rise to object recognition through action. Primary circular reactions inform the infant about self, but they do not differentiate between information obtained from self or another. The tendency of newborns to cry when others are crying is explained by reflex triggering and later, in the second month, by contagion. There is no ability visually to establish an emotional correspondence between self and other. Smiling, at between 2 and 3 months, is explained as pseudo-imitation originating in contagion and maintained by mutual stimulation (Piaget, 1962 obs. 1, obs. 3, pp. 7, 9, 18).

Piaget was very careful to eliminate from consideration behavioural correspondence which comes about merely as a result of training. Only behaviours obviously mediated by primary circular reactions are considered true examples of early imitation. The first interpersonal imitative abilities begin at about the sixth month. For example, the baby may see the model move the hand and imitates, if that movement is already in the baby's repertoire (Piaget, 1962 obs. 17, p. 25). To imitate facial movements is considered an advanced achievement, possible only from about 1 year. The ability to match facial movements is thought to require representation (a mental model) of the appearance of the face (e.g., Piaget, 1962 obs. 46, p. 37). He describes the baby, from about 8 months, building up the motor schemes necessary for invisible imitation by correlating touch with vision, as if to establish the correspondence between invisible parts of her own body and the visible parts of the adult's face. True imitation of facial expressions develops late because the infant must first establish, through inference, the relationship between visible and invisible movements (Piaget, 1962, p. 61). Finally, deferred imitation begins at about 1 year. Deferred imitation differs from immediate imitation in that reproduction of a behaviour occurs in the absence of the model; it involves the symbolic evocation of absent realities and includes complex sequences of action (Piaget, 1962, p. 68). Deferred imitation has many of the characteristics which Donald (1991) ascribes to mimesis.

The evidence already reviewed on neonatal imitation contradicts Piaget's general progression from visible to invisible imitation. Solving the problem of the origins of hetero-imitation clearly requires an alternative mechanism. Modern theory needs to take into account evidence from prenatal development to explain the abilities of the newborn. Ultrasonic scanning studies of foetuses have shown that at least fifteen different, well-co-ordinated movement patterns can be discerned as early as 15 weeks gestational age (De Vries, Visser and Prechtl, 1984). These include independent finger movements, rapid and slow mouth opening, movements of the hand, repetitive contacting of the mouth with the fingers, opening and closing of the jaws, and leg movements. Movements of the fused eyelids are observed at 20 weeks, and conjugate lateral eye movements with open eyelids by 24–25 weeks. Finely modulated facial expressions can also be observed in foetuses of 24 weeks (Hofer, 1981). Many of these are behaviours that have been reported in neonatal imitation studies.

To penetrate the question of mechanism further it is necessary to consider the neuromuscular development of the foetus. Contemporary theories of brain development suggest that the detailed circuitry of the nervous system may depend on feedback from intra-uterine activity and also on intra-uterine sensory feedback (Purves, 1994). Such experience-dependent growth processes may begin very early in development. By 8 weeks, the spinal cord has formed and contains motor neurons which will innervate the developing motor system. Primary afferent nerves which bring information from the periphery, and interneurons, are not yet interconnected. At this age, general, writhing movements are observed which transform into more graceful movements by 10 weeks, as the spinal reflex arc is closed. From 11 weeks, there is an eightfold increase in the number of synapses on the motor neurons. Myelinisation of the nerve fibres in the ventral part of the spinal cord begins at 12 weeks and coincides with the clear differentiation between the various independent movement patterns which De Vries et al. (1984) observed in the twelfth to fifteenth week. By 13 weeks, many mid-brain structures are already physically arranged as in the adult, and electrical activity can be detected in the hippocampus and diencephalon (O'Rahilly and Müller, 1994). Between 16 and 24 weeks, descending fibres, originating in the dorsal thalamus and striatum, first inhibit and then reactivate mid-brain systems, as connections are established with the cortical plate, where intensive synaptic formation is also occurring (Hofer, 1981). The patterns of firing at the synapses may depend on feedback from activity, both in sensory and motor systems, which contributes to the further differentiation of the emerging central nervous system (Purves, 1994).

There is a high level of activity (estimated to be as many as 20,000 movements per day in the foetus to 15 weeks) followed by a period of quiescence between 16 and 24 weeks and resumption of more finely modulated activity thereafter (Hofer, 1981). Given the very early appearance of co-ordinated movements, it is apparent that much foetal behaviour must be regulated by systems within the spinal cord, brain stem and mid-brain. These basic action systems are progressively integrated with cortical systems as development proceeds. This process continues well into postnatal life, with the mid-brain serving different behaviours, as a multifunctional core, as new postures, different neurotransmitters, new sources of perceptual information, cortical systems and descending pathways are progressively integrated with the mid-brain (Bekoff, 1995; Hofer, 1981).

The neural basis for the action patterns reported in neonatal imitation studies may therefore be well established long before birth. The repetitive nature of foetal activity fits in some respects the concept of a circular reaction, but a crucial difference for developmental theory is that the newborn can immediately relate at least some of her own movement patterns to those of another person. This requires a theory of perception–action coupling, such as that of Gibson (1966), which solves the problem by postulating an information-based dynamical systems account. Many of the characteristics of the body in action are specified by objective information, which are simultaneously self-specific and exterospecific (Gibson, 1987). Much of this information is kinetic; it consists of structures which both change and remain invariant over time and which are equivalent across several perceptual systems.

There is good agreement between various theories that some such mechanism might be involved in innate imitation. Meltzoff and Borton (1979) argue that the mechanism of imitation, with its essential defining property of 'transfer', is logically equivalent to matching information across modalities of input (the active intermodal matching AIM hypothesis (Meltzoff and Moore, this volume). Meltzoff and Moore (1994) suggest that there may a limited innate set of actions, such as tongue protrusion, which can home in rather precisely on the observed target behaviour which sets the goal for proprioceptive matching. Trevarthen (this volume) argues for 'transfer of an amodal perceptual effect' and Donald (1991) also postulates a supramodular 'mimetic controller' which serves to model perceptual events. Kugiumutzakis (1985), on the other hand, argues that face recognition must occur between the visual exploration of the facial model and before the first effort to imitate. He argues that this is mediated by some form of facial 'memory engram' which carries information for the corresponding facial action.

These lines of argument may entail a theory of the embodied foundations of self-perception, which can then be extended to interpersonal perception. Such theories make special reference to amodal aspects of proprioception which are informative about the self, especially in maintaining postural control (Butterworth, 1995; Rochat, 1994). A similar analysis might help to establish how the newborn succeeds in hetero-imitation. In dynamical systems theory, development is self-organising around various attractors, or state spaces, on which the configurations of the system tends to converge (Butterworth, 1993; Hopkins and Butterworth, 1997). Dynamical systems tend to be cyclic, but they do not literally copy themselves in the manner of circular reactions. Rather, their dynamics are constrained within limits set by the elasticity of the musculature, by biomechanical, neurological and other contextual factors, to function within typical regimes of variation.

Although principles of dynamical systems theory have not yet been widely applied to newborn imitation, there is evidence that neonatal imitation may involve matching the dynamic patterns of perceptible input to patterned proprioceptive output (Vinter, 1986). On the evidence available so far, behavioural matching occurs both from vision and audition to the actions of the hand, mouth and tongue, and through the dynamics of social interaction to the expression of emotions. Strictly speaking, the dynamic systems approach does not require any translation from perception to action, or cross-modal matching, since the equivalence between input and output processes is established at a more abstract level of spatiotemporal patterning. Thelen and Smith (1993) suggest that, while perceptual modalities involve qualitatively different takes on reality, there are multiple interactions between systems from the outset.

Many examples of perception–action coupling in babies, in locomotion and postural control, are discussed by Bertenthal and Pinto (1993) in an analysis which might usefully be applied to imitation. In a dynamic systems account of imitation, the aim would be to explain how co-ordinated behaviour emerges between individuals. If perception and action are opposite poles of a functional, goal-directed system, it is possible to envisage that both perceptual and motor sources may project information, at an appropriately abstract level, to common regions of the brain. What applies intra-individually in feedback control of action might equally apply inter-individually, as Andrew (1998) maintains. It is of particular significance that dynamic principles may be applied to the bimodal perception of speech in relation to the visual configurations of the mouth (Kuhl and Meltzoff, 1982, 1986). The visual contribution to decoding speech, even in early infancy, is good evidence for the importance of perceptual mechanisms which link visual, kinaesthetic and auditory patterning in the service of communication. Furthermore, newborns actually do distinguish between the sound of their own cries and those of another baby crying (Martin and Clark, 1982).

Thus, the long-held distinction between imitating visible and invisible movements proves to have been a red herring because, on a dynamic systems analysis, what really matters is that the infant should be sensitive to the categorical equivalence of input and output processes. As Goldfield (1995) explains, the dynamics of the articulators, whether perceived in another or produced by the self, uniquely specify the same information. In Trevarthen's research (this volume), intermodal mapping occurs over more extended intervals but, again, the dynamics can be understood in terms of a temporal mesh between prosodic (melodic) and pragmatic (turn-taking) sequences of infant and adult behaviour.

In summary, a dynamic systems analysis suggests that the infant is capable of imitating visual, auditory and proprioceptive information because prenatal patterns of activity have been involved in selectively laying down the mid-brain structures at the heart of the embodied action system. These mid-brain systems, perhaps in combination with cortical processes, contribute to the control of manual, vocal and facial systems of expression in the newborn. Since the individual functions as an organised totality, the information controlling action, from whatever modality it is obtained, can be self-specifying and self-referent, or, indeed, other-specifying and other-referent. Postnatal social interaction carries visual information for the equivalence, between individuals, of species-typical action patterns and forms of emotional expression. Such a mechanism for the 'transfer' of information between self and other lies at the heart of our definition of imitation.

Motives for imitation in the newborn

This leads to the question of the motives for imitation. As Kugiumutzakis (1985) notes, how does the newborn understand that the models were presented in order to be imitated? He proposes that the infant reads the invitational quality of the adult's behaviour as an opportunity to communicate. Even allowing a much greater role for perception in early action control still requires motivating principles for imitation.

The fact that newborn infants show visual and auditory preferences, has laid the foundations for the modern study of infant perception. Such preferences suggest that there is an innate aesthetic basis to an infant's relative approach or withdrawal from stimulation (Fantz, 1965; Schneirla, 1962). With respect to natural visual models for imitation, it has long been shown that newborn babies prefer faces over other patterns (e.g., Johnson and Morton, 1991). More recently it has been demonstrated that babies prefer beautiful faces over less beautiful ones (Samuels and Ewy, 1985; Samuels, Butterworth, Roberts, Graupner and Hole, 1994) and that this preference is innate (Slater, Von der Schulenberg, Brown, Badenoch, Butterworth, Parsons and Samuels, 1998). In these experiments, black-and-white photographs were used, which suggests that the inbuilt preference must be for the configuration of the face.

We do not need to argue that the infant has innate expectations about faces, since every infant is born with her own face innervated in the species-typical manner. The dynamical organisation of the infant's own facial musculature could provide a proprioceptive foundation on which to specify when a visual percept is categorically similar (and perhaps whether this perceptual configuration is relatively well formed). Dynamical systems analyses consider variation to occur around 'attractor basins', in relation to which configurations of muscular movements can occur. This account requires that there is a finite set of permissible categories of configuration of the facial musculature so that the newborn will perceive a facial expression and generate a response within the equivalence class. A similar perception-based account would be sufficient for the ability categorically to imitate sounds. With respect to the innate auditory preference for the mother's voice, intra-uterine 'eavesdropping' may lay the basis for an aesthetic preference for the particular pattern of the mother's voice over that of a stranger (DeCasper and Fifer, 1988; Fifer and Moon, 1995).

However, there is more to imitation than simply seeking pleasure. Why does the infant oblige the curious psychologist and produce an imitative response? Kugiumutzakis (1993) and Trevarthen (this volume) both suggest that a deep-seated need to communicate is the strongest motive. Some of the specific imitative phenomena of newborns, such as mouth or tongue movements, emotional expressions and hand movements may certainly be understood as the expressive components of vocal and gestural communication. Compatible arguments have been made by Fridlund (1997), who distinguishes between facial displays revealing social motives and the experience of emotions. The infant's motives for affiliation, companionship and communication, in the context of reciprocal exchanges between co-operating partners, may be the setting for the emergence of emotional experience as an intersubjective phenomenon. Perhaps the newborn baby perceives the adult's model, in the particular procedures which have proved effective in eliciting neonatal imitation, to be an invitation to take a turn (Kugiumutzakis, this volume). The essentially interpersonal aspect of such exchanges once again meets our criteria for the definition of innate imitation.

The development of imitation in infancy and early childhood

In laying so much stress on newborn imitation in this chapter, there is no intention to devalue the developmental progress still to come. With development in the first year the capacity for imitation undergoes further changes. Babies can now reproduce a response having seen only the end result. They can imitate after a significant delay and imitation can take on symbolic properties. Piaget (1962, obs. 57, p. 65) showed further qualitative differences in that imitation at 12 months can take on a symbolic aspect. He described his daughter Jacqueline trying to work out how the drawer of a matchbox operates by systematically sliding her tongue in and out of her mouth.

The relation between the dynamics and statics of imitation, and between immediate and deferred imitation, may prove a much more interwoven process than previously envisaged. From the outset, perception of the model without concurrent action is sufficient for oral imitation, which means there is no necessity for immediate motor activity to ensure imitation (Meltzoff and Moore, 1977).

An issue not yet fully resolved concerns the course of development between neonatal and subsequent imitation. Maratos (1998) and Vinter (1985) found that the probability of imitation of facial models declines over the first 3 months. Meltzoff and Moore (this volume) caution that the apparent disappearance of oral imitation at two months may be illusory, since babies of this age can be induced to imitate if the imitation game is prolonged sufficiently. However, the question of development need not require any absolute regression. Vinter (1985) for example, found that the frequency of full tongue protrusion declined significantly between 8 and 12 weeks, whereas imitation of hand movements declined between 5 and 8 weeks. Kugiumutzakis (this volume) reports that what will be imitated changes during the first 6 months. Imitation of tongue protrusion and mouth opening develops according to a U-shaped curve, whereas vocal imitation develops in an inversely U-shaped function, which increases as oral imitation declines. The differential time course of imitation in different expressive systems might be consistent with postnatal experience dependent on brain development in which feedback loops are successively integrated with innate control systems. Imitation would thereby acquire qualitatively new properties which initially incorporate iconic memory and eventually, at the end of infancy, conceptual processes (Mounoud and Vinter, 1981).

Of particular interest to this question, is recent evidence for imitation from memory. Meltzoff and Moore (1994) showed that 6-week-old babies can imitate tongue protrusion to one side (a novel response) not only immediately, but also 24 hours after having seen it being modelled. It made no difference whether the mother or a stranger modelled the stimuli (mouth opening or tongue protrusion) and infants imitated from both dynamic and static models. From a dynamic systems perspective this means that the statics are sufficient to specify the dynamics, which might constitute a reasonable definition of recognition memory. The authors argue that the infant uses imitation as a means of identifying the particular experimenter on successive encounters, which implies that imitation is embedded within processes of person individuation.

Meltzoff (1988a) also observed deferred imitation in babies of 8 months, 1 week after they saw the experimenter perform a completely novel action (banging the forehead on a platform). By 14 months, infants show deferred imitation across changes in context and object size (Barnat, Klein and Meltzoff, 1996). Infants will imitate an action, even when they have not been allowed to perform it, 2 months after observing the target act being modelled for only 1 minute (Meltzoff, 1995). Thus, by the end of infancy, brief perceptual learning is sufficient to result in long-term, non-verbal, memory which is sufficient for the baby to reproduce specific actions after long delays.

Donald (1991) suggests that imitation from memory may involve both episodic and procedural aspects. Episodic memory is rich in perceptual content, whereas procedural memory is for the generalisable aspects of action (Tulving, 1983). Imitation from memory clearly involves both types, since what is remembered is a particular action first encountered as a perceptual event. While there has been a great deal of research on event perception in infancy, very little has been done on event memory in the neonatal period (Butterworth, 1989). Promising research, consistent with very early memory formation, is evidence for visual recognition of the mother in babies less than 4 days old (Bushnell, Sai and Mullin, 1989). More needs to be known about the necessary exposure time for memory to be established. Bushnell (1998) estimates that neonates have had 40 hours of exposure to the mother's face by day 3, whereas deferred imitation typically involves just a few minutes of exposure to the model.

All of this is consistent with the thesis that several mechanisms are involved in the development of imitation in the first year which may interact in repeated cycles, eventually giving rise to deferred, symbolic responses of the kind noted by Piaget. First, imitation may involve perceiving not only the dynamics but also the form of the facial (oral or manual) display. Certainly by 6 weeks (but perhaps not at birth, Vinter, 1986) infants can reproduce mouth opening merely by observing the endstate (mouth wide open, Meltzoff and Moore, 1994). Second, imitation may be both immediate and also based on representation from remarkably early in development. The delay over which imitation can occur increases with development, but the important new findings are that deferred responding is possible from very early on (6 weeks). This requires a theory of memory formation in early infancy for which perceptual input is a sufficient condition (Meltzoff and Moore, 1994). Third, the profoundly social and interpersonal nature of early imitation is well illustrated by the fact that babies recognise the actual individual who presented the model, and they attempt to recreate the action they previously saw being made by that person. Fourth, imitation from memory may require an even more complex analysis, since it may involve elements of analogical reasoning and long-term recall, as Piaget's own studies showed (1962, obs. 57).

An innate capacity for imitation serves not only learning, but also communication. Nadel and colleagues have outlined a theory of communication development beyond infancy through synchronous, immediate imitation between peers. Imitation on this theory acts as a stepping-stone in the development of referential communication (Nadel and Fontaine, 1989; Nadel and Pezé, 1993; Nadel, Guerini and Rivet, this volume). In experimental studies of babies, imitation is usually elicited by adult models (although spontaneous mutual imitation does occur in everyday life). In toddlers, however, mutual imitation extends to the peer group, and it is spontaneous and especially evident around identical objects. The toddler, with limited language competence, makes use of immediate imitation to share referents with peers and this helps to bridge the gap between non-verbal and verbal communication. In a sense, toddlers spontaneously generate a mimetic culture around the artefacts provided for them, to serve the purpose of communication. Around the age of 4 years, this mimetic system, which depends upon the immediate context, is normally supplanted by the linguistic system.

Conclusion

In conclusion, this chapter has focused on recent research on imitation in newborns to clarify questions about the existence, mechanisms and motives of innate imitation in humans. The emphasis has been on the contribution of perceptual systems as channels of information which enable the baby to imitate. It seems safe to say that immediate imitation is innate in humans. From these perceptual origins, immediate imitation enables emotional sharing, learning and communication. Further study will enable a better understanding of how humans, through information exchange, perceive themselves not only to be members of the same species, but also to share the same language and culture.

ACKNOWLEDGMENTS

Figure 3.1 is reproduced from Whiten, A. and Ham, R. (1992). On the nature and evolution of imitation in the animal kingdom, reappraisal of a century of research. *Advances in the Study of Behaviour.* 21, 239–83 with the permission of the authors and Academic press.

Thanks to Richard Andrew and Jacqueline Nadel for helpful comments on earlier drafts of this chapter.

REFERENCES

Andrew, R. (1962). Evolution of intelligence and vocal mimicking. *Science*, 137, 585–9.

(1998). Cyclicity in speech derived by call repetition rather than from intrinsic cyclicity of ingestion. *Behavior and Brain Sciences*, in press.

Anisfeld, M. (1996). Only tongue protrusion modelling is matched by neonates. *Developmental Review*, 16(2), 149–61.

Baldwin, J. M. (1894). Imitation, a chapter in the natural history of consciousness. *Mind*, 3, 26–55.

(1901). *Dictionary of philosophy and psychology*. London: Macmillan.

(1902). *Development and evolution*. London: Macmillan.

(1903). *Mental development in the child and the race*. 3rd edn.

Barnat, S. B., Klein, P. J. and Meltzoff, A. N. (1996). Deferred imitation across changes in context and object: Memory and generalisation in 14 month infants. *Infant Behavior and Development*, 19, 241–51.

Bavelas, J. B., Black, A., Lemery, C. R., MacInnis, S. and Mullett, J. (1986). Experimental methods for studying 'Elementary motor mimicry'. *Journal of Nonverbal behavior*, 10, 102–19.

Bekoff, A. (1995). Development of motor behaviour in chick embryos. In J. P. Lecanuet, W. P Fifer, N. A. Krasnegor and W. P. Smotherman (eds.), *Fetal development: a psychobiological perspective* (pp. 191–204). New Jersey: Erlbaum.

Bertenthal, B. and Pinto, J. (1993). Complementary processes in the perception and production of human movements. In L. B. Smith and E. Thelen (eds.), *A dynamic systems approach to development: Applications* (pp. 208–39). Cambridge MA: MIT Press.

Bugnyar, T. and Huber, L. (1997). Push or pull: an experimental study on imitation in marmosets. *Animal Behavior*, 54, 817–31.

Bushnell, I. W. R. (1998). The origins of face perception. In F. Simion and G. E. Butterworth (eds.), *The development of sensory, motor and cognitive capacities in early infancy* (pp. 65–82). Hove: Psychology Press.

Bushnell, I. W. R., Sai, F. and Mullin, J. T. (1989). Neonatal recognition of the mother's face. *British Journal of Developmental Psychology*, 7, 3–15.

Butterworth, G. E. (1989). Events and encounters in infant perception. In A. Slater and G. Bremner (eds.), *Infant development* (pp. 73–82). Hove: Lawrence Erlbaum

(1993). Dynamic approaches to infant perception and action: Old and new theories about the origins of knowledge. In L. B. Smith and E. Thelen (eds.), *A dynamic systems approach to development: Applications* (pp. 171–87). Cambridge, MA: MIT Press.

(1995). An ecological perspective on the origins of self. In J. Bermudez, N. Eilan and A. Marcel (eds.), *The body and the self* (pp. 97–105). Cambridge, MA: MIT Press.

Byrne, R. (1995). *The thinking ape: Evolutionary origins of intelligence*. Oxford University Press.

Darwin, C. (1859). *The origin of species*. London: John Murray.

Davis, J. D. (1981). Imitation. In D. McFarland (ed.), *The Oxford companion to animal behavior*. Oxford University Press, 298–302.

DeCasper, A. W. and Fifer, W. P. (1980). Of human bonding: newborns prefer the mother's voice. *Science*, 208, 1174–6.

De Vriess, J. I. P., Visser, G. H. A. and Prechtl, H. F. R. (1984). Fetal motility in the first half of pregnancy. In H. F. R. Prechtl (ed.), *Continuity of neural function from prenatal to postnatal life*. London: Spastics International Medical Publications.

Donald, M. (1991). *Origins of the modern mind: Three stages in the development of culture and cognition*. Cambridge, MA: Harvard University Press.

Fantz, R. L. (1965). Visual perception from birth as shown by pattern selectivity. *Annals of the New York Academy of Sciences*, 118, 793–814.

Field, T. M., Woodson, R. W., Greenberg, R. and Cohen, C. (1982). Discrimination and imitation of facial expressions by neonates. *Science*, 218, 179–81.

Fifer, W. P. and Moon, C. M. (1995). The effects of fetal experience with sound. In J. P. Lecanuet, W. P. Fifer, N. A. Krasnegor and W. P. Smotherman (eds.), *Fetal development: a psychobiological perspective* (pp. 351–68). Hillsdale, NJ: Erlbaum.

Fontaine, R. (1984). Imitative skills between birth and six months. *Infant Behavior and Development*, 7, 323–33.

Fridlund, A. J. (1997). The new ethology of human facial expressions. In J. A. Russell and J. M. Fernandez-Dols (eds.), *The psychology of facial expression* (pp. 103–32). Cambridge University Press.

Galef, B. G. Jr. (1988). Imitation in animals: history, definition and interpretation of data from the psychological laboratory. In T. R. Zentall and B. G. Galef Jr. (eds.), *Social learning: Psychological and biological perspectives* (pp. 1–27). Hillsdale, NJ: Erlbaum.

Gibson, J. J. (1966). *The senses considered as perceptual systems*. Boston: Houghton-Mifflin.

(1987). The uses of proprioception and the detection of propriospecific information. In E. Reed and R. Jones (eds.), *Reasons for realism: Selected essays of James J. Gibson* (pp. 164–70). Hillsdale, NJ: Erlbaum.

Goldfield, E. (1995). *Emergent forms: Origins and early development of human action and perception*. New York: Oxford University Press.

Gottlieb, G. (1992). *Individual development and evolution: The genesis of novel behavior*. New York: Oxford University Press.

Guillaume, P. (1926). *Imitation in children* (Elaine P. Halperin, trans). University of Chicago Press, 1968.

Hayes, L. A. and Watson, J. S. (1981). Neonatal imitation: fact or artefact? *Developmental Psychology*, 17, 655–60.

Heyes, C. M. (1996). Introduction: Identifying and defining imitation. In C. M. Heyes and B. G. Galef (eds.), *Social learning in animals: The roots of culture* (pp. 211–19). London: Academic Press.

Heyes, C. M., Dawson, G. R. and Nokes, T. (1992). Imitation in rats: initial responding and transfer evidence. *Quarterly Journal of Experimental Psychology*, 45b, 59–71.

Heyes, C. M. and B. G. Galef (eds.) (1996). *Social learning in animals: The roots of culture*. London: Academic Press.

Hofer, M. A.(1981). *The roots of human behavior*. San Francisco: Freeman.

Hopkins B. and Butterworth G. E. (1997). Dynamic systems approaches to infant development. In J. G. Bremner, A. Slater and G. E. Butterworth (eds.), *Infant development: Recent advances* (pp. 75–97). Hove: Erlbaum.

Johnson, M. H. and Morton, J. (1991). *Biology and cognitive development. The case of face recognition.* Oxford: Blackwells.

Kaitz, M., Meschulach-Sarfaty, O. and Auerbach, J. (1988). A re-examination of newborns' ability to imitate facial expressions. *Developmental Psychology,* 24(1), 3–7.

Kugiumutzakis, G. (1985). The origin, development and function of early infant imitation. Ph.D. thesis. Department of Psychology, University of Uppsala, Sweden.

    (1993). Intersubjective vocal imitation in early mother–infant interaction. In J. Nadel and L. Camaioni (eds.), *New perspectives in early communicative development* (pp. 23–47). London and New York: Routledge.

Kuhl, P. and Meltzoff, A. N. (1982). The bimodal perception of speech in infancy. *Science,* 218, 1138–41.

    (1986). The intermodal representation of speech in infants. *Infant Behavior and Development,* 7, 361–81.

Lhermitte, F., Pillon, B. and Serdaru, M. (1986). Human autonomy and the frontal lobes. Part 1. Imitation and utilisation behavior: A neuropsychological study of 75 patients. *Annals of Neurology* 19(4), 326–34.

Lloyd-Morgan (1896). *Habit and instinct.* London: Edward Arnold.

Maratos, O. (1973). The origin and development of imitation during the first 6 months of life. Unpublished Ph.D. thesis, University of Geneva.

    (1998). Neonatal, early and later imitation: same order phenomena? In F. Simion and G. E. Butterworth (eds.), *The development of sensory, motor and cognitive capacities in early infancy* (pp. 143–58). Hove: Psychology Press.

Martin, G. B. and Clark, R. D. (1982). Distress crying in neonates: Species and peer specificity. *Developmental Psychology,* 18, 3–9.

Masters, J. (1979). Interpreting 'imitative' responses in early infancy. *Science,* 205, 215.

McDougall, W. (1931). *Social psychology.* 22nd edn. London: Methuen.

McFarland, D. (1981). *The Oxford companion to animal behavior.* Oxford University Press.

Meltzoff, A.N. (1988a). Infant imitation and memory: Nine month olds in immediate and deferred tests. *Child Development,* 59, 217–25.

    (1988b). Infant imitation after a 1-week delay: Long-term memory for novel acts and multiple stimuli. *Developmental Psychology,* 24, 470–6.

    (1995). What infant memory tells us about infantile amnesia: Long-term recall and deferred imitation. *Journal of Experimental Child Psychology,* 59, 497–515.

    (1996). The human infant as imitative generalist: a 20-year progress report on infant imitation with implications for comparative psychology. In C. M. Heyes and B. G. Galef (eds.), *Social learning in animals: The roots of culture* (p. 347). London: Academic Press.

Meltzoff, A. N. and Borton, R. W. (1979). Intermodal matching by human neonates. *Nature,* 282, 403–4.

Meltzoff, A. N. and Moore, M. K. (1977). Imitation of facial and manual gestures by human neonates. *Science,* 198, 75–8.

    (1994). Imitation, memory, and the representation of persons. *Infant Behavior and Development,* 17, 83–99.

Moore, B. R. (1992). Avian movement imitation and a new form of mimicry: tracing the evolution of a complex form of learning. *Behavior*, 122, 231–63.

Mounoud, P. and Vinter, A. (1981). Representation and sensori-motor development. In G. Butterworth (ed.), *Infancy and Epistemology* (pp. 200–35). Brighton: Harvester Press.

Myowa, M. (1996). Imitation of facial gestures by an infant chimpanzee. *Primates*, 37(2), 207–13.

Nadel, J. (1994). Wallon's framework and influence. In A. Vyt, H. Bloch and M. H. Bornstein (eds.), *Early child development in the French tradition: Contributions from current research* (pp. 177–90). New Jersey: Erlbaum.

Nadel, J. and Fontaine, A.-M. (1989). Communicating by imitation: a developmental and comparative approach to transitory social competence. In B. H. Schneider, G. Attili, J. Nadel and R. P. Weissberg, (eds.), *Social competence in developmental perspective* (pp. 131–44). Dordrecht: Kluwer Academic Publications.

Nadel, J. and Pezé, A. (1993). What makes immediate imitation communicative in toddlers and autistic children? In J. Nadel and L. Camioni (eds.), *New perspectives in early communicative development* (pp. 139–58). London and New York: Routledge.

O'Rahilly, R. and Müller, F. (1994). *The embryonic human brain: An atlas of developmental stages.* New York: Wiley-Liss.

Piaget, J. (1954). *The construction of reality in the child.* New York: Basic Books.

(1962). *Play dreams and imitation in the child.* New York: Norton.

Preyer, W. (1892). *The mind of the child.* New York: Appleton.

Provine, R. R. (1997). Yawns, laughs, smiles, tickles and talking: Naturalistic and laboratory studies of facial action and social communication. In J. A. Russell and J. M. Fernandez-Dols (eds.), *The psychology of facial expression* (pp. 158–75). Cambridge University Press.

Purves, D. (1994). *Neural activity and the growth of the brain.* Cambridge University Press.

Reissland, N. (1988). Neonatal imitation in the first hour of life. Observations in rural Nepal. *Developmental Psychology*, 24, 464–9.

Richards, R. J. (1988). *Darwin and the emergence of evolutionary theories of mind and behavior.* University of Chicago Press.

Rochat, P. (1995). *The self in infancy: Theory and research.* Amsterdam: Elsevier.

Romanes, G. J. (1884). *Mental evolution in animals.* New York: AMS Press.

(1889). *Mental evolution in man.* New York: Appleton.

Russon, A. E. and Galdikas, B. M. F. (1993). Imitation in ex-captive orangutans. *Journal of Comparative Psychology*, 107, 147–61.

Samuels, C. J., Butterworth, G., Roberts, A., Graupner, L. and Hole, G. (1994). Facial aesthetics: Infants prefer attractiveness to symmetry. *Perception*, 23, 823–32.

Samuels, C. J. and Ewy, R. (1985). Aesthetic perception of faces during infancy. *British Journal of Developmental Psychology*, 221–8.

Schneirla, T. C. (1962). Psychology, comparative. Encyclopaedia Britannica. Reprinted in L. Aronson, E. Tobach, J. S. Rosenblatt, D. S. Lehrman (eds.), *Selected writings of T. C. Schneirla.* San Francisco, Freeman 1972.

Slater, A., Von der Schulenberg, C., Brown, E., Badenoch, M., Butterworth, G.

E., Parsons, S. and Samuels, C. (1998). Newborn infants prefer attractive faces. *Infant behavior and development*. 21, 2, 345–54.

Slater, P. (1990). Causes of development in ethology. In G. E. Butterworth and P. E. Bryant (eds.), *Causes of development* (64–81). Hemel Hempstead: Harvester.

Spencer, H. (1870). *Principles of psychology*. 2nd edn. London: Williams and Norgate.

Tarde, G. (1895). *Laws of imitation*. 2nd edn. Preface xiv. (E. C. Parsons, trans.). Massachusetts: Peter Smith 1962.

Thelen, E. and Smith, L. B. (1993). *A dynamic systems approach to the development of cognition and action*. Cambridge, MA: MIT Press.

Thorpe, W. H. (1963). *Learning and instinct in animals*. 2nd edn. London: Methuen.

Tiedemann, D. (1787). Observations on the mental development of a child. In W. Dennis (ed.), *Historical readings in developmental psychology*. New York: Appleton Century Crofts 1971.

Tomasello, M. (1996). Do apes ape? In C. M. Heyes and B. G. Galef (eds.), *Social learning in animals: The roots of culture* (pp. 319–46). London: Academic Press.

Trevarthen, C. (1993). The functions of emotions in early infant communication and development. In J. Nadel and L. Camaioni (eds.), *New perspectives in early communicative development*. London: Routledge.

Tulving, E. (1983). *Elements of episodic memory*. New York: Oxford University Press.

Vinter, A. (1985). *L'imitation chez le nouveau-né*. Lausanne: Delachaux & Niestle.
   (1986). The role of movement in eliciting early imitation. *Child Development*, 57, 66–71.

Visalberghi, E. and Fragaszy, D. M. (1990). Do monkeys ape? In S. T. Parker and K. R. Gibson (eds.), *Language and intelligence in monkeys and apes* (pp. 247–73). Cambridge University Press.

Voneche, J. (1982). Evolution, development and knowledge. In J. M. Broughton and D. J. Freeman-Moir (eds.), *The cognitive developmental psychology of James Mark Baldwin*. Norwood, NJ: Ablex.

Wallon, H. (1934). *Les origines du caractère chez l'enfant*. Paris: Presses Universitaires de France.
   (1942). *De l'acte à la pensée*. Paris: Flammarion.

Whiten, A. (1998). Evolutionary and developmental origins of the mind reading system. In J. Langer and M. Killen (eds.), *Piaget, evolution and development*. Hillsdale, NJ: Erlbaum.

Whiten, A. and Custance, D. (1996). Studies of imitation in chimpanzees and children. In C. M. Heyes and B. G. Galef (eds.), *Social learning in animals: The roots of culture* (pp. 291–318). London: Academic Press.

Whiten, A. and Ham, R. (1992). On the nature and evolution of imitation in the animal kingdom: Reappraisal of a century of research. In P. J. B. Slater, J. S. Rosenblatt, G. Beer and M. Milinski (eds.), *Advances in the study of behavior* (vol. 21, pp. 239–83). New York: Academic Press.

Xitco, M. J. Jr. (1988). Mimicry of modelled behaviors by bottlenose dolphins. Unpublished MA thesis, Department of Psychology, University of Hawaii.

Zazzo, R. (1957) Le problème de l'imitation chez le nouveau né. *Enfance*, 10, 135–42.

(1988) Imitation et compétences du nouveau-né. Janvier 1945: Découverte de l'imitation neo-natale? *Psychologie Française*, 33(1/2), 5–7.

Zentall, T. R. (1996). An analysis of imitative learning in animals. In C. M. Heyes and B. G. Galef (eds.), *Social learning in animals: The roots of culture* (pp. 221–43). London: Academic Press.

Zentall, T. R., Sutton, J. and Sherburne, L. M. (1998). True imitative learning in pigeons. *Psychological Science*, in press.

4 Evolutionary foundations of imitation: social, cognitive and developmental aspects of imitative processes in non-human primates

Kim A. Bard and Connie L. Russell

Imitation in non-human primates has recently become both a focus of attention and a point of debate. Recent experiments, however, have found that imitation is a difficult phenomenon to measure (Tomasello, Kruger and Ratner, 1993a; Whiten and Ham, 1992). The popular assumptions about imitation and its evolutionary foundations include the following analysis of species differences: imitation occurs 'naturally' in human infants, imitation must be taught with considerable effort to great apes, and imitation does not exist in monkeys and prosimians, no matter how many years of training are given. These assumptions have taken us on a search for characteristics common to human and ape, and dissimilar between these species and monkeys.

Questions addressed by this review include: (1) whether there are differences in imitation among primate species; (2) whether primates have an innate predisposition to imitate; (3) what the communicative characteristics of the social environment that appear necessary for imitation are; (4) what the cognitive requirements of imitation are; and (5) whether there are developmental changes in imitation in non-human primates. Discussion of these questions will expand our knowledge of the ontogeny and evolutionary bases of imitation (see also Russon, Bard and Parker, 1996; Heyes and Galef, 1996, for further discussion). Primates are interesting subjects to study for their own sake (Bard, Platzman, Lester and Suomi, 1992; de Waal, 1982), and, in addition, by understanding them better, we expand our knowledge of our own primate heritage. Knowledge of the evolutionary and biological roots of human behaviour provides an important adaptive context that enriches our appreciation of all primate behaviour (e.g., Harlow and Harlow, 1965; Yerkes, 1943).

Definitions in comparative perspective

Many claims have been made about the imitative abilities of different species. The evaluation of these claims is complicated by the definitional and methodological issues in this area of research. Before it can be determined which species learn by imitation, imitation must be defined. As with many concepts of interest to scientists, agreement upon a single definition has not yet been reached. Heyes (1993) defines imitation as learning about *behaviour* from conspecific observation, as distinguished from social learning (or non-imitative social learning), defined as learning about the *environment* through conspecific observation. Whiten and Ham (1992), in their attempt at a complete taxonomy of 'mimetic processes' define imitation as a form of social learning in which 'B learns some aspect(s) of the intrinsic *form* of an act from A' (p. 250). This definition is an acknowledgment that any imitative act will not be an exact replication of the behaviour observed. Thorpe's (1963) definition is more strict in requiring both exact replication and that the behaviour that is copied is novel or improbable and there is not an instinctive tendency for the behaviour. Many others have put forth definitions of imitation, but these are sufficient to illustrate that the acceptance of something as evidence for imitation can depend on the definition used. This is the first difficulty encountered in our quest to identify primate species that learn by imitation.

The requirement for novelty put forth by Thorpe (1963) presents a problem in imitation research. How can it be determined if a behaviour is novel? It seems impossible to know the complete behavioural history of any subject participating in a study of imitation. Also, some species have a limited range of potential actions and many of these will have been performed previously in some form or another. Whiten and Ham (1992) suggest two objective criteria for judging pre-existing acts to be novel: previously performed behaviours are combined or adjusted in a novel way, or already existing behaviours are combined in a novel way with action on environmental objects.

Another issue in the study of imitation is to rule out alternative explanations. Many lower-level alternative explanations must be ruled out before imitation can be claimed unequivocally. The most important of these are response facilitation, stimulus (or local) enhancement, observational conditioning and goal emulation. Response facilitation (or social facilitation) is the temporary increase in the probability of an individual engaging in a behaviour that already exists in their repertoire as a result of observing a conspecific engage in the behaviour. This 'contagious' behaviour should not be labelled as imitation if no new behaviour is learned. Stimulus (or local) enhancement involves learning as to which object or location in the environment one should orient (Whiten and Ham, 1992). If it is the case that once attention is directed to the appropriate environmental stimuli then action A results, the behaviour could be attributed to individual learning rather than imitation.

Observational conditioning is the learning of an association between an object and an emotional evaluation. An example of this is a fearful response to snakes by monkeys who observed the same reactions in another monkey (Mineka, Davidson, Cook and Keir, 1984). The contagion aspect of observational conditioning appears related to the beginnings of empathetic responses (i.e., 'contagious crying' found in human newborns), but should be distinguished from social referencing which is the solicitation of emotional information about an ambiguous object (see Russell, Bard and Adamson, 1997 for further details of the development of social referencing in chimpanzees).

Köhler (1927) distinguished imitation of 'substance' from imitation of 'form' (Galef, 1992). This distinction is now discussed as 'emulation' versus 'imitative copying'. Goal emulation was proposed as an alternative explanation for behaviour that led to achieving the same goal without copying all aspects of the model's behaviour (Tomasello et al., 1993a). In goal emulation, the end result is achieved more quickly as a result of observation, but the exact actions used by the model are not used by the observer. There is disagreement about the cognitive basis underlying goal emulation versus imitative copying: is goal emulation in fact a lower-level process than imitative copying? (see Byrne, 1996b for further discussion).

The term imitation is generally reserved for the demonstration of imitative copying, the exact replication of both means and ends. There continue to be questions, however, about the significance of imitation in comparison with individual learning, in terms of the development of new behaviours (e.g., Byrne, 1996a; Russon, 1996). Some would argue that imitation is the highest-level ability, one that clearly is human species-specific. In tool tasks, for instance, subjects are given higher credit for replicating the means ('slavish copying' à la Byrne, 1996a) rather than replicating the end result (which, by previous definitions, is goal emulation and not imitation). This only makes sense if imitation, *per se*, is the goal rather than solving the task. It is likely that different subjects bring different characteristic interpretations to a problem-solving task. For instance, language-trained apes were superior to both 18-month-old and 30-month-old human subjects in a study of delayed imitation of tool tasks (Tomasello, Savage-Rumbaugh and Kruger, 1993b). The researchers suggested that the children's lack of delayed imitation was more a reflection of lack of explicit instruction (they were not told explicitly that the task was to imitate), than lack of ability relative to the apes. When measuring the ability to imitate in other species, therefore, researchers must be clear as to the 'instructions' given to non-human primates because the instructions may determine the interpretation of the nature of the problem (e.g., Bard, 1990; Custance and Bard, 1994; Mathieu and Bergeron, 1981).

Methodologies in comparative perspective

Evidence for imitation in non-human primates is based on several methodologies. Naturalistic observations and anecdotal reports of imitative abilities in primates have led to more systematic experimental studies. Studies have taken the following tacks to address the question of whether imitative copying occurs in non-human primates: (1) teaching imitation of arbitrary actions and testing imitative ability with novel actions; (2) testing imitation of actions on objects; (3) testing imitation of complex problem-solving tasks such as imitation of tool use; and (4), more recently, exploring the possibility of neonatal imitation in non-human primates. The results of each of these procedural approaches to the study of imitation in non-human primates is discussed in the following sections.

Neonatal imitation

One method used to study imitation is the study of the very earliest imitation, neonatal imitation typically of facial actions. The investigation of neonatal imitation in non-human primates is important to further our knowledge of the evolutionary and developmental foundations of brain and behaviour relations (Hallock, Worobey and Self, 1989). Can the cross-species study of similar capacities at birth reveal significant comparative relations between behavioural flexibility and plasticity in cortical development? Are similar developmental mechanisms responsible for changes in behaviour across primate species? Many questions remain unanswered with respect to the extent of similarity in behavioural and brain capacities.

Imitation may serve emotional, cognitive, and/or communicative functions (e.g., Nadel and Pezé, 1993). The findings of imitation in human newborns highlighted predispositions to imitate facial and manual actions, vocalisations and emotionally laden facial expressions. The communicative purpose of imitation was proposed by Trevarthen (1979) and Maratos (1982), and supported by the research of Kugiumutzakis (1985). We knew that very young apes were able to open their mouth, produce tongue-clicking noises and protrude their tongue (Bard, in press; Chevalier-Skolnikoff, 1982; Jacobsen, Jacobsen and Yoshioka, 1932; Redshaw, 1989; Turney, 1978). Moreover, while conducting tests of neonatal neurobehavioural integrity (Bard, 1994a) we found that chimpanzees appeared to imitate both vocalisations and facial actions (Figure 4.1). Debbie, a 19-day-old chimpanzee neonate, is shown in Figure 4.1a to be pursing her lips concurrently with the neonatal examiner, K. A. Bard. Moments later the second photograph was taken during which Debbie opened her mouth apparently in response to the examiner opening her mouth. During the neonatal

Figure 4.1. It is not clear if it is infant imitation or examiner responsiveness that is captured in the photographs of Debbie, 19-day-old chimpanzee and K. A. Bard, neurobehavioural examiner, during neonatal testing sessions. Figure 4.1a illustrates pursed lips and 4.1b illustrates mouth opening in both adult human and newborn chimpanzee. Photo by Josh Schneider.

examinations, the best performance of the infant was encouraged so it was not certain that the infant was imitating, rather the examiner could have been extraordinarily responsive (see similar reasoning for human neonatal performance: Meltzoff and Moore, 1977). We had reasons to suspect that newborn chimpanzees were imitating, but it was time to conduct rigorous testing (Myowa, 1996).

Perhaps in non-human primates, in contrast to humans, the capacity for imitation is not present at birth. If the null hypotheses was correct then no evidence of imitation would be found: infant behaviours would occur at random with respect to the adult model. Alternatively, the capacity may require 'exercise' through social interactions which support and nurture its continuing development (Trevarthen, 1979). Thus, the capacity may be present in non-human primates at birth, but without exercise the imitative ability will cease to be expressed.

There is a possibility that the proportion of chimpanzee infants that can imitate is small. Careful consideration of the human data reveals that not all human infants exhibit imitative ability. Only 50% of the 18 neonates in Meltzoff and Moore's (1977) *Science* article were found to imitate. When the setting is more relaxed, natural and communicative, a higher percentage of newborns imitate (80%: Kugiumutzakis, 1985). Both of these experimental settings were used with chimpanzee subjects in order to maximise the likelihood that imitation if present would be found in newborn chimpanzees. We were prepared for the possibility that imitation would not be demonstrated by every chimpanzee infant, but equally we were intrigued by the possibility that some chimpanzee newborns would imitate facial actions and sound production.

This section of the chapter is devoted to a discussion of our unpublished study of neonatal imitation in chimpanzees, designed to test the following four hypotheses: (1) chimpanzees have an innate predisposition to imitate facial actions of human adults. Imitation in chimpanzees is tested at 1–3 days of age. This early test reflects primarily inborn tendencies for imitation. If imitation does not occur in chimpanzees at 1–3 days of age then this hypothesis will be rejected. (2) Developmental change in imitation occurs within the first 30 days of life. Developmental changes in imitation will be determined by comparing the performance of chimpanzees tested at 1–3 days of age, a period in which extra-uterine environmental influences are minimal, with the performance of the chimpanzees tested at 7–11 days. These comparisons will document developmental changes in imitation. (3) A communicative test procedure fosters enhanced imitation compared with the non-interactive test procedure. Each infant at each age is given two tests of imitation in counterbalanced order. If imitation is equivalent in the two tests that differ in communicative interaction, then this hypothesis will be rejected. (4) Repeated tests will foster enhanced imitative performance. At each age, each subject is given initial tests and repeated tests. If imitation is learned, then practice should enhance performance. If performance has not improved on the repeated test compared with the initial test, then this hypothesis will be rejected.

We assessed imitation in nine chimpanzees born at the Yerkes Research Center and one subject born at the Southwest Foundation for Biomedical Research. Five chimpanzees were tested during the first 72 hours of life and five chimpanzees were tested when 7–11 days old. Although this is still a relatively small sample size, it is considered quite large for studies with chimpanzees. Recall that the original report of neonatal imitation in humans by Meltzoff and Moore (1977) was based on 6 infants in one experiment and 12 infants in the second experiment.

Every effort was made at the Yerkes Center to have every infant chimpanzee raised by the biological mother. The overarching goal of current chimpanzee management and behavioural research programme at the Yerkes Center was to maximise the likelihood of full species-typical competence in adulthood. For chimpanzees, it is both cost-efficient and most effective to maximise competence by having infants remain with their biological mothers whenever possible and for as long as possible. Despite our best efforts, however, there were mothers who exhibited no behavioural competence with their newborns. These infants were placed in the nursery. Infants were placed in the nursery only as a result of insufficient or inadequate maternal care (see Bard, 1994b, 1995 for further details of inadequate maternal care).

The nursery environment was designed with lots of peer contact and interactions with adult humans to encourage the development of chimpanzee species-typical skills (see Bard and Gardner, 1996 for details of rearing environment). Note, however, that face-to-face interactions and extended periods of mutual gaze are not chimpanzee species-typical (Bard, 1994b: Goodall, 1986), and were consciously minimised in interaction with the chimpanzee newborns. Maternal behaviours modify infant attention in both humans (e.g., Pecheux, Findji and Ruel, 1992) and chimpanzees (Bard, 1995).

It might be considered ideal to remove an infant temporarily from its mother in order to test the mother-reared chimpanzee newborn. Chimpanzee mothers with good maternal competence, however, do not place their infants out of contact at any time within the first 30 days of life (Bard, 1994b). Access to infants, therefore, requires sedation of the mother. The process of sedation can provoke stress in the mother, recovery from sedation can provoke stress in the mother, and the chemical properties of sedation can provoke disorientation, stress, hallucinations and a lack of physical co-ordination. Each of these effects alone can be considered risk factors. In combination, there is an unacceptably high risk of disruption of continued maternal care. The first 30 days is considered the high-risk period in chimpanzee maternal care. Any process by which an infant is obtained from the mother places the continued maternal rearing at risk. The Yerkes Center was dedicated to maternal rearing of chimpanzees. Therefore, at Yerkes, chimpanzee infants were not removed from maternal care for experimental protocols. The risk of a mother not accepting her infant upon return from even a brief temporary separation was too great to justify.

Two groups of neonatal chimpanzees were selected based on age in order to assess the effect of age (maturation plus experience) on imitative ability. Both groups were given repeated tests within 24 hours of the initial test to assess the effect of limited imitative experience on imitation. Each subject was exposed to at least two modelled actions. The infant's response to one model is compared to its response to the other model. Thus each infant acts as its own matched control. In this repeated measures paradigm, the imitative actions can not be attributed to general arousal or responsiveness to the presentation of a model. Both the infant and the model were videotaped in order to precisely document the similarity or dissimilarity in actions by model and by the neonate.

In order to assess the effect of development, imitation was assessed at two points within the neonatal period, within the first 72 hours and between 7 and 11 days of age. The first period was chosen to correspond to the standard assessment for imitative ability of newborns (e.g., Field, Woodson, Greenberg and Cohen, 1982; Kugiumutzakis, 1985; Meltzoff and Moore, 1977). This period is also shortly after birth. Imitation evident in this period indicates an innate predisposition as extra-uterine environmental influences are minimal. The second period was chosen as the period during which chimpanzees show a decline in reflexive actions and appear to be responding to the social environment (e.g., the beginning of social smiles; see Bard et al., 1992).

In general terms, the procedures involved in testing neonatal imitation include a quiet alert infant placed in a position facing an adult model who has a predetermined list of target actions with video cameras focused on the faces of each participant. A prototypical set-up is illustrated in Figure 4.2. The target actions were modelled by the adult human and the responses of the infant were coded from videotape.

Two test procedures were utilised for imitation tests at both of the age points. The first test procedure (referred to as *Structured*) is identical to that used by Meltzoff and Moore (1977). This procedure is standardised,

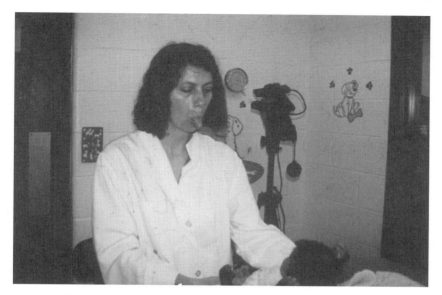

Figure 4.2. A video camera focuses on the face of Nugget, infant
chimpanzee while K. A. Bard models facial actions of tongue
protrusion (shown here), mouth opening, and sounds of tongue clicks
on a predetermined schedule. Photo by Dr Linda Brent.

rigorous and not interactive. The second procedure (referred to as
Interactive) is identical to that used by Kugiumutzakis (1985, this volume)
and assessed the communicative aspect of imitation in a setting that is
comfortable and relaxed with the pace geared to the newborns'
responsiveness. This procedure was used in addition to the Structured
procedure because it appears that a higher percentage of newborns
exhibit imitation in the more natural situation (i.e., approximately 50% of
infants demonstrate imitation in Meltzoff and Moore's (1977) procedures, whereas up to 80% of the infants tested in Kugiumutzakis' procedures imitated). A list of the facial expressions in random order was
made in advance of the test session. In this way the model is not allowed
to choose which actions to produce based on the infant's behaviour. The
order of the actions to be modelled was decided in advance.

For both procedures, scoring was conducted by two independent
coders. Coding from both sets of procedures was treated with the same
rigorous validation of reliability. The assessment of inter- and intra-
observer reliability provided records of accuracy and stability of the coding
system (e.g., Bakeman and Gottman, 1986). The primary coders were
trained in advance to agree with each other to at least a 90% agreement

with a Cohen's Kappa of over 0.80 (Cohen's Kappa is the preferred method of assessing agreement because the statistic deducts chance agreement from the observed agreement; Bakeman and Gottman, 1986).

Structured procedure

The infant was seated in an infant seat (well padded to adjust for smaller chimpanzee bodies compared with human infants') facing the model. The demonstrator sat facing the infant but was not responsive to the infant nor interactive. The order of the actions to be modelled was determined in advance and the timing of the actions was predetermined in an absolutely standardised fashion. The facial act was modelled for 4 seconds, 1 second was given between demonstrations so that each 20-second period consists of 4 demonstrations. These 20-second Demonstration periods were followed by 20-second No Model periods and continued for a total of 4 minutes. Meltzoff and Moore (1977) found that a response period without modelling was important for maximising infants' imitative responses. Then the second facial act was modelled in the same manner (4 times in 20 seconds followed by a 20-second No Model period) for an additional 4 minutes.

The number of times that each modelled action occurred was summed for each 4-minute period. Operational definitions of mouth opening and tongue protrusion given by Meltzoff are valid for chimpanzees as well. Figures 4.3a and 4.3b illustrate newborn chimpanzees mouth opening (MO) response. Tongue protrusion (TP) is illustrated in Figure 4.4. All occurrences of both behaviours were recorded by a coder who was unaware of the hypotheses of the research and unaware of the timing and order of modelled actions. If the number of TP which occurred when TP were modelled, exceeded the number of TP which occurred when MO were modelled, then it was concluded that the infant matched the TP action, i.e., imitated. Similarly, if the infant emitted more MO during the period when MO were modelled, compared to the number of mouth openings emitted when TP were modelled, then it was concluded that the infant matched the MO action. The Wilcoxon matched-pairs signed-ranks test (Siegel, 1956) was used in order to make a judgment that one performance was greater than the other. Recall that each infant acted as their own matched control in this repeated-measures analysis.

Interactive procedure

In a dimly lit room, the experimenter either held the newborn in her arms or supported the infant with blankets on a low table according to the

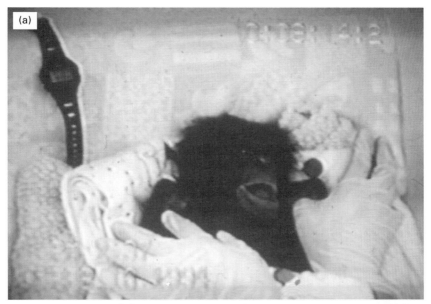

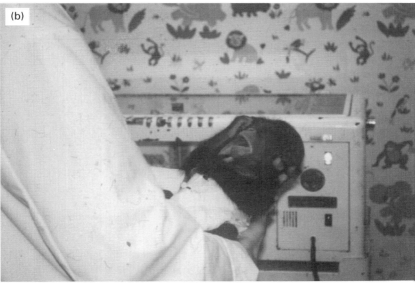

Figure 4.3. A neonatal chimpanzee is pictured emitting a mouth opening during assessment of imitation (a) in the Structured (Meltzoff and Moore, 1977) protocol; and (b) in the Interactive (Kugiumutzakis, 1985) protocol. Photo from videotape.

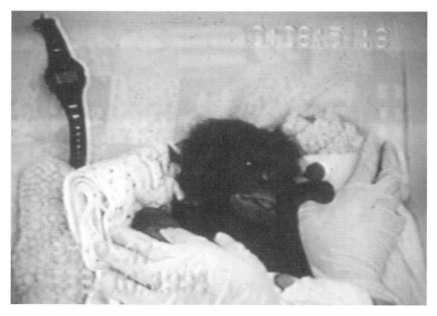

Figure 4.4. Tongue protrusion in a neonatal chimpanzee is illustrated in this photograph taken from videotaped session of the Structured protocol.

procedures which maximise the infant's comfort. The position of the infant was changed as needed to maintain the infant in a calm, quiet and alert behavioural state (Brazelton, 1984).

The procedure began with a 60-second adaptation period. When the demonstrator determined that the infant was looking, was vocally quiet, and the infant's mouth and tongue were not moving, then the first target action was modelled. Target facial displays were MO, TP, and tongue clicks – TC. The demonstration period consisted of presenting one facial action, pausing briefly with a calm face and then continuing with the same action until either: (1) the infant produced any of the target actions regardless of whether it was the action currently demonstrated; or (2) five demonstrations of the same target action were given. When these conditions were met, a 10-second period of a calm face was given. The next target action was modelled until the above conditions were met and each demonstration period was interspersed with a 10-second calm face. Note in the Interactive procedure, unlike the Structured procedure, the timing of the actions could vary based on the responsivity of the infant to either faster actions or slower actions.

The MO and TP models were identical to those used in the Structured procedure. The TC, however, was a three note series, click, click, click. It is important to know that one demonstration of a TC included three rhythmic clicks, thus presenting a rather complex model for the newborn consisting of both sound production and a series of three actions. This total test lasted less than 10 minutes.

In Interactive procedure, the coder observed first the face of the model. The time and type of each modelled action was recorded on a sheet of paper. The coder made a second pass through the videotape in order to record the time and type of each of the infant's facial actions. The coder was blind to the hypotheses of the study. The experimenter then matched the time of occurrence of the model's action with the infant's facial actions. If the infant exhibited the target action within 10 seconds of the demonstration, then a match was determined to have occurred. A Cochran's Q test (Siegel, 1956) was conducted to determine the significance in the number of subjects matching the modelled actions.

The results from the Standardised and the Interactive testing are presented in Table 4.1. For the subjects who were given their first test within the first 72 hours of life in the Structured procedure, 4 out of 5 subjects matched one or both of the modelled actions and in the Interactive procedure 2 of the 5 subjects imitated a single modelled action.

We were curious to know if repeated testing improved performance in this early newborn period. In the Structured procedure, 3 out of 4 matched one or both of the modelled actions. In terms of individual change, 2 subjects improved their performance, 1 subject stayed the same, and the performance of 1 subject was worse in the repeated test. In the Interactive procedure, 2 of the 4 subjects matched 1 or 2 modelled actions, and 2 subjects responded with non-matching actions. Two subjects performed the same on the repeated testing and one subject improved.

Two-week-old chimpanzees are very attentive and responsive to environmental stimuli (Bard et al., 1992). Imitation tests on 5 additional subjects, who were tested for the first time when they were 7 to 11 days of age revealed performance only slightly better than initial testing. Rather than improving matching performance *per se*, initial testing at this age seemed to allow chimpanzees greater likelihood of responding. In the Structured procedure, all 5 chimpanzees matched one of the modelled actions. In the Interactive procedure, 1 subject matched 1 modelled action, 3 subjects matched 2 modelled actions, and 1 subject matched all 3 modelled actions. In other words, all 5 subjects, when tested at 7–11 days of age, matched at least 1 modelled action, using either test procedure. At this age every subject responded with at least 1 matching

Table 4.1. *Imitative performance by chimpanzees at two ages with two test procedures*

	No Response	No Match	Match 1	Match 2	Match 3
FIRST TEST ≤ 3 DAYS					
Structured	Merlin	*No Match*	Drew Brooks Andi	Faye	
Interactive	Lucas	Andi	Drew Merlin		
REPEATED TEST ≤ 3 DAYS					
Structured		Brooks	Merlin Andi	Drew	
Interactive		Andi Brooks	Merlin	Drew	
FIRST TEST 7–11 DAYS					
Structured	*No Response*	*No Match*	Lindsey Rosemary Wilson Claus★ Nugget!		
Interactive	*No Response*	*No Match*	Wilson	Rosemary Claus★ Nugget!	Lindsey
REPEATED TEST 7–11 DAYS					
Structured		Andi	Merlin Claus★	Nugget!	
Interactive			Brooks Merlin	Andi Claus★ Nugget!	

Note:
★! Special cases, see explanation on p. 103

response, unlike younger subjects some of whom did not emit any response at all.

The best performance during the neonatal period was attained by Lindsey when she was 7 days of age during the Interactive procedure. She was given models in the following order: tongue protrusion, tongue click and mouth opening; and the series was repeated twice. The examiner demonstrated TP, but Lindsey did not respond. Four seconds later the examiner gave a second demonstration, and Lindsey responded 4 seconds later with a tongue protrusion. The examiner waited 10 seconds and then demonstrated tongue clicks, pausing 7 to 8 seconds in between each of the 5 demonstrations. Five seconds after the last TC demonstration, Lindsey gave her response, a single very soft tongue click. The examiner paused 10 seconds and then demonstrated mouth opening, paused 8 seconds and demonstrated another mouth opening, and her response, 4 seconds later, was to open her mouth, ending the first series.

It is noteworthy that the tongue click model was a series of 3 tongue click sounds produced by the release of suction when the tongue was moved quickly away from the roof of the mouth. In the first series, Lindsey made a small sound by moving her tongue away from her mouth in response to the examiner's tongue click. During the second series, the examiner gave only 4 demonstrations of the 3-note tongue click, and she responded with a 3 behaviour sequence, mouth opening, mouth opening and tongue click. All of her body seemed to participate in maintaining her attention, with concentration and slow rhythmic hand and leg waving, and cycles of focused visual attention alternating with short periods of looking away, as if to regroup, take a short pause from the effort, and then return to the game (paralleling descriptions of human mother–human infant face-to-face interactions as described in Bullowa, 1979).

There was a slight improvement in performance at 7–11 days that might be interpreted as due to an extended period of human influence, since these chimpanzee newborns were tested in a nursery setting with adult human caregivers. Claus and Nugget are two special cases. Claus was, and continues to be, raised by his chimpanzee mother. He was in the nursery for less than a week, while being treated for a slight infection of the belly button. While in the nursery, the only human faces to which he was exposed had the mouth area completely obscured with blue biosafety face masks. Similarly, Nugget, the infant born and raised at the SW Foundation, had only been exposed to human faces with the mouth area completely covered by a white face mask. The similar imitative performance of all of these infants provides sufficient evidence to conclude that prior exposure to human faces is not required for chimpanzee newborns to imitate facial actions.

In conclusion, these preliminary results suggest that newborn chimpanzees imitate facial actions. Although these results are based on a small sample of subjects, we think that they provide sufficiently strong evidence to conclude that newborn chimpanzees share the human predisposition to imitate facial and vocal actions. When we consider both potential effects of development, and potential effects of repeated exposure, we can conclude that there is only a suggestion of small improvements in performance due to development within the neonatal period.

Observational studies of imitation

Observations of the spread of innovations in groups of monkeys have been put forth as evidence for cultural transmission through imitation (Itani and Nishimura, 1973; Nishida, 1987). A very popular example of innovations in food washing occurred in a group of Japanese macaques (*Macaca fuscata*) in Koshima Islet. These monkeys were provisioned with sweet potatoes on a sandy beach. The behaviour of carrying the potatoes to the water and washing them was first observed in a 1-year-old named Imo. This behaviour was then observed in Imo's playmates and family members during the next few years.

Galef (1992) acknowledges that this innovation could have been spread in part by imitation, but cautions that alternative explanations cannot be ruled out. One reason that imitation has been accepted as an explanation for potato washing is due to its 'bizarreness'. However, potato washing has also been reported in four other troops of Japanese macaques, suggesting that individual innovation of this behaviour is not so 'bizarre'. Another explanation that must be considered is that caretakers selectively provisioned those monkeys who washed potatoes, hence reinforcing this behaviour (Green 1975 as cited by Galef, 1992). Galef also pointed out that the behaviour spread relatively slowly, slower than would be expected if imitation was the mechanism of transmission rather than trial-and-error learning. Possibly the most convincing alternative explanations for the spread of potato washing is a combination of stimulus enhancement and response facilitation. Individuals could find bits of sweet potato in the water and come to associate the sand-free potatoes with the water. Imo's playmates and family would be the individuals most likely to come into contact with Imo and thus come into contact with the results of Imo's washing behaviour. Logically, these individuals would be the first to acquire this new innovation. Food washing can be learned very quickly and is most likely due to individual learning, based on observations of tufted capuchin monkeys (*Cebus apella*) and crab-eating macaques (*Macaca fascicularis*) in a laboratory setting, making this explanation for potato washing among the Japanese macaques more plausible (Visalberghi and Fragaszy, 1990).

Claims of cultural transmission, potentially through imitation, have been proposed to explain differences in tool use such as that seen in termite and ant fishing among different groups of chimpanzees (see Boesch, 1996; Galef, 1992; McGrew, 1992). Goodall (1986) proposed that 'Young chimpanzees learn the tool using patterns of the community during infancy, through a mixture of social facilitation, observation, imitation, and practice – with a good deal of trial and error learning thrown in' (p. 561). In contrast, Boesch (1996) suggests that there is sufficient evidence to rule out alternative hypotheses and to conclude that nut-cracking, leaf-clipping and leaf-grooming are culturally determined.

Quite a few observational reports of imitation by chimpanzees exist (see Whiten and Ham, 1992 for extensive review). Convincing evidence of imitation has occurred in the context of play or exploration. For example, Köhler (1927) and more recently, de Waal (1982) observed young chimpanzees imitating the locomotory patterns of others, e.g., limping just like they observed an injured adult limp. Also, Hayes and Hayes (1952) described an incident in which their home-raised chimpanzee, Viki, used a mirror to apply lipstick to her lips. Even the details of Viki's actions, such as smoothing the cosmetic after having applied it, were similar to the model.

Russon and Galdikas (1995) have reported impressive spontaneous reproductions of human activities by rehabilitant orang-utans that seem to be best explained by imitation. A female orang-utan cleaned her teeth with a toothbrush and toothpaste, and she even imitated the action of spitting out the contents of her mouth over the veranda railings. In addition, she imitated the camp cooks' fire-making techniques, including some of the details, such as scooping fuel from a container with a cup, placing the tip of a smouldering stick in the fuel, and fanning the stick with a metal lid by holding it vertically and waving it briskly back and forth. Moreover, this imitation occurred in the absence of the model and, therefore, constitutes delayed imitation. Other observed behaviours such as painting, making bridges, hanging hammocks and the use of boats are suggestive of imitative abilities in orang-utans. Multiple instances of 'true imitation' have been documented in free-ranging orang-utans although Russon (1996) argues that exact matches of means and ends rarely occur in the spontaneous imitative behaviour of either humans or non-human primates. In the face of such strong observational evidence, it is curious that laboratory experimental studies have failed to demonstrate imitation in orang-utans.

Few claims have been made about the imitative ability of gorillas, the remaining great ape. Anecdotal evidence for imitation in gorillas is sparse (see Whiten and Ham, 1992; Byrne, 1996a). Free-ranging mountain gorillas eat plants that are protected by stings and spines. The gorillas have learned certain ways of processing the plants for eating, in order to reduce the amount of contact with these aversive portions of the plants. While the individual gorillas' techniques vary at a fine level of description, on a grosser level the techniques are the same in the majority of observed cases. Based on our earlier definitions, we might call this goal emulation. It appears, however, that there is greater similarity in the gorilla's actions than would be expected if goal emulation was the learning mechanism. Byrne and Byrne (1993) make a convincing argument for what they call programme-level imitation, a form of imitation in which 'what is imitated is the logical order of elements and the inter-relationships of processing stages' (p. 259). Their argument is actually strengthened by the fact that there are variations on the most common technique, because these variations demonstrate that there is more than one potential way to process the food. Thus, the lower-level explanations of stimulus enhancement are discounted. They acknowledge that genetic constraints or trial-and-error learning could be responsible, but consider these to be improbable explanations.

As Visalberghi and Fragazsy (1990) stated, 'The problem of demonstrating imitation in spontaneous situations is not adequate observation; the problem is exclusion of alternative hypotheses' (p. 257). It is for this reason that claims about imitative abilities based on naturalistic observation have been met with scepticism (e.g., Tomasello et al., 1993a). Naturalistic observation is useful as an initial mode of investigating animal behaviour, but it is necessary that some of the questions raised by the descriptive investigations be answered under the controlled conditions of the laboratory. These controlled conditions have taken several forms in the study of imitation in primates.

Imitation of arbitrary actions: 'do-as-I-do' studies

The goal of studies using the method of teaching imitation of arbitrary actions, teaching primates to 'do-as-I do', is to ascertain 'whether a species can imitate when actively encouraged to do so' (Whiten and Custance, 1996, p. 294). This type of investigation is conducted informally in everyday interactions with young human children in western cultures who comply with the prompts, 'where's your nose', 'touch your elbow', etc. With non-human species, especially those individuals reared with conspecifics and not language-trained, we want to test the ability to imitate the arbitrary action that is demonstrated apart from their understanding of spoken language (see Fouts, Hirsch and Fouts, 1982, for discussion of the role of imitation for learning sign language in apes). Many reviews (i.e., Galef, 1992; Visalberghi and Fragaszy, 1990) have concentrated on the imitation of relatively complex functional behaviours, and have found surprisingly little evidence of imitation among non-human species. Therefore, it is particularly significant that imitation was documented when the focus was changed from imitation of tool use, a skill with cognitive challenges, to imitation of arbitrary actions (Custance, Whiten and Bard, 1995).

Hayes and Hayes (1952) devised such an experimental procedure to test imitative abilities. The Hayeses trained Viki to imitate such that on the command 'do this' she attempted to copy the arbitrary or non-functional action the human demonstrator performed next, such as pulling the mouth wide open. After teaching Viki 12 training actions, the Hayeses demonstrated that Viki imitated a total of 55 of a series of 70 novel actions (i.e., with no direct training). Unfortunately, thorough descriptions of each of the 70 actions were not presented and it appeared that some of the behaviours were 'shaped' by the Hayeses so that processes other than imitation may have been involved. As Whiten and Ham (1992) pointed out 'presumably one cannot "train" an animal to imitate in this way unless it has some inherent imitative capacity' (p. 255). Yet, unfortunately, Hayes and Hayes did not provide a detailed account of the procedure.

Custance and her colleagues (Custance and Bard, 1994; Custance et al., 1995) replicated the study by Hayes and Hayes (1952) with two 4-year-old nursery-reared chimpanzees using more rigorous methods. The chimpanzees were first taught 15 gestures to be done on the command 'Do this!' They were then presented with 48 arbitrary novel gestures that did not involve objects. The chimpanzees imitated 13 and 17 actions each, as identified by two coders who were blind to the specific gestures which had been observed by the chimpanzees. The coders' ability to identify the actions was significantly better than could be explained by chance.

The orang-utan, Chantek, who was involved in a language study, was taught to imitate some actions on the command 'Do the same thing' (similar to the 'Do this' studies mentioned above: Miles, Mitchell and Harper, 1996). He successfully followed the 'where's your nose?' game and was successful when the 'do-the-same-thing' command was extended to actions on objects. As is the case with human infants, however, these reports are suggestive that orang-utans are capable of imitating, but are not conclusive.

Imitation of actions on objects

The distinction has been made between studies that demonstrate that a species *can* imitate and those that demonstrate that a species *does* imitate (Whiten, Custance, Gomez, Teixidor and Bard, 1996). The Do-as-I-do studies demonstrated that chimpanzees *can* imitate (see also Tomasello et al., 1993b). Another study was designed to determine if chimpanzees imitate spontaneously without tuition to do so (Whiten et al., 1996). In this study, an artificial fruit that simulated food processing was presented to children and chimpanzees. The subjects observed 1 of 2 demonstrated actions on 1 of 2 locking mechanisms. For example, a threadless bolt was removed either with a poking technique or a twisting technique. This method ruled out the potential explanation of stimulus enhancement by 'enhancing' the same location in both techniques. Blind observers were able to distinguish the 2 techniques on the bolt for the chimpanzees, but not on the other locking mechanism. Chimpanzees were sometimes more efficient than the children in solving the problem due to the children's more faithful imitation of the unnecessary elements of the observed techniques. This brings up the interesting issue that emulation may be the more competent solution to a problem in some circumstances (Whiten and Custance, 1996). Whiten and Ham (1992) noted the lack of evidence of imitation in monkeys that could not be alternatively explained by other mechanisms such as social enhancement, social facilitation, observational conditioning or trial-and-error learning. They suggest that future research with different monkey taxa using a food-processing analogue may yet provide more definitive evidence of imitation in monkeys.

There have been some experimental tests of imitation based on Piagetian tasks, modified from the procedures outlined by Užgiris and Hunt (1975). Separate experiments found evidence for delayed imitation of facial actions and delayed imitation of actions on objects in a 4-year-old gorilla (Chevalier-Skolnikoff, 1982), 4- to 6-year-old chimpanzees (Mathieu and Bergeron, 1981; Mignault, 1985), and a 4-year-old orangutan (Miles et al., 1996). Unfortunately, none of the apes' behaviour with respect to instances of delayed imitation were described in detail. What is very clear is that more research is needed.

Studies on the imitation of tool use

Tool using tasks have been presented to monkeys without any evidence of imitative learning (see Visalberghi and Fragaszy, 1990, for a thorough review). Some monkeys did learn to use the tools in the task, though they did not seem to benefit from observing another individual solving the task. Visalberghi and Fragaszy present potential explanations for the lack of imitation in experimental situations, but conclude that it is most likely due to cognitive constraints, such as the lack of 'understanding of the causal relations between the actions performed by the model and the outcome' (Visalberghi and Limongelli, 1996, p. 73).

Preliminary experimental studies of imitation in older chimpanzees suggest that goal emulation rather than imitative copying was the primary mechanism involved in the observational learning of tool use (Tomasello et al., 1993b). The subjects learned, through observing an expert model, to put the tool and the goal into a functional relation, but did not copy the exact actions that they observed. In a study of imitation of tool manufacture in an orang-utan, Wright (1972) concluded that the manufacture of stone tools was within the capability of prehistoric humanoids. The orang-utan was able to copy the goal and also copied the intermediate goal of tool manufacture prior to tool use. The author notes that the imitation was not 'parrot-fashion learning' (p. 305), but, rather, the orang-utan used innovative alternative techniques, which Wright interpreted as an indication of the intelligent nature of orang-utan problem-solving.

More recently, a study of the acquisition of tool use in young chimpanzees, utilising familiar social partners, provided some evidence of enhanced performance as a result of modelling, but again imitative copying was not definitive (Bard, Fragaszy and Visalberghi, 1995). The task was to insert a stick into a clear tube and push out the grape. Imitation in this study was defined in terms of 'savings': i.e., the observers learned to solve the task in fewer trials than the individuals who learned through trial-and-error. We found that observing a model did not facilitate performance if the subject was too young to learn the tool task, i.e. in 2-year-old chimpanzee infants. But 3-year-olds and 4-year-olds did exhibit savings: in 3-year-olds, solution occurred in 27 trials for the observer and 47 trials for the individual learner; and, in 4-year-olds, solution occurred in the first trial for the observer and in the 25th trial for the individual learner. Moreover, the method by which the chimpanzees learned the task had a modest effect on their comprehension of the tool task; when complex tools were given, those subjects who observed a model during acquisition had greater success and fewer errors than individual learners. This study is important in highlighting the interaction of age with task difficulty and with imitation.

Five questions on imitation in non-human primates

We return to the five questions with which we opened our chapter to discuss the evidence obtained from non-human primates on imitation. Often the search for characteristics that are unique to the human species provides as much valuable information on commonalities as on differences. Research efforts to explore the mechanisms that support the development of imitative capacity are needed because there continues to be debate as to whether a singular mechanism is responsible for imitation throughout development. Chimpanzees can be productively utilised to investigate social communicative foundations for imitation since in 'natural experiments' (such as the necessity of hand-rearing infants), the environment is designed to foster learning communicative signals, either of a chimpanzee species-typical or of a human species-typical (i.e., language) nature (see Bard, 1994a; 1995; and Bard and Gardner, 1996 for further discussion of the effects of rearing environment).

Is imitation part of our primate heritage or is it unique to the human species?

From the evidence gathered thus far, it seems that very few primate species learn by imitation, although humans are by no means unique in this ability. Chimpanzees, in particular among primate species, are comparable to humans in the realms of extended pre-adult development (e.g., Bruner, 1972; Goodall, 1986), communication and language skills (e.g., Gardner and Gardner, 1969; Plooij, 1984; Premack, 1972; Savage-Rumbaugh, Rumbaugh and Boysen, 1978), cognitive skills (e.g., Mathieu and Bergeron, 1981) and behavioural performance (e.g., Gallup, 1970; Plooij, 1984). Although caution is advised in overgeneralisations based on parallels in performance, there is no doubt that chimpanzees are our closest evolutionary relatives (e.g., King and Wilson, 1975). Thus, it is not surprising that the evidence for imitation is strongest for chimpanzees among the non-human primates. Observational studies report the likelihood that chimpanzees imitate. Experimental studies have demonstrated chimpanzees' ability to imitate arbitrary actions (Custance et al., 1995), imitate actions on objects (Tomasello et al., 1993b; Whiten et al., 1996) and imitate complex tool-use tasks (Bard et al., 1995; Visalberghi and Limongelli, 1996). The evidence is suggestive for the other ape species, orang-utans and gorillas. The reproduction of complex human activities by orang-utans suggests that they are also able to learn tool use by imitation, though this is yet to be demonstrated experimentally. Orang-utans and a gorilla have been shown to engage in 'do-as-I-do' activity although systematic testing of imitative ability with novel arbitrary actions has not been conducted. There has been no evidence of imitation in any species of monkey, despite deliberate attempts to teach behaviour through imitation processes, and providing situations in which learning would be facilitated through observation of successful solution by another (e.g., Chevalier-Skolnikoff, 1982; Parker, 1991; Visalberghi and Fragaszy, 1990).

One problem in asking the question 'Which primate species imitate?' is that the absence of evidence for a particular species cannot be taken as proof that the species is not capable of imitating. Some species for which this ability seems probable, such as the gorilla, have not been studied extensively in this domain. Some monkey species have been studied extensively without any demonstration of imitation. Clearly, here the issue is one of 'proving the null'. When is the lack of evidence sufficiently large enough to conclude that a particular species does *not* imitate?

Much work remains to be done before strong conclusions can be made about which species can and cannot imitate. Studies need to be designed in such a way that alternative explanations can be ruled out. Greater attention should be given to making the comparative research on imitation more ecologically relevant, such as the simulation of food processing exemplified by the artificial fruit (Whiten et al., 1996) and using data collected from field studies (e.g., Boesch, 1996; McGrew, 1992; Russon, 1996). Apes may show stronger evidence of imitation if conspecific demonstrators are used, such as seen in orang-utans (Russon and Galdikas, 1995) and chimpanzees (Bard et al., 1995). Methodologies better suited for eliciting imitation in the great apes may be used in the future. Experimental evidence for imitation in great apes may be sparse because of the lack of a personal relationship between the ape and the demonstrator, use of very young subjects, demonstration of actions that are beyond the apes' capabilities, and single demonstration of actions to be imitated rather than repeated demonstration (Russon and Galdikas, 1995). In order to optimise the likelihood of a species demonstrating its capability to imitate, these issues need to be addressed.

So much emphasis has been placed on determining whether species have 'true imitation' that an important finding may have been given very little attention. Social learning other than imitation may be very important for many species, including human children. Being in a group with more experienced individuals may facilitate learning through response facilitation, local enhancement, observational conditioning and goal emulation. Group dynamics may favour co-operation in problem-solving tasks, such that individuals solve different types of tasks, or different aspects of the same task (e.g., one capuchin works the mechanisms, the other capuchin captures the food: Fragaszy and Visalberghi, 1989), and rewards are shared. These processes may be adequate for the kinds of things that many species need to learn in order to survive.

Is a communicative environment required for imitation?

Currently, there is controversy concerning the influence of the human cultural environment on imitative learning in non-human primates. It is particularly worrisome that there are some who argue that there can not be convincing evidence of imitative ability obtained in any study of wild non-human primates, even in chimpanzees (e.g., Galef, 1992, Tomasello et al., 1993a). Documented occurrences of imitation, some argue, have been a result of human enculturation (typically this means language-training). The argument follows that tutorials in a human-type communicative system are necessary for imitation, especially for the more sophisticated imitative performances evident in deferred imitation or imitation of tool use.

We know that social learning begins to exert an influence on development in humans and apes even within the newborn period (Bard, 1994a; Nugent, Lester and Brazelton, 1989). In chimpanzees, differences in rearing environment relate to differences in emotional expressions and to differences in emotionally reactive interpretations of standard environmental events (Bard, in press; Bard and Gardner, 1996). Inborn temperamental characteristics interact with environmental consequences in the expression of both imitative and emotional responses. The comparison group in these ape studies is the mother-reared chimpanzees in the laboratory. It may be that the communicative environment in the wild supports the social factors involved in imitation in ways not reflected in the mother–infant relationship in captive conditions. Some argue that captive conditions can never be as challenging as the wild, and so, by definition, the most advanced skills of any sort must be found in wild subjects (e.g., Boesch, 1996). Recent evidence suggests that, when common eliciting conditions are met, common communicative abilities such as intentional and referential pointing emerge in both chimpanzee and human subjects (e.g., Leavens, Hopkins and Bard, 1996).

Recent theories of imitation assert a social–communicative origin to imitation, in contrast to the perceptual–kinesthetic matching hypothesis (e.g., Field et al., 1982; Mitchell, 1994; Meltzoff and Moore, 1977). Kugiumutzakis (1993) found that newborns (minutes after birth) were able to imitate a vocalisation with expressions indicative of the great effort which is exerted in order to engage in a communicative fashion. Trevarthen (1979), for example, has advocated that imitations of vocalisation serve as the basis for primary intersubjectivity in early communicative exchanges (Kugiumutzakis, this volume). Finally, imitation has been proposed as the necessary means for developing a sense of self (e.g., Hart and Fegley, 1994; Parker, 1991), a sense of interpersonal self (e.g., Trevarthen, this volume) and a 'theory of mind' (e.g., Butterworth, 1991). In summarising the data, Meltzoff (1996) suggested that imitation is an important mechanism in social learning.

In parallel with the shift in interpretation of imitation in human literature, there is a renewed consideration of social–communicative variables in demonstrations of imitation in non-human primates (e.g., Bard, in press; Bard et al., 1995; Fragaszy and Visalberghi, 1989). It has long been the contention of primatologists that chimpanzee intellect excels in its social application (e.g., Byrne and Whiten, 1988; Goodall, 1986; de Waal, 1982). In fact, the discovery of 'theory of mind' in chimpanzees by Premack and Woodruff (1978) sparked a new research area in child psychology. Social–communicative experiences do not necessarily coincide with developing cognition, especially in laboratory chimpanzees, thus comparative investigations of the development of imitation are particularly important.

When two nursery-reared chimpanzees were assessed for imitative abilities at 4½ years of age, using procedures similar to those used by Hayes and Hayes, they were initially unable to imitate vocal or manual arbitrary actions (Custance and Bard, 1994, Custance et al., 1995). Initially, the chimpanzees acted as if the 'game' was to touch the experimenter's hands. They had to learn the 'rules' of the imitation game involving taking turns, watching the model and doing the same action on their own body as they observed in the model. These 'rules' of the game are identical to those learned by human infants during development. These same chimpanzees at a slightly younger age did show evidence, however, of spontaneous imitation of actions on objects (Whiten et al., 1996). Human infants and chimpanzee infants reared in human homes do exhibit imitation of arbitrary actions at relatively early ages. Thus, there is good evidence that important cultural factors, missing in standard laboratory conditions, are necessary for imitation to occur. We argue that scaffolding is required for the development of a robust imitative capacity (Custance and Bard, 1994).

We are still very unsure about how this early proclivity relates to later imitative capacity. Does imitation atrophy, like muscle tissue, if not regularly exercised? Does neonatal imitation need to be actively nurtured, through a social communication system, in order to develop further? Are *human* social communication systems, the *only* type that support the development of imitation? The demonstration of neonatal imitation in chimpanzees challenges our notions of unique human propensities to imitate. These are not the only questions about imitation that remain unanswered. Further experimental research will bring us closer to understanding imitation and the functional mechanisms that underlie and support imitation in human and non-human primates.

Is imitation an innate predisposition in chimpanzees?

Competing theories explain the occurrence of neonatal imitation: (1) facial actions act as innate releasing mechanisms, akin to the innate responsiveness to sign stimulus discovered by ethologists (e.g., Tinbergen and Lorenz); (2) a learned response, shaped through early interactive experience; (3) active intermodal matching mediated by a representational system (e.g., Field et al, 1982; Meltzoff and Moore, 1977); and (4) innate intersubjectivity (Kugiumutzakis, 1993; Trevarthen, 1979). There are three strong arguments against the innate releasing mechanism explanation of neonatal imitation. First, not all human infants exhibit imitation: approximately 50% of the infants tested by Meltzoff exhibit imitation. Second, there are numerous imitative responses exhibited by neonates (lip protrusion, mouth opening, eye blinks, finger movements, sound production, head movements, emotional expressions, hand gestures). It seems unlikely that there are innate releasers for each of the numerous imitative responses. Finally, neonates do not produce an immediate and perfect matching response (e.g., Kugiumutzakis, 1985). The hypothesis that shaping mechanisms underlie neonatal imitation garners some support with the fact that some infants do show a pattern of improving performance through the course of repeated imitation testing (Kugiumutzakis, 1993). Some infants, however, show an opposite pattern of less-correct matching during the same imitation tests. There is a great likelihood, which no researcher denies, that environmental experiences contribute to changes in imitative performance. That shaping is the primary underlying mechanism, however, is not supported by the findings that immediately after birth, prior to any interactive experience, infants exhibit imitation, and that videotaped records of the model's behaviour show that differential responses are *not* given in response to the infants' imitative behaviour.

The multiple studies of imitation by Meltzoff and Moore (e.g., 1977) have repeatedly concluded that active intermodal matching mediated by a representational system is the only explanation of neonatal imitation that remains when all other mechanisms are considered and rejected. Recently, however, Meltzoff (1996) argued convincingly that the intermodal matching system functions only in social–communicative settings. Kugiumutzakis has presented strong evidence that neonatal imitation is a result of an innate intersubjectivity. Intersubjectivity, according to Trevarthen, 'provides internal images of face and hand movements for the identification and imitation of the expressions of others' (Trevarthen and Hubley, 1978, p. 213). Intersubjectivity provides the innate basis of the intention to communicate which these researchers suggest is the function served by imitation. Regardless of the mechanism, either a special form of learning or an innate predisposition for communication, the function served by imitation is becoming both more clear and more commonly agreed.

Newborn behavioural capacities are strongly comparable in human and chimpanzee. Some neonatal chimpanzees imitated facial actions (tongue protrusion and mouth opening) and sound production (tongue clicks). The presence of neonatal imitation in chimpanzees highlights the evolutionary origins of imitation. The presence of imitation in the neonatal period has been assumed to be indicative of an innate predisposition (Meltzoff and Moore, 1977: Trevarthen, 1979). Evidence of imitation in neonatal chimpanzees, therefore, must be considered indicative of a predisposition for imitative learning in this species, as well.

Imitation of facial expressions by chimpanzee neonates represents a chimpanzee capacity to imitate that is similar to that of humans. Chimpanzees appeared more capable of imitating when tested in a communicative paradigm rather than a rigid non-interactive format, which suggests that imitation serves a communicative function for chimpanzees as well. How this predisposition relates to later imitative capacity in chimpanzees is unknown. The evidence presented here suggests that social environment is important in the nurturing of imitative capacity in the child and the chimpanzee.

Are there cognitive constraints on imitation in non-human primates?

Traditionally, imitative abilities in child and chimpanzee were attributed solely to cognition. According to Piaget (1962), the development of imitative skills followed a sequence of development that was parallel to that of other sensorimotor domains. In human infants, the studies of Meltzoff (1996), have found very early imitation capacities, thus demonstrating a human proclivity for intermodal co-ordination (i.e., to match perceptual stimuli with kinaesthetic feedback). Imitation of facial actions occurs in newborns, which obviously challenges many of Piaget's notions. Theoretical challenges to Piagetian theory continued with the discovery of deferred imitation as early as 9 months of age (Meltzoff, 1996). Thus, imitation is now known to develop in human infants in a sequence that is out of synchrony with the other cognitive domains.

In non-human primates, some of the earliest studies of the development of cognition investigated intelligence within a Piagetian perspective. The evidence is quite dramatic that cognition is not the mechanism which supports imitation. Cognitive development was documented to follow Piagetian stages in the sensorimotor period in both monkeys and apes. Imitation, in contrast, was found to be at very rudimentary levels in monkeys, but at levels comparable to humans in the apes (Chevalier-Skolnikoff, 1982; Parker, 1991). When viewed within a comparative perspective, it seems that cognitive ability may be a necessary condition for the occurrence of imitation, but it is not a sufficient condition.

Early interpretation of neonatal imitation stated that neonates used mental representation to match their facial actions to those of a visually perceived model (Field et al., 1982; Meltzoff and Moore, 1977), thus agreeing with Piaget that imitation arose through cognitive capacities but disagreeing about the time at which the cognitive capacity arose. Subsequently the emphasis changed to the importance of social factors in the development of imitation. Current conclusions are that neonatal imitation is indicative of innate intersubjectivity. The presence of neo-natal imitation in humans and chimpanzees, therefore, dispels the notion that advanced cognitive ability is a necessary condition for imitation. Moreover, an argument could be made that neonatal imitation in chimpanzees is indicative of 'innate interspecies intersubjectivity' (Kugiumutzakis, personal communication, 1994).

Theories have been advanced that imitation is related to other cognitive abilities, such as self-recognition, empathy and tool use (Gallup, 1970; McGrew, 1993; Piaget, 1962). If imitation of complex skills is a necessary condition for the development of self-recognition, one would expect to find imitation of tool use, for instance, only in those species that exhibit self-recognition, i.e., humans and apes, and not among species which do not exhibit self-recognition, for example, monkeys. Cross-species comparisons do confirm this expectation. However, if one considers research that combines the cross-species and the developmental per-spectives, a different picture emerges.

There are repeated suggestions in the developmental literature that imitation requires learning a self–other distinction such that imitation leads to the development of self-awareness (e.g., Meltzoff, 1996). If imita-tion is a cognitive prerequisite for self-recognition then one would expect to find imitation developmentally preceding self-recognition. In human infants, Hart and Fegley (1994) found that the age at which self-recogni-tion developed could be predicted by the degree of social imitation in an earlier test. Parker (1991) suggests that imitation is necessary for the development of self-recognition even in non-human primates. The Facial Imitation Model, as proposed by Parker (1991), states that, through the production and monitoring of contingent facial actions, the one-to-one correspondence between self and mirror-image is discovered. There are both empirical and theoretical reasons for disputing these arguments. First, Lin, Bard and Anderson (1992) found very little evidence of mirror-monitored facial and head movements (contingent behaviour) in young chimpanzees either before or after the development of self-recog-nition. So, although by 2½ years of age the chimpanzees seemed to recognise the contingency between their head and its mirror-image (since they passed the mark test), they did not engage in elaborate facial actions in order to learn the contingency involved. Moreover, there were not more facial contingent actions in the youngest subjects. Lin et al.'s study was particularly interesting since it identified an age range (2 to 2½ years) as the period when mirror self-recognition develops in nursery-reared chimpanzees. In older chimpanzees (3½ years) imitative behaviour was demonstrated after a period of tuition (Custance and Bard, 1994; Whiten et al., 1996). One of these nursery-reared chimpanzees was tested for mirror self-recognition immediately prior to the imitation assessments. There was no doubt about his understanding that the reflected image was himself (see Figures 1 and 2 in Custance and Bard, 1994). Cognitive capacity related to self-recognition and, at a level equivalent to 18–24-month human infants, was found to be present in chimpanzees without tuition (Lin et al., 1992). In contrast, imitative behaviour, even of the lowest cognitive level, i.e., imitation of arbitrary actions, required a period of social tuition (Custance and Bard, 1994). Thus, there are strong arguments to be made that imitative behaviour in chimpanzees does not rely solely upon underlying cognitive capacities (e.g., Custance and Bard, 1994).

Often researchers have claimed we have little evidence of imitation in non-human species (e.g., Tomasello et al., 1993a) because the ability to imitate *per se* is confounded with the ability to imitate complex manipulative behaviour (Custance and Bard, 1994). Most researchers have tended to concentrate on the imitation of complex functional behaviours related to food-processing, such as tool use, and communicatory gestures. However, these are cognitively demanding behaviours in their own right and one would expect that fact to increase the overall difficulty of imitating them.

Are there developmental changes in imitation in non-human primates?

There are important developmental considerations with regard to imitative ability. Piaget argued that the cognitive substrate for imitation of invisible actions, such as tongue protrusion and mouth opening, developed between 8 and 12 months of age in human infants. Meltzoff and Moore (1977) found newborn infants were capable of imitating mouth opening and tongue protrusion. Kugiumutzakis (this volume) and Heimann (this volume) have each documented how imitation of facial and vocal actions changes from birth through the first 6 months of life. Piaget argued that the cognitive substrate for delayed imitation was mental representation which developed between 18 and 24 months in human infants. Meltzoff has documented delayed imitation in infants as young as 9 months of age.

In summary, there may be a disparity in imitative ability in chimpanzees raised in different circumstances. Do we find equal levels of imitation across cultures that vary in the nurturing of facial imitation? We argue that similar disparities would be found in human infants raised in different circumstances (e.g., children in cultures with different emphases on imitative skills, see for example Ochs and Schieffelin, 1984). It is likely that early imitation that is not nurtured or supported will drop out of an infants repertoire, atrophying like muscle tissue through disuse (e.g. Whiten and Custance, 1996). When we consider imitation across cultures is there information that suggests neonatal imitation is related causally to imitation of arbitrary actions and/or imitation of tool tasks? Is imitation a unitary ability? These questions remain to be answered.

Conclusions

After reviewing the literature and presenting new data on neonatal imitation in chimpanzees, we conclude that apes and humans have similarities in the development of flexible social and communicative skills that could account for the similarities found in their early imitative ability. The chapters in this volume attest to the intricate communicative interchanges which occur between infant and adult that support the development of imitation in human infants. We believe that this same developmental system which nurtures intersubjectivity exists in apes and humans. Thus, the naturalness of imitation in apes approximates that in human infants and considerable 'effort' is expended to support the development of imitative exchanges in both human and ape infants. We argue against the notion of reflexive type of imitation in either human or ape infants. In contrast, monkey species appear to have more inflexible, or more hardwired communicative and social skills. The assumption that imitation can not be taught to monkeys appears to be true. Consideration of the cognitive substrate for imitation ability does not appear to account for the differences in imitative ability across species.

ACKNOWLEDGMENTS

The research was supported in part by NIH grants from the National Center for Research Resources RR-00165 to Yerkes, RR-03591 to R. B. Swenson and T. Insel, and RR-01658 to K. A. Bard. We are grateful to the following students, research assistants and collaborators for their invaluable contributions to the chimpanzee research: Erika Yeager, Josh Schneider, Kathy Gardner, Kelly

McDonald, Dr Debbie Custance, Dr Dorothy Fragaszy and Dr Linda Brent. The Yerkes Center is fully accredited by the American Association for Accreditation of Laboratory Animal Care.

REFERENCES

Bakeman, R. and Gottman, J. (1986). *Observing interaction: An introduction to sequential analysis*. New York: Cambridge University Press.
Bard, K. A. (1990). 'Social tool use' by free-ranging orang-utans: A Piagetian and developmental perspective on the manipulation of an animate object. In S.T. Parker and K. R. Gibson (eds.), *'Language' and intelligence in monkeys and apes: Comparative developmental perspectives* (pp. 356–78). New York: Cambridge University Press.
  (1994a). Very early social learning: The effect of neonatal environment on chimpanzees' social responsiveness. In J. J. Roeder, B. Thierry, J. R. Anderson and N. Herrenschmidt (eds.), *Current primatology: Volume III Social development, learning, and behavior* (pp. 339–46). Strasburg, France: Université Louis Pasteur.
  (1994b). Evolutionary roots of intuitive parenting: Maternal competence in chimpanzees. *Early Development and Parenting*, 3, 19–28.
  (1995). Parenting in primates. In M. Bornstein (ed.), *Handbook of Parenting: Vol. II Ecology and biology of parenting* (pp. 27–58). Hillsdale, NJ: Erlbaum.
  (in press). Social-experiential contributions to imitation and emotion in chimpanzees. In S. Bråten (ed.), *Intersubjective communication and emotion in early ontogeny: A source book*. Cambridge University Press.
Bard, K. A., Fragaszy, D. M. and Visalberghi, E. (1995). Acquisition and comprehension of a tool-using behavior by young chimpanzees: Effects of age and modeling. *International Journal of Comparative Psychology*, 8, 47–68.
Bard, K. A. and Gardner, K. H. (1996). Influences on development in infant chimpanzees: Enculturation, temperament, and cognition. In A. Russon, K. A. Bard and S. T. Parker (eds.), *Reaching into thought: The minds of the great apes* (pp. 235–56). Cambridge University Press.
Bard, K. A., Platzman, K. A., Lester, B. M. and Suomi, S. J. (1992). Orientation to social and nonsocial stimuli in neonatal chimpanzees and humans. *Infant Behavior and Development*, 15, 43–56.
Boesch, C. (1996). Three approaches for assessing chimpanzee culture. In A. Russon, K. A. Bard and S. T. Parker (eds.), *Reaching into thought: The minds of the great apes* (pp. 404–29). Cambridge University Press.
Brazelton, T. B. (1984). *Neonatal behavioral assessment scale.* (2nd edn.). *Clinics in Developmental Medicine No. 88.* Spastics International Medical Publications. Philadelphia: Lippincott.
Bruner, J. (1972). Nature and uses of immaturity. *American Psychologist*, 27, 687–708.
Bullowa, M. (1979). *Before speech: The beginning of interpersonal communication.* New York: Cambridge University Press.
Butterworth, G. (1991). The ontogeny and phylogeny of joint visual attention. In A. Whiten (ed.), *Natural theories of mind.* Oxford: Basil Blackwell.
Byrne, R. W. (1996a). The misunderstood ape: Cognitive skill of the gorilla. In

120 K. A. Bard and C. L. Russell

A. E. Russon, K. A. Bard and S. T. Parker (eds.), *Reaching into thought: The minds of the great apes* (pp. 111–30). Cambridge University Press.

(1996b). *The thinking ape: Evolutionary origins of intelligence.*

Byrne, R. W. and Byrne, J. M. E. (1993). Complex leaf-gathering skill of mountain gorillas (*Gorilla g. beringei*): Variability and standardization. *American Journal of Primatology*, 31, 241–61.

Byrne, R. W. and Whiten, A. (1988). *Machiavellian intelligence: Social expertise and the evolution of intellect in monkeys, apes, and humans*. Oxford University Press.

Chevalier-Skolnikoff, S. (1982). A cognitive analysis of facial behavior in Old World monkeys, apes, and human beings. In C. T. Snowdon, C. H. Brown and M. R. Petersen (eds.), *Primate communication* (pp 303–68). New York: Cambridge University Press.

Custance, D. M. and Bard, K. A. (1994). The comparative and developmental study of self-recognition and imitation: The importance of social factors. In S. T. Parker, R. W. Mitchell and M. L. Boccia (eds.), *Self-awareness in animals and humans: Developmental perspectives* (pp. 207–26). Cambridge University Press.

Custance, D. M., Whiten, A. and Bard, K. A. (1995). Can young chimpanzees (*Pan troglodytes*) imitate arbitrary actions? Hayes & Hayes (1952) revisited. *Behavior*, 132, 837–59.

Field, T., Woodson, R., Greenberg, R. and Cohen, D. (1982). Discrimination and imitation of facial expressions by neonates. *Science*, 218, 179–81.

Fouts, R. S., Hirsch, A. D. and Fouts, D. H. (1982). Cultural transmission of a human language in a chimpanzee mother–infant relationship. In H. E. Fitzgerald, J. A. Mullins and P. Gage (eds.), *Psychobiological perspectives* (pp. 159–93). Child Nurturance Series, vol. 3. New York: Plenum.

Fragaszy, D. M. and Visalberghi, E. (1989). Social influence on the acquisition of tool-using behaviors in tufted capuchin monkeys (*Cebus apella*). *Journal of Comparative Psychology*, 103, 159–70.

Galef, B. G., Jr. (1992). The question of animal culture. *Human Evolution*, 3, 157–78.

Gallup, G. G. (1970). Chimpanzees: Self-recognition. *Science*, 167, 86–7.

Gardner, R. A. and Gardner, B. T. (1969). Teaching sign language to a chimpanzee. *Science*, 165, 664–72.

Goodall, J. (1986). *The chimpanzees of Gombe: Patterns of behavior*. Cambridge, MA: Belknap Press of Harvard University Press.

Hallock, M. B., Worobey, J. and Self, P. S. (1989). Behavioral development in chimpanzee (*Pan troglodytes*) and human newborns across the first month of life. *International Journal of Behavioral Development*, 12, 527–40.

Harlow, H. F. and Harlow, M. K. (1965). The affectional systems. In A. Schrier, H. Harlow and F. Stollnitz (eds.), *Behavior of nonhuman primates*. New York: Academic Press.

Hart, D. and Fegley, P. (1994). Social imitation and the emergence of a mental model of self. In S. T. Parker, R. W. Mitchell and M. L. Boccia (eds.), *Self-awareness in animals and humans: Developmental perspectives* (pp. 149–65). Cambridge University Press.

Hayes, K. J. and Hayes, C. (1952). Imitation in a home-raised chimpanzee. *Journal of Comparative and Physiological Psychology*, 45, 450–9.

Heimann, M. (1989). Neonatal imitation, gaze aversion, and mother–infant inter-action. *Infant Behavior and Development*, 12, 495–505.

Heyes, C. M. (1993). Imitation, culture, and cognition. *Animal Behavior*, 46, 99–1010.

Heyes, C. M and Galef, B. G., Jr. (1996). *Social learning in animals: The roots of culture*. San Diego, CA: Academic Press.

Itani, J. and Nishimura, A. (1973). The study of infrahuman cultures in Japan. In E. W. Menzel (ed.), *Precultural primate behavior* (pp. 26–50). Basle: Karger.

Jacobsen, C. F., Jacobsen, M. M. and Yoshioka, J. G. (1932). Development of an infant chimpanzee during her first year. *Comparative Psychology Monographs*, 9, 1094.

King, M. C. and Wilson, A. C. (1975). Evolution at two levels in humans and chimpanzees. *Science*, 188, 107–16.

Köhler, W. (1927). *The mentality of apes*. London: Routledge & Kegan Paul.

Kugiumutzakis, G. (1985). The origin, development, and function of the early infant imitation. *Abstracts of Uppsala Dissertations from the Faculty of Social Sciences*.

(1993). Intersubjective vocal imitation in early mother–infant interaction. In J. Nadel and L. Camaioni (eds.), *New perspectives in early communication development* (pp. 23–47). London: Routledge.

Leavens, D. A., Hopkins, W. D. and Bard, K. A. (1996). Indexical and referential pointing in chimpanzees (*Pan troglodytes*). *Journal of Comparative Psychology*, 110, 346–53.

Lin, A., Bard, K. A. and Anderson, J. R. (1992). Development of self-recognition in chimpanzees (*Pan troglodytes*). *Journal of Comparative Psychology*, 106, 120–7.

Maratos, O. (1982). Trends in the development of imitation in early infancy. In T. Bever (ed.), *Regression in mental development: Basic phenomena and theories*. Hillsdale, NJ: Erlbaum.

Mathieu, M. and Bergeron, G. (1981). Piagetian assessment on cognitive development in chimpanzee (*Pan troglodytes*). In A. B. Chiarelli and R. S. Corruccini (eds.), *Primate behavior and sociobiology*. New York: Springer-Verlag.

McGrew, W. (1992). *Chimpanzee material culture: Implications for human evolution*. Cambridge University Press.

(1993). Brains, hands and minds: puzzling incongruities in ape tool use. In A. Berthelet and J. Chavaillon (eds.), *The use of tools by human and non-human primates*. Oxford: Clarendon Press.

Meltzoff, A. N. (1996). The human infant as imitative generalist: A 20-year progress report on infant imitation with implications for comparative psychology. In B. G. Galef and C. M. Heyes (eds.), *Social learning in animals: The roots of culture* (pp. 347–70). London: Academic Press.

Meltzoff, A. N. and Moore, M. K. (1977). Imitation of facial and manual gestures by human neonates. *Science*, 198, 75–8.

Mignault, C. (1985). Transition between sensorimotor and symbolic activities in nursery-reared chimpanzees (*Pan troglodytes*). *Journal of Human Evolution*, 14, 747–58.

Miles, H. L., Mitchell, R. W. and Harper, S. E. (1996). Simon says: The development of imitation in an enculturated orang-utan. In A. E. Russon, K. A. Bard and S. T. Parker (eds.), *Reaching into thought: The minds of the great apes* (pp. 278–99). Cambridge University Press.

Mineka, S., Davidson, M., Cook, M. and Keir, R. (1984). Fear of snakes in wild and lab-reared rhesus monkeys. *Journal of Abnormal Psychology*, 93, 355–72.

Mitchell, R. W. (1994). Multiplicities of self. In S. T. Parker, R. W. Mitchell and M. L. Boccia (eds.), *Self-awareness in animals and humans: Developmental perspectives* (pp. 81–107). Cambridge University Press.

Myowa, M. (1996). Imitation of facial gestures by an infant chimpanzee. *Primates*, 37, 207–13.

Nadel, J. and Pezé, A. (1993). What makes immediate imitation communicative in toddlers and autistic children? In J. Nadel and L Camaioni (eds.), *New perspectives in early communicative development* (pp. 139–56). New York: Routledge.

Nishida, T. (1987). Local traditions and cultural transmission. In B. B. Smuts, D. L. Cheney, R. M. Seyfarth, R. W. Wrangham and T. T. Struhsaker (eds.), *Primate Societies* (pp. 462–74). University of Chicago Press.

Nugent, J. K., Lester, B. M. and Brazelton, T. B. (1989). *The cultural context of infancy: Volume 1: Biology, culture and infant development*. Norwood, NJ: Ablex.

Ochs, E. and Schieffelin, B. (1984). Language acquisition and socialization. Three developmental stories and their implications. In R. Shweder and R. LeVine (eds.), *Culture theory* (pp. 276–320). Cambridge University Press.

Parker, S. T. (1991). A developmental approach to the origins of self-recognition in great apes. *Human Evolution*, 6, 435–49.

Pecheux, M. G., Findji, F. and Ruel, J. (1992). Maternal scaffolding of attention between 5 and 8 months. *European Journal of Psychology of Education*, 7, 209–18.

Piaget, J. (1962). *Play, dreams and imitation in childhood*. New York: Norton & Co.

Plooij, F. X. (1984). *The behavioral development of free-living chimpanzee babies and infants*. Monographs on Infancy, vol. 3, Norwood, NJ: Ablex.

Premack, D. (1972). Teaching language to an ape. *Scientific American*, 227, 921–99.

Premack, D. G. and Woodruff, G. (1978). Does the chimpanzee have a theory of mind? *Behavioral and Brain Sciences*, 1, 515–26.

Redshaw, M. E. (1989). A comparison of neonatal behavior and reflexes in the great apes. *Journal of Human Evolution*, 18, 191–200.

Russell, C. L., Bard, K. A. and Adamson, L. B. (1997). Social referencing by young chimpanzees (*Pan troglodytes*). *Journal of Comparative Psychology*, 111, 185–93.

Russon, A. E. (1996). Imitation in everyday use: Matching and rehearsal in the spontaneous imitation of rehabilitant orang-utans (*Pongo pygmaeus*). In A. E. Russon, K. A. Bard and S. T. Parker (eds.), *Reaching into thought: The minds of the great apes* (pp. 152–76).Cambridge University Press.

Russon, A. E. and Galdikas, B. M. F. (1995). Constraints on great apes' imitation: Model and action selectivity in rehabilitant orang-utan (*Pongo pygmaeus*) imitation. *Journal of Comparative Psychology*, 109, 5–17.

Savage-Rumbaugh, E. S., Rumbaugh, D. M. and Boysen, S. T. (1978). Symbolic communication between two chimpanzees (*Pan troglodytes*). *Science*, 201, 641–4.

Siegel, S. (1956). *Nonparametric statistics for the behavioral sciences.* New York: McGraw-Hill.

Thorpe, W. H. (1963). *Learning and instinct in animals.* Cambridge, MA: Harvard University Press.

Tomasello, M., Kruger, A. and Ratner, H. (1993a). Cultural learning. *Behavioral and Brain Sciences*, 16, 495–552.

Tomasello, M., Savage-Rumbaugh, S. and Kruger, A. C. (1993b). Imitative learning of actions on objects by children, chimpanzees, and enculturated chimpanzees. *Child Development*, 64, 1688–105.

Trevarthen, C. (1979). Communication and cooperation in early infancy: A description of primary intersubjectivity. In M. Bullowa (ed.), *Before speech: The beginning of interpersonal communication.* New York: Cambridge University Press.

Trevarthen, C. and Hubley, P. (1978). Secondary intersubjectivity: Confidence, confiding, and acts of meaning in the first year of life. In A. Lock (ed.), *Action, gesture, symbol: The emergence of language* (pp. 183–229). New York: Academic Press.

Turney, T. H. (1978). Human neonatal and infant behavioral assessment scales being applied to chimpanzees. *Laboratory Primate Newsletter*, 17, 14–5.

Užgiris, I. Č. and Hunt, J. V. (1975). *Assessment in infancy: Ordinal scales of psychological development.* Chicago: University of Illinois Press.

Visalberghi, E. and Fragaszy, D. M. (1990). Do monkeys ape? In S. Parker and K. Gibson (eds.), *'Language' and intelligence in monkeys and apes: Comparative developmental perspectives* (pp. 247–73). Cambridge University Press.

Visalberghi, E. and Limongelli, L. (1996). Acting and understanding: Tool use revisited through the minds of capuchin monkeys. In A. E. Russon, K. A. Bard, and S. T. Parker (eds.), *Reaching into thought: The minds of the great apes* (pp. 57–79). Cambridge University Press.

Waal, F. de (1982). *Chimpanzee politics: Power and sex among apes.* New York: Harper & Row.

Whiten, A. and Custance, D. (1996). Studies of imitation in chimpanzees and children. In B. G. Galef and C. M. Heyes (eds.), *Social learning in animals: The roots of culture* (pp. 291–318). New York: Academic Press.

Whiten, A., Custance, D. M., Gomez, J-C., Teixidor, P. and Bard, K. A. (1996). Imitative learning of artificial fruit processing in children (*Homo sapiens*) and chimpanzees (*Pan troglodytes*). *Journal of Comparative Psychology*, 110, 3–14.

Whiten, A. and Ham, R. (1992). On the nature and evolution of imitation in the animal kingdom: Reappraisal of a century of research. In P. J. B. Slater, J. S. Rosenblatt, G. Beer and M. Milinski (eds.), *Advances in the study of behavior.* (vol. 21, pp. 239–83). New York: Academic Press.

Wright, R. (1972). Imitative learning of a flaked stone technology – the case of an orang-utan. *Mankind*, 8, 296–306.

Yerkes, R. M. (1943). *Chimpanzees: A laboratory colony.* New Haven: Yale University Press.

Part III

Social motives for imitation in infancy

5   What infants' imitations communicate: with mothers, with fathers and with peers

Colwyn Trevarthen, Theano Kokkinaki and Geraldo A. Fiamenghi Jr.

Imitative reactions, sympathetic emotions and human learning

If we observe children closely, we see that culture is propagated, not so much by training in skills, as a 'behaviouristic' theory assumes, nor even by instruction putting knowledge into human information stores, but by learners' and teachers' active mimicry. However it is cultivated, institutionalised and managed, education of culture is a conversational, intersubjective process in which the learners make active contribution.[1]

Everyday life in human society is animated in *mutual interest between persons* who, in their conversations, and depending on their status and companionship, express reciprocity of intentions, interco-ordination of skilful movements, convergent imaginings and conscious recognition. All human communities and societies are like this, however different they may be in size, structure and technical sophistication, and in whatever form the history of their knowledge and beliefs are coded, stored and transmitted. Reasons and explanations, facts, institutions and powerful roles are attractive and explored because human individuals find them potentially of interest to other human beings. They are social knowledge produced by interaction (Barnes, 1995). It follows that the 'context', 'content' or 'construction' of a culture, its ethnography and its language, cannot be the cause of its meanings. Meanings come from the human need for individuals to communicate interests, purposes and feelings. This requires a psychological means of representing knowledge in sociable forms, and even infants have the rudiments of this ability (Trevarthen, 1994). *Mimesis*, the ability to mimic or 'become' objects, natural events, animals, human purposes, remembered actions of other persons, even fantasies that go beyond possible real experience, to represent experiences for oneself and to others in metaphorical simulation, has, in fact, been identified as the defining feature of the first evolutionary step to the human level of mind (Donald, 1991). Mimetic behaviour, called fantasy play, is also the driving force of learning in early childhood. Victor Turner (1982) called it 'the human seriousness of play'.

Human imitative 'acting out' is done with *emotions* that respond immediately, open to the real or imagined gaze of other human beings – emotions that can make and break relationships of trust. Sometimes we display painstaking 'conscientious' deceptively self-centered concern. But, if failure threatens, our self-confidence may be clouded by shame, fear or anger. Often we imitate in a confident happy way with infectious exuberance and *esprit*, and when this joy is shared it strengthens companionship. The need for display of evaluative emotion distinguishes imitations between persons from all other accommodations each of them may make as a rational subject who bends purposeful activity to the constraints and opportunities of the impersonal or indifferent physical world. There is no point in showing emotions to things, except as part of the game of being an imitating and imitated actor in the human world. Imitations have a communicative purpose, and they attend to human evaluations of their motives.

A capacity to imitate instructive models or exemplars has always been regarded as important in education of the young and formation of a socially approved character and intelligence. None the less, human imitation, especially that of unsophisticated infants who are too young to follow explanations, remains problematic in a psychology that concentrates most of its effort on measuring the rational, cognitive functions of the minds in single adult subjects. Imitative behaviours still evoke intense theoretical controversy. Intersubjective, 'other-sensitive' imitation of actions, roles and narrative displays is typical of infants and toddlers long before they master language. Newborns are willing and selective imitators from the first contacts they have with the expressions of other persons. We use imitations interactively to motivate one another reciprocally from the start. These earliest imitations offer the greatest challenge to psychological theory.

We begin an account of this fundamental human psychological characteristic in terms of the *theory of innate sympathy* developed by Adam Smith (1759), the Scottish philosopher of society and morals (who was much more than the father of market economics). Smith saw that imitations are sympathetic responses, and to explain this he described how persons watching a street gymnast treading a high wire tend to move their bodies as if participating in the balancing. In his account, as in that of his teacher in Glasgow, the theologian and moral philosopher Frances Hutcheson (1755), sympathy is clearly qualified by *emotion generated by others' attitudes*. For example, Smith defined the moral conscience as the 'impartial observer' who may criticise one's acts, conveying feelings of approval or disapproval. We are inhabited by a kind of internal imitator who can make judgments of the good or bad nature of our actions. Thus Smith believed that each person can assume at least part of the feelings, purposes and judgments of others, different from his own. Imitation of a behaviour appears to be *one* kind of response in this sympathetic relating, among many. Imitating has many functions, depending on the give and take of the interpersonal transactions, and the rise and fall of trust and understanding in relationships, and depending, too, on the level of cognitive representation at which it is operating.

What is imitated?

In modern psychological terms, sympathy could be defined as the mutual elaboration of behaviours by individuals who match their separate dynamic cognitive images, judgments and memories. They construct models, schemata or representations of one another and the world they know, creating matching patterns that can be recreated and stored. But the notion of a cognitive scheme or process, or any acquired representation that assimilates and remembers perceptual information about the effects of acting in a particular way in the past, is not sufficient to explain how *the intended act itself* can be perceived and immediately imitated, as it often seems to be, without practice and trial and error. How could an *intention* pass at the first occasion from one person to another? We will defend the hypothesis that *endogenous motives* or 'images of action', which are at the source of all intentions and of the recognitive processes that assimilate perceptions to guide and regulate what is done, must be taken in directly, and reciprocated or 'reflected back', for sympathetic mimesis to begin. Our task is to explain how this could be, how behaviours and their motives can be translated intersubjectively. Our psychology offers little help. It gives us no clear explanation for fundamental motives, or for their intersubjective transfer. The emotional forces of human semiosis, correspondingly, remain obscure.

The facts are that motives in individuals do affect the awareness and intentions motivated in other individuals. The understandings (and misunderstandings) of talk, and of all symbolic and representational forms of language, are carried upon intuitive interpersonal regulations, and upon mimetic representations that cross intersubjective space easily. They are woven into narratives of sympathetic intentionality charged with emotions. We believe that research on how, without being able to speak, infants begin communication, and how they develop a capacity to share understanding of what they and other persons mean by what they do and by what they say, can give essential information. The evidence has been coming in over the past three decades from research on infants' interactions with other persons, and especially from detailed analysis of what expressions infants are sensitive to and how they move in response. The protoconversational reactions of infants about 2 months of age (Bateson, 1975, 1979; Trevarthen, 1974, 1979) show that humans have a dual representation of self and other that permits them to enter into immediate relation with one another's emotions in 'dialogic closure' (Bråten, 1988, 1992). Such a capacity is evident immediately after birth.[2]

Within the first year, an infant gains understanding of meaning in 'co-operative awareness' with 'joint purpose' (Bakeman and Adamson, 1984; Bretherton, McNew and Beeghley-Smith, 1981; Bruner, 1976; Hubley and Trevarthen, 1979; Scaife and Bruner, 1975; Trevarthen, Murray and Hubley, 1981; Tomasello, 1988). This is a new and striking change in the infant's motives, which we described as the development of 'secondary intersubjectivity' (Trevarthen and Hubley, 1978). It involves the infant in active co-ordination of his or her (praxic) interests in objects with the directions of attention and the apparent intentions of a partner who becomes a companion in task performance (Hubley and Trevarthen, 1979). These terms imply both an interest in 'reading', and representing, others intentions from their attentions, gestures and expressions, and a capacity for mimesis, if this is defined as the matching of motives between individuals who reflect one another's social affordances and dynamics of thinking, and a transfer of ideas about what the motives intend to do (Donald, 1991). A 1-year-old will use this new understanding to aquire many ways of acting that demonstrate deferred imitation of others' purposes and meanings (Meltzoff, 1995; Trevarthen et al., 1981; Trevarthen, 1990).

We do not believe that the conversational and imitative ability of infants comes from learned intermodal associations between feedback effects of moving, nor do we believe that the primary function of imitation is to establish emotional coherence and self-awareness, or to identify who other individuals are, though both these acquired understandings, and many others, can be explored and elaborated in reciprocal imitation games. Some direct *intermotive attraction* is involved when imitations occur. This is manifest in the ability of newborn infants to communicate, including their ability to attend to and *complement or copy*, eye contact and a variety of facial, vocal and gestural expressions. It is important that the behaviours which newborns imitate are specifically adapted in their form and timing to guide interpersonal motive transactions. Facial, gestural and vocal expressions are inherently richer in humans than in any other species. They equip the infant as a potential partner in dynamic emotional narratives. The immediate appearance at birth of this conversational interest means that its mechanism must reside in brain systems that were organised to be regulations of such experience before birth, i.e., in adaptive anticipation.

Constitutional foundations for imitation of motives

Seeking for a unified psychobiological theory of how imitation is possible for any sentient and active organism, we first define motives as spontaneous processes generated in the interneuronal core of the brain that result in *motor sets*, on which are built both co-ordinated movements and coherent perceptions to fit the movements to surroundings, prospectively. On the one hand, the effect of these sets is to direct initial co-ordinations between efferent neuromuscular outputs – to produce acts that aim the body in adaptive patterns and directions of movement. They are also inseparably coupled with *perceptual sets* that ready the afferent and cognitive brain systems for certain act-related inputs of information (affordances) that may guide the movements once they are made, increasing their efficiency and efficacy (Gibson, 1979; Neisser, 1976; Sperry, 1950, 1952; Von Holst and Mittelstaedt, 1950). Perception informs 'prospective control' for the actor's moving (Lee, 1993).

Figure 5.1 presents a summary of the place of motives in the generation of action and perception. Motives (M) organise *act intentions* (A) and *perceptual attentions* (P) as one adaptive process. The set of motor initiatives (m) that activate *sensory-accessory muscle systems* (a), which orient, focus and modulate pick-up of information by the special receptor systems of the head, eyes, ears, mouth and hands, are of special importance in communication of motives, because they offer advance information about what the actor is *becoming interested in* or is *going to do*. They make motives apparent.

'Motor images' can be detected in the brain in the form of neuronal activity that precedes a movement and perception, and they are also evident from the intrinsic programmed characteristics of movement. In a recent review of the evidence from neurophysiology and experimental studies of behaviour, Jeannerod (1994) concludes that, in what he calls the 'representing brain', 'the content of motor representations can be inferred from motor images at a macroscopic level, based on global aspects of the action (the duration and amount of effort involved) and the motor rules and constraints which predict the spatial path and kinematics of movements'. In other words, the brain represents, in one integrated time–space field, the *rhythm*, *effort* and whole-body-related *direction* of moving, and starts to do so before the execution of any act, predictively. These are generative features of brain activity and movements.

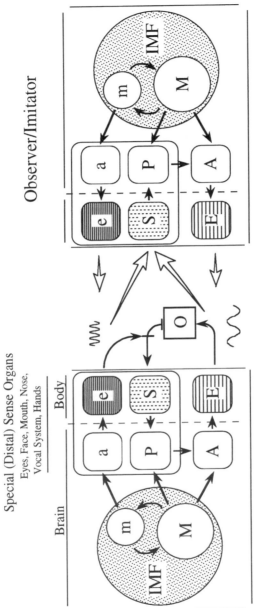

Figure 5.1. Motives are generated in the core of the brain in an interneuronal system, the Intrinsic Motive Formation (IMF). This co-ordinates all neural centres in one generative space–time field of behaviours. Motives to move the body (M) integrate mechanisms of perception (P) and action (A) in cycles of perceptuo–motor activity that are performed by effectors (E) and monitored by receptors (S). A subset of the motor system (a + e) is motivated (m) to regulate the orientation and focusing of special sense organs. Effector activity may make use of objects (O) and at the same time transmit rhythmically coherent effects that may inform the motives of an observer or imitator, who has similar (sympathetic) motive principles, about the purposes, interests and feelings of the actor.

In the puzzle of imitation, it is of great interest that activity of a group of prefrontal neurone units in the brain of a monkey that appears to formulate the motor image for a particular act of manipulation (an m-system output, Figure 5.1) has been shown to be excited when another individual, for example the human experimenter, is observed by the monkey to be making *the same manipulation with the same preparatory hand positioning* (Di Pelligrino, Fadiga, Fogassi, Gallese and Rizzolatti, 1992). 'This very striking result supports the idea of representation neurons as a common substrate for motor preparation and imagery' (Jeannerod, 1994, p. 190). It also shows that, with appropriate body-to-body mediation, neurone activity in one brain can *imitate* neurone activity in another brain.

Motor images may also be inferred from biomechanical analysis of the organisation, economy and efficiency of forces in the body when it is moving about or acting against the environment. They may be inferred to form an essential purposeful component of organised neuromuscular events (the forces and their transitions in 'biodynamic systems' of the body) upon which all skilful movements depend (Bernstein, 1967). As with the electrophysiological indices of the aim and form of the monkey's manipulations, the economy and harmony of movements and their generative impulses can be 'read' by another voluntary agent directly. Indeed, human observers are remarkably good at detecting the effort or rhythmic grace of another person moving, sensing their comfort or pain. An observer can perceive a whole moving body from fragments of information about the coactive displacements of joints and segments of limbs of persons walking, running, dancing, picking up objects, etc. (Johanssen, 1975; Runeson, 1977). For example, we can see the human body in a display of spots of light that are attached to the limbs of a walking or dancing person who is observed in the dark, and it is even possible for us to identify a familiar person from the way the lights move.

As shown in Figure 5.1, the m-component of motives makes preparations for effective action – it *attends to (directs) perceptual exploration (investigative behaviour)*, employing both distance and surface receptors. The *special accessory motor systems*, for looking, listening, palpating, sniffing, tasting, get detailed perceptual information about goals for more general and more definitive action, *before* irrevocable commitment is made by displacement of the whole body. The ethologists long ago distinguished these two stages of motivation by their manifestations in 'orienting' and 'consummatory' behaviours (Craig, 1918). At the same time as orienting of reception is taking place, motives estimate the potential effects of behaviour inside the body. The *self-regulatory emotions* assess and define the 'pleasures and pains' and 'benefits and risks' of acting *for the organism*, and make appropriate anticipatory adjustments in the physiological systems of the body. In a behaving animal, activity of the heart and respiratory organs is adjusted appropriately, again *before* muscular activity is excited (Jeannerod, 1994, p. 192). Thus, in dealing with situations and objects, the sentient and voluntary subject is both selectively orienting to pick up information in an array of receptor modalities, and readying the physiology of the body for action. Because the affordances of objects and circumstances differ, they become associated with differing 'aesthetic values' or *object-related emotions*. Intentions are projected in orienting and preparatory movements adapted to the location, form, size, etc. of the object, and expressions of feelings about the object's uses or properties accompany this phase of purposefulness. Finally, the anticipatory activities of the brain/mind, their rhythms and externally detectable patterns, are potentially important sources of information for another subject who needs to interact with the one whose motives are changing. Human facial and vocal expressions of *interpersonal emotions* have evolved from these early signs of purposeful action (Buck, 1984; Darwin, 1872; Izard, 1971, 1980). These emotions about and for persons are not just for self-regulation; they are the natural source of 'moral values' in 'self–other' relationships. Thus may be defined three facets of orienting and emotion, depending upon their functional aim or purpose; related, (1) to the body, (2) to physical circumstances or objects, and (3) to persons (Trevarthen, 1993a).

Antenatal developments

If we wish to imagine how a newborn brain could be equipped with this constellation of intrinsic behaviour-regulating mental powers that predict an active existence of the body in interaction with objects and other individuals, we can invoke the classical embryological principle of 'prefunctional morphogenesis', assuming that a mechanism for motives and emotions formed in the embryo, which is prefunctional in relation to psychological activity, will constrain and organise all 'emergent' processes and representations that neuronal nets acquire as a result of stimulation from the world.

Given recent attention to the generative powers that, in theory, can be attributed to epigenetic 'dynamic systems' between body, brain and environment that come into action only after birth (Fogel and Thelen, 1987), it is necessary to emphasise that, in the 'complex adaptive system' of an animal, prenatal brain and body development, and especially development in the brain that has already set up important body-mapping and body-motivating conditions before birth, are ready to 'investigate' effects of acting, seeking purposeful co-ordination in the body and beneficial goals in the environment, selectively. A famous example in peripheral anatomy is the eye, which, formed as a potential optical sensing device before there are any visual inputs, remains the organ for pick-up of information from light throughout life, scanning the prospective space for behaviour in intermittent steps with systematic brain-directed precision. In many animals, and most notably in humans, the eye is also simultaneously an organ of expression and of imitation, and, with a highly visible white schlera, it is anatomically adapted for this function as well.

In the brain, cells first interact and become organised in systems of neurons in the immobile body of the embryo, out of contact with the sensory receptors. The 'chaos' that a vast overproduction of neuroblasts, axon outgrowths, dendrites and synapses is assumed to create in the cortex and elsewhere in the brain of an infant (Changeux, 1985; Edelman, 1987) is deeply and productively constrained by structures and processes of brain tissue and body that were already elaborated in the embryo brain stem before any part of the nerve net was electrically active or receptive to the environment (O'Rahilly and Müller, 1994). Selective retention of neuronal assemblies that have been favoured in a competition for trophic substances or effects of stimulation from the environment postnatally is neither random nor passive. The embryo brain contains an interconnected set of ordered representations of the body's form before sensory motor nerves are formed. The 'initial state' of neural organisations in the fetal mind/brain, and their continuation as functions of an Intrinsic Motive Formation (IMF) in the brain of the child, are fundamental in all future behavioural adaptations and learning, including the elaborations in humans of symbolic thought and of language (Aitken and Trevarthen, 1997; Trevarthen and Aitken, 1994). The IMF is represented in Figure 5.1 as the integrative matrix of the CNS in which consummatory and investigative motives (M and m) are formulated.

We look to research on infants to clarify how initial, prenatally active, embryogenic motive states assist in the emergence of skilled mimesis and the generation of mimetic meanings. A first step will be to make an accurate description of intersubjective or communicative interactions of a non-verbal and emotive kind between young infants and their adult caregivers. But it is also necessary to see the antecedents of human mimesis in the imitative behaviours of many animal species.

Evolution of imitation by motive reflection of mirror affordances

Social co-operation between even the simplest animals requires recognition and co-ordination between motive impulses in different individuals.

In the least elaborated forms with rudimentary brains there is little mental activity to transmit, just periods of restlessness and the present direction of moving. Matching sensibilities and ways of locomoting allow environmental events and simple non-psychogenic signals (for example, gravitation, the fluctuating heliocentric field of light, or chemical markers) to serve as an immediate frame for parallel action, as when plankton swarm on the surface of the ocean on one night with a full moon, or ants or moths follow the same pheromone trail. But, even in molluscs, insects and lower vertebrates, there is some recognition by individuals of the correspondence between the motives of the perceiver and perceptible features of *body form or rhythm* that motives regulate in other actors. Sign stimuli embodied in animals' surface features coupled to the ways they move the body or its parts elicit specific reactions, and are invited by complementary specific signalling behaviours of social partners (Lorenz, 1965; Sebeok, 1990; Tinbergen, 1951). With this degree of intersubjective recognition, more complex imitative and complementary reactions, and more subtle social learning, are possible.

Imitating animals pick-up signals of their partners by the same collection of modalities that they use to guide their locomotion, or to project their movements to fit objects in the environment. Visually driven imitation has been assumed to be more difficult to explain than the more self-stimulatory effects in audition or vibration sense because it can be imagined that in the latter case the model's behaviour is experienced *in the same form* as the imitator's reproduction. This, however, is a misconception. Even auditory signals are different for the emitter, who hears them through the body and inside the head, than for a distant perceiver. Moreover, the body of the former is moving to make sound, and is, therefore, making other proprioceptive inputs as well. Visual imitation is not, in reality, the most esoteric form of behavioural mirroring, and it is common in animal social life. Many species with small brains but efficient sight not only guide their actions by reafference feed-forward mechanisms, but also imitate actions they see in other individuals. For example, Siamese fighting fish display to a mirror, becoming excited to fight the reflected image. Jumping spiders court their mirror-image.

Translation between the affordances of *proprioception* ('self-as-agent' feeling) and *alteroception* ('other-agent' feeling) always requires intervention of some mechanism of intersubjective closure to affirm a correspondence or matching. This could be called 'affordance mirroring'. Each subject's actions to perceive or make use of what the partner affords become affordances for the partner. 'Constancies' in perception take origin from the impulse to act in the form of 'corollary discharges' (Sperry, 1950) or 'efference copy' and 'reafference signals' (Von Holst and Mittelstaedt, 1950). This same trace of an impulse to act could be used to detect acting by another individual.

In birds and mammals, rhythmic invariants in other individuals' acting and differentiated forms and surface adornments of body parts are reacted to in specific ways, and moves of one individual are often repeated by partners. This is equally true for both *orienting or exploratory movements*, on the one hand, and for *consummatory acts* that are aimed to use objects in the environment in particular ways. Many of the orienting movements, as *intention movements* (Tinbergen, 1951), have become specialised as predictive expressions of motive energy or emotion to which conspecifics are ready to respond. Exchanges of intention movements evolve into ritual displays and routines of interaction in which the motive states of participants are transformed, to aid mating, feeding of young, collaborative foraging, etc. Reptiles, birds and mammals transmit socially important messages of purpose or feeling to other members of their group by means of postural, gestural and vocal signals (Marler, Evans and Hauser, 1992; Ploog, 1992). In species of birds and primates with high social intelligence there is a powerfully developed insight into the rhythm and directedness of group members' mental processes picked up from what they do. They manifestly share, and imitate, intentions.

The primates, and especially the apes, with their extraordinary manipulatory intelligence and uniquely developed focal visual assessment of surroundings with precisely co-ordinated saccadic eye-and-head movements, are capable of highly discriminating imitation of acts that exploit environmental resources (Byrne, 1995; Galef, 1988; Gomez, 1991; Visalberghi, Fragaszy and Savage-Rumbaugh, 1995). They also imitate the gestures their partners make, and can subtly reflect or exploit social behaviours of their partners, taking account of social partners' preferences and aversions as they orient to and manipulate the environment (Cosmides, 1989; Menzel, 1971; Tomasello, Savage-Rumbaugh and Kruger, 1993b; Whiten and Byrne, 1997). The brains of primates have evolved in relation to the size, and therefore the intersubjective complexity, of their social groups (Dunbar, 1992; Goody, 1995; Humphrey, 1976; Passingham and Ettlinger, 1974). Apes can be trained to use a token system or a gesture sign system to gain social co-operation (Premack, 1987; Savage-Rumbaugh, 1986). They have a degree of connectedness and flexibility of purposes, a curiosity about the narrative gestures of their social partners and a self-consciousness of agency that goes beyond that of the monkeys (Donald, 1991; Whiten and Byrne, 1997).

It has been claimed that captive apes, like humans, demonstrate *conversational intelligence* when they repeat arbitrary coded gestures or symbol manipulations that human partners make for various co-operative purposes in a game-like exchange (Greenfield and Savage-Rumbaugh, 1993). Even so, it is clear that sympathetic (intersubjective) awareness and conversation-like exchange of expressions have a new level of complexity and efficacy in humans. Human cultural learning by mimesis, beginning in the 'socio-dramatic' protoconversations and games of infancy, generates acquisition of an infinity of new skills and understandings, and it prepares the path to the imitative exploration of speech and the mastery of language (Clark, 1977; Locke, 1993). When other species observe and imitate intentions, demonstrating what has been called 'theory of mind', they show limitations in curiosity and goal selection. They acquire stereotyped action sequences deploying a limited repertoire of signs to accomplish defined social functions, or they learn, by imitating, how to manipulate environmental resources for immediate consumption. Human toddlers and older children, in contrast, observe, learn and re-enact social mannerisms, ethical principles, cognitive interests and investigative, problem-solving behaviour. Before they walk, they pick up, and represent to themselves in imaginitive play, elaborate routines of execution for technical and artistic use of environmental affordances for goals that are remote in time and space, goals that the community has learned over generations to invest with special value and meaning. All these purposes are assisted by intentionally supportive guiding behaviours of more experienced partners (Rogoff, 1990). They are further enriched and differentiated by language, which fixes words to the actions and objects of co-operative understanding, and to the feelings and qualities of acting and experiencing. In the first stages of language learning, imitation, immediate and deferred, has many important functions (Clark, 1977), but not so much in the aquisition of grammatical forms of expression as in the negotiation of purposes and interests, and in the exploitation of, and experimentation with, the activity of speech.

Humans live and learn by sharing the myths and rituals of a cosmos of meaning created historically and dramatically. The icons, signs and symbols by which they encode this communal awareness may or may not be taken into speech or other language. They are remembered from anecdotal moments when ideas and their expressions were shared by subtle and largely unconscious forms of sympathetic mimesis. We express purposes and convey meanings to one another elaborately, and with emotion.

How psychological theory has failed to explain human mimesis

Imitation, the transfer of forms of behaviour between subjects, is regarded in quite different ways by different theories of behavioural co-ordination and behavioural development. As fashions in mind theory change, so imitative phenomena change in credability, simplicity and apparent explanatory importance. In the past two centuries, the psychometric and psychophysical preoccupations of empirical psychological science, conspiring with the intellectual/literate basis and clinical and ethical preoccupations of psychodynamic theory, have actually led thinking and practice in psychology away from consideration of all but the simplest innate processes of motivation, making them a problem. The newborn infant has been conceived as irrational and, therefore, psychologically empty, preoccupied with the needs for survival and striving to regulate physiological arousal, to attain pleasure and escape pain. The infant's emotions have been inferred through analysis of mental pathology in adults. They have been portrayed as generators of dissolution and pain that need external regulation (Dollard and Miller, 1950; Sroufe, 1996). More recently, positive emotions have been given more importance. Moments of coherent joy are said to be infused into the baby from a sympathetic caregiver (Emde, 1992; Emde, Biringen, Clyman and Oppenheim, 1991; Hofer, 1990; Schore, 1994; Stern, 1990). But when infants are observed responding to caregivers with calm and affectionate mutual concern, they demonstrate active emotional initiative in a great variety of expressions, and they show communicative purpose.

In the behaviourist perspective, which sought to minimise assumptions about internal representations and endogenous motives, imitation is an impossibility, except as a consequence of the elimination of random and often misdirected responses, and by the emergence of an association learned step by step between originally unconnected reflex reactions, the selection process being reinforced by social rewards because imitations are noticed and valued by parents and teachers. Discovery of the matching response is still supposed, by some, to develop by construction of new intermodal matches (Anisfeld, 1996). Similarly, in structural linguistics and the machine intelligence of cognitive theory, imitation may result unintentionally from accommodative tracking, or in problem-solving strategies from a matching of schemata or symbolic representations that are accumulated from experience. Imitations become solutions to theoretical problems of social action and reaction, or of semantics. These theories, fundamentally rational as they are, focus on the individual who is educated by the senses, and who either re-acts by moving in response to certain structures or processes in the stimulus field, or who acts in a way that will cause the sensed milieu to generate stimuli of recognisable spatial and temporal configuration. Their interest is in perception, and the processing of cognition. Internal processes are formulated as categorisations, and categorisations of categorisations, all coded as formal effects of stimuli.

In cognitive theory, the model for an imitator can be conceived as entirely artificial, as a mechanical event with no human properties. Piaget (1962) studied infants moving their mouths open and shut to imitate a matchbox that he was manipulating. But, wait! Was he not moving the box to imitate a mouth opening and shutting? This possible 'person-like-ness' of his model was, apparently, overlooked. Piaget presents visual tracking of a moving object as the paradigm of 'imitation', an accom-modative problem-solving activity of reason that is coupled with the expression of a *self-regulatory* emotion of 'serious intent'. This function he contrasted to 'play', which is triumphantly assimilative and performed with *self-satisfying* 'pleasure in mastery' (Piaget, 1962). Piaget was disre-garding the communicative function of these displays while he minimised the role of emotions in regulations of interpersonal consciousness. His notions of the 'biological' functions that form the basis for pleasure and unpleasure correspond with those of Freud.

We conclude that the source of a subject's insight into what other minds attend to, what they intend to do and how they feel about it has been made into a mystery by reductive assumptions of how the mind reasons about, or experiments with, experience as the embodied subject regulates feelings of pleasure and pain. Recent speculations about how a 'Theory of Mind' develops in children constitute a real advance by recog-nising that what goes on in minds is naturally of interest to humans. But, these models have not, we believe, much clarified the problem of how sympathetic awareness begins. They merely rephrase the verbal repre-sentational hypothesis in mentalistic or cognitive science (machine intelli-gence) language. The Theory of Mind debate is leading to clarification of important steps in the development of human intersubjectivity after lan-guage has been mastered. However, the basic ability to imitate remains to be understood. It is independent of both linguistic and rational repre-sentations, and it is not a symbolic formulation of machine 'thinking'. Mimesis generates symbols, not the other way round. Imitation is a part of the needed explanation.

This is made abundantly evident when we see very young infants engaging systematically with expressions of motives in other individuals to whom they pay attention in highly selective ways. It is important, first, that, many months before the threshold of linguistic skills is attained, a young infant displays powers of imitative representation and conversa-tional reciprocity of expressions far more complex than any other species of animal (Tomasello, Kruger and Ratner, 1993a). Furthermore, human mimetic abilities develop rapidly in the first year. Sharing of ritual per-formances that are displayed as significant artifacts, with that 'self-satis-faction' and socio-dramatic awareness of others' evaluations which

Wallon (1928; 1970, p. 173) described as *réactions de prestance*, are typical of infants' play with trusted others in the second half of the first year (Trevarthen, et al., 1981; Trevarthen, 1990). And co-operative manipulation of objects, with orientation to observe, and co-operate with the probable intentions of companions in an arbitrary task, appear months before the first word is uttered, around the end of the first year (Bakeman and Adamson, 1984; Bretherton and Bates, 1979; Trevarthen and Hubley, 1978).

By definition, an imitated act corresponds *in some degree* with the form and/or timing of the act of another individual. (It is important to emphasise that imitations are of greater interest when they are *not exactly the same* as the identified model act, because differences between model and the reproduction may constitute, not errors, but significant information in their co-operation.) The imitator must generate movement by a cerebral process that has critical elements that match those involved in the model subject's action. How could this come about? For an empiricist, this problem must be solved by finding the same pattern of stimulation in the 'model' and the imitator, unconditioned or the consequence of shaping and internalisation by a learning process. Thus the simplest, or crudest, imitation must be one that reacts in the same way to the same stimulus as the one that the model reacted to. Alternatively, the stimulus created by the model (a signal or goal-directed act of some kind) must be the same as the one the imitator experiences when he acts in imitation. This is the 'contagion' or 'pseudo-imitation' of Piaget (1962) or the 'emulation' of Tomasello (1990), where the goal or end-effect is reproduced but not the (intended) form of action (Byrne, 1995). Parallel acts can be generated by two or more subjects tracking the same event, chasing the same goal, or tracking one another.

Significant (or 'true' or 'immediate') imitation somehow goes beyond these short-cuts or parallel reactions. It involves a transfer of some amodal perceptual effect beneath or inside modalities, or a substitution of equivalent movements that differ in superficial anatomy but are similar in stimulatory potential; for example, the same in timing, with the same in dynamic (emotive) configuration or 'attunement' (Stern, Hofer, Haft and Dore 1985; Stern, 1993; Trevarthen, 1986). Human mimicry exhibits those cardinal features of conscious intentional behaviour; flexibility of both sensory confirmation (intermodal equivalence) and rhythmic motor execution (motor equivalence) (Trevarthen, 1978; 1993b).

In what way could the imitative form be translated between subjects? The empiricist assumes it must be constructed by trial and error, or by successive approximation, that it must be guided by reinforcements that the imitating subject experiences as positive for forms of action that are to be strengthened, or negative for non-imitative components. This is a tautological theory, and, with all simple 'mechanistic' theories, it cannot explain neonatal imitation which is naive and immediate. The special generative features of motives and emotions and their communicability must be taken into account.

The only way to explain why an animal acts in a particular way, or changes the way it has been acting by developing new interests or tactics, is to take account of its motives, the internally generated impulses that propel activity. When the act depends on what the stimulating environment can afford, information from the environment is essential to the progress and successful culmination of acting. Almost all acts are investigative, or at least selectively reactive. But distinctly different forms of action are not simply different because the environment makes them that way. The subject's motives specify *in advance* what environmental affordances are to be the object of acting.

Imitation as communication

With Užgiris (1981, 1984), we see infant imitation as effective and functional in interpersonal communication from the start. Imitating is an integrative psycho-social generator of learning, even for a newborn, and it operates with many well-differentiated emotions. It is not just the tracking and study of novelty to solve general problems of acting and a way to construct new cognitive schemata. It is not a reaction that serves merely to regulate arousal. As the infant's mind develops, interpersonal or intersubjective imitation manifests itself as the developmental source of the peculiar narrative or discursive (propositional) and potentially 'socio-dramatic' form of human rationalising. We imagine thinking to be extended to impersonal, unimpassioned abstract or general categories of event by a metaphorical analogy, by a subject taking the objective event or form (in 'episodic' experience) to be an extension of the body and its movements, but doing so in a creative recollective manner, detached from actual communication.[3]

Kinds or grades of imitation are related to motives, attentions and intentions of differing complexity, involving more or less cognition or more or less experience and memory, and imitations also differ in their fundamental aims and generative progression. Their meaning changes. Their form and time differ in corresponding ways, and the *gist* or *style* becomes essential and fundamental information for partners in interaction about what companions are doing. Imitation is thus not simply a way one individual acquires a new behaviour, it is a regulatory interpersonal (intersubjective) process that brings motives of different individuals into productive engagement (Užgiris, 1981). In consequence, imitator and

imitatee are always ready to exchange roles – to reflect one another, and to
show and negotiate initatives that way.[4]

The neonate's inborn plan for matching with the bodies and actions of persons: how they behave when they imitate

Newborn infants, though weak and inexperienced, are sentient and
intending agents. They have a coherent prospective world for moving in
which, for example, they perform 'prereaching' with arm and hand aimed
to points outside the body and co-ordinated with head and eye rotations
(Trevarthen, 1975, Trevarthen et al., 1981; Von Hofsten, 1983a). These
movements can occur without a perceived object, perceptually speaking
'in vacuo' (or rather 'in corporo', by activating the body's field of activity),
but the newborn can also 'lock on' to within a few degrees to an 'out-of-
the-body' object that the infant is looking at, and the synchronised
head–eye–hand co-ordination can be modified to track a moving exterior
target. This 'imitation' of an outside event is clearly built upon the
generation within the infant's mind of a coherent, 'in one time', body-
related *behavioural field*, an 'action space' radiating from a single 'ego
centre' (Trevarthen, 1980). Generative goals for an infant's acting can be
perceptually confirmed and elaborated, but they do not originate as
effects of stimuli popping up in a formless field of awareness, and they are
not made up of disjointed and unsynchronised bits.

The newborn human also generates many 'expressions' appropriate for
communication with another human – head rotations and tilts, patterned
expressions of upper and lower face that involve displacement of receptive
eyes, lips and tongue, vocalisations, and elaborate gestures of the hands.[5]
The hands of a newborn are already organs with two distinct modes of
purposeful operation; for intentions of the self directed to objects, and for
expressions to others (Rönnqvist and Von Hofsten, 1994). In the latter
case the movements of the hands 'belong' as much to the motives of the
other as to the motives of the baby. Indeed, all the expressive behaviours
have this 'double aspect' motivation – they are *both self-regulatory and
other-regulatory*.

Each of the expressive forms of movement can be imitated if a human
partner acts in a particular way that is timed and formed to interact with
the rhythms of attending and intending that the infant is displaying. Each
is isomorphic with movements the subject may make to sense the body
and/or the environment in a special focused way. That is, each is also a
component of intentional awareness, and that is why they are rich in
information for a sympathetic other seeking co-operative awareness.

The dynamics of movement is a critical stimulating element for a model to be imitated by newborns (Vintner, 1986), and neonates may attempt to imitate the rhythmic pattern of a repeated model (Kugiumutzakis, this volume). As we shall show, even a premature newborn is ready to engage in a reciprocal, rhythmic vocal interaction with a sympathetic, imitative partner. The movements of expression exhibit pronounced rhythmic cohesion, and rhythmically measured repetition of a model expression in a spontaneous communication game with a parent or in an imitation test with an experimenter seems to add to the salience of the model for the infant correspondent. However, neonates do not imitate well when models are presented with mechanical regularity and insensitive insistence, as can be the case in 'well-controlled' experiments that aim to reduce the factors that might be involved in triggering a matching response (see Kugiumutzakis, 1993; this volume).

All the evidence points to the conclusion that, as for pre-reaching, engagement with a person as object for an imitative communication depends on the presence in the infant of a latent motive or prediction to respond in that kind of way and in that general direction. That said, there is good evidence that infants can track an unexpectedly changing model when they imitate, and they can improve matching by a successive approximation after the motion of the model has ceased. Again this resembles the situation in reaching beyond the body where the goal is located in a common representation of the space for moving such that all modalities of proprioception (mechanoreceptive and exproprioceptive) are in concordance, and where final realisation of the act may be assisted by adjustments to the goal object at a second phase of execution. A tongue protrusion matching sight of another person's performance must match the infant's expected reafferent 'feel' of making a movement of that form, in that part of the body-movement space. As Kugiumutzakis (this volume) has explained, imitated movements of the upper face may involve less adjustment because the motor field is relatively simple there, with fewer muscles, in comparison with movements of the mouth and tongue for which there are many more motor possibilities and a much larger neural representation in the cerebral cortex. Neonatal behaviours in imitation tests confirm this idea. Newborns make relatively simple reproductions of eye closure, but more effortful and varied attempts, with successive approximation, for tongue protrusion.

Newborns indicate their special awareness of other persons by their reactions to being held and moved by a person, and by their visual orienting to, and fixation on, the face of a person near them. But they are especially sensitive to the human voice, and show a preference, possibly already established antenatally, for the voice of the mother (DeCasper and Fifer, 1980; Fifer and Moon, 1995). Eye-to-eye contact, which is firmly established around the end of the first month, but which is adumbrated by a searching of the upper face for eye-contact that newborns make in spite of their immature foveae, is of special interest because this amounts to a mutual imitation of acting and experiencing, simply because mutually oriented eyes are both stimuli and receptors. One-month-olds also clearly see mouths and hands of their partners. Tests of imitating in infants within a few hours after birth prove that an inexperienced newborn can see, and differentially recognise, eyes, mouth, tongue and hands. This is the conclusive evidence that immediate (not learned and not symbolically mediated) imitation of conversational expressions is an innate faculty in humans.

The above observations and explanations confirm that every movement and every perception of a goal for moving is formulated around a core *motor image*, with its dynamic (kinematic and energetic) and physiognomic (body-form related) characteristics, and with predictive regulation of the reafferent effects that its expression will have in perception (Trevarthen, 1986).

Imitation cycles microanalysed in communication with infants

'Conversational analysis' of films or video recordings of non-verbal components in natural interactions between communicating adults have demonstrated the precision of synchrony between movements of expression, both within subjects (intrasynchrony) and between them (inter-synchrony). Application of the same micro-analytic techniques has shown that mother–infant interactions achieve similar levels of efficiency in coordination and similar precision of timing (Beebe, Jaffe, Feldstein, Mays and Alson, 1985; Condon and Sander, 1974; Jaffe, Stern and Peery, 1973; Mayer and Tronick, 1985; Stern, 1974; Stern, Beebe, Jaffe and Bennett, 1977; Trevarthen, 1974, 1977, 1979). Imitations occur between adults as part of the regulation of transactions of feelings and intentions between them. The same function is served by natural reciprocal imitations between infants and their partners.

To appreciate the remarkable *timing* features of imitative behaviour in infancy, which we feel have been seriously neglected, it is necessary to recall that all sentient and voluntary behaviour has a tendency to cyclic patterns in which rate of movement and repetition of movements are strictly controlled in a prospective intracerebrally determined plan of bodily action. Skills are attained by repetition of moves measured in a neurogenic action-time. Central coherence of the timing of movements and the processing of sensory data is essential to biomechanical efficiency and unity of consciousness (Bernstein, 1967; Pöppel, 1994), and this internal source becomes the origin of intersubjective sympathy and co-operative intentions.[6]

Baldwin (1894) called cyclic or iterated behaviours, where an act is repeated to explore sensory effects and improve performance, 'self-imitations'. Piaget (1953) adopted Baldwin's concept in his formulation of a theory of how body awareness and object concepts are achieved in infancy by mutual assimilation of schemata for *circular reactions* of differing complexity and degree of conceptual determination ('primary', involving only the body, 'secondary' involving a manipulated object, 'tertiary' involving a symbolic representation). By concentrating on individual self-regulation first, both Baldwin and Piaget and other investigators of infant intelligence and imitation (e.g. Guillaume, 1971; Wallon, 1970), with most modern developmental psychologists working in the behaviourist and cognitive traditions, have failed to take account of the precocious efficiency of cyclic 'self–other' regulations between subjects. This is why imitations of newborns have been ruled out as 'theoretically impossible'. The problem has been created by the theory that infants are born without integrated psychological powers, and are incapable of organising themselves as (rhythmically) coherent intentional psychological subjects, and by the corollary that they are incapable of having any consistent relation with any object and its properties.

To dispel these false beliefs, we first describe the behaviours of an infant in dynamic emotional interaction of protoconversation with an adult. From this analysis we can form a description of the rhythmic cycles and phases of motivation that generate and regulate such phenomena, which are essentially psychological because they are organised by and sensitive to states of mind that are given a primary regularity by motive states in the brain in three fundamental dimensions of embryogenic origin: *morphology* (structure), *intensity* (energy) and *timing* (process) (Trevarthen, 1986). The communicative interactions of young infants show that regulators of all three of these dimensions are installed in the brain and body before birth.

Imitation can then be seen to be one of many dynamic intersubjective patterns of behaviour that arise at definite places in the dynamic configurations that two mutually interested subjects tend to create. That the two subjects have a natural readiness or predisposition to 'dialogic closure in felt immediacy' (Bråten, 1988; 1997) is proved by the efficiency, productivity and regularity of events in protoconversations between infants and their intuitively responsive mothers or fathers. That this process is dynamically negotiated or 'worked out' on the interpersonal stage is shown by the systematic perturbations or risks that the interactants tend to introduce as soon as dialogic 'confluence' has been achieved, especially when it is between familiar partners in familiar territory and with familiar routines of play (Nakano & Kanaya, 1993; Reddy, 1991). These perturbations expose and engage the dynamic regulations of motives in the two individuals. Nakano (1996) calls them 'incidents' and describes the motives for them in humans, particularly infants and parents, as manifestations of 'incident affinity' within 'the space of the We'.

Protoconversational interaction with imitation

A microanalysis of a conversational development over 30 seconds between a mother and her 6-week-old daughter will serve to illustrate essential features of primary intersubjective dialogues or protoconversations that emerge in the second month after a full-term birth (Figure 5.2).

This example exhibits a remarkable precision of timing in the alternation of utterances between the infant and the adult, which indicates that they share a rhythmic 'time-base' for expression, and perhaps that they have matching *cycles of motivation* leading to regular sequences of active expression (*assertion*) and attentive reception (*apprehension*), or of 'intention' and 'attention' (these terms for phases of expression and awareness are discussed below and diagrammed in Figure 5.8). Estimated bar lengths are remarkably regular (mean = 1.55 sec; sd. = 0.04 sec), and the infant enters into precise co-ordination with the mother's rhythm. This spectograph, and those shown in Figures 5.3 and 5.4, have been prepared in the course of a detailed acoustic analysis of mothers' speech to infants (Malloch, Sharp, Campbell, D., Campbell, A. and Trevarthen, 1997).

It will be seen, also, that imitations can be identified in both directions, but most frequently of the infant by the mother when she makes vocalisations of sympathetic encouragement, and that they occur at particular points in the interaction. They appear to play a role in the development of co-ordinated mutuality. The mother's imitations are protracted, amplified or enhanced versions of the infant's sounds (Papousek and Papousek, 1989). They seem to be intended as supportive emotionally coloured 'attunements' (Stern et al., 1985) of dynamic emotional forms (Stern, 1993). In this sample, imitation clearly serves a between-subjects communicative function, in association with many other sympathetic reactions of a non-imitative kind, such as smiles, hand gestures and various vocal expressions of feeling.

Throughout this interaction, mother and infant maintained mutual gaze, broken only briefly when the infant was excited to make a vigorous utterance, or when the mother's attention was distracted. Mutual gaze, being a potent sign of intersubjective reciprocity, is, as mentioned above, a kind of imitation. It is used to regulate the degree to which the partner

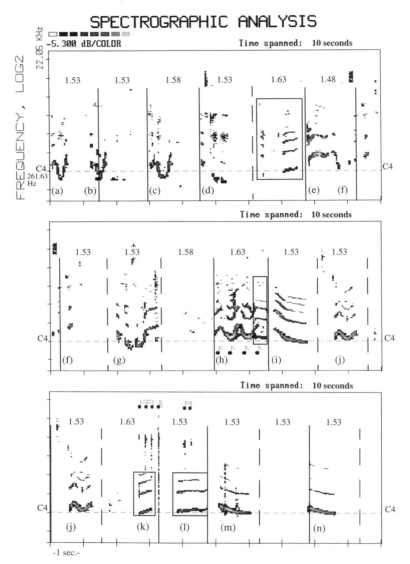

Figure 5.2. Mother speaking to her 6-week-old daughter who is seated opposite her in a baby chair and paying close attention, and occasionally smiling, vocalising and gesturing. This example of an extended (30 seconds) protoconversation, ending in a rhythmic nonsense game with the mother bouncing the baby, illustrates the rhythmic pattern of 'intuitive motherese'. A musical bar structure is set up in which the short, repetitive utterances of the mother, and the

'intrudes' (Robson, 1967; Stern, 1974). Removal of gaze from a partner can indicate avoidance, or it can show a change of interest towards another object. The latter becomes an increasingly important signal with older infants as they begin active exploration of surroundings and start to seek goals for observation and manipulation.

In interactions between young infants and their companions, one observes many behaviours that are triggered by actions of those other persons. Some of the infant's expressions are obviously adapted to soliciting human aid to help the infant feed, sleep or maintain comfort. They engage caregiving motives of the adults, and are responded to with actions that minister to the infant's apparent need, or that give emotional solace or support, as when a mother makes comforting sounds and lifting, rocking or patting movements to calm a fretting baby. Others, however, like Laura's utterances in the dialogue with her mother, are addressed as contributions to explore a communicative interaction, and they are responded to in that guise. They are seeking reciprocal, dynamic engagement of motives for their own sake in expressive forms of facial movements, vocalisations, posture changes, limb movements and hand gestures, including touching movements. Imitations that take the form of emotional expressions are easily seen as part of the regulation of interpersonal contact itself. More methodical or 'studious' imitations may have a self-stimulatory, self-regulatory purpose. They reproduce the other's act to test its regulation in the self. They may or may not convey a message about the balance of intersubjective purpose.

The state of the imitative mechanism before term

Innate principles of imitative reprocity in neonate imitation are indicated in a remarkable recording that Saskia van Rees has made of a precocious proto-conversation with imitation between a father and an 8-week premature infant that was born 5 weeks previously at 27 weeks gestational age (Van Rees and De Leeuw, 1987; Trevarthen, 1993a, Figure 3.2). In this

Caption to Figure 5.2 (*cont.*)
infant's responses, are inserted. The infant's vocalisations (*), which overlap or replace the mother's in the pauses she leaves, are enclosed in rectangles.

Mother's speech:
(a) Come on; (b) Again; (c) Come on then; (d) That's clever!; ****
(e) Oh, yes!; (f) Is that right?; (g) Well, tell me some more then; (h) Tell me some more then *; (i) Orrh!; (j) Come on; (k) ch-ch-ch-ch **;
(l) ch-ch ***; (m) E-gooo!; (n) Goo!

example, the father, who has the infant under his clothes resting against his chest, is gently touching the infant's hands and face, imitating expressions and gestures, 'showing' them to the infant, and exchanging vocalisations. His sounds clearly imitate the infant's coos in duration and pitch, but they are a little stronger and more sustained, with deeper formant components. Infant and father do not actually have eye contact or mutual gaze because the infant lies with eyes closed, but the father holds the baby to him with the right ear against his chest, and he studies the baby's face and hands closely. They share timing of movements, and especially of vocalisations, with remarkable precision (Figure 5.3). The infant's quick responses to the father's sounds appear themselves as imitations, because they are clearly responses in the same form. This shows how in reciprocal interaction the roles of imitator and imitatee may blend so that who is imitating whom becomes indeterminate. It is interesting, too, that the infant makes a slight rise in pitch when the father fails to respond.

Father and infant alternate vocalisations at approximately equal intervals on a clear pulse. In Figure 5.3, a and b, it can be seen that the father imitates Naseera 14 times with an interval about 0.75 seconds, and Naseera imitates him with about the same timing, or even more quickly, on 10 occasions. In the enlarged portion, Figure 5.3, c, the father follows Naseera 7 times at an average interval of close to 0.75 seconds (0.65 to 0.85 sec) and Naseera reacts to him twice with the same interval (0.7 sec). When they are interacting, the intervals of either the father's or Naseera's vocalisations are usually either 2 or 3 times 0.75 seconds (c. 1.5 sec, or 2.1–2.5 sec). When they are vocalising on their own, however, both seem to generate a longer phrasing interval. At the beginning of Figure 5.3, 'a' the utterances of Naseera are 6.6 seconds apart, and the father's imitated replies are 6.8 seconds apart. In the middle of 'a' the father waits 4.5 seconds before calling Naseera again. At the end of 'a' and the beginning of 'b' Naseera makes a series of vocalisations separated by 4.1, 3.7 and 4.7 seconds, with no supportive vocalisations from the father.

The cycles of attending and intending of the infant and father appear to form a two level hierarchy, the different durations being approximately 0.75 seconds and 4 seconds, levels which match remarkably well the 'utterance' (0.64 ± 0.18 sec) and 'phrase' ($3.7 \pm .066$ sec) components recently reported to be characteristic of spontaneous vocalisations of infants from early months (Lynch, Oller, Steffens and Buder, 1995). The mean 'utterance' (0.83 ± 0.62 sec) and 'phrase' (4.10 ± 2.50 sec) elements were also found to be preserved without much lengthening in the case of an infant born totally deaf because of atrophy of the cochleas (Lynch, 1996). Matching elements and phrases of perception and action are found in adult speech, in poetry and in music, indeed in the cognitive

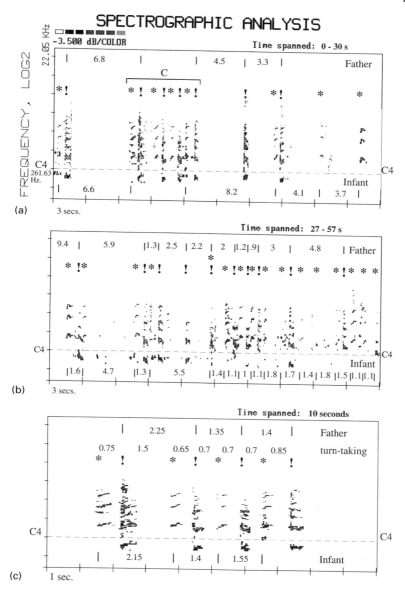

Figure 5.3. Sound track from the original uncut rushes of a video made by Saskia van Rees (Van Rees an de Leeuw, 1987) of a father with his 8 week premature daughter who is 'kangarooing' inside his clothes against his chest. The two vocalise rhythmically together, the father imitating the short, high pitched coos of his daughter.

and motoric processes of human perceivers or actors of all ages (Fraisse, 1984; Pöppel, 1994; Turner and Pöppel, 1983).

The imitations of this premature infant with the father are part of a longer temporally organised performance in which the two participants exchange parts and wait to correspond, with matching sense of timing. Both are apparently acting voluntarily or predictively. They appear to be mutually aware and seeking to recover the interaction when, for some reason, one or other fails to sustain an exchange. They each wait for several seconds for the remembered responses.

Developments in infant's motives to communicate, and changing imitations

Imitation evidently has dynamic, intersubjective regulatory functions from the beginning of human interactive life, but the messages it conveys change as the infants motives undergo age-related developments. These changes relate to developments in memory, in 'self-awareness' and in discrimination of cognitive categories, but they cannot be explained by a cognitive/associative theory. More fundamental internally generated changes in motivation for co-operative action and intersubjective play must be invoked.

The above examples are characteristic of Primary or Innate Intersubjectivity, where the motivation is focused on immediate regulation of communication itself. Beyond 3 months, an infant has increasing interest to explore surroundings, with the rapidly maturing abilities to make selective visual inspection and with more precisely directed and more deliberately selective movements of manual prehension. At the same time the body is stronger and many movements are of a kind that engage the different body parts in rhythmic and endlessly varied patterns of activity. Evidently bodily self-stimulation and acquisition of more efficient perceptuo-motor control is one purpose of these behaviours that contributes to their development.

The development in range and vigour of attending and acting at this age correlates with a more playful reaction to a partner's attempts to obtain communication. Games develop where the timing of moves is more complex than in the early weeks, and where the risks of incompatible expressions and 'teasing' provocations multiply. The emotional expressions of infants become more subtle, too, including coy or shy evasions of the attempts of familiar persons to engage them in play (Reddy, 1991). Expressions as of distressed 'shame' appear in interactions with strangers, or with familiar individuals who are not responding in their normal way, or who are behaving in an inaccessible way (Murray and Trevarthen, 1985; Trevarthen, 1990; Weinberg and Tronick, 1996).

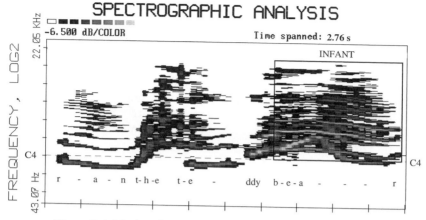

Figure 5.4. Mother singing the baby song, 'Round and round the garden, like a teddy bear' to her 24-week-old daughter, who joins in to vocalise, with matching pitch, on the final syllable of the word 'bear', an extended vowel. See the rhythmic structure of the song in Figure 5.9.

One highly characteristic feature of this period is the development of *rituals of play*, in which patterns of expressive behaviour and turn taking are formulated and repeated many times, and greeted with signs of pleased recognition on the part of the infant (Bruner and Sherwood, 1975; Hubley and Trevarthen, 1979; Papoušek, Papoušek and Harris, 1987; Ratner and Bruner, 1978; Stern, 1974, 1985; Stern and Gibbon, 1980; Trevarthen and Hubley, 1978; Trevarthen et al., 1981; Trevarthen, 1990). Parents play *teasing games* and begin to perform *baby songs* that enable the mother to excite attention to repeating patterns of rhythm and melody (Papoušek, Papoušek and Symmes, 1991; Trehub, Trainor and Unyk, 1993) and *action games* in which the infant's body is moved rhythmically to melodic patterns. The rhythms and prosody of these performances lead the infant to make contributions that are timed to alternate with the mother, or to coincide with climaxes in excitement (Stern, Jaffe, Beebe and Bennett, 1975).

Baby songs have regularities of timing and intonation which seem to imitate the infant's capacities to predict a sequence of cyclical expressive events, the 'emotional narrative' or 'dynamic emotional envelope' (Stern, 1993). They are imitated at certain points by the attending infant. We offer a typical example in which the baby imitates the mother's singing of a well-known song by sharing in an emphasised climax feature, the final vowel of a phrase, one that rhymes with the ending of a line that comes later in the verse of the song (Figure 5.4).

Maratos (1982), Kugiumutzakis (1985, 1993, this volume), Heimann, Nelson and Schaller (1989) and Heimann (1991) have charted age-related changes within the first 6 months in what infants are willing to imitate. Towards the end of the first year, infants first become attracted to imitate *ritual performances* that are made into often repeated games or jokes, such as waiving goodbye and clapping hands. These imitations are often deferred; that is they are often reproduced by the infant, unprompted, after an interval of days. They may also be employed 'instrumentally' by the child as an 'opener' for interaction with a different person (Trevarthen et al., 1981; Trevarthen, 1990). Such features led me to call these imitations 'discretionary', because they have a new flexibility of intention or deliberativeness in comparison with early imitations, which are more ingenuous or 'magnetic' (Trevarthen, 1982).

After 9 months, infants start to attend more deliberately to the gestures that a partner makes as indicators of their intentions in performance of a task, or to the expressions of emotion that indicate how they, the partner, evaluates a new or uncertain object or situation (emotional referencing) (Heimann and Ullstadius, this volume). A one-year-old is more willing to co-operate in a joint task, or to 'comply with' it, by 'completing an instruction' than he or she is willing to imitate a demonstration (Hubley and Trevarthen, 1979). In other words, into the second year the baby accepts information from gesture and vocalisation about an incomplete intended action, and he or she is eager to complete it. This is the behaviour that identifies purposeful joint attention in Secondary Intersubjectivity (Trevarthen and Hubley, 1978), the generative step in development of protolinguistic collaboration (Bretherton and Bates, 1979; Bruner, 1983; Halliday, 1975). Meltzoff has made an experimental demonstration of this completion of intentions in infants by 18 months (Meltzoff, 1995). The way imitation changes with age because the child's motives change is beautifully demonstrated by Nadel in her studies of 'immediate imitation' by toddlers, following principles enunciated by Wallon (Nadel, 1986; Nadel-Brulfert and Baudonnière, 1982; Wallon, 1970).

Imitation in different relationships, I: fathers and mothers with infant boys and girls

Imitation is always an interaction between acting subjects, even in the simplest case of contagious parallel movement, and therefore it depends on the motives of the partners. For this reason we should expect imitation to be different with different partners, both on the side of the infant and on the side of the partner.

If it is correct that infants are born imitators, in possession of a human motive system that can respond to intentional and emotional expressions of human partners, and that is motivated to learn from repeated experiences of mimetic interactions with familiar individuals, they should be willing and interesting partners for communication not only with their mothers, but also with their fathers who are also likely to address them with sympathetic affection. But traditional psychological theories gave fathers a minor role in the development of infants' communication. This appears to reflect a preoccupation with the physical or organic needs of the young infant, and the idea that the father is the representative of rationally ordered society.

In a sophisticated society where fathers felt distanced from their young children, Freud conceived of motives of infants in interaction with their mothers as primarily for gaining physiological benefits of comfort and nourishment. He thought that more elaborate emotions developed later, around sexual desire. The father had no place in the first stage, but, for a boy around the age of 4 or 5 years, a father becomes significant as a sexual rival for the mother's affections. Freud described the emotions of father–son relationships as competitive, agonistic ones, mixed, as the boy becomes more self-aware, with positive feelings that identify the father as an exemplar of socially (sexually) effective behaviours.

Freud defined *identification* as 'the assimilation of one ego to another one, as a result of which the first ego behaves like the second in certain respects, imitates it and in a sense takes it into itself' (Freud, 1933, p. 94), or, 'the endeavour to mould a person's own ego after the fashion of one that has been taken as a model' (Freud, 1921, p. 63). Like Baldwin and Piaget, he believed that the integrated feelings of the infant's ego were acquired first from the body by self-stimulation. In the sexual sphere this means 'libidinal aims' are satisfied by 'auto-eroticism'. A representation of an 'object' emerges as part of the self in 'narcissistic identification' when self and non-self are confused or merged. First the mother, and subsequently the father become separately conceived objects of identification.

It is clear that there is no place in Freud's theory of early infancy for imitative self–other reciprocity (primary intersubjectivity). When the infant's mind is beginning to separate a world of objects from the self, the dependence of both boys and girls on the mother is absolute. Her comforting presence is sought in actions and in fantasy. Later, the boy experiences a desire for his mother, at the same time identifying with the father defensively or aggressively, wanting to be like him, but fearing him as a competitor for the mother's care and affection. For a girl there is no such conflict, her identification with the mother being secure.

Psychoanalytic work by Anna Freud and Dorothy Burlingham explored the idea that the father can become a significant role model and source of self-regulating impulses earlier than Freud had thought, in the pre-Oedipal stage. 'The infant's emotional relationship to its father . . . is an integral part of its emotional life and a necessary ingredient in the complex forces which work towards the formation of its character and personality' (Burlingham and Freud, 1944). According to Anna Freud (1965), imitation of parents begins in early infancy and increases as awareness of the object world expands and motor skills improve. She considered that the infant develops an identification with a parent from pleasurable experiences of being imitated by them in the pre-Oedipal phase, and that this identification, being motivated by a wish to change the self, is a forerunner of the super-ego (Machtlinger, 1976, p. 300). The conscience (conceived as a learned representation of an 'internal legislator) is a later development from merely desirable ideas of the self which are transformed by the introjection that follows from identification. In reaction to paternal aggression, the little boy changes from a threatened passive person to a threatening active one, imitating the father (Kugiumutzakis, 1983).

Burlingham observed that the emotional handling a father had experienced as a child from his father can have a strong influence on the way he feels and acts with his own child. Fathers may say they are imitating their own fathers, even continuing to act as their fathers did against their better judgment (reported by Machtlinger, 1976, p. 293). Such 'echoes of intimacy' carried over from childhood have been confirmed in the work on transgenerational effects in attachment of Main and Goldwyn (1984) and Fonagy, Steele, Steele, Moran and Higgitt (1991). This research has shown that an infant's attachment to each parent depends on the way that parent relates emotionally to the infant. Burlingham also noted that girls and boys are treated differently by both fathers and mothers; 'I cannot help feeling that, in spite of and beyond the complexities of parental characters, and also in spite of the alleged modern equality of the sexes, many of the either female or male characteristics of the parents will continue to exist and, in response to them, the infants' differentiated emotional reactions and differentiated experiences of pleasure' (Burlingham, 1973).

Like psychoanalytic theory, social learning theories and more recent cognitive developmental theories have assumed that the father contributes little to child development before 4 years, when he offers a sex role identity for boys. He has little to offer for the early socialisation of girls. For both Thorndike (1898) and Watson (1908), imitation is not instinctive; it starts from perception of the chance similarity between a vocalisation and a sound the infant hears, and Watson added that adults imitate young infants more than the infants imitate them. Parton (1976) exemplifies the standard associative view that imitation is constructed from responses already in the child's repertoire by classical conditioning –

the adult copies the infant's behaviour and the infant tends to repeat the reiterated response, and this encourages an increase in the infant's tendency to imitate (Kugiumutzakis, 1983). Gewirtz and Stengle (1968) claimed that boys imitate their fathers because they are rewarded for doing so, and Baer and Sherman (1964) add that imitation gains reinforcement value because it is rewarded, and thus becomes its own reward. Such theorising dismisses any innate tendency to imitate, and denies a specific adaptive value to imitation.

A tendency of infants to accept rewards more readily from models that resemble themselves was demonstrated by Sears (1953), Kagan (1958) and Mussen and Rutherford (1963), but for Mowrer (1950) and most other learning theorists identification with a parent depends on the nurturance and reward that the parent supplies, thus boys are likely to imitate fathers who are loving and warm, even if the imitations are not rewarded directly.

In the cognitive developmental view, moral identifications are not made by imitation until a relatively advanced stage of development, and accordingly a theory of identification with parents must be part of a much broader account of mental development (Kohlberg, 1969). According to this theory, imitation is motivated not only by interest in the dimensions of the activity itself (its complexity, novelty, etc.), but also by the effects of the act upon other objects. Major developments in what will be accepted as a model for imitation are due not to the formation of new motives for imitation, but to cognitive–structural changes in concepts of role competence. These result in a rechannelling of primary competence motivation into varying channels of selective imitation (Kohlberg, 1969). The cognitive–developmental theory claims that the child learns to sex-type himself and his activities during the second and third year. By the age of 3 to 4 the boy knows quite well he is a boy and prefers 'boy things' to 'girl things' simply because he likes himself and those who are familiar and similar to himself. Before this point in his development, he was mother-oriented. Tending now to prefer masculine activities, he seeks a model for these activities. Thus he is led to select his father rather than his mother as a model. Imitation, in turn, leads to emotional dependency upon the father (Kohlberg, 1969). Emulating fathers' skills, thinking and vocabulary aids the cognitive development of boys (Radin, 1976).

Thus, learning theories and cognitive developmental theories, while emphasising different processes, both claim that the father starts to be an imitated model for a boy only when the boy is around 3 to 4 years of age.

Ethologists seek to explain the inherited phylogenetic roots of paternal behaviour (Lynn, 1974). The permanent social groups of primates comprise both sexes and have characteristics like those of human families.

It is beneficial for the male to stay with the family to assist and protect the female through a long and demanding pregnancy. It has been proposed that the male's sexual attachment to the female may have led to the development of fathering behaviour. This would suggest that human fathers stay with the family and derive satisfaction from their offspring for biological rather than cultural reasons. As a permanent member of the family, the male primate confers a combination of benefits, assisting in parental care and in defence of the group while gaining maximum access to receptive females (Eisenberg, 1966; Rypma, 1976). It has been suggested that male humans inherit a 'fathering instinct' that is satisfied and reinforced by features of the child, who is a source of pleasure. Motivated by curiosity, a new father is attracted to the child and through his senses comes to recognise the child as his. He finds that when he fondles and nurtures the child, it becomes attracted to him, mimicking and responding to him. 'To early man, as to today's man, imitation is the sincerest form of flattery, and it was flattering to see an image of himself mirrored in the behaviour of his child' (Biller and Meredith, 1975, p. 14).

In the plethora of studies on father–infant interaction in the last 25 years, not one is concerned exclusively with the development of imitative patterns in father–infant interaction in early infancy. The field continues to be dominated by preoccupations with development of social roles and acquisition of socially approved, or disapproved, behaviours. Differences in the behaviours of fathers and mothers, or of fathers' behaviour with sons and daughters have usually been related to contrasting cultural beliefs about the importance of a father in the development of young children. Nevertheless some detailed observations have been made which strongly suggest that very young infants can communicate with fathers, and that fathers may derive great pleasure from this.

In a study of medication in labour and the sex of the infant as factors affecting the interaction of the newborn with mother and father, Parke, O'Leary and West (1972) found that infants that had been exposed to tranquillising medication, being more lethargic, caused mothers to increase their efforts at interaction. Fathers, however, preferring an active awake infant, interacted less with neonates born with medication. It was also established that the father can be a very active participant in the family triad. Mothers smiled more than fathers, who may have been inhibited by the observation of their behaviour, but fathers tended to imitate more. Brazelton, Yogman, Als and Tronick (1979) observed that fathers can regulate, reciprocate and interchange behaviours with their infants, but fathers' behaviours showed qualitative differences in comparison with mothers' interactions with their infants. In the case of a 3-month-old boy with his father, these authors reported the following: the father enters with a neutral facial expression and begins a narrative vocalisation while the infant stills, sits upright and watches the father intently and quietly. The infant appears 'set' to interact. After about 6 seconds, the infant then greets his father with a wide grin and punctuates this with large, abrupt movements of his foot. Infant vocalisations are likely to be in the form of laughs, short and intense, followed by long pauses, while the father imitates and amplifies his infant's facial expressions. Episodes of mutual play are followed by pauses in which the father becomes less animated (Brazelton et al., 1979, p. 32).

Greenbaum and Landau (1979) studied young infants' exposure to speech by mothers, fathers and siblings in different environments at 2, 4, 7 and 11 months. Vocal imitations appear to have been low compared to other kinds of verbal response. Imitations of consonants uttered by the child, however, increased at 7 and 11 months in contrast to the preceding ages. Papoušek, Papoušek and Harris (1987) found no significant differences in maternal and paternal vocal matching with young infants. Episodes of playfulness were described in the following categories: (1) infant vocalisation accompanied by a facial expression of pleasure, (2) vocalisations repeated after some aspect of the partner's behaviour and thus potentially contingent upon it, (3) reciprocal matching of vocal sounds or some of the parameters of vocalisations, (4) repetitive strings of reciprocal sounds imitative of the infant's sounds, and (5) prosodic features in parental baby-talk in games with the infant. After analysing laboratory recordings of spontaneous 6-minute interactions of infants with their parents at 2, 3 and 4 months in this way, they identified 128 episodes of vocal play, 82% of which were initiated by the infants. There were no significant differences between mothers and fathers, and no changes with the infants' age. Parents answered the infants' sounds by matching turns in 61.9% of cases, and there were no sex differences. Infants answered only 17.4% of parental sounds with matching turns. Infants imitated only mothers' sounds; no paternal sounds in vocal play were followed by infants' matching turns, even though, by definition, parental vocalisations in play were in the infants' repertoire. This difference between fathers and mothers was interpreted as evidence that some factor in the fathers, possibly their relative unfamiliarity, discouraged the infants from imitating. The families, it should be noted, represented the traditional German pattern, in which fathers spend most of the day in professional work while mothers care for their infants. Field (1978) has compared infants' interactions with fathers who are primary and secondary caretakers, and she concluded that familiarity is, indeed, a significant factor. It seems generally believed now that fathers and mothers interact in similar ways with their infants, provided thay have equal contact (White and Wollett, 1987).

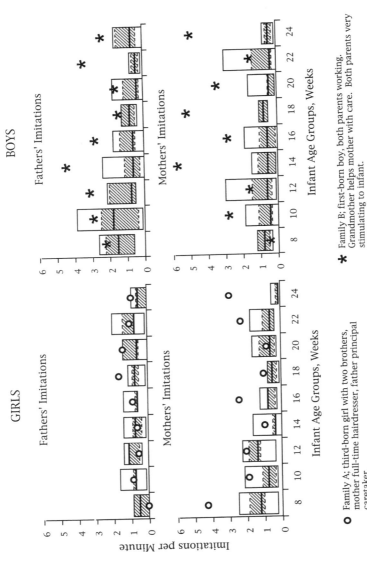

Figure 5.5. Parents imitations of infants in Crete. Rates of imitation of female and male infants by fathers and mothers at 2-week intervals from the 8th to the 24th week after the infant's birth. Two exceptional families (A O and B ★) in which at least one parent imitated at a consistently high level, generally well outside the range of the other parents, are indicated separately. The bars indicate the whole range of imitations for the remaining adults (white), the interquartile range (cross-hatched), and the median rate (thicker horizontal line).

O   Family A; third-born girl with two brothers, mother full-time hairdresser, father principal caretaker.

★   Family B; first-born boy, both parents working. Grandmother helps mother with care. Both parents very stimulating to infant.

While there has been a significant change in the way fathers' relationships with infants are viewed, the above findings cannot be satisfactorily integrated or interpreted because there is no comprehensive theory of the role of the father in early infancy (McGreal, 1981). None of the classical theories (psychoanalytic, genetic epistemological, social learning or ethological) reveals either the true role of the father or the ways the infant affects the father. They all focus on the father's contribution to child development, especially psycho-sexual development, giving a one-sided and incomplete picture. None of the theories gives a place to differentiated emotional regulations that might be shared between a father and his infant, and their changes in the short or long term. They are not studying communication and its emotional regulations.

Varieties of early companionship of infants with fathers and mothers in Cretan families

We have preliminary results from a project recording spontaneous play in the home between mothers and fathers and their boy or girl infants between the second and sixth month. These results come from Kokkinaki's analyses of video recordings made in Rethymnon, Crete.[7] Nine video recordings were made at 15-day intervals, in each family, and at each visit both parents were recorded playing for 8–10 minutes with their son or daughter while the other parent was out of the room; father and mother in alternating order on successive visits. There were 6 girls and 7 boys in all. Parents were asked simply to play as usual with the baby in a comfortable position on the parent's lap, lying on a sofa or in a baby seat. The researcher behind the camera tried to be inobtrusive and out of the line of sight of the infant, and did not speak. Visits were made when the parents felt it would be most convenient and when the baby was fed, rested and expected to be in a good mood. Recording was interrupted if the infant was tired or distressed.

A digital time signal was added to the video recordings, which were then processed by microanalysis to encode imitations of all communicative vocalisations and non-speech sounds, all facial, hand and head movements, as well as all possible combinations of these behaviours. Parental imitations were defined as simple reproductions of any single vocal, kinetic or facial expression of the baby which were at least in part the same as the infant's preceding behaviour. This allowed identification of 'partial' and 'expanded' imitations as well as 'accurate' matches. Synchronous or immediate replies in a different form (e.g., a head movement in reaction to a vocalization) were not accepted as imitations.

Figures 5.5 to 5.7 show the rates of parental imitation (imitations per

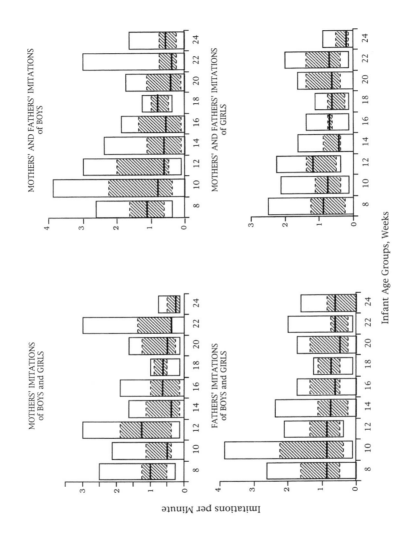

Figure 5.6. Rates of imitation of mothers and fathers with infants of both sexes, and the rates for boys compared with those for girls. In these graphs, the two families with exceptionally high rates of imitation (families A and B in Figure 5.5) are excluded.

minute) for an 8-minute portion of each recording. While these data must be regarded as preliminary until further details of the timing of responses, and the information from a similar population in Scotland, are available, we see interesting differences between the behaviours of fathers and mothers, differences in communications with boy and girl infants, and some parents who behave very differently from the majority. It appears, from Figure 5.5, that fathers of boys start by imitating more than fathers of girls, and that parents imitate less as the babies approach 6 months of age. In one family, exceptionally high rates of imitation may be related to the fact that neither father nor mother were principal caregivers. We will be interested to see if, in a larger population, there is a significant tendency for imitation to be more intense when the communication appears to require more effort on the parent's part.

When, as in Figure 5.6, left, the results from families with boys and girls are combined, there is little difference between parents. When the results for both parents are combined for boys and girls separately (Figure 5.6, right), it is clear that the boys are not only imitated by some parents more than girls, but the period at which the variance in imitation is reduced comes about 2 weeks later in boys (18 weeks) than it does for girls (16 weeks). This is an interesting confirmation that, at this stage of infancy, girls' development is a few weeks ahead of that of boys'. The same result has been obtained for binocular stereopsis (Held, Shimono and Gwiazda, 1984), for reaching (Von Hofsten, 1983b) and for communicative gestures (Trevarthen, 1996). If the effect is confirmed with more subjects, this will strongly support the hypothesis that developmental changes in infants affect the rate at which parents imitate their babies in play.

In Figure 5.7 there is a slight fall in the rate of imitation for the whole population, and a more conspicuous change in the variability of parents imitative behaviours with a minimum at 18 weeks. Put alongside indications of the occurrence of one of the temperamental, 'difficult' or regressive periods of infant behaviour, which have been reported by Dutch mothers (Rijt-Plooij and Plooij, 1993), and in comparison with measurements indicating how head circumference changes in the same period of infancy (Fischer and Rose, 1994), the data indicate that changes in the infants' brain and communicative behaviour may influence parents' imitations. This hypothesis will be directly examined by forthcoming analysis of developmental changes in the imitations made by the *infants* in Kokkinaki's tapes. Altogether the results of this study give clear indication that in playful engagements, in Crete at least, both parties, infants and parents (and this means mothers *and* fathers)

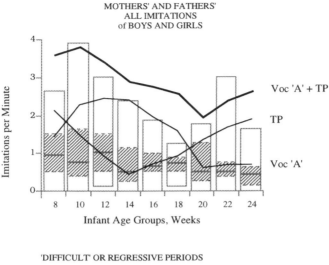

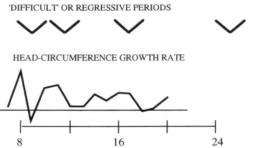

Figure 5.7. All imitations by parents, fathers and mothers, combined for all families, with boys and with girls. The relative frequency of imitative responses of two kinds, tongue protrusion (TP) and a vowel sound (Voc 'A'), obtained by Kugiumutzakis (1985, 1997) in his recordings of babies in Crete are shown, as well as the sum of these two frequencies, to obtain an indication of the overall imitativeness of the infants for these expressions.

contribute to the regulation of imitative communication that is truly intersubjective.

Imitation in different relationships, II: infants imitating infants

The greater part of work done in the last years on imitation is focused on mother–infant and child–child imitation. Experimental studies of infants'

ability to imitate adults have multiplied, especially around the controversy about the reality and nature of neonatal imitation. There are also
many studies of imitation between toddlers and older children, but few of
infants' imitations of other infants. If we want to fully understand the
intrinsic capacities of infants to initiate communication in a mutually
emotional way, the best strategy would seem to be to observe how they
react to strangers of the same age as themselves, who have no language,
and no cultural stereotypes or conventions. This would prove how much a
communicating infant needs 'scaffolding' from an older, more mature,
more culturally experienced and speaking partner.

It has often been asserted that the apparent abilities of infants to reciprocate in conversation-like exchanges are in reality 'random' and 'unintentional'; the appearance of reciprocity is essentially the result of the
mother filling in, extending and interpreting rather aimless and
undifferentiated actions of their babies not 'meant' as communications.
On the other hand, detailed descriptions of the efficiency and appropri-
ateness of infants' responses to familiar adults, and especially studies of
the emotion-rich efforts infants make to call attention or to avoid after the
contact with an adult is perturbed or interrupted, have led to the conclusion that they are born well-motivated to play an active, emotionally
charged and discriminating role in interaction with sympathetic human
partners (Beebe, 1982; Beebe et al., 1985; Murray and Trevarthen, 1985;
Reddy, Hay, Murray and Trevarthen, 1997; Stern, 1974, 1985;
Trevarthen, 1979, 1984; Tronick, 1982, 1989; Tronick, Als, Adamson,
Wise and Brazelton, 1978, 1980; Weinberg and Tronick, 1994). Of
course, the main difference between the infant and an adult partner is
that the latter is likely to be talking. Given that the infant is not understanding the semantic content of speech and yet is reacting in a sympathetic and effective manner to qualities of the partner's expression in
many forms, it is possible that similarly motivated infant–infant interactions will occur by non-verbal means.

A number of studies have recorded interactions between infants over 6
months of age. For example, these have investigated imitation (Hanna
and Meltzoff, 1993; Patrick and Richman, 1985), differences between
mother–infant and infant–infant interactions (Adamson and Bakeman,
1985), the effect of the presence of toys (Hay, Nash and Pedersen, 1983;
Vandell, Wilson and Buchanan, 1980) and the differences between reactions to familiar and unfamiliar peers (Jacobson, 1981). It appears that, in
this age range, infants who are strangers to each other are often wary and
avoid one another at first, but, in spite of this suspicious reaction, negotiated play is soon enjoyed, with mutual sensitivity of responses. Mutual
touching, as a positive response by 6-month-olds to one another, may be

inhibited by the presence of toys, but a toy may become more interesting if it is held by a peer, especially for a boy (Hay et al., 1983). One-year-olds point to, show and offer toys to one another (Hay, Caplan, Castle and Stimson, 1991). It would appear that at this age peer interactions do indeed have many of the features of infants' interactions with adults.

Apart from investigations of 'contagious crying' between young infants and the different reactions of newborns to recordings of their own crying (Hay, Nash and Pedersen, 1981; Martin and Clark, 1982; Sagi and Hoffman, 1976; Simner, 1971) and one study of how pairs of infants 1 to 3 months old interact when seated confronting one another on their mothers' laps (Fogel, 1979), there has been no analysis of the earliest possible face-to-face exchanges between peers. There has been one comparison of young infants' reactions to peers with how they respond to the reflection of themselves in a mirror (Field, 1979).

Although the above studies report only diffuse animation or quiet attending, and not the subtleties described for mother–infant proto-conversations, the evidence we do have indicates that infant–infant interaction could be a way of testing the idea that infants naturally regard other humans of any age as potential partners in an emotionally charged communication game, and that they can communicate feelings and interpersonal initiatives without the aid of mothers or toys. Observations by Reddy (1992) of how a 3-month-old, who is familiar with the mirror-image, behaves in front of the mirror indicate that a rich playfulness is possible with a reflected self. It seems to us that meetings with peers must be a common event in everyday life of many infants, and we expect they are of some interest to them.

We have begun a study of how pairs of infants at between 5 and 9 months use immediate or repeated imitation as a means of communicating. This is preparatory to studies of even younger subjects' interactions. Infants were brought by their mothers to the laboratory and placed in front of one another in their push-chairs. Their behaviour is recorded with the aid of two video cameras and a split-image generator that gives us a picture of the two infants side-by-side on one monitor, with sound. We are beginning a computer-assisted microanalysis of the behaviours of the two infants, measuring their timing. The babies readily start a *conversation of movements* in which imitations play a conspicuous part. As the interaction progresses, they take turns and then we can observe a nicely patterned dance involving initiatives by both infants.

Take, for example, two 8-month-old infants, a boy and a girl. They have never met before and are seated in their push-chairs, facing each other. Suddenly, while they look at each other the boy starts to kick his foot up and down and the girl imitates him immediately. He kicks back and she does the same, but she also vocalises, smiles and points at him. He is absolutely stunned by the presence of another infant in front of him who is behaving in this obviously friendly way. Reciprocal expressive behaviours while the infants are gazing at one another, like this, are typical of our corpus. Another interesting phenomenon in the infant's communication is *synchronisation between matching behaviours*. They do the same movements with their bodies at precisely the same time. In the above example, in 1 minute of interaction, there were 2 successive imitations and 5 synchronisations.

Imitation can be used *to keep the 'movement-conversation' going*, as in the case of two 9-month-old infants, a girl and a boy. He, like the previous boy, kicks and moves his legs up high while looking at the girl, and she imitates him, but not with the exactly matching body movement; first, because she is not as mobile as he is (he can put his legs in a higher position than she can) and also because as he kicks he vocalises in a long and loud way (Tarzan-like), while she smiles at him. As his attention shifts to other things, like investigating his push-chair screws, she tries to re-call his attention by repeating the movement she imitated before, kicking and moving her legs up while looking intently at him. She succeeds – he looks back, imitates her kick and emits his 'Tarzan' call again.

Imitation may serve to express *recognition and pleased sympathy*. With two other 9-month-old infants, a boy and a girl, he looks at her, vocalises an 'a-haa' sound and waves his hand, jumping in his push-chair. She smiles at him and waves back, vocalising a 'uu' sound. He laughs at her and waves back again.

Imitation may also be used to *tease* the other. Another 9-month-old pair, a boy and a girl, shared interest in a toy which he is holding in his hand. He keeps shaking the toy, holding it out in front of her, and she imitates his hand movements, and vocalises 'uu', pointing as well. He jumps and shakes the toy again, as she tries to reach it. He evidently is finding pleasure in provoking her fruitless efforts.

We note that the timing of these interactions is well controlled and different pairs express themselves and respond in closely similar rhythms.

Imitation in different relationships, III: infants and mirrors

Reddy (1991; Reddy et al., 1997) has recorded that playful reactions may be provoked by infants seeing their mirror-images as young as 3 months. Zazzo (1957, 1993) made similar observations in his extensive studies of the reactions of infants and young children to mirrors. We have made recordings of older infants reacting to a mirror box in which a TV camera facing the infant is concealed behind the partially silvered glass front. In this mirror, self-imitation is used for play, which is apparently provoked by the infant's awareness of the reflection of him- or herself, and the surface of the mirror becomes a toy. One 9-month-old boy looks at the mirror, shakes his mug and smiles to his image, and then, still smiling, hits the mirror with his mug. A 9-month-old girl, who is sitting on the floor facing the mirror, starts to make a series of kiss-like pouts, and then increases the speed of them and smiles, until she is really sending kisses. After that, still smiling and kissing, she makes jumping movements with her bottom and moves her arms up and down, apparently feeling a great pleasure in doing so while watching her image. In many cases, the infants are obviously 'showing off' self-expression with the 'mirror other'.

Infants also used self-imitation as a means of *self-recognition* or *self-exploration*, as in the example of a 7-month-old boy, who waved to the mirror, then, recognising the hand as his, looked directly at it while moving it in front of his eyes. There have, of course, been many experimental studies aimed at determining when infants see the mirror-image as a representation of themselves, 'self-awareness' being conceived as a developmental outcome of experience with the sensory feed-back effects of acting (Lewis and Brooks-Gunn, 1979; Rochat, 1995). We have taken more interest in the impersonations of social interactions that mirrors stimulate.

Conclusions and a model: imitations are driven by sympathetic fluctuations in motives that regulate the balance of initiative in intersubjective encounters

The studies we have reviewed, and the new results we have presented, show that infants are born ready to reciprocate in rhythmic engagements with the motives of sympathetic partners, and that imitations are made communicatively, as part of this mutual, reciprocal involvement. Expressive acts are reproduced as responses. They carry a message of acceptance or interest and take place in a sequence of behaviours that exhibit precise temporal patterning, with synchronisations and turn taking. What can we infer about the motive processes of intersubjectivity in humans from this data?

Figure 5.8 shows an analysis of the rhythms of a Scottish mother's song in English. Her infant showed rapt attention to her performance, and moved and vocalised with sympathetic attunement. The baby concentrated vocalisations on the protracted vowels with which the mother

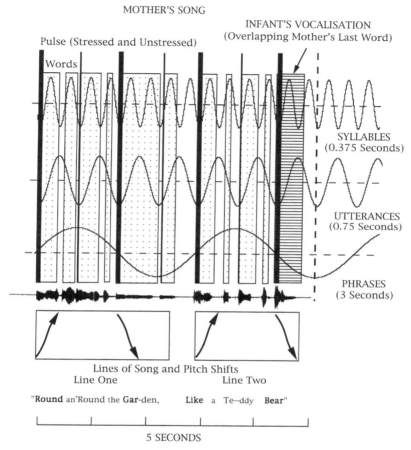

Figure 5.8. Rhythms of the baby song 'Round and round the garden'. Mono and bisyllabic words in the text are shown in the microphone signal immediately above the boxes in which major pitch shifts are indicated. Each 2-and-a-half second musical phrase (or line of the verse) has a rise and a fall of pitch, and four utterances (beats), which are alternately stressed and unstressed. The infant vocalises on the last syllable (see Figure 5.4), and this rhymes with the final syllable of the song, which ends, 'One step, two step; And a tickly under there!'

ended her phrase pairs, the second and fourth lines of her song. The baby thus demonstrated sensitivity to the rhythmic 'structure' or 'syntax' of the song and its 'semantic emphasis' or points of high significance, in direct reflection of the dynamic motives mother and infant were experiencing together.

The prominence of the rhythmic synchrony, which has drawn the attention of all who have made sufficiently detailed microanalytic descriptions of mother–infant interactions (Beebe, 1982; Beebe et al., 1985; Papoušek and Papoušek, 1981, 1987, 1989; Stern et al., 1977; Stern and Gibbon, 1980; Trevarthen, 1979, 1993a, b), appears to show that the mind of an infant is endowed with a mechanism that causes oscillations in motives at certain preferred intervals. Three periodicities manifest in vocalisations, which, following Lynch et al. (1995) we will call 'syllables', 'utterances' and 'phrases', seem to be of cardinal importance in all forms of expression. We propose that each of these represents a phasic alternation of the intrinsic motives between an active state of 'assertive' effort and a more receptive state of 'apprehension', in which activity is reduced in favour of reception and concentrated around organs that are engaged in taking in and 'processing' information from the environment. In an intersubjective encounter, this means that in each subject assertive expression alternates with apprehensive attending, and the two subjects either alternate or synchronise these phases between them. Imitations, we would propose, occur at one place in alternation, when assertiveness of one subject is waning, and the other is still highly apprehensive or acceptive.

This idea is diagrammed in Figure 5.9. We would predict that, in conversations between humans, and other kinds of co-operative voluntary behaviour, a rhythmic pattern of expressions will be displayed. Generally vocal or verbal imitations, sounds of agreement (such as 'uhuh'), eyebrow raising, nods, smiles. etc. will be fitted in between declarative or assertive speech turns with their gestural accompaniments. Changes in eye contact should also be coupled to the same motive fluctuations.

In 'motherese', rhythmic games, nonsense chants and baby songs, the parent is mirroring the manifestations of these rhythms in the baby, encouraging the infant's participation. Our analyses confirm that infants begin life highly sensitive to the periodic expressions of other persons, and that they are born skilled in reacting with rhythmic 'attunement' to the patterns of 'emotional narrative' that are produced. The rhythms of a Scottish mother singing 'Round and round the garden' with her 5-month-old, and the baby's musical collaboration by vocalising on the final syllable of the second line, are demonstrated in Figure 5.8.

Kokkinaki has, as presented above, shown that fathers can join in these games as well as mothers. Fiamenghi (above, and 1997) confirms that infants can set up rhythmic intersubjective play with other same-age infants, even before 6 months. In forthcoming work, we will be examining communications between much younger infants, and we will be extend-

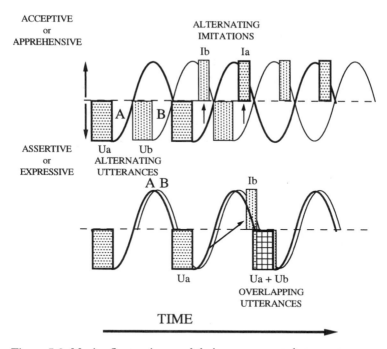

Figure 5.9. Motive fluctuations and their engagements between two subjects in communication. Utterances (U), or other periodic expressions, occur as assertiveness is increasing and cease as the motive for assertion falls. Imitations (I) are triggered in the other subject when the utterer has started to lose assertion and is becoming more apprehensive or acceptive. They may be followed immediately by an utterance from the second subject who thus takes a turn. Synchronisation of utterances may be set up (below) when one subject (B) tracks the expressive pulses of the other subject (A), imitates (Ib) and immediately makes an utterance (Ub overlapping Ua).

ing the study of fathers' imitations to a population of Scottish families matched with those in Crete.

ACKNOWLEDGMENTS

This chapter was prepared while Colwyn Trevarthen held a fellowship at the Centre for Higher Studies of the Norwegian Academy of Science and Letters, and has benefited from discussions there with members of the Study Group on Infant Communication; Stein Bråten, Mikael Heimann, Karsten Hundeide and Caroline Pope-Edwards.

Theano Kokkinaki is supported in her Ph.D. research at The University of

Edinburgh by The Alexander S. Onassis Public Benefit Foundation: Greek Section of Scholarships and Research. Her project has been made possible by the generous collaboration of Professor Giannis Kugiumutzakis of the University of Crete at Rethymnon.

Geraldo Fiamenghi is supported by CNPq – Brazil (grant number 201633/93–0) for his research toward a Ph.D. in Psychology at The University of Edinburgh. The spectrographs presented in Figures 5.2, 5.3 and 5.4 were preparted by Dr Stephen Malloch, who also made the analysis of the bar structure of the mother's speech shown in Figure 5.2.

NOTES

Rizzolatti and Arbib cite 'mirror neurons' in monkey frontal cortex as evidence for pyschological matching of perceived external events to internally generated actions, or observer to actor, and find PET scan evidence for a mirror system for gesture recognition in Broca's area of humans that links 'doing' with 'communicating', actor and observer and sender and receiver of messages (Rizzolatti, G. and Arbib, M. A. (1998). Language within our grasp. *Trends in Neuroscience*, 21, 188–94).

1 In his recent book on 'The Culture of Education', Jerome Bruner (1996) proposes that the future of educational theory lies in a better comprehension of its intersubjective nature. Awareness of culturally defined objects, tasks and manners is alive in infants at one year, and eagerly shared (Trevarthen, 1988, 1992).

2 We considered the significance of reciprocal imitations between mothers and infants in protoconversations first in response to a presentation by Olga Maratos of her pioneering study of imitation in early infancy (Maratos, 1973; Trevarthen, 1974).

3 This can be true of creative thought even at its highest level of complexity. Einstein reported to Hadamard (1945) that his mathematical invention was initially in the form of 'sensations of bodily movement', and that formal 'symbolising' was a difficult later stage. The converse imaginative ability to *become something else*, the embodiment of an object or event of interest, i.e., to move from objective awareness to subjective awareness, is what we understand Merlin Donald (1991) to mean by 'mimesis', and we accept his estimate of its central importance in the evolution of representational processes in the human mind, and their communication.

4 Wallon's theory of imitation emphasised this reciprocity (Wallon, 1970), which is documented and analysed developmentally in Nadel's studies of the functions of immediate imitation in the play of toddlers (Nadel-Brulfert and Baudonniere, 1982; Nadel, 1986; Nadel and Pezé, 1993).

5 It is of interest that the ability to imitate hand presentations in the same form as another person intends them is confused in autism. Autistic children, when they are asked to perform this kind of imitation, often make 'ego-centric' ('perceptual') rather than 'allo-centric' ('intersubjective') reproductions of hand postures. They match what they see, failing to mirror the orientation of the hands as if they were in the place of the other person (Ohta, 1987).

6 Piaget (1966) acknowledged the place of rhythm 'at the junction of organic and

mental life' in the earliest 'sensations' and he observed that, 'rhythm . . . involves a way of linking elements together which already heralds an elementary form of what appears as the reversibility characteristic of higher mental processes'. Donald (1991, p. 186), recognising the communicative significance of human moving, makes the very different claim that rhythm is a special feature of human *expressive* behaviour, and central to human mimesis. He says: 'Rhythm is an integrative mimetic skill relating to both verbal and visuomotor mimesis. Rhythm is a uniquely human attribute; no other creature spontaneously tracks and imitates rhythms in the way humans do, without training. Rhythmic ability is supramodal; that is, once a rhythm is established, it may be played out with any motor modality, including the hands, feet, head, mouth or the whole body . . . Rhythm is therefore evidence of a central mimetic controller that can track various movement modalities *simultaneously* and in parallel.' Here are two different definitions of rhythm.

7 Unpublished research for Doctoral Thesis, University of Edinburgh. The thesis, completed in 1998, also includes data from a matching sample of families in Edinburgh, Scotland.

REFERENCES

Adamson, L. and Bakeman, R. (1985). Affect and attention: Infants observed with mothers and peers. *Child Psychology*, 56, 582–93.

Aitken, K. J. and Trevarthen, C. (1997). Self–other organization in human psychological development. *Development and psychopathology*, 9, 651–75.

Anisfeld, M. (1996). Only tongue protrusion modeling is matched by neonates. *Developmental Review*, 16, 149–61.

Baer, D. M. and Sherman, J. A. (1964). Reinforcement control of generalized imitation in young children. *Journal of Experimental Child Psychology*, 1, 37–49.

Bakeman, R. and Adamson, L. (1984). Coordinating attention to people and objects in mother–infant and peer–infant interactions. *Child Development*, 55, 1278–89.

Baldwin, J. M. (1894). *Mental development in the child and the race*. New York: Macmillan.

Barnes, B. (1995). *The elements of social theory*. London: UCL Press.

Bateson, M. C. (1975.) Mother–infant exchanges: The epigenesis of conversational interaction. In D. Aaronson and R. W. Rieber (eds.), *Developmental psycholinguistics and communication disorders*; Annals of the New York Academy of Sciences, vol. 263. New York: New York Academy of Sciences.

(1979). 'The epigenesis of conversational interaction': A personal account of research development. In M. Bullowa (ed.), *Before speech: The beginning of human communication* (pp. 63–77). Cambridge University Press.

Beebe, B. (1982). Micro-timing in mother–infant communication. In M. Key (ed.), *Non-verbal communication today: Current research*. New York, Mouton.

Beebe, B., Jaffe, J., Feldstein, S., Mays, K. and Alson, D. (1985). Inter-personal timing: The application of an adult dialogue model to mother–infant vocal and kinesic interactions. In F. M. Field and N. Fox (eds.), *Social perception in infants* (pp. 249–68). Norwood, NJ: Ablex.

Bernstein, N. (1967). *Coordination and regulation of movements*. New York: Pergamon.

Biller, H. B. and Meredith, D. L. (1975). *Father power*. New York: David McKay.

Bråten, S. (1988). Dialogic mind: The infant and adult in protoconversation. In M. Cavallo (ed.), *Nature, cognition and system* (pp. 187–205). Dordrecht: Kluwer Academic Publications.

(1992). The virtual other in infants' minds and social feeling. In A. H. Wold (ed.), *The dialogic alternative* (Festschrift for Ragnar Rommetveit), (pp. 77–97). Oslo/Oxford: Scandinavian University Press/Oxford University Press.

(1998). Companion space theorems: Imitational learning from (e)motional memory. In S. Bråten (ed.), *Intersubjective communication and emotion in early ontogeny*. Cambridge University Press (in press).

Brazelton, T. B., Yogman, M. W., Als, H. and Tronick, E. (1979). The infant as a focus for family reciprocity. In M. Lewis and L. Rosenblum (eds.), *The child and its family*. New York and London: Plenum Press.

Bretherton I. and Bates, E. (1979). The emergence of intentional communication. In I. C. Užgiris (ed.), *Social interaction and communication during infancy*. New directions for child development, vol. 4, 81–100.

Bretherton, I., McNew, S. and Beeghley-Smith, M. (1981). Early person knowledge as expressed in gestural and verbal communication: When do infants acquire 'theory of mind'? In M. E. Lamb and L. R. Sherrod (eds.), *Infant social cognition*. Hillsdale, NJ: Erlbaum.

Bruner, J. S. (1976). From communication to language – A psychological perspective. *Cognition*, 3, 255–87.

(1983). *Child's talk. Learning to use language*. New York: Norton.

(1996). *The culture of education*. Cambridge, MA: Harvard University Press.

Bruner, J. S. and Sherwood, V. (1975). Early rule structure: the case of peekaboo. In J. S. Bruner, A. Jolly and K. Sylva (eds.), *Play: Its role in evolution and development*. Harmondsworth: Penguin Books.

Buck, R. (1984). *The communication of emotion*. New York: The Guilford Press.

Burlingham, D. (1973). The pre-Oedipal infant–father relationship. *Psychoanalytic Study of the Child*, 28, 23–47.

Burlingham, D. and Freud, A. (1944). *Infants without families*. London: George Allen & Unwin.

Byrne, R. W. (1995). *The thinking ape: The evolutionary origins of intelligence*. Oxford University Press.

Byrne, R. W. and Whiten, A. (1997). Machiavellian intelligence. In A. Whiten and R. W. Byrne, *Machiavellian Intelligence: Evaluations and Extensions*. Oxford University Press.

Changeux, J.-P. (1985). *Neuronal man: The biology of mind*. New York: Pantheon Books.

Clark, R. (1977). What's the use of imitation? *Journal of Child Language*, 4, 341–58.

Condon, W. S. and Sander, L. W. (1974). Neonate movement is synchronized with adult speech: interactional participation and language acquisition. *Science*, 183, 99–101.

Cosmides, L. (1989). The logic of social exchange: has natural selection shaped how humans reason? Studies with the Wason selection task. *Cognition*, 31, 187–276.

Craig, W. (1918). Appetites and aversions as constituents of instincts. *Biological Bulletin, Woods Hole,* 34, 91–107.

Darwin, C. (1872). *The expression of emotion in man and animals.* London: Methuen.

DeCasper, A. J. and Fifer, W. P. (1980). Of human bonding: Newborns prefer their mother's voices. *Science,* 208, 1174–6.

Di Pelligrino, G., Fadiga, L., Fogassi, L., Gallese, V. and Rizzolatti, G. (1992). Understanding motor events: A neurophysiological study. *Experimental Brain Research,* 91, 176–80.

Dollard, J. and Miller, N. E. (1950). *Personality and psychotherapy: An analysis in terms of learning, thinking and culture.* New York: McGraw-Hill.

Donald, M. (1991). *Origins of the modern mind.* Cambridge, MA and London: Harvard University Press.

Dunbar, R. I. M. (1992). Neocortex size as a constraint on group size in primates. *Journal of Human Evolution,* 20, 469–93.

Edelman, G. M. (1987). *Neural Darwinism: The theory of neuronal group selection.* New York: Basic Books.

Eisenberg, S. F. (1966). The social organization of mammals. *Handbook of Zoology,* 10, 1–92.

Emde, R. N. (1992). Positive emotions for psychoanalytic theory: Surprises from infancy research and new directions. In T. Shapiro and R. N. Emde (eds.), *Affect: Psychoanalytic perspectives* (pp. 5–44). Madison, CT: International Universities Press.

Emde R. N., Biringen, Z., Clyman, R. B. and Oppenheim, D. (1991). The moral self in infancy: Affective core and procedural knowledge. *Developmental Review,* 11, 251–70.

Fiamenghi, G. A. (1997). Intersubjectivity and infant–infant interaction: Imitation as a way of making contact. Annual Report, Research and Clinical Center for Child Development, No. 19, 15–21. Hokkaido University, Sapporo, Japan.

Field, R. (1978). Interaction patterns of primary versus secondary caretaking fathers. *Developmental Psychology,* 14, 183–5.

Field, T. (1979) Infant behaviors directed towards peers and adults in the presence and absence of the mother. *Infant Behavior and Development,* 2, 47–54.

Field, T. N., Woodson, R., Greenberg, R. and Cohen, D. (1982). Discrimination and imitation of facial expressions by neonates. *Science,* 218, 179–81.

Fifer, W. P. and Moon, C. M. (1995). The effects of fetal experience with sound. In J.-P. Lecanuet, W. P. Fifer, N. A. Krasnegor and W. P. Smotherman (eds.), *Fetal development: A psychobiological perspective* (pp. 351–66). Hillsdale, NJ: Erlbaum.

Fischer, K. W. and Rose, S. P. (1994). Dynamic development of coordination of components in brain and behavior: A framework for theory and research. In G. Dawson and K. W. Fischer (eds.), *Human Behavior and the Developing Brain* (pp. 3–66). New York: The Guilford Press.

Fogel, A. (1979). Peer- vs. mother-directed behavior in 1- to 3-month-old infants. *Infant Behavior and Development,* 2, 215–26.

Fogel, A. and Thelen, E. (1987). Development of early expressive action from a dynamic systems approach. *Developmental Psychology,* 23, 747–61.

Fonagy, P., Steele, M., Steele, N., Moran, G. S. and Higgitt, A. C. (1991). The capacity for understanding mental states: the reflective self in parent and child and its significance for security of attachment. *Infant Mental Health Journal*, 12(3), 201–18.

Fraisse, P. (1984). Perception and estimation of time. *Annual Review of Psychology*, 35, 1–36.

Freud, A. (1965). *Normality and pathology in childhood.* New York: International Universities Press.

Freud, S. (1921/1955). *Group psychology and the analysis of the ego.* (Standard edn), vol. 18. London: Hogarth Press.

Freud, S. (1933/1979) *New introductory lectures in psychoanalysis.* London: Penguin Books.

Galef, B. G. (1988). Imitation in animals: History, definitions, and interpretation of data from the psychological laboratory. In T. Zentall and B. G. Galef Jr. (eds.), *Social learning: Psychological and biological perspectives* (pp. 3–28). Hillsdale, NJ: Erlbaum.

Gewirtz, J. L. and Stengle, K. G. (1968), Learning of generalized imitation as the basis for identification. *Psychological Review*, 75, 374–97.

Gibson, J. J. (1979). *The ecological approach to visual perception.* Boston: Houghton Mifflin.

Gomez, J. C. (1991). Visual behavior as a window for reading the mind of others in primates. In: A. Whiten (ed.), *Natural theories of mind: Evolution, development and simulation of everyday mindreading* (pp. 195–207). Oxford: Blackwell.

Goody, E. (1995). *Social intelligence and interaction.* Cambridge Universioty Press.

Greenbaum, C. W. and Landau, R. (1979). The infant's exposure to talk by familiar people: Mothers, fathers, and siblings in different environments. In M. Lewis and L. Rosenblum (eds.), *The child and its family.* New York and London: Plenum Press.

Greenfield, P. M. and Savage-Rumbaugh, E. S. (1993). Comparing communicative competence in child and chimp: the pragmatics of repetition. *Journal of Child Language*, 20, 1–26.

Guillaume, P. (1971). *Imitation in children.* University of Chicago Press.

Hadamard, J. (1945). *The psychology of invention in the mathematical field.* Princeton University Press.

Halliday, M. A. K. (1975). *Learning how to mean: Explorations in the development of language.* London: Edward Arnold.

Hanna, E. and Meltzoff, A. (1993). Peer imitation by toddlers in laboratory, home, and day-care contexts: Implications for social learning and memory. *Developmental Psychology*, 29(4), 701–10.

Hay, D. F., Caplan, M., Castle, J. and Stimson, C. A. (1991). Does sharing become increasingly 'rational' in the second year of life? *Developmental Psychology*, 27, 987–93.

Hay, D., Nash, A. and Pedersen, J. (1981). Responses of six-month-olds to the distress of their peers. *Child Development*, 52, 1071–5.

(1983). Interaction between six-month-old peers. *Child Development*, 54, 557–62.

Heimann, M. (1989). Neonatal imitation, gaze aversion and mother–infant interaction. *Infant Behavior and Development*, 12, 495–505.

Heimann, M. and Schaller, J. (1985). Imitative reactions among 14–21 days old infants. *Infant Mental Health Journal*, 6, 31–9.

Heimann, M., Nelson, K. E. and Schaller, J. (1989). Neonatal imitation of tongue protrusion and mouth opening: Methodological aspects and evidence of early individual differences. *Scandanavian Journal of Psychology*, 90, 90–101.

Held, R., Shimono, S. and Gwiazda, J. (1984). Gender differences in the early development of human visual resolution. (Proceedings of the ARVO Meeting, April–May, 1984, Abstract No. 90). *Investigative Ophthalmology & Visual Science*, 25, 220.

Hofer, M. A. (1990). Early symbolic processes: Hard evidence from a soft place. In R. A. Glick and S. Bone (eds.), *Pleasure beyond the pleasure principle* (pp. 55–78). Newhaven, CT: Yale University Press.

Hubley, P. and Trevarthen C. (1979). Sharing a task in infancy. In I. Užgiris (ed.), *Social interaction during infancy: New directions for child development*, 4, 57–80. San Francisco: Jossey-Bass.

Humphrey, N. (1976). The social function of intellect. In P. P. G. Bateson and R. A. Hinde (eds.), *Growing Points in Ethology*. Cambridge University Press.

Hutcheson, F. (1755). *A system of moral philosophy*. Glasgow.

Izard, C. E. (1980). The emergence of emotions and the development of consciousness in infancy. In J. M. Davidson and R. Davidson (eds.), *The psychobiology of consciousness*. New York, Plenum Press.

(1971). *The face of emotion*. New York: Appleton-Century-Crofts.

Jacobson, J. (1981). The role of inanimate objects in early peer interaction. *Child Development*, 52, 618–26.

Jaffe J., Stern D. N. and Peery, J. C. (1973). Conversational coupling of gaze behavior in prelinguistic human development. *Journal of Psycholinguistic Research*, 2, 321–30.

Jeannerod, M. (1994). The representing brain: Neural correlates of motor intention and imagery. *Behavioral and Brain Sciences*, 17, 187–245.

Johanssen, G. (1975). Visual motion perception. *Scientific American*, 232(6), 76–88.

Kagan, J. (1958). The concept of identification. *Psychological Review*, 65, 296–305.

Kohlberg, L. (1969). Stage and sequence: The cognitive-developmental approach to socialization. In D. Goslin (ed.), *Handbook of socialization theory and research*. Chicago: McNally.

Kugiumutzakis, G. (1983). Imitative phenomena: A new challenge. MA thesis, Department of Psychology, University of Uppsala.

(1985). The origins, development and function of early infant imitation. Ph.D. thesis, Uppsala University, *Acta Universitatis Uppsaliensis, 35*.

(1993). Intersubjective vocal imitation in early mother–infant interaction. In J. Nadel and L. Camaioni (eds.), *New perspectives in early communicative development*. London: Routledge.

(1998). Neonatal imitation in the intersubjective companion space. In S. Bråten (ed.), *Intersubjective communication and emotion in early ontogeny*. Cambridge University Press. (in press).

Lee, D. N. (1993). Body–environment coupling. In U. Neisser (ed.), *The perceived self: Ecological and interpersonal sources of the self-knowledge* (pp. 43–67). New York: Cambridge University Press.

Lewis, M. and Brooks-Gunn, J. (1979). *Social cognition and the acquisition of self.* New York: Plenum.

Locke, J. L. (1993). *The child's path to spoken language.* Cambridge, MA and London: Harvard University Press

Lorenz, K. (1965). *Evolution and the modification of behavior.* Chicago University Press.

Lynch, M. P. (1996). The case of total deafness II: Phrasing of prelinguistic vocalizations of a child born with congenital absence of cochleas. *Applied Psycholinguistics*, 17, 293–312.

Lynch, M. P., Oller, D. K., Steffens, M. L. and Buder, E. H. (1995). Phrasing in prelinguistic vocalizations. *Developmental Psychobiology*, 28, 3–25.

Lynn, D. C. (1974). *The father: His role in child development.* Belmont, California: Wadsworth.

Machtlinger, V. (1976). Psychoanalytic theory: Preoedipal and oedipal phases with reference to the father. In M. Lamb (ed.), *The role of the father in child development.* New York: Wiley.

Main, M. and Goldwyn, M. (1984). Predicting rejection of her infants from mother's representation of her own experience. Implications for the abused–abusing intergenerational cycle. *International Journal of Child Abuse and Neglect*, 8, 203–17.

Malloch, S., Sharp, D., Campbell, D. M., Campbell, A. M. and Trevarthen, C. (1997). Measuring the human voice: Analysing pitch, timing, loudness and voice quality in mother/infant communication. *Proceedings of the Institute of Acoustics*, 19(5), 495–500.

Maratos, O. (1973). The origin and development of imitation in the first six months of life. Ph.D. dissertation, University of Geneva.

(1982). Trends in development of imitation in early infancy. In T. G. Bever (ed.), *Regressions in mental development: Basis phenomena and theories* (pp. 81–101). Hillsdale, NJ: Erlbaum.

Marler, P., Evans, C. S. and Hauser, M. (1992). Animal signals: Motivational, referential, or both? In H. Papoušek, U. Jurgens and M. Papoušek (eds.), *Nonverbal vocal communication.* Cambridge and New York: Cambridge University Press.

Martin, G. B. and Clark, R. D. (1982). Distress crying in neonates: Species and peer specificity. *Developmental Psychology*, 18(1), 3–9.

Mayer, N. K. and Tronick, E. Z. (1985). Mother's turn-giving signals and infant turn-taking in mother–infant interaction. In T. M. Field and N. A. Fox (eds.), *Social perception in infants.* Norwood, NJ: Ablex, 199–216.

McGreal, C. E. (1981). The father's role in the socialisation of his infant. *Infant Mental Health Journal*, 2(4), 216–25.

Meltzoff, A. N. (1995). Understanding the intentions of others: Reenactment of intended acts by 18-month-old children. *Developmental Psychology*, 31(5).

Menzel, E. W. (1971). Communication about the environment in a group of young chimpanzees. *Folia Primatologica*, 15, 220–32.

Mowrer, O. (1950). *Learning theory and personality dynamics.* New York: Roland Press.

Murray, L. (1980). The sensitivities and expressive capacities of young infants in communication with others. Ph.D. thesis, University of Edinburgh.

(1992). The impact of postnatal depression on infant development. *Journal of Child Psychology and Psychiatry*, 33(3), 543–61.

Murray, L. and Trevarthen C. (1985). Emotional regulation of interactions between two-month-olds and their mothers. In T. Field and N. Fox (eds.), *Social perception in infants*. Norwood, NJ: Ablex.

(1986). The infant's role in mother–infant communication. *Journal of Child Language*, 13, 15–29.

Mussen, P. and Rutherford, E. (1963). Parent–child relations and parental personality in relation to young children's sex-role preferences. *Child Development*, 34, 589–607.

Nadel, J. (1986). *Imitation et communication entre jeunes enfants*. Paris: PUF.

Nadel, J. and Pezé, A. (1993). What makes immediate imitation communicative in toddlers and autistic children? In J. Nadel and L. Camaioni (eds.), *New perspectives in early communicative development* (pp. 139–56). London: Routledge.

Nadel-Brulfert, J. and Baudonnière, P.-M. (1982). The social function of reciprocal imitation in 2-year-old peers. *International Journal of Behavioral Development*, 5, 95–109.

Nakano, S. (1996). 'I' don't know what's happening, but 'we' do. Paper presented at the conference on 'New Psychologies', Tarbert, Scotland, June, 1996.

Nakano, S. and Kanaya, Y. (1993). The effects of mothers' teasing: Do Japanese infants read their mothers' play intention in teasing? *Early Development & Parenting*, 2(1), 7–17.

Neisser, U. (1976). *Cognition and reality: Principles and implications of cognitive psychology*. San Francisco: Freemans.

O'Rahilly, R. and Müller, F. (1994). *The embryonic human brain: An atlas of developmental stages*. New York: Wiley-Liss.

Ohta, M. (1987). Cognitive disorders of infantile autism: A study employing the WISC, spatial relationship conceptualisation, and gesture imitations. *Journal of Autism and Developmental Disorders*, 17, 45–62.

Oster, H. (1978). Facial expression and affect development. In M. Lewis and L. A. Rosenblum (eds.), *The development of affect* (pp. 43–75). New York: Plenum.

Papoušek, H. and Papoušek, M. (1987). Intuitive parenting: A dialectic counterpart to the infant's integrative competence. In J. D. Osofsky (ed.), *Handbook of infant development*. 2nd edn. New York: Wiley.

Papoušek, M. and Papoušek, H. (1981). Musical elements in the infants vocalization: their significance for communication, cognition and creativity. In L. P. Lipsitt and C. K. Rovee-Collier (eds.), *Advances in infancy research*, vol. 1. Norwood, NJ: Ablex.

(1989). Forms and functions of vocal matching in interactions between mothers and their precanonical infants. *First Language*, 9, 137–58.

Papoušek, M., Papoušek, H. and Harris, B. J. (1987). The emergence of play in parent–infant interactions. In D. Görlitz and J. F. Wohlwill (eds.), *Curiosity, imagination and play: On the development of spontaneous cognitive and motivational processes* (pp. 214–46). Hillsdale, NJ: Erlbaum.

Papoušek, M., Papoušek, H. and Symmes, D. (1991). The meanings and melodies in motherese in tone and stress languages. *Infant Behavior and Development*, 14, 415–40.

Parke, R. D., O'Leary, S. E. and West, S. (1972). Mother–father–newborn interaction: Effects of maternal medication, labor, and sex of infant. Proceedings, 80th Annual Convention, APA.

Parton, D. A. (1976). Learning to imitate in infancy. *Child Development*, 47, 14–31.

Passingham, R. E. and Ettlinger, G. (1974). A comparison of cortical function in man and other primates. *International Review of Neurobiology*, 16, 233–99.

Patrick, K. and Richman, C. (1985). Imitation in toddlers as a function of motor and verbal aspects of modeling. *The Journal of Genetic Psychology*, 146(2), 507–18.

Pawlby, S. J. (1977). Imitative interactions. In H. R. Schaffer (ed.), *Studies in mother–infant interaction: The Loch Lomond symposium*. London: Academic Press.

Piaget, J. (1953). *The origins of intelligence in children*. London: Routledge & Kegan Paul.

    (1962). *Play, dreams and imitation in childhood*. London: Routledge & Kegan Paul.

    (1966). *The psychology of intelligence*. Totowa, NJ: Littlefield Adams.

Ploog, D. (1992). The evolution of vocal communication. In H. Papoušek, U. Jurgens and M. Papoušek (eds.), *Nonverbal vocal communication*. Cambridge and New York: Cambridge University Press.

Pöppel, E. (1994). Temporal mechanisms in perception. *International Review of Neurobiology*, 37, 185–202.

Premack, D. (1987). *Gavagai*. Cambridge, MA: MIT Press.

Radin, N. (1976). The role of the father in cognitive, academic and intellectual development. In M. Lamb (ed.), *The role of the father in child development*. New York: Wiley.

Ratner, N. and Bruner, J. S. (1978). Games, social exchange and the acquisition of language. *Journal of Child Language*, 5, 391–400.

Reddy, V. (1991). Playing with others' expectations; teasing and mucking about in the first year. In: A. Whiten (ed.), *Natural theories of mind: Evolution, development and simulation of everyday mindreading* (pp. 143–58). Oxford: Blackwell.

    (1992). The rudiments of shyness in two-month-olds? Visual cutoff, head turning and arm curving in intimate interactions. Poster presented at the European Developmental Conference, Seville, August–September, 1992.

Reddy, V., Hay, D., Murray, L. and Trevarthen, C. (1997). Communication in infancy: Mutual regulation of affect and attention. In G. Bremner, A. Slater and G. Butterworth (eds.), *Infant development: Recent advances*. Hove, East Sussex: Psychology Press.

Rijt-Plooij, H. H. C. van de and Plooij, F. X. (1993). Distinct periods of mother–infant conflict in normal development: sources of progress and germs of pathology. *Journal of Child Psychology and Psychiatry*, 34, 229–45.

Robson, K. S. (1967). The role of eye to eye contact in maternal–infant attachment. *Journal of Child Psychology and Psychiatry*, 8, 13–25.

Rochat, P. (1995). *The self in early infancy.* New York: North-Holland-Elsevier Science Publishers.

Rogoff, B. (1990). *Apprenticeship in thinking: Cognitive development in social context* New York: Oxford University Press.

Rönnqvist, L. and Hofsten, C. von (1994). Neonatal finger and arm movements as determined by a social and an object context. *Early Development and Parenting*, 3, 81–94.

Runeson, S. (1977). On the possibility of 'smart' perceptual mechanisms. *Scandanavian Journal of Psychology*, 18, 172–9.

Rypma, C. B. (1976). Biological bases of the paternal response. *The family coordinator*, 25, 335–9.

Sagei, A. and Hoffman, M. (1976). Empathic distress in the newborn. *Developmental Psychology*, 12(2), 175–6.

Savage-Rumbaugh, E. S. (1986). *Ape language: From conditioned response to symbol.* New York: Columbia University Press.

Scaife, M. and Bruner, J. S. (1975). The capacity for joint visual attention in the infant. *Nature*, 253, 265–6.

Schore, A. N. (1994). *Affect regulation and the origin of the self: The neurobiology of emotional development.* Hillsdale, NJ: Erlbaum.

Sears, P. S. (1953). Childrearing factors related to the playing of sex-typed roles. *American Psychologist*, 8, 431 (Abstract).

Sebeok, T. A. (1990). *Essays in zoosemiotics.* Monograph Series of the Toronto Semiotic Circle, Number 5. Toronto Semiotic Circle, Victoria College in the University of Toronto.

Simner, M. (1971). Newborn's response to the cry of another infant. *Developmental Psychology*, 5(1), 136–50.

Smith, A. (1759). *The theory of moral sentiments.* Glasgow, 6th edn. 1790 (D. D. Raphael and A. L. Macfie, General Editors. Oxford: Clarendon, 1976; Reprint, Indianapolis: Liberty Fund, 1984).

Sperry, R. W. (1950). The neural basis of the spontaneous optokinetic response produced by visual inversion. *Journal of Comparative & Physiological Psychology*, 43, 482–9.

(1952). Neurology and the mind–brain problem. *American Scientist*, 40, 291–312.

Sroufe, L. A. (1996). *Emotional development: The organisation of emotional life in the early years.* Cambridge University Press.

Stern, D. N. (1974). Mother and infant at play: the dyadic interaction involving facial, vocal and gaze behaviors. In M. Lewis and L. A. Rosenblum (eds.), *The effect of the infant in its caregiver* (pp. 187–213). New York: Wiley.

(1985). *The interpersonal world of the infant: A view from psychoanalysis and development psychology.* New York, Basic Books.

(1990). Joy and satisfaction in infancy. In R. A. Glick and S. Bone (eds.), *Pleasure beyond the pleasure principle* (pp. 13–25). Newhaven, CT: Yale University Press.

(1993). The role of feelings for an interpersonal self. In U. Neisser (ed.), *The perceived self: Ecological and interpersonal sources of self-knowledge.* New York: Cambridge University Press,

Stern, D. N. and Gibbon, J. (1980). Temporal expectancies of social behaviors in mother–infant play. In E. Thoman (ed.), *Origins of infant social responsiveness* (pp. 409–29). New York: Erlbaum.

Stern, D. N., Beebe, B., Jaffe, J. and Bennett, S. L. (1977). The infant's stimulus world during social interaction: a study of caregiver behavior with particular reference to repetition and timing. In H. R. Schaffer (ed.), *Studies in mother–infant interaction*. New York: Academic Press.

Stern, D. N., Hofer, L., Haft, W. and Dore, J. (1985). Affect attunement: The sharing of feeling states between mother and infant by means of intermodal fluency. In T. N. Field and N. Fox (eds.), *Social perception in infants*, Norwood, NJ: Ablex.

Stern, D. N., Jaffe, J., Beebe, B. and Bennett, S. L. (1975). Vocalization in unison and alternation: Two modes of communication within the mother–infant dyad. *Annals of the New York Academy of Science*, 263, 89–100.

Thelen, E. (1985). Expression as action. In G. Zivin (ed.), *The development of expressive behavior: Biology–environment interactions*. Orlando: Academic Press.

Thorndike, E. L. (1898). Animal intelligence: An experimental study of the associative process in animals. In A. J. Riopelle (ed.) (1967). *Animal problem solving*. London: Penguin Books.

Tinbergen, N. (1951). *The study of instinct*. Oxford: Clarendon Press.
   (1952). Derived activities: Their causation, biological significance, origin, and emancipation during evolution. *Quarterly Review of Biology*, 27(1), 1–32.

Tomasello, M. (1988). The role of joint attentional processes in early language development. *Language Sciences*, 10, 69–88.
   (1990). Cultural transmission in the tool use and communicatory signalling of chimpanzees? In S. T. Parker and K. R. Gibson (eds.), *'Language' and intelligence in monkeys and apes*. New York: Cambridge University Press.

Tomasello, M., Kruger, A. C. and Ratner, H. H. (1993). Cultural learning. *Behavioral and Brain Sciences*, 16(3), 495–552.

Tomasello, M., Savage-Rumbaugh, E. S. and Kruger, A. C. (1993b). Imitative learning of actions on objects by children, chimpanzees and enculturated chimpanzees. *Child Development*, 64, 1688–705.

Trehub, S. E.,Trainor, L. J. and Unyk, A. M. (1993). Music and speech processing in the first year of life. *Advances in Child Development and Behavior*, 24, 1–35.

Trevarthen, C. (1974). The psychobiology of speech development. In E. H. Lenneberg (ed.), *Language and brain: Developmental aspects*. Neurosciences Research Program Bulletin, 12, 570-85. Boston: Neurosciences Research Program.
   (1975). Growth of visuomotor coordination in infants. *Journal of Human Movement Studies*, 1, 57.
   (1977). Descriptive analyses of infant communication behavior. In H. R. Schaffer (ed.), *Studies in mother–infant interaction: The Loch Lomond symposium* (pp. 227–70). London: Academic Press.
   (1978). Modes of perceiving and modes of acting. In J. H. Pick (ed.), *Psychological modes of perceiving and processing information* (99–136). Hillsdale, NJ: Erlbaum.

(1979). Communication and cooperation in early infancy. A description of primary intersubjectivity. In M. Bullowa (ed.), *Before speech: The beginning of human communication* (pp. 321–47). London: Cambridge University Press.

(1980). Functional organization of the human brain. In M. C. Wittrock (ed.), *The brain and psychology* (pp. 33-91). New York: Academic Press.

(1982). The primary motives for cooperative understanding. In G. Butterworth and P. Light (eds.), *Social cognition: Studies of the development of understanding* (pp. 77–109). Brighton: Harvester Press.

(1984). Emotions in infancy: Regulators of contacts and relationships with persons. In K. Scherer and P. Ekman (eds.), *Approaches to emotion* (pp. 129–57). Hillsdale, NJ: Erlbaum.

(1986). Development of intersubjective motor control in infants. In M. G. Wade and H. T. A. Whiting (eds.), *Motor development in children: Aspects of coordination and control* (pp. 209–61). Dordrecht: Martinus Nijhof.

(1988). Universal cooperative motives: How infants begin to know language and skills of culture. In G. Jahoda and I. M. Lewis (eds.), *Acquiring culture: Ethnographic perspectives on cognitive development* (pp. 37–90). London: Croom Helm.

(1990). Signs before speech. In T. A. Sebeok and J. Umiker-Sebeok (eds.), *The semiotic web, 1989* (pp. 689–755). Berlin, New York, Amsterdam: Mouton de Gruyter.

(1992). An infant's motives for speaking and thinking in the culture. In A. H. Wold (ed.), *The dialogical alternative* (Festschrift for Ragnar Rommetveit). Oslo and Oxford: Scandanavian University Press/Oxford University Press.

(1993a). The function of emotions in early infant communication and development. In J. Nadel and L. Camaioni (eds.), *New perspectives in early communicative development* (pp. 48–81). London: Routledge.

(1993b). The self born in intersubjectivity: An infant communicating. In U. Neisser (ed.), *The perceived self: Ecological and interpersonal knowledge of the self* (pp. 121–73). New York: Cambridge University Press.

(1994). Infant semiosis. In W. Nöth (ed.), *Origins of semiosis* (pp. 219–52). Berlin: Mouton de Gruyter.

(1996). Lateral asymmetries in infancy: Implications for the development of the hemispheres. *Neuroscience and Biobehavioral Reviews*, 20, 571–86.

Trevarthen, C. and Aitken, K. J. (1994). Brain development, infant communication, and empathy disorders: Intrinsic factors in child mental health. *Development and Psychopathology*, 6, 599–635.

Trevarthen, C. and Hubley, P. (1978). Secondary intersubjectivity: Confidence, confiding and acts of meaning in the first year. In A. Lock (ed.), *Action, gesture and symbol: The emergence of language* (pp. 183–229). London: Academic Press.

Trevarthen, C., Murray, L. and Hubley, P. A. (1981). Psychology of infants. In J. Davis and J. Dobbing (eds.), *Scientific foundations of clinical paediatrics.* (2nd edn. pp. 211–74) London, Heinemann Medical.

Tronick, E. Z. (1982) (ed.). *Social interchange in infancy.* Baltimore: University Park Press.

(1989). Emotions and emotional communication in infants. *American Psychologist*, 44(2),112–26.

Tronick, E. Z., Als, H. and Brazelton, T. B. (1980). Monadic phases: A structural description analysis of infant–mother face-to-face interaction. *Merrill-Palmer Quarterly*, 26, 3–24.

Tronick, E. Z., Als, H., Adamson L., Wise, S. and Brazelton T. B. (1978). The infant's response to entrapment between contradictory messages in face-to face interaction. *Journal of the American Academy of Child Psychiatry*, 17, 1–13.

Tucker, D. M. (1991). Developing emotions and cortical networks. In M. Gunnar and C. Nelson (eds.), *Minnesota Symposium on Child Psychology, Vol. 24: Developmental Behavioral Neuroscience*. Hillsdale, NJ: Erlbaum.

Turner, F. and Pöppel, E. (1983). The neural lyre: Poetic meter, the brain and time. *Poetry*, August, 1983, 277. (Republished in Turner, F. (1985). *Natural classicism: Essays on literature and science*. New York: Paragon House.)

Turner, V. (1982). *From ritual to theatre: The human seriousness of play*. New York: Performing Arts Journal Publications.

Užgiris, I. Č. (1981). Two functions of imitation during infancy. *International Journal of Behavioral Development*, 4, 1–12.

   (1984). Imitation in infancy: Its interpersonal aspects. In M. Perlmutter (ed.), *Parent–child interaction and parent–child relations in child development*. The Minnesota Symposia on Child Psychology, vol. 17. Hillsdale, NJ: Erlbaum.

Van Rees, S. and de Leeuw, R. (1987). *Born too early: The kangaroo method with premature babies*. Video by Stichting Lichaamstaal, Scheyvenhofweg 12, 6092 NK, Leveroy, The Netherlands.

Vandell, D., Wilson, D. and Buchanan, N. (1980). Peer interaction in the first year of life: An examination of its structure, content and sensitivity to toys. *Child Development*, 51, 481–8.

Vinter, A. (1986). The role of movement in eliciting early imitations. *Child Development*, 57, 66–71.

Visalberghi, E., Fragaszy, D. M. and Savage-Rumbaugh, E. S. (1995). Performance in a tool-using task by common chimpanzees (*Pan troglodytes*), bonobos (*Pan paniscus*), an orang-utan (*Pongo pygmaeus*) and capuchin monkeys (*Cebus apella*). *Journal of Comparative Psychology*, 109, 52–60.

Von Hofsten, C. (1983a). Developmental changes in the organization of pre-reaching movements. *Developmental Psychology*, 20, 378–88.

   (1983b). Catching skills in infancy. *Journal of Experimental Psychology: Human Perception and Performance*, 9, 75–85.

Von Holst, E. and Mittelstaedt, H. (1950). Das Reafferenzprinzip. *Naturwissenschaften*, 37, 256–72.

Vygotsky, L. S. (1967). Play and its role in the mental development of the child. *Soviet Psychology*, 5(3), 6–18.

Wallon, H. (1928). La maladresse. *Journal de Psychologie, Janvier 1928*, 61–78. (Republished in *Enfance*, 1959, Nos. 3–4, 264–78).

   (1970). *Les origines du caractère chez l'enfant*. 4th edn. Paris: Presses Universitaires de France. (Originally published 1934.)

Watson, J. B. (1908). Imitation in monkeys. *Psychological Bulletin*, 5(6): 169–178.

Weinberg, M. K. and Tronick, E. Z. (1994). Beyond the face: An empirical study of infant affective configurations of facial, vocal, gestural and regulatory behaviors. *Child Development*, 65, 1503–15.

(1996). Infant affective reactions to the resumption of maternal interaction after the still-face. *Child Development*, 67, 905–14.

White, D. G. and Wollett, E. A. (1987). The father's role in the neonatal period. In D. Harvey (ed.), *Parent–infant relationships*. New York: John Wiley & Sons Ltd.

Whiten, A. and Byrne, R. W. (eds.) (1997). *Machiavellian intelligence: Evaluations and extensions*. Oxford University Press.

Zazzo, R. (1957). Le problème de l'imitation chez le nouveau-né. *Enfance*, 10, 135–42.

(1993). *Reflets de miroir et autres doubles*. Paris: Presses Universitaires de France.

6 Imitation as activity: its developmental aspects

Ina Č. Užgiris

The study of imitation has a long history in psychology (see Aronfreed, 1969; Nadel, 1986; Scheerer, 1985; Užgiris, 1979). Throughout this history, there has been a tension between those looking at imitation mainly as an individual mental ability or disposition and those linking imitation primarily with social life, with the position in ascendancy shifting more than once. In recent decades, interest in the social–communicative aspects of imitation has again gained prominence. But implicit in this tension is also a difference in focus on the internal or external aspects of imitation, the mental processes involved versus overtly manifest conduct. A growing appreciation of the embodiment of mental life (e.g., Butterworth, 1994) suggests that conceptualising imitation as a form of activity may provide a way to integrate some of the divergent perspectives on imitation and to formulate new questions about its role in the course of development.

The concept of activity is usually associated with a tradition in Soviet psychology (Leont´ev, Luria, Vygotsky) and its recent elaborations within the sociocultural approach (e.g., Wertsch, del Rio and Alvarez, 1995), although a number of other theoretical currents have also encouraged acceptance of the concept of action for analysing how people engage with the world and each other (e.g., Bruner, 1986). An aim of this chapter is to look at imitation from the perspective of activity theory and to examine what has been learned in empirical work about imitation during infancy in terms of characteristics that are considered with respect to actions. This leads, minimally, to the inclusion of questions about motives, goals, the effect of conditions on specific acts of imitation, and the role of meaning in structuring imitation. Moreover, taking imitation action as a unit for analysis also adds to the kind of questions that need to be considered in empirical research.

A second aim of this chapter is to view imitation developmentally, that is, to examine changes in imitation with respect to a certain directionality. A developmental perspective considers both continuities and transformations, claiming that a fuller understanding is gained by locating specific functioning within a developmental trajectory. The directionality indicates which aspects of imitation actions are important to note and to examine. Probably the best-known developmental view of imitation is that of Piaget (1945/1962), but transformations in imitation have been suggested by other theorists as well. Selected studies on infant imitation will be reviewed for a picture of both continuities and transformations in imitation as the child develops. Although longitudinal studies are still relatively few, consideration of imitation with respect to a longer time-span helps to highlight the changes that imitation as action may undergo in development.

Finally, once imitation is viewed as action, it becomes evident that the cultural embeddedness of imitation has to be considered. Being largely interpersonal in nature, imitation is subject to cultural formation even in infancy. With respect to imitation, as with respect to most phenomena considered by psychology, an awareness of the cultural meanings for imitation will enrich our understanding of its developmental course and its functions.

In the first section of the chapter, some theoretical ideas from activity theory, Piaget's developmental perspective and my own interpersonal approach to imitation will be briefly presented. The notion of action will be discussed in order to facilitate an examination of recent empirical studies of imitation from an action perspective. A developmental trajectory for imitation will be outlined, based largely on Piaget's conception of development in imitation. Moreover, the implications of recognising the interpersonal nature of imitation will be reviewed. In the next section of the chapter, some selected empirical studies on infant imitation will be examined in terms of the concepts highlighted in the first section. The chapter concludes with a discussion of imitation as a culturally situated activity.

Theoretical perspectives on imitation

Because of its extended history, there have been numerous interpretations of the phenomenon of imitation. In empirical studies, similar operational criteria are generally used to identify instances of imitation: a recognisable similarity between the acts of two persons is attributed to imitation if the match does not seem explainable on some other basis. In contrast, there is not much theoretical agreement about the processes involved in leading to the match. The review that follows is not comprehensive, but is directed toward a presentation of a few conceptions that will be used in the subsequent examination of recent empirical work on imitation.

Activity theory

At a very basic level, concern with action focuses attention on persons as agents, as motivated beings seeking to attain particular outcomes through their conduct and taking into consideration the means available in the situation. Action is thus contrasted to movement (e.g., reaching versus arm motion) and to being passively subjected to some occurrence (e.g., stepping into a shower versus being caught in a burst of rain). Obviously, there are many fine points about action to be argued by philosophers, but a focus on action provides a distinct lens for viewing the multiformity of human engagement with each other and the world.

A specific approach to examining activity was proposed by Leont'ev and his followers (see Wertsch, 1981). It suggested that human conduct has to be analysed at different levels. Activity is taken as the highest-order concept, defined in terms of motives that remain in force over long periods of time, although they are not necessarily innate and may vary in the course of life. Labour has been viewed as the prototypical human activity and analysed in terms of its social organisation during different historical periods, but other spheres of endeavour sustained by broad need/motive complexes have been also discussed as activities (Glassman, 1996). Such broad motives as wanting social contact, wanting to acquire knowledge, or wanting to relax and have fun gain specificity when operating towards concrete objects in a historical time and place.

Analysis of ontogenetic changes has contributed to the acknowledgment of spheres of activity besides labour (e.g., play or learning). The concept of dominant or leading activity has been proposed as a way to delineate important developmental periods. El'konin (1972) has suggested that establishing emotional contact with adults is the dominant activity in early infancy, followed by instrumental mastery of objects and then by socially constituted use of objects. However, '[w]hen a new activity becomes dominant, it does not cancel all previously existing activities: it merely alters their status within the overall system of relations between the child and his [her] surroundings' (p. 247). This suggests that an infant or child may engage in one of several activities at any given time and the relations between them could be a topic for study.

The next level concept is that of action, delineating the goal-directed undertakings that people pursue. Activities are carried out through actions that have more specific and shorter-range goals. Moreover, similar actions may be part of several different activities. In Leont'ev's system, actions are instantiated in terms of specific operations, that is, means that are appropriate, available, or chosen by an actor. The cultural situatedness of actions derives not only from their inclusion in activities linked to the larger social structure, but also from their instantiation in a concrete context as construed by an actor.

In analysing actions, Leont´ev and his colleagues have placed greater emphasis on the material tools available to members of a society and, thus, gave their conception a more materialistic tone. In contrast, the discussion of cultural tools that has been stimulated by Vygotsky's (1978) writings has been more attentive to language and cultural meanings involved in action (e.g., Wertsch, 1995) and has had a greater impact on the sociocultural approach currently being elaborated. Both similarities and differences between these two strands of the theory of activity have been adeptly explicated by Zinchenko (1995). In the case of both strands, however, the essential part played by society in shaping human action has been given theoretical prominence.

In order to facilitate discussion of infant conduct in controlled settings, the term act will be used to refer to units that may or may not qualify as operational instantiations of actions. The aim of using this term is to assert the organised nature of even the earliest infant conduct and to suggest the desirability of linking it to goal-directed action. An illustration is given to indicate how the activity theory perspective might be applied to organise observations of infant conduct.

If learning through exploration (motive) and the experience of new sights and sounds (object) is taken as an activity of infants and young children, then the actions of throwing small objects (with the goal of seeing what happens) or approaching interacting adults (with the goal of being able to observe what they are about) may be viewed as constituents of the activity, being carried out by different means and in different manners depending on a specific context in the culturally structured world of the infant. Considered as acts, the throwing of utensils, toys or other objects by infants would be viewed in relation to the availability of such objects in different settings and to the meaning given to such throwing acts by the cultural group. Thus, the frequency with which infants engage in particular acts would be expected to depend not only on their ability and goals, but also on the meaning of these acts in specific situations.

In work guided by activity theory, even though the importance of the sociocultural context is highlighted, its operation is treated at a rather global level. The interactions through which cultural understandings are made evident to young children and the means through which they are maintained in the social group are not often examined in step-by-step detail. The child is positioned in relation to the social group as a whole rather than to concrete encounters with other persons, whose acts embody the relevant cultural understandings. Language and verbal interactions are given a major role, but even the verbal structuring of acts is more often assumed than substantiated. Thus, the formation of actions by preverbal infants remains largely unexamined (but see Lisina, 1985; Rogoff, Mistry, Goncü and Mosier, 1993). The tacit structuring of inter-personal actions by the adult partner together with the infant needs to be considered in order to gain a fuller picture of infant functioning during interactions with others.

Similarly, presentations of activity theory strongly emphasise the importance of developmental (genetic) analysis for understanding all phenomena, but empirical work from this perspective has dealt as much with historical development and microgenetic analyses as with develop-ment during ontogenesis. Consequently, Piaget's developmental theory will be used as the framework for examining imitation developmentally.

Piaget's theory

In analysing psychological functioning, Piaget considered the origins of various competencies, the directionality of changes in those competen-cies, and the continuity that may persist through the observed changes and transformations of those competencies. Speaking in very global terms, it can be said that Piaget generally posited the origins of competen-cies in sensorimotor functioning, described the changes in structural or organizational terms, and derived the continuity from processes and functional invariants. The developmental direction was towards greater mental (internal) activity, reflectivity and equilibration of increasingly complex and integrated cognitive structures.

The phenomenon of imitation was taken up by Piaget in relation to a broader analysis of cognitive development, with a particular concern for the achievement of symbolic functioning. Piaget sought the origins of imitation in sensorimotor functioning and linked imitation specifically to the process of accommodation of the assimilatory schemes. Although for observational purposes Piaget defined imitation as 'the act by which a model is reproduced' (Piaget, 1945/1962, p. 6), his conceptual analysis was focused on cognitive activity, which need not always include overt imitation. 'Imitation is thus seen to be merely a continuation of the effort at accommodation, closely connected with the act of intelligence, of which it is one differentiated aspect, a temporarily detached part' (Piaget, 1945/1962, p. 5). In this way, Piaget avoided claiming that imitation as such is an innate tendency, as well as that 'true imitation' appears at some particular point in development, as was done by Baldwin (1895) and Guillaume (1926/1971). Although Piaget observed definite changes in his children's imitations during the first 2 years of life, he linked them together through the accommodation function.

Thus, the factors of the familiarity of the acts modelled and of the internality of the child's attempts to reproduce the modelled acts were central for Piaget's developmental trajectory. As the infant's schemes become more varied and the process of accommodation becomes more differentiated from assimilation, more novel and complex models come to be imitated by the child. Similarly, as the child's schemes become more varied and integrated, the accommodation to an observed model can be carried out covertly and the reproduction can take place at a later time, without an overt instigation. The trajectory of imitation is toward its interiorisation as a mental process, although it remains capable of organising overt reproductions of observed models as well.

The six stages in sensorimotor functioning were used by Piaget as a framework to structure the developmental course in imitation as well. Major junctures in this course are the firmer differentiation of accommodation from assimilation at stage IV, enabling the infant to proceed to imitate some novel acts, and the interiorisation of accommodation at stage VI, starting the formation of mental symbols and enabling the infant to imitate presently absent models even without prior overt imitation.

Piaget also addressed the issue of the motive for children's imitation. He tied it to interest arising from an incomplete assimilation of an observed model. 'The interest thus appears to come from a kind of conflict between the partial resemblance which makes the child want to assimilate, and the partial difference which attracts his attention the more because it is an obstacle to immediate reproduction. It is therefore this twofold character of resemblance and opposition which seems to be the incentive for imitation' (Piaget, 1945/1962, p. 51). The motive, thus, is a cognitive one, grounded in the nature of the child's meaning-giving schemes.

Because Piaget considered imitation primarily in relation to the development of symbolic functioning, he had little to say about overt imitation beyond the sensorimotor period. It is possible to extrapolate that, for Piaget, overt imitation would continue to serve cognitive understanding by facilitating accommodation to somewhat discrepant events. But the relation of a child's other goals to the goal of better understanding with respect to overt imitation and the broader situatedness of imitative acts are not addressed by Piaget's theory.

An interpersonal perspective

An interpersonal perspective highlights the engagement of individuals with each other as persons, as actors sharing or potentially sharing an understanding of their actions and the situation in which they are engaged. In addition, it emphasises the joint construction of ongoing interchanges by the participants and the centrality of communication in this construction. When the participants are an infant and an adult, the contribution of the two participants is not equal, but their joint engagement has the characteristics of interpersonal interaction.

Athough descriptions of imitation by infants and children usually consist of their responses to an adult modelling gestures, vocalisations or acts with objects, analyses of imitation have traditionally focused on the acts of the individual child. Piaget's descriptions are no exception; he sometimes even alludes to his different relationships with his three children, but characteristics of relationships do not have a fundamental place in his conception of development in imitation. In contrast, Wallon (1934) linked imitation to the development of an awareness of self and the goal of social interaction with others. Wallon's ideas, however, have not influenced the empirical work on infant imitation except in the French-speaking world (e.g., Nadel-Brulfert and Baudonnière, 1982; Nadel, 1986). This social–communicative function of imitation has come to be explicitly recognized only fairly recently.

My studies of infant imitation convinced me that even in relatively controlled settings, imitative acts have not only a cognitive function, but also a social–communicative function (Užgiris, 1981). We found that even when tasks required only minimal accommodation, infants continued to imitate and maintain a dialogic interaction with the experimenter (Killen and Užgiris, 1981). Observational studies of mother–infant interaction also confirmed the presence of imitative interchanges between mothers and their preverbal infants. Thus, imitation needs to be recognised not only as serving cognitive understanding, but also as being a component of the child's social life.

From an interpersonal perspective, imitation is treated as a form of social engagement, extending in time, consisting of acts by both mutually influencing partners, and carrying meaning within the interaction. If imitations between an infant and an adult are taken as prototypical, one can say that they serve to establish a mutually constructed, shared world between the participants and to bring the culturally constituted world known to the adult into the infant's experience.

An interpersonal view highlights several characteristics of imitation (Užgiris, 1984, 1990). First, imitation is seen to be bidirectional. The act of imitation can be observed by both participants, and the model is potentially influenced by the observer's acts at the same time as the observer is influenced by the model's acts. If the interaction continues, the model may become the imitator, as the roles are reversed. Through the very shifting of roles, reciprocity is introduced into the interaction. Second, in the context of interpersonal engagement, imitative acts are relevant to the ongoing interaction. The acts that are modelled and imitated are not arbitrary, but are related to the interests and goals of the partners. Moreover, by being selective, imitation can give a certain emphasis and direction to the interaction. Selectivity may work not only in terms of the acts of the other that are picked up for imitation, but also in terms of the specific aspects of complex acts that are included in the imitation.

The interpersonal perspective also provides an avenue for bringing the cultural dimension into considerations of imitation. Not only is the pattern of interactions with infants structured by culture, but the meaning given to specific infant acts is formed in relation to cultural expectations. Moreover, the objects that are introduced into the interactions and around which many modelling-imitation sequences are built are usually cultural artifacts and embody culturally meaningful possibilities. The way imitation is included in social interactions and the meanings that are given to imitative acts in different settings can be expected to result in the cultural formation of imitation itself.

Recognition of the social-communicative function of imitation makes it interesting to examine imitation from the perspective of activity theory. This perspective brings into central stage questions about motives for imitation, the goals of imitation actions and the interplay between children's available means to carry out actions and their use of imitation. The activity theory perspective also suggests an examination of imitation in terms of a developmental trajectory, ranging from its origins through its transformation in relation to other competencies. Piaget's focus on only the cognitive function of imitation yields a description of the developmental trajectory (toward symbolic functioning) that appears incomplete, but its origin in sensorimotor functioning is a starting-point for looking at imitation as situated activity.

A selective review of imitation research

Data about imitation during infancy is provided by both experimental and observational studies. Although all studies ultimately use a coder's judgment to identify instances where an infant's act resembles the model's act enough to be called a match, the experimental studies usually include some check on the likelihood that the infant would have acted in the same way even without the model being present (baseline or different-model controls). In contrast, observational studies usually make a more intuitive evaluation that the infant's act is related to the model's, relying on the temporal contiguity of the two matching acts as well as other features of the interaction (e.g., attentiveness) to make a judgment of imitation. Studies viewing imitation interactively tend to be observational and to code the acts of both participants.

It might be noted that experimental studies generally report very low rates of modelled acts in the control conditions, suggesting that data from studies without such controls can be treated as reliable. Clearly, concern with different kinds of questions has led investigators to favour either observational or experimental methods.

It is important to note that controlled studies of imitative acts and observational studies of naturally occurring interactions yield different kinds of data. The controlled studies give information about what an infant does when the situation is purposefully designed to enhance the likelihood of an imitative act. Whether one concludes that the imitation ability is the infant's or the infant's in conjunction with the researcher's arrangements is a matter of theoretical orientation. In contrast, data from observational studies tell more about what typically happens in settings deemed appropriate for infant–adult social interaction. Activity theory would recognise the situational embeddedness of imitation in studies applying either method. It would prompt questions about what goals acting to imitate serves and when imitating others may become goals in themselves, rather than about the capability to perform one or another act.

A review of some empirical studies of imitation in infancy will be organised around three topics: the origin of imitation and age-related trends; the goals of imitation actions; and the motives forming imitation activity. The review of studies is not comprehensive and serves mainly to illustrate the conceptual issues being raised.

Origins and trajectory

The question about the origins of imitation has motivated studies of very young infants in an attempt to ascertain whether imitation is an innately given ability. The answer, however, has not been based purely on empirical data; it has hinged as much on the investigator's conception of imitation.

Observations of very young infants seemingly performing acts of imitation can be found in a number of early studies (e.g., Valentine, 1930; Zazzo, 1957); even Piaget (1945/1962) noted vocal contagion during the first week of life. The interpretations of these observations, however, have tended to cast them as some sort of pseudo-imitation, due to some other process than the one assumed to support genuine acts of imitation. Thus, for Piaget, early matches of a familiar modelled act are an enhancement of circular activity, because accommodation is said not to be differentiated from assimilation in the early stages. Piaget (1945/1962) concludes that 'imitation is learnt' (p. 80), although not at some concrete moment, but through continuous sensorimotor activity, as initial schemes integrate new elements, become differentiated, and enhance the accommodation function.

Several more recent studies have documented the reproduction of a number of gestures by neonates and very young infants (e.g., Fontaine, 1984; Maratos, 1973; Meltzoff and Moore, 1977; 1983; Vinter, 1985) in fairly controlled or highly structured experimental situations. Although these results have received various interpretations, Meltzoff and Moore (1983) concluded that the ability to imitate is part of the biological endowment of normal children at birth. They focused on imitation as a behavioural phenomenon, and, noting its presence, searched for processes to account for it, relating it to the capacity for amodal representation. Their stance leads to an adevelopmental conception of imitation, favouring questions about individual differences in imitation ability or disposition rather than questions about a developmental trajectory for imitation itself.

The occurrence of imitative acts also has been reported in observational studies of adult interaction with young infants (e.g., Papoušek and Papoušek, 1977; Trevarthen, 1977; Užgiris, 1984). These imitations were taken to indicate the social engagement of the participants and were noted to be a small proportion of the total interaction. Moreover, it was consistently found that imitations by the adult (the mother) are more frequent than such acts by the infant. These types of observations have been given in support of the social–communicative function of imitation in addition to the accommodative function emphasised by Piaget. They also lend support to the treatment of imitation as an interpersonal phenomenon rather than as an individual capability or disposition. Viewed interpersonally, the unit to be analysed is the back-and-forth interchange, not the act of one person; as the interchange is mutually formed, its goal also need not be individually assigned to each participant (Užgiris, 1989).

In spite of the differing interpretations regarding a developmental course for imitation, the empirical research on age-related trends during the first two years of life is fairly consistent. As infants become older, they imitate a greater variety of acts, acts of more complex structure, and attain closer reproductions of the model's acts in imitation tasks (e.g., Abravanel, Levan-Goldschmidt and Stevenson, 1976; McCall, Parke and Kavanaugh, 1977; Rodgon and Kurdek, 1977; Užgiris, 1972). These studies generally support the expectation that cognitive development would lead infants to find a greater variety of models within their accommodation range, promoting imitation. They do not begin to account for differences in responsivity to specific models or trends over shorter periods of time.

For example, the trend in vocal imitation is not exactly parallel to imitation of gestures or acts with objects, although few studies have examined imitation of both types of models by the same infants (but see Masur, 1993). In vocal imitation, infant responsivity seems to increase fairly linearly and follow the trajectory toward imitation of more novel models and with less overt approximation, as Piaget's theory suggests. In contrast, the trend in gestural imitation is less straightforward. A number of studies report that, during the first 6 months of life, imitation of some models increases, while imitation of others decreases or remains level (e.g., Fontaine, 1984; Maratos, 1982; Vinter, 1985). In the second half of the first year, imitation of specific acts seems to depend on various characteristics of the acts modelled (e.g., gestures versus acts with objects). The complexity of acts and their content contributes to the likelihood of imitation during the second year of life. Even the recent studies of deferred imitation report a greater facility with such tasks in the second year of life (Barr, Dowden and Hayne, 1996; Meltzoff, 1985, 1988). These kinds of findings indicate that at the level of acts, imitation is greatly affected by the specifics of the situation and the meaning that the modelled acts have for the infant.

Observations of imitation during interactions with an adult (the mother) suggest a trend toward greater frequency and reciprocity in imitative interchanges. We found that within the first year of life, infants increasingly imitated their mothers' acts and the mothers continued to imitate their infants' acts, resulting in an overall rise of imitative interchanges and a greater reciprocity between the partners (Užgiris, 1984; Užgiris, Benson, Kruper and Vasek, 1989). Moreover, some of these interchanges consisted of more than one turn for each partner, suggesting a differentiation of their structure. Pawlby (1977) also found an increase in the frequency of imitations during free play between infants and their mothers and a greater tendency to engage in vocal imitations towards the end of the first year. From the middle of the first year, parent–infant games often include imitative turns and speak to the inclusion of imitation in a greater variety of social actions with older infants.

These age-related changes in the occurrence of imitative acts have several implications. First, if imitation is an innate capability present at birth, a great deal of work remains to be done to account for the jagged trajectory of imitative acts during infancy. Second, if imitation at the level of acts appears to be so situation-dependent, examination of imitation within a framework of goals may yield a more cohesive developmental picture. Third, a consideration of imitation in relation to the functional organisation of children's activity may be more useful than the traditional separation of studies into experimental and observational.

Goals of imitation

At the level of empirical investigation, very few studies can be stretched to say something about the goal of imitation actions. Studies that have looked at imitation of acts with and without objects and those that varied the interaction context yield some tentative suggestions.

Some imitation actions seem to have the goal of exploring events that appear interesting to the infant. From the second half of the first year, infants are reported to imitate acts performed with objects more readily than acts performed as gestures. For example, Abravanel et al. (1976) found that infants imitated relatively novel acts performed with objects, but not acts without objects during the second year of life. In one of our studies, we found that infants imitated modelled acts when they were done with an object (e.g., striking a bell), but hardly at all when the same act (i.e., striking) was modelled as a gesture (Užgiris, 1979). It may be possible to explain such findings in terms of Guillaume's (1926/1971) claim about the motivating role of interesting effects or Piaget's (1945/1962) ideas about imitation as an effort to accommodate incompletely understood events.

However, the significantly different imitation of specific acts led us to consider the meaningfulness of the act to the infant as the main factor. In a different study (Killen and Užgiris, 1981), we performed the same gesture with a socially appropriate object (e.g., drinking from a cup) and with an inappropriate object (e.g., drinking from a car). In both instances, the act was performed with an object and had some outcome. Even infants in the youngest group (10 months old) imitated acts with the appropriate objects, but only the oldest group of infants (22 months old) reliably imitated the acts with inappropriate objects, although even the younger infants showed an appreciation for the two kinds of acts through their demeanour. This suggests that the infants' goals in imitating the two types of acts may have been different, with the goal of exploration of an unusual possibility evident in the imitation of acts with incongruous objects.

The clearest examples of imitation serving the goal of mastery come from instances where a child goes through several overt attempts to match the model's act. Piaget (1945/1962) described a number of such episodes, especially ones where the infant was attempting to imitate a new model. For example, he describes how L. imitated the act of hitting oneself on the stomach by first clapping her hands (to make the sound) and then patting her stomach (p. 54, obs. 42). Similar approximations occurred in imitating new sounds (obs. 41). This kind of effort to gradually match a model has been informally noted by a number of investigators, but it is rarely a part of empirical coding plans. Even when partial imitations are coded, they are usually included in one quantified score, without attention to any progressivity in matching over successive attempts. However, this kind of effortful approximation has not been reported during ongoing interpersonal interactions. It may be that the structure of interpersonal engagement does not support the goal of exploring what is happening in the same way (through imitation), because it would disrupt the co-ordination with the interaction partner.

Piaget has also reported several instances of young infants seemingly imitating in order to cause the repetition of an event. For example, in the middle of the first year, J. imitated her mother's hand movement in order to get her mother to beat a quilt (Piaget, 1937/1954, p. 250, obs. 137). These kind of instances may say more about the child's limited understanding of causality than about the goals of imitation, but they do illustrate the general goal-directedness of imitations. Even older children, when they do not quite understand the causal mechanism for an event may imitate some irrelevant acts when trying to reproduce the event, but stop imitating them once they grasp its cause (Sibulkin and Užgiris, 1978). Moreover, from a very broad perspective, the ritual enactment of events in anticipation of causing them to happen speaks to causation as being a possible goal of imitation actions.

Imitation occurring during early interpersonal interactions seems to have a very simple goal: to be in accord, agreement or shared feeling with the other. Although most adults do not set out consciously to imitate their partners when they interact with young infants, they do recognise a 'shared togetherness' in the imitation episodes. This may explain the preponderance of one-round imitations during these early interactions (Užgiris, 1984). In contrast, imitations occurring during interactions with older infants seem to be more conscious and strategic, and may test the partner's responsivity through variations on specific acts. These later imitations may have a game-like quality of variation on a theme known to both partners. Infant appreciation of the fact that they are being imitated by an adult has been demonstrated in experimental studies as well (Eckerman and Stein, 1990; Meltzoff, 1990).

Imitation may also serve the goal of empathic understanding, but it seems unlikely to be a conscious goal in those situations. Interpersonal interactions with young infants include affective matching as well as attunement (Stern, 1985), and imitation of facial expressions by very young infants has been reported (Field, Woodson, Greenberg and Cohen, 1982; Field, Woodson, Cohen, Greenberg, Garcia and Collins, 1983). Adults match not only facial expressions, but body postures and the muscular tone of others in what has been called emotional contagion (Hatfield, Cacioppo and Rapson, 1994). Hoffman (1984, 1990) has proposed that early imitations constitute the developmental origins of later empathic understanding. Moreover, we have found that 1-year-old infants who engage in more affective imitation with their mothers seem to better grasp the expressions of others; they tend to respond more with congruent expressions to sad and happy affective displays (Lacks and Užgiris, 1995).

In sum, observational studies suggest that infants may have several goals for imitating the actions they observe. In experimental studies, the goals of the infant have not been explicitly considered. It may be enlightening to make the goals of imitation more evident in experimental studies as well and to attend to their effect on the occurrence of imitation.

Motives for imitation

The two broad functions of imitation already discussed can be considered to be the main motives that organise imitation activity. Cognitively motivated imitation activity seems to be more closely aligned with the developmental trajectory proposed by Piaget, making imitation less overtly evident in cognitive endeavours after infancy, except where overt matching is specifically encouraged. In contrast, imitation activity with a social–communicative motive may have a less evident developmental trajectory, but vary more in relation to other means available for communicative interaction. As children's repertoires of skills increase, imitation still remains evident in their social interactions throughout infancy and early childhood.

Piaget's observations provide support for cognitively motivated imitation in infancy. Among the most salient examples are attempts based on the use of analogy; in one sense they are errors, but they also demonstrate a search for understanding. Piaget (1945/1962) has described a number of episodes where attempts at reproduction start with an analogous act (e.g., closing and opening the hand to a modelling of eye blinking; p. 36, obs. 25) and eventually reproduce what has been modelled. The instance of L. opening and closing her mouth while attempting to find a solution to the problem of getting a chain out of a box through a narrow opening (p. 65, obs. 57) has become widely cited. This kind of action bridges the reproduction of models by analogy and the reproduction of whole problem situations. An example of the latter is J.'s behaviour upon getting the legs of a doll caught in the neck of her dress (p. 65, obs. 56). Upon managing to extricate the doll, she immediately tried to recreate the problem in order to attempt its solution again. The reproduction of fortuitous problem solutions may be observed among older children as well, but, as Piaget's interest was in linking imitation to the development of symbolic functioning, he did not investigate cognitively motivated imitation much past infancy.

At the level of themes and scenarios, but not at the level of simple acts, the symbolic play of young children might be examined for elements of a search for understanding through reproduction of certain events. Moreover, the search for analogies and the making of symbolic models for phenomena that are not well understood seem to be readily recognisable adult modes of thinking. These kind of extensions of cognitively motivated imitation activity are not usually linked to the simple, overt imitations of infants.

Imitation activity with a social–communicative motive has been recognised not only during the interactions between young infants and their partners, but also during peer interactions in early childhood. Coordination of joint play among young peers seems to rely a great deal on communication achieved through imitation. Nadel (1986; Nadel-Brulfert and Baudonnière, 1982) has described how the availability of opportunities for imitation enhances social engagement during peer play. Similarly, studies by Eckerman (1993; Eckerman, Davis and Didow, 1989) and her colleagues show the communicative function of imitation and its gradual integration with early verbal communication. In peer interactions, imitation continues to communicate affiliation and fellowship (Grusec and Abramowitch, 1982), but becomes embedded within other activities.

Although these two motives may seem to structure activity in different contexts (solitary versus social), they may come together during apprenticeship or tutoring interactions. These joint learning interactions include imitation to gain understanding of the task at hand, but, being interpersonal, they also depend on social co-ordination and mutual appreciation of the efforts by each partner. Thus, the demonstrations and reproductions involved in such activity may intertwine the two motives for imitation.

Imitation, as a conscious activity, clearly becomes situation-bound and linked with its cultural valuation. Thus, the role of imitation activity among other types of activities during the childhood years needs to be considered in relation to the cultural understanding and valuation of imitation.

The cultural embeddedness of imitation

At the level of acts, imitation is probably observable among the most varied cultural groups. However, the meaning given to imitative acts of infants and young children and to imitations of older children and adults can be expected to differ greatly. There are not many systematic observations of imitation that take its cultural situatedness into account. A few reports may be pointed to, however, in order to highlight the need for research that would take the cultural understanding of imitation into account.

The possibility has been raised that the imitation embedded in interactions with young infants may depend on a symmetrical view of adult–child relationships (Ochs and Schieffelin, 1984). If imitative acts signify mutuality and reciprocity, they would not be expected during communicative interactions between persons considered to have a different status. However, imitative acts for achieving a goal specified by an older person may still occur. For example, although Kaluli adults do not engage infants as communication partners, they explicitly invoke imitation as a technique for infants to learn acceptable conversational routines. Interaction routines with young children that specifically request imitation by the child have been reported for other groups as well (e.g., Watson-Gegeo and Gegeo, 1986). In such instances, imitation is organised to serve a cognitive function, but its very explicit structuring negates the shared mutuality that imitation seems to communicate among these cultural groups.

In the western world, imitation activity is not much valued as a learning technique in most settings. There are numerous negative terms applied to imitation (aping, mimicry), suggesting the unfavourable attitude toward the reproduction of the acts of others rather than finding one's own solutions. Demonstration and observation are not much favoured as modes of interaction when the goal is increased understanding by at least one of the participants, except when this happens informally, without much reflection. In contrast, it has been reported that, in many cultural groups, observation and reproduction of what has been observed are favoured as modes for teaching and learning (Whiting and Edwards, 1988).

Although few in number, observations from other cultural groups point to two important dimensions of imitation. As a reflected and conscious activity, imitation becomes circumscribed to certain settings or status groups (e.g., young children) and is structured by the valuation attached to such activity. As such, it functions in mainly cognitive endeavours to increase understanding and skills as well as in social interactions to structure relationships between participants. But imitation as a conscious activity probably does not account for many imitative acts. Little is known about the effect of conscious valuation and unreflected imitation on each other in the course of development.

The social–cognitive interplay during imitation activity is not much explored in the literature looking at other cultural groups. Although our current views distinguish the cognitive and social functions of imitation, from an interpersonal perspective, it would seem that the two functions are always intertwined, with one being more dominant or more conscious. Given different cultural valuations of imitation activity, it is clear that the larger framework for imitative acts needs to be considered in order to better understand the place of imitation in human interactions.

Concluding comments

It has been suggested throughout the chapter that activity theory may help to conceptualise imitation as a phenomenon in human life and to organise the diverse literatures on imitation. The theory suggests that imitation may be viewed at the level of acts, as they make up the operational instantiation of actions, at the level of actions, and at the level of activities.

Most empirical studies of imitation approach the phenomenon at the level of acts, where the effect of conditions on the occurrence of imitation are examined. In these types of studies, large individual differences in the amount of imitation are typically reported even among infants at a similar developmental level. It seems possible that at least some of these individual differences are due to variation in the goals of the participants or in the meaning attached to imitation. If imitative acts are viewed as constituents of goal-directed actions, then they need to be examined in relation to other options available for that situation. Moreover, this implies that the effect of situational variables (presence of objects, possibility of a clear effect, mode of modelling) may also need to be considered in relation to the goal of the whole action.

Because imitation is fundamentally interpersonal, it can be expected that the cultural valuations of imitation would begin to influence reliance on imitative acts even in infancy. These valuations may be specific to the age or status of the participants. Thus, analyses going beyond the level of acts would also help to understand the course of imitation in ontogenesis.

At the level of actions, imitation is related to the goals of the participants and the possibilities for meeting them. Imitation actions may depend a great deal on what the complement of actions possible for the participants is. Adults clearly have more varied possibilities for action than children, and the seemingly greater prevalence of imitation among infants and young children may reflect their narrower range of possibil-

ities. In social interactions, the congruence of goals between the participants may be a requirement for imitation to be a possible action. From
this perspective, the level of action may be the most productive level of
analysis for further research on imitation.

Viewed as activity, imitation seems to have two major functions, the
cognitive and the communicative. At this level, the cultural meaning of
imitation is clearly central in determining whether it becomes a recognised and encouraged activity, or is submerged within other culturally
valued pursuits. Even so, imitation as activity does not seem to be prevalent and is practised only in very specific contexts.

In social interactions, considerable imitation seems to be tacit and not
consciously recognised, until some specific set of conditions makes the
choice of imitation actions the conscious means for reaching a desired
goal. One can speculate that among groups that are less individualistic in
their value orientations and more inclined toward conservation of existing ways, imitation activity may more often have a conscious and well-
defined place.

An individualistic and cognitive orientation to the study of imitation in
infancy tends to consider imitation in relation to the picking up of minor
novelties in instances where other means for doing so may not be
effective. It is suggested that a more encompassing view of imitation as a
motivated and goal-directed pattern of action pursued within a cultural
meaning system would help to construct a fuller developmental picture.
Imitation in infancy would not be treated as an isolated ability, but would
be linked with the developmental trajectory of various culturally embedded competencies constructed in interaction with others.

ACKNOWLEDGMENTS

My thanks go to Catherine Raeff, Julia Lacks and Jim Wertsch for their helpful
comments on an earlier version of this chapter.

REFERENCES

Abravanel, E., Levan-Goldschmidt, E. and Stevenson, M. B. (1976). Action
    imitation: The early phase of infancy. *Child Development*, 47, 1032–44.
Aronfreed, J. (1969). The problem of imitation. In L. P. Lipsitt and H. W. Reese
    (eds.), *Advances in child development and behavior* (vol. 4, pp. 209–319). New
    York: Academic Press.
Baldwin, J. M. (1895). *Mental development in the child and the race*. New York:
    Macmillan.
Barr, R., Dowden, A. and Hayne, H. (1996). Developmental changes in deferred
    imitation by 6- to 24-month old infants. *Infant Behavior and Development*, 19,
    159–70.

Bruner, J. (1986). *Actual minds, possible worlds*. Cambridge, MA: Harvard University Press.

Butterworth, G. (1994). Theory of mind and the facts of embodiment. In C. Lewis and P. Mitchell (eds.), *Children's early understanding of mind* (pp. 115–32). Hillsdale, NJ: Erlbaum.

Eckerman, C. O. (1993). Imitation and toddlers' achievement of co-ordinated action with others. In J. Nadel and L. Camaioni (eds.), *New perspectives in early communicative development* (pp. 116–38). London: Routledge.

Eckerman, C. O., Davis, C. C. and Didow, S. M. (1989). Toddlers' emerging ways of achieving social coordination with a peer. *Child Development*, 60, 440–53.

Eckerman, C. O. and Stein, M. R. (1990). How imitation begets imitation and toddlers' generation of games. *Developmental Psychology*, 26, 370–8.

El´konin, D. B. (1972). Toward the problem of stages in the mental development of the child. *Soviet Psychology*, 10, 225–51.

Field, T. M., Woodson, R., Cohen, D., Greenberg, R., Garcia, R. and Collins, K. (1983). Discrimination and imitation of facial expressions by term and preterm neonates. *Infant Behavior and Development*, 6, 485–9.

Field, T., Woodson, R., Greenberg, R. and Cohen, D. (1982). Discrimination and imitation of facial expressions by neonates. *Science*, 218, 179–81.

Fontaine, R. (1984). Imitative skills between birth and six months. *Infant Behavior and Development*, 7, 323–33.

Glassman, M. (1996). Understanding Vygotsky's motive and goal: An exploration of the work of A. N. Leontiev. *Human Development*, 39, 309–27.

Grusec, J. E. and Abramovitch, R. (1982). Imitation of peers and adults in a natural setting: A functional analysis. *Child Development*, 53, 636–42.

Guillaume, P. (1971). *Imitation in children*. University of Chicago Press. (Original work published 1926).

Hatfield, E., Cacioppo, J. T. and Rapson, R. L. (1994). *Emotional contagion*. Paris: Cambridge University Press.

Hoffman, M. L. (1984). Interaction of affect and cognition in empathy. In C. E. Izard, J. Kagan and R. B. Zajonc (eds.), *Emotion, cognition and behavior* (pp. 103–31). Cambridge University Press.

(1990). Empathy and justice motivation. *Motivation and Emotion*, 14, 151–72.

Killen, M. and Užgiris, I. Č. (1981). Imitation of actions with objects: The role of social meaning. *Journal of Genetic Psychology*, 138, 219–29.

Lacks, J. M. and Užgiris, I. Č. (1995, March). Affective imitation in relation to the genesis of empathy. Paper presented at the meeting of the Society for Research in Child Development, Indianapolis, IN.

Lisina, M. I. (1985). *Child–Adults–Peers: Patterns of communication*. Moscow: Progress Publishers.

Masur, E. F. (1993). Transitions in representational ability: Infants' verbal, vocal, and action imitation during the second year. *Merrill-Palmer Quarterly*, 39, 437–56.

Maratos, O. (1973). The origin and development of imitation in the first six months of life. Paper presented at the British Psychological Association annual meeting, Liverpool.

(1982). Trends in the development of imitation in early infancy. In T. G. Bever (ed.), *Regressions in mental development: Basic phenomena and theories* (pp. 81–101). Hillsdale, NJ: Erlbaum.

McCall, R. B., Parke, R. D. and Kavanaugh, R. D. (1977). Imitation of live and televised models by children one to three years of age. *Monographs of the Society for Research in Child Development*, 42, (whole no. 173).

Meltzoff, A. N. (1985). Immediate and deferred imitation in fourteen- and twenty-four-month-old infants. *Child Development*, 56, 62–72.

(1988). Infant imitation and memory: Nine-month-olds in immediate and deferred tests. *Child Development*, 59, 217–25.

(1990). Foundations for developing a concept of self. In D. Cicchetti and M. Beeghly (eds.), *The self in transition: Infancy to childhood* (pp. 139–64). University of Chicago Press.

Meltzoff, A. N. and Moore, M. K. (1977). Imitation of facial and manual gestures by human neonates. *Science*, 198, 75–8.

(1983). Newborn infants imitate adult facial gestures. *Child Development*, 54, 702–9.

Nadel-Brulfert, J. and Baudonnière, P. M. (1982). The social function of reciprocal imitation in 2-year-old peers. *International Journal of Behavioral Development*, 5, 95–109.

Nadel, J. (1986). *Imitation et communication entre jeunes enfants* [Imitation and communication between young children]. Paris: Presses Universitaires de France.

Ochs, E. and Schieffelin, B. B. (1984). Language acquisition and socialization. In R. A. Shweder and R. A. LeVine (eds.), *Culture theory* (pp. 276–320). New York: Cambridge University Press.

Papoušek, H. and Papoušek, M. (1977). Mothering and the cognitive head-start: Psychobiological considerations. In H. R. Schaffer (ed.), *Studies in mother–infant interaction* (pp. 63–85). New York: Academic Press.

Pawlby, S. J. (1977). Imitative interaction. In H. R. Schaffer (ed.), *Studies in mother–infant interaction* (pp. 203–24). New York: Academic Press.

Piaget, J. (1937/1954). *The construction of reality in the child*. New York: Basic Books.

(1962). *Play, dreams and imitation in childhood* (C. Gattegno and F. M. Hodgson, trans.). New York: Norton (Original work published 1945).

Rodgon, M. M. and Kurdek, L. A. (1977). Vocal and gestural imitation in 8-, 14- and 20-month-old children. *Journal of Genetic Psychology*, 131, 115–23.

Rogoff, B., Mistry, J., Göncü, A. and Mosier, C. (1993). Guided participation in cultural activity by toddlers and caregivers. *Monographs of the Society for Research in Child Development*, 58 (8, Serial No. 236).

Scheerer, E. (1985). Pre-evolutionary conceptions of imitation. In G. Eckardt and W. G. Bringmann (eds.), *Contributions to a history of developmental psychology* (pp. 27–53). Berlin: Mouton Publishers.

Sibulkin, A. E. and Užgiris, I. Č. (1978). Imitation by preschoolers in a problem-solving situation. *The Journal of Genetic Psychology*, 132, 267–75.

Stern, D. N. (1985). *The interpersonal world of the infant*. New York: Basic Books.

Trevarthen, C. (1977). Descriptive analyses of infant communicative behavior. In H. R. Schaffer (ed.), *Studies in mother–infant interaction*. New York: Academic Press.

Užgiris, I. Č. (1972). Patterns of vocal and gestural imitation in infants. In F. J. Monks, W. W. Hartup and J. deWitt (eds.), *Determinants of behavioral development* (pp. 467–71). New York: Academic Press.

(1979). Die Mannigfaltigkeit der Imitation in der frühen Kindheit. In L. Montada (ed.), *Brennpunkte der Entwicklungspsychologie* (pp. 173–93). Stuttgart: Verlag W. Kohlhammer.

(1981). Two functions of imitation during infancy. *International Journal of Behavioral Development*, 4, 1–12.

(1984). Imitation in infancy: Its interpersonal aspects. In M. Perlmutter (ed.), *The Minnesota Symposia on Child Psychology: Vol. 17. Parent–child interactions and parent–child relations in child development* (pp. 1–32). Hillsdale, NJ: Erlbaum.

(1989). Infants in relation: Performers, pupils, and partners. In W. Damon (ed.), *Child development today and tomorrow* (pp. 208–311). San Francisco: Jossey-Bass.

(1990). The social context of infant imitation. In M. Lewis and S. Feinman (eds.), *Social influences and socialization in infancy* (pp. 215–51). New York: Plenum Press.

Užgiris, I. Č., Benson, J. B., Kruper, J. C. and Vasek, M. E. (1989). Contextual influences on imitative interactions between mothers and infants. In J. Lockman and N. Hazen (eds.), *Action in social context* (pp. 103–27). New York: Plenum Press.

Valentine, C. W. (1930). The psychology of imitation with special reference to early childhood. *British Journal of Psychology*, 21, 105–32.

Vinter, A. (1985). *L'Imitation chez le nouveau-né*. Paris: Delachaux and Niestle.

Vygotsky, L. S. (1978). *Mind in society*. Cambridge, MA: Harvard University Press.

Wallon, H. (1934). *Les origines du caractère chez l'enfant*. Paris: Boivin & Co.

Watson-Gegeo, K. A. and Gegeo, D. W. (1986). Calling-out and repeating routines in Kwara'ae children's language socialization. In B. B. Schieffelin and E. Ochs (eds.), *Language socialization across cultures* (pp. 17–50). New York: Cambridge University Press.

Wertsch, J. V. (1981). The concept of activity in Soviet Psychology: An introduction. In J. V. Wertsch (ed.), *The concept of activity in Soviet Psychology* (pp. 3–36). Armonk, NY: M. E. Sharpe, Inc.

(1995). The need for action in sociocultural research. In J. V. Wertsch, P. del Rio and A. Alvarez (eds.), *Sociocultural studies of mind*. New York: Cambridge University Press.

Wertsch, J. V., del Rio, P. and Alvarez, A. (eds.). (1995). *Sociocultural studies of mind*. New York: Cambridge University Press.

Whiting, B. B. and Edwards, C. P. (1988). *Children of different worlds*. Cambridge, MA: Harvard University Press.

Zazzo, R. (1957). Le problème de l'imitation chez le nouveau-né. *Enfance*, 10, 135–42.

Zinchenko, V. P. (1995). Cultural-historical psychology and the psychological theory of activity: Retrospect and prospect. In J. V. Wertsch, P. del Rio and A. Alvarez (eds.), *Sociocultural studies of mind*. New York: Cambridge University Press.

Part IV

Imitation, communication and
developmental psychopathology

7   The evolving nature of imitation as a format for communication

Jacqueline Nadel, Caroline Guérini, Ann Pezé and Christine Rivet

This chapter will stress the evolving nature of immediate imitation as a format for communication. We will propose that immediate imitation can be considered not only as a primary interactive means but also as a milestone for intentional communication in normal, disabled and impaired development.

From birth to death we are imitating, and this is part of our own bodily creativity (Wallon, 1934). Immediate imitation is a primary ability, so simple, deep inside us, that it is one of the most difficult aspects of our behaviour to discover, scrutinise and finally consider objectively. Moreover, as stated in the Introduction to this book, Plato's negative opinion of mimesis still affects the study of imitation. Plato's viewpoint is especially obvious when we examine the following phenomenon: *two people performing the same action simultaneously*. Immediately, we think that the imitator shows poor interactive skills and personal goals. The only case when immediate imitation has been considered to have some evolutionary and developmental value is when matching a novel act, perhaps because it includes the goal of acquiring new behaviour. Although Užgiris (1981) proposed a heuristic distinction between the cognitive and the social functions of imitation, we usually recognise the first and ignore the second. We generally also fail to consider and distinguish the immediate and the deferred aspects within each of these two functions of imitation.

Deferred imitation may be cognitive or social in function. When serving an acquisitive purpose, deferred imitation is generally called *observational learning* (Bandura, 1971), regardless of whether it is elicited or spontaneous. For instance, a previously observed procedure may allow us to solve a problem we had never faced before. Deferred imitation may serve another function, as a way to evoke an abstract object or person or to make the past be present via pantomime: for example by facial expressions, bodily evocations of events and emotions connected with events. These are directly understandable by our social partners and allow us to develop and share a memory of events without language (Wallon, 1942).

Immediate imitation also has two functions. It may be prompted by purposes of learning: the 'look-at-me and do-like-me' procedure is a key for elementary academic and other kinds of acquisitions. But immediate imitation may also be of use for purposes of communication. Consider our previous example of two persons doing the same act quasi-simultaneously, let us say putting on sun-glasses: a familiar gesture with no acquisitive goal. Are we right if we think that the imitator shows poor interactive skills and develops no personal goals? Or are we assuming, a priori, that similarity equates with conformism? Maybe the imitator, when putting on the glasses to be the same as the imitatee, is telling the imitatee: 'I *am interested in you.*' In this case, the imitator has a different goal from the imitatee – who put on sun-glasses against the sun – since the imitator does not want to be protected from sun but to attract the imitatee's attention. Then the act of imitating is a message, with a here-and-now meaning that links the imitatee and the imitator. All this is a very simple functional analysis. It does not fully confirm the statement that immediate imitation could be a communicative tool.

What exactly is the function of such behaviour? Is there any developmental change in it? What is its role in communicative development? This chapter will focus on these points in normal, disabled and psychopathological development. It will be shown that, through early childhood, immediate imitation evolves from an elementary behavioural unit of bodily matching with undetermined function, to complex sequences of matching activities which support long-lasting referential exchanges. Our contention is that immediate imitation is an interactive format underlying the shift from primary to pragmatic communication. By primary communication, is meant an expressive system which is not denuded of semantic and intentional content, but which does not imply any monitoring or prediction of the partner's behaviour. By contrast, pragmatic communication is intentional, referential, predictive (hence, inferential) and coded. This kind of communication implies that the emitter has a goal concerning the partner, chooses means to achieve this target on the basis of predictive relationships between means and ends, and corrects the results if needed. Primary communication must precede pragmatic communication, but the latter is not an inevitable development. For instance, one model of autism claims that intentional communication is impaired in children with autism, but their capacity for primary interaction is not impaired (Baron-Cohen, Leslie and Frith, 1985). Two processes are involved in the role which, we argue, immediate imitation has in supporting the transition from primary to pragmatic communication; these are *mastering interpersonal timing* and *sharing topics.*

Neonatal imitation and the emergence of a social function

Early after birth, imitation can be elicited, as first shown by Zazzo (1957) and by Maratos (1973). In their famous studies, Meltzoff and Moore (1977; 1983a) systematically demonstrated the capacity of newborns to imitate certain adult facial and gestural behaviours, and highlighted the cognitive consequences of this innate ability. Their important findings were first considered as controversial and initiated a burst of research in the area. It is worth noting that this seminal set of studies does not document the functional use of imitation, since the main purpose of the paradigm was to elicit the phenomenon (see Meltzoff and Moore, 1983b). However, more recent findings show that neonatal imitation demonstrates two remarkable characteristics: selectivity of human stimuli (Kugiumutzakis, 1993, this volume; Ohta, 1987), and ontological detection of identity (Meltzoff and Gopnik, 1993; Meltzoff and Moore, this volume). Both features are basic for social development, and several authors have emphasised the importance of imitation in intersubjective development (Papoušek and Papoušek, 1977; Stern, 1985; Trevarthen, 1977). However the construct of intersubjectivity is not directly testable. Although Heimann (1989) has shown that neonatal imitation is a good predictor of further face-to-face interactions, his important contribution highlights the potential, but not the effective, intersubjective function of neonatal imitation. To operationalise intersubjectivity, it is necessary to take into account the other facet of the imitative phenomenon: Sensitivity to being imitated. In a microanalysis of the dyadic behaviours of 9-week-olds and their mother communicating through an audio-video system (Nadel, 1996), we found very few examples of imitative sequences such as the following: the mother imitates one of her baby's gestures (for instance, raising the arm), then adds a kinetic component to the gesture (for instance, turning the wrist, arm raised), and then the baby imitates the mother's new gesture (i.e. turning the wrist, arm raised). More generally, the functional role of early imitation in communication has to be demonstrated in a free social context, rather than under modelled conditions. Kugiumutzakis (this volume) is working in this direction. Several authors have reported naturalistic studies of imitation in mothers' interactions, but with older infants. They showed that immediate imitation increasingly enters into dyadic exchanges between mother and baby and increasingly takes the form of imitative sequences (Maratos, 1973; Papoušek and Papoušek, 1989; Pawlby, 1977; Užgiris, Benson, Kruper and Vasek, 1989a; Užgiris, Broome and Kruper, 1989b) with 'rounds' (Pawlby, 1977), where a first imitation is imitated and so on.

Turn taking, role taking and imitation: imitating and being imitated

Interactive sequences imply alternation. In the case of imitative sequences, two kinds of alternation have to be distinguished: turn taking, where each partner alternately imitates the same act x: A does x, then B does x, then A does x again, and B does x again, and so on . . ., and role shifting, where each partner alternates imitating and being imitated: A does x and B does x, A does y and b does y, A does z and B does z, then B does j and A does j, B does k and A does k . . ., a kind of second-order alternation implying interpersonal regulation of role shifting. Only simple imitative turn taking is found in the studies of early imitative sequences quoted above. However this first-order alternation already marks an important difference from simple matching, since the two partners actively use imitation as a means to emit and answer: in this way, imitation becomes a tool for social exchanges. Of course, this does not mean that turn taking is already mastered. The mother is usually monitoring and supporting imitative sequences with babies younger than 9 months (Užgiris et al., 1989a), and it is only after 18 months that she begins to be more demanding about the rules of turn taking and role respecting (Bruner, 1982, p. 32.). From this perspective, imitative sequences between peers are interesting to consider, since no scaffolding would be expected between agemates. Imitation of a peer has been reported before the end of the first year, 10–12 months, but mostly as short-lasting episodes requiring only two turns, i.e., one round (Eckerman, Whatley and Kutz, 1975). Longer imitative sequences between peers are described as emerging at a much older age. Extensive use of imitation in social exchanges between peers reaches its peak at roughly 30 months of age, when there is a rapid rise in extended imitative sequences during long-lasting interactions (2 rounds or more) (Nadel, 1986a, b; Nadel-Brulfert and Baudonnière, 1982). A longitudinal study conducted by Eckerman and her group indicates that extended sequences are not found earlier (Eckerman, 1993).

The important difference between short-lasting and long-lasting episodes lies in the fact that long-lasting episodes involve role shifting. Older toddlers demonstrate the alternate use of two facets of the imitative phenomenon, one concerning the imitator, the other concerning the imitatee. The imitator is involved in a selective process of choosing the person to imitate and the act to be imitated. The imitatee generally receives the effect of being imitated as a positive signal of interest. Social research on the effects of being imitated has shown its universal value as a strong elicitor of social attention towards the imitator (Fouts, Waldner and Watson,

1976; Roberts, Wurtele, Boone, Metts and Smith, 1981; Thelen, Dollinger and Roberts, 1975). This effect of being imitated is already observed in very young babies: it enhances eye-to-eye contact (Field, 1977). After 18 months of age, being imitated prompts further imitation of the imitator by the model (Eckerman and Stein, 1990); this implies an alternation in roles, and suggests that the effect of being imitated is an important factor in role shifting.

Role shifting in imitation was demonstrated in one of our studies with triads of 2-year-old toddlers (Nadel-Brulfert and Baudonnière, 1982). A triadic context was considered as more relevant for this, since alternation is inherent to dyads and may thus lead one to overestimate the early capacity for role shifting (Tremblay-Leveau and Nadel, 1996). A significant positive correlation was found between the number of imitative behaviours and the number of imitated behaviours for 39 children participating in 13 triads without an adult present. This indicates a conversational symmetry between the role of imitator and the role of model. A striking point is that this symmetry is reached in triads, and indicates a complex capacity in the interpersonal regulation of timing, since there are only 2 roles: imitator and imitatee, for 3 children. Other indices of interpersonal timing were found in our study, such as the time-span between the act imitated and the imitation. Taking into account that taking hold of a matching object may be a starter for an imitative sequence, and that the discarding of an identical object may be the signal for cutting off the imitative sequence, two situations were recorded: the time-span before imitating by taking hold of an identical object, and the time-span before imitating by discarding an identical object (Nadel-Brulfert and Baudonnière, 1982). The histograms of time-spans concerning 284 holds and 311 discards are remarkably similar (see Figure 7.1). They support the hypothesis that these toddlers are showing a temporal co-ordination which implies continual attention to the other(s)' activities. Again these results are particularly revealing since they were obtained in triads.

A qualitative demonstration of this search for synchrony is given by the initiators of a new hold waiting for their partner(s) while they are rushing to the identical object, or by the initiator of a discard, waiting until the partner(s) have put down the identical object before picking up another object. To summarise, role shifting in imitative sequences is achieved by switching from imitatee to imitator and back, in a co-constructed timing of alternation. This co-construction might be an important prelinguistic basis for linguistic turn taking and role shifting between young peers without adult scaffolding.

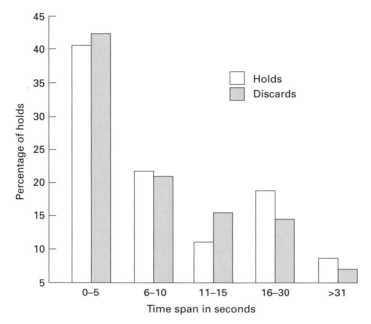

Figure 7.1. Lapses between two paired object holds and between paired discards. This illustration shows that the lapses between two paired object holds and the lapses between two paired object discards are similar and account for the search of synchrony between children during imitative interactions.

Sharing topic and imitation

Another important difference between first tongue protrusion matching and further immediate imitation lies in the fact that later imitation involves objects. For instance, Užgiris (1976) showed that imitations are more likely to appear if actions involving concrete objects are modelled. This, of course, serves the cognitive function of imitation. Numerous studies using modelling in an experimental context have shown the increasing capacity to imitate more and more sophisticated procedures (Yando, Seitz and Zigler, 1978). Furthermore, Meltzoff (1995) showed that 18-month-old toddlers are even able to violate literal imitation, when the modelled procedure fails to achieve the end. In this case, the children performed the target act, demonstrating that they could infer the adult's target act by watching the failed attempts. This means that the motive for imitating was to reach the same target act, and that the relevant procedure was extracted by a process of vicarious inference: what Meltzoff nicely proposed to interpret as an early capacity to attribute intentionality to the model (Meltzoff, 1995). In our studies of spontaneous imitation in a communicative context, we never noticed this kind of behaviour. On the contrary, we quoted numerous imitations reproducing failures to achieve an obvious and familiar goal (i.e.: falling from the chair you try to kneel on, putting the glasses upside-down etc.). Although quoted, these cases had classically been neglected as 'task-irrelevant imitation'. However they are irrelevant if and only if we consider the motive of imitation to be behaviour acquisition, as is obviously the case in Meltzoff's experiment. On the contrary, if the motive of imitation is to show an interest in the partner, it is relevant to imitate the procedural aspects of the other's activity, that is to say his/her gestures, even if they fail to achieve the goal. According to Wallon (1934), a bodily state of identity is necessary for sustained mutual interest to develop in young children (see Nadel, 1994, for further explanation of Wallon's framework). If Wallon is right, simultaneous gestural imitations should be the predominant means of long-lasting interactions in prelinguistic children, and identical objects should provide the ideal supports for gestural matchings. To test these hypotheses, we created the following design (Nadel-Brulfert and Baudonnière, 1982). Let the reader imagine a room with different kinds of attractive toys, some aimed at developing bodily postures (cowboy hats, sun-glasses, umbrellas), others at pretending (dolls, towels, stuffed animals), others at demonstrating physical abilities (balls, inflated balloons, clinging mobiles) . . . All the objects can be used solitarily, for their intrinsic value, or as mediators of social interest. Suppose now that 3 acquainted 2-year-olds are invited to enter the room. Now we close the door. They are alone in the room without an adult present and no instructions other than: 'You can use the toys.' What will happen? Each of them can choose between two centres of interest: the object or the partner. And a third option is available to combine the two interests in using objects as mediators of social exchanges. The children are filmed with a hidden camera, and we can thus evaluate moment by moment the choice made by each of the partners between these 3 possible options. Let us now complete our experimental design by putting in the room 3 identical sets of the objects above described. This will allow us to describe very easily what each child is doing, second by second, among 4 possible states: (1) the child is not holding an object; (2) the child is holding an object that is different from the object held simultaneously by one or both partners; (3) the child is holding an object identical to the one held by one or both partners; (4) the child is holding several objects either as in (2) or as in (3) or as in (2) + (3). When we carried out a study of this kind, we found that the toddlers only spent, on average, 8% of the sessions of 15 minutes duration without

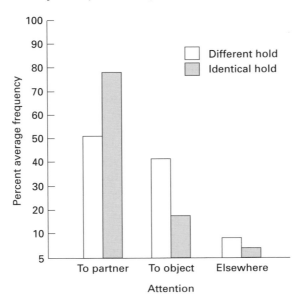

Figure 7.2. Focus of attention according to the type of hold: percentage average frequency. This illustrates a significant drop in attention to the partner when different objects are held and a significant increase in attention to the object.

objects in their hands. Simultaneous holds of identical objects were three times more numerous and longer (70% versus 21% of the time) than holds of different objects (Nadel-Brulfert and Baudonnière, 1982).

We next looked to see whether toddlers were object- or partner-centered. We used 6 codes: (1) no detectable centre of interest; (2) object-centered (i.e. manipulating the object and looking at the object) while holding a different object; (3) object-centered while holding an identical object; (4) partner-centered without object (i.e. emitting a behaviour while looking at one or both partners); (5) partner-centered and acting on an object different from the one held by the other peer(s) while looking at the partner(s); (6) partner-centered and acting on an identical object while looking at the partner(s). We found that toddlers spent, on average, only 6% of the time without a detectable centre of interest. Their attention was mainly partner-centered (72% of the time) when holding identical objects, but equally split between partner-centered and object-centered during the holds of different objects (see Figure 7.2).

Finally, in a third coding we looked at the activities supported by holding different or identical objects, in order to detect imitative activities. Imitation without an object or with a different object in hand only represented 4% of the total time. This highlights the role of objects in imitative sequences, and the privileged status of identical objects to achieve imitative activities.

We carried out further studies with dyads observed in two conditions: 1 set of 20 different objects and 2 identical sets of 10 objects (Nadel, 1986a, b). Comparing these two conditions allowed us to demonstrate that the importance of imitative activities previously shown in triads was not a bias linked to the presence of identical sets of objects. In fact, with one set of 20 different objects, the partners were equally split between partner-centered and object-centered orientation (as has been found in triads during the hold of different objects). This general finding when different objects are held is borne out by other studies documenting the frequency of interactions between peers around the age of 2 years (Bronson, 1981; Rubenstein and Howes, 1976). Moreover, in the different objects condition, the majority of exchanges were short-lasting, while in the identical objects situation they were long-lasting (4 turns or more), and mostly with an imitative format (Nadel and Fontaine, 1989). This means that at age 2 years, long-lasting interactions without an adult scaffolding are not supported by other formats when imitation is not available.

More recently, we decided to analyse further interactions via an identical object. Sequences of interactions mostly involve objects (Jacobson, 1981), and are linked to cognitive progress in co-ordinating attention to several foci of interest, generally a person and an object (Bakeman and Adamson, 1984; Butterworth and Jarrett, 1991). Communicating through imitative sequences also implies the ability to share attention to an object with somebody. However, in imitation, attention is not focused on an object but rather on 2 identical items of an object. How is this processed? We turned to this question in studying the effects of formatting imitative sequences with deaf-and-blind students. In an experiment carried out by Christine Rivet (1994), 6 young profoundly deaf and severely visually impaired adults were selected on the basis of their (moderate) capacities to communicate with their teacher and their inability to communicate with their peers. Two deaf-and-blind students were randomly assigned to the control condition, and 4 to the experimental condition. The experimental group was trained by a familiar teacher to use the imitative system of communication. A table was specially built to contain 2 symmetrical rows of 4 identical and familiar objects: hats, towels, cups, and balls. In parallel, the control group was familiarised by a familiar teacher with the experimental design, the 2 sets of identical objects, their symmetrical position and their possible uses, but did not receive any imitative formatting.

As the first step in the training, the teacher had to prompt imitative responses in the deaf and blind students, by modelling simple uses of the 4 objects, until the students were able to imitate what the teacher did. Then modelling by the teacher became more complex, including a sequence of several acts – including symbolic use – involving one or several objects. Six to 8 sessions were enough for the 4 students rapidly to learn to answer by imitation. They were then considered as trained (T). Once the trained students were able to answer by imitating, the second step was to teach them how to monitor role shifting from imitator to imitatee. The teacher first prompted each student to imitate him/her, then shifted to imitating each student, and finally stopped doing anything, and waited for the students' initiatives. The teacher waited until each student gave obvious indices of prompting imitation, like repeated use of the object while looking at the teacher, and/or touching the teacher's arm. These attempts were considered as indices of intentional initiations of imitation. The teacher then imitated in return. When the students were able to monitor role shifting 3 times in each of 3 successive sessions, they were considered as experts (E). While the 4 students learned to answer by imitating, only 2 of the 4 learned to manage role shifting. Two results are worthy of notice. The two experts did adapt their communicative skills to the partner: this is particularly evident for E1, who displayed very different patterns according to the partner (see Figure 7.3). The two experts communicating together offer the best example of role switching. The second interesting result lies in the development of special gestures of showing in the 2 experts (E), but not in the trained (T) nor in the control (C) persons. These special gestures were mixed gestures indicating first a request (something like 'I want this object') by extending the hand toward the identical item next to them on the table for the partner to take it, and then turning the hand towards the partner several times, meaning something like: 'for yourself'. Then this complex gesture seemed to mean: 'I intend that you take this object for yourself.' Gómez, Sarria and Tamarit (1993) developed a heuristic distinction between a proto-imperative group of gestures and a proto-demonstrative group. Proto-imperatives are aimed at attracting attention to achieve an observable behaviour, while proto-demonstratives are aimed at attracting attention as the ultimate goal of the communicative act. Camaioni (1993) showed that the use of proto-imperatives appears 2 to 3 months before the use of proto-demonstratives. Taking into account this developmental finding, we propose that the mixed gesture observed in persons with deaf-blindness in order to prompt their partner's imitation, is intermediate between requesting and showing. In fact, pointing towards an item identical to the object you hold leads to a special kind of joint attention, since

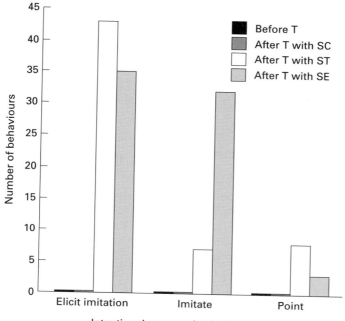

Figure 7.3. The effect of imitative training on intentional communication in a deaf-and-blind student. This illustration shows the use of pointing after imitative training, linked with new capacities of eliciting the partner's imitation and imitating the partner. It shows also different levels of communication according to the partner: SC (control), ST (trained), or SE (expert).

attention is attracted by the same object, but this object is in two samples. This leads to a joint activity of a special kind: namely, similar activity exerted simultaneously on two distinct items. This complex gesture induces both a change in the partner's behaviour, like a proto-imperative, and a change in the partner's interest, like a proto-demonstrative. Normally developing toddlers also use pointing or a verbal deictic 'there', and a demonstrative like 'the hat', or an imperative like 'take it'. Often they offer the identical item, which leads the partner to imitate (Nadel-Brulfert and Baudonnière, 1982). These active invitations to be imitated, therefore, appear not only to be intentional but also to be referential.

Going a step further in examining the referential aspect of imitation, an experiment carried out by Caroline Guérini (Guérini and Nadel, 1996) explored the relationships between matching activities with a co-referent and sharing a topic. We started the study with the hypothesis that, although the simplest way of sharing a topic is classically described as 'joint activity' on the topic of joint attention (Bakeman and Adamson, 1984), it might well be that another way is to focus on the same topic by simultaneously performing the same imitative activity with two identical items which can be considered as co-referents. Taking into account the children's verbal comments allows us to know more about the link between gestural imitations and shared topics. We invited 8 dyads of 30-month-olds and 8 dyads of 42-month-olds to repeated meetings in an experimental setting with several duplicated objects and several single objects. These were either gathered in thematic corners (tea-party corner, fountain corner) or randomly placed in the room (note that the random arrangement was constant for each meeting and each dyad). We arranged repeated meetings, because we supposed that older children without adult scaffolding might construct shared topics by establishing routines and variations in routines, as do mother-and-baby dyads (Bruner, 1982). Each dyad met 5 times for 10 minutes without an adult present. The meetings were videotaped with a hidden camera. Prior to the experiment, subgroups of 4 children were chosen on the basis of MLU level, age (difference: less than 3 months), gender (same-sex dyads) and familiarity (same group in the day-care centre). This matching allowed us to switch partners between the 2 similar dyads in a sixth session. In the sixth session, the 2 partners met each other in the experimental setting for the first time, as in session 1, but had already experienced 5 sessions playing in the experimental room with another partner.

The questions were: did the partners increase shared topics throughout the 5 meetings (comparison between session 1 and session 5)? Which interactive format did they use to construct their shared topics (imitation/co-operation/scaffolding)? Were they able to share their previous topics with a new partner? If so, there would be an increase of shared topics during the 6th session (session 5 < session 6). On the other hand, was it necessary to construct new topics? If so, it would be a handicap compared to a first session with no previous topic built (session 1 > session 6), and would reveal the process of co-construction of shared topics. The results are summarised in Figure 7.4a for acted out shared topics and in Figure 7.4b for verbal shared topics. During the first session, at 30 months as well as at 42 months, shared topics revealed by acts without language were mainly imitative and included the use of identical items (e.g., both partners simultaneously pretending to pour water from the fountain in to a cup and having the doll drink; or pretending to let the rattle glide along the water while in the boat). Sometimes the shared topics led to a co-operative activity with different objects, like one

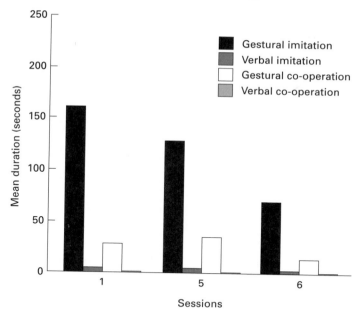

Figure 7.4a. Formats of shared topics in 30-month-olds. This illustration shows no increase in imitative nor in co-operative format of shared topics between the first and the fifth session with the same partner. However, imitative shared topics drops significantly during the sixth session with another partner. Imitative shared topics are significantly more numerous than the co-operative ones.

child taking a doll and putting it in a baby buggy, while the partner is putting an umbrella on the buggy and a hat on the doll's head. At 30 months, shared verbal topics were almost never found, whereas, at 42 months, they were numerous and mainly imitative (80%): – 'I will pour water from the fountain' – 'I too will pour water from the fountain. My baby is thirsty' – 'Yes, my baby is thirsty also. I will take her cup' – 'I will take my baby's cup and pour water in it' – 'yes, pour water in it and give it to the baby' – 'and I will give it to my baby. She wants to drink.' Some shared verbal topics, however, were used to enhance different roles, like: – 'it is vacation. I will put the picnic bag in the boat' – 'yes and I will wake the babies and dress them' – 'meanwhile I will pour water in the bottle and put it in the boat' – 'and now I will sit the babies in the boat' – 'yes, do sit with them in the boat to look after them' – 'go and fetch their hats because it is sunny' . . . Thirty-month-olds did not significantly change the amount of their imitative or co-operative shared topics by the 5th

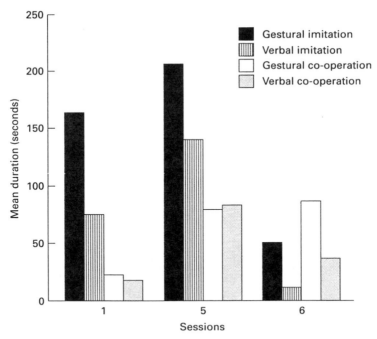

Figure 7.4b. Formats of shared topics in 42-month-olds. This illustration shows that imitative verbal as well as co-operative verbal formats of shared topics increase significantly between the first and the fifth session with the same partner, and decrease significantly at session 6. However, imitative shared topics still remain significantly more numerous than the co-operative ones except when partner changes and new topics have to be established.

session nor with the switch of partners at the 6th session. This means that they had not really co-constructed the shared topics but just agreed with their partner's proposal. On the other hand, at 42 months of age, all verbal shared topics increased by the 5th session, with numerous recurrent themes. At the 6th session, a dramatic decrease of imitative topics with the switch of partner shows the importance of imitation in the co-construction of themes.

To summarise: immediate imitation can be considered as an evolving format allowing young children first to develop selective matching movements from the human repertoire; then to interact through the alternation of imitating and being imitated, to build long-lasting interactions about an identical object; then to use the identical object as a co-referent, and finally to construct shared topics with the co-referent. Imitation thus provides a means towards developing referential communication. Moreover, monitoring role shifting between imitator and imitatee allows the child to learn how to exert intentional invitations and to control the mental state of interest in the partner. For these reasons, we propose that the imitative format also provides a means towards developing referential and inferential communication. Within this framework, the communicative function of immediate imitation can be seen as essential in filling the gap from primary to pragmatic communication.

Imitation and sensitivity to being imitated in children with autism

Are children with autism able to use imitation as a means of primary communication? Are they capable of spontaneous imitation as a way to attract attention or to answer? Are they sensitive to being imitated as a way to understand imitative behaviour? Are they capable of monitoring role shifting between imitator and imitatee as a means of secondary communication? It is very difficult to answer these questions clearly, since, classically, they are not ones that have been addressed.

Imitation

First of all, there has been very little study of spontaneous gestural imitation in children with autism. To date, there have only been a handful of observational studies of autistic imitation during dialogic meetings (see Dawson and Adams, 1984), and even less is known about imitation during encounters between autistic and non autistic-agemates. What then about their ability to spontaneously imitate as a means to initiate (when they are not addressed) or to respond (when they are addressed)?

Speculation on the social function of imitation has been indirect through clinical evaluations of imitation level, such as the Užgiris–Hunt scales of imitation (1987), or scores in imitation tasks used for the assessment of apraxia (Rogers, Bennetto, McEvoy and Pennington, 1996). When experimental designs have been used, they obviously addressed the behaviour acquisition function of imitation under conditions where an adult prompts the imitation of an action being modelled (Charman and Baron-Cohen, 1994). One reason why results in studies of imitation in autism are highly contradictory, therefore, may be that the distinction between the different types and functions of imitation are not clearly taken into account. For example, some authors claim that children with autism are deeply impaired in imitation (DeMyer, Hingtgen and Jackson, 1981; Prior, 1979; Wing, 1976). More precisely, Curcio (1978), Hammes and Langdell (1981) and Sigman and Ungerer (1984) demonstrate strong relationships between gestural imitation level, symbolic play and language development. But these influential works were principally concerned with deferred imitation (level 6), which is considered by Piaget (1945) to indicate emerging representational capacity which normally appears around 18 months of age, simultaneously with symbolic play and language. When the criterion becomes immediate imitation of very familiar actions, Hammes and Langdell (1981) show that autistic children of a mean mental age of 54 months were all able to imitate, while Rogers and Pennington (1991) suggest autism-specific impairments in imitation without consideration of mental age. More recently, Charman and Baron-Cohen (1994) found that, even with unfamiliar objects, children with autism showed intact gestural and procedural imitation as compared to children with mental handicap matched on verbal mental age (notice however, that matching on VMA is an advantage for autistic children since their NVMA is generally higher). Using the same material, Brown (1996) did not find evidence of a general deficit in imitation in her group of 24 persons with autism compared to 3/4-year-old normal children.

But what about younger ages, where the absence of a deficit in imitation may hinder further social development? Until recently, it was not possible to study younger autistic infants, because their condition was not diagnosed before 30 months. However, Charman, Swettenham, Baron-Cohen, Cox, Baird and Drew (1997) took advantage of their new prospective screening instrument for autism in infancy (Baron-Cohen, Cox, Baird, Swettenham, Nightingale, Morgan, Drew and Charman, 1996), to carry out a study comparing empathy, joint attention, imitation and pretend play in normally developing children age 20 months, in developmentally delayed children and in children with autism. They found no significant difference between the mean number of imitation trials completed by each group, but imitation trials on which subjects successfully imitated the modelled action were lower in the autistic group than in both the MA matched group of developmental delay and the normal group. The materials and method used to assess imitation capacities were similar to those employed by Meltzoff (1988) with normal infants, and by Charman and Baron-Cohen (1994) with older subjects with autism. The child sat opposite the experimenter. Four tasks were modelled 3 times on objects designed to be unfamiliar to the child. At the end of the modelling period, the objects were placed in front of the child. If the child did not manipulate the object, a non-specific prompt ('what can you do with this?') was given. The response period was 20 seconds per task. Obviously, behaviour acquisitive function of imitation is being explored in this kind of study. Imitation is prompted in a school-like design (child sitting opposite the adult) with a non familiar object to manipulate and no social relationship to develop with the experimenter. However, the authors were interested in the development of social communication in infants with autism. If this was the case, then why not use a communicative context and study spontaneous imitation?

To explore the use of imitation as a communicative means, we carried out a study in which 8 autistic children met 8 non-autistic familiar age-mates. Each dyad was observed in a room at their day-care centre, which had been rearranged with 2 sets of 10 identical attractive toys (as was done previously with normal young children). No instructions were given to the children as they entered the rearranged room; they were just told: 'you can play with all the toys'. The autistic children were 6 to 12 years old. They had been diagnosed according to established criteria. None had any gross motor or perceptual handicaps. All were mute and had severe mental retardation (mean MA: 19 months; SD: 8 months; range: 10 months to 36 months). All showed object permanence level 5 or 6 with the Užgiris–Hunt's scales (Užgiris and Hunt, 1975). The non-autistic children were attending the same day-hospital as their autistic agemates. They were mentally deficient (non-verbal IQ range: 0.50 to 0.70), and they came from at risk families. All were able to use non-verbal and verbal communication. The results showed that 1 child with autism was unable to display any other than disruptive behaviour towards the partner. The 7 others in addition showed passive acceptance of social initiations. They also displayed positive social behaviours, such as taking the offering or offering on request, seeking proximity or following the partner. Six of the 7 displayed gestural imitations. The correlation between the amount of imitative and non-imitative positive social behaviour was significant ($r = +0.67$, $p < 0.05$), indicating that imitation is a good predictor of social capacities in children with autism, and is part of their positive communicative repertoire. Moreover, imitation was one of the major communicative tools, as we previously showed in prelinguistic toddlers where it represents more than 50% of interactive time (Nadel and Pezé, 1993) (see Figure 7.5).

Sensitivity to being imitated

We know that autistic children improve their social responsiveness when they are imitated (Dawson and Adams, 1984; Tiegerman and Primavera, 1981), and especially their face-to-face interaction with the mother (Dawson and Galpert, 1988). The imitation of an autistic child by the adult also allows the child to continue the relationship when the adult pauses with a blank face (Nadel, 1996; Nadel, Croué, Kervella, Mattlinger, Canet, Hudelot, Lécuyer and Martini, submitted). Nine

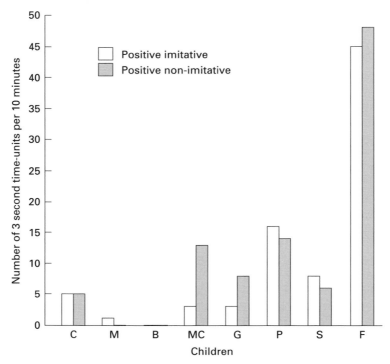

Figure 7.5. Positive imitative and non-imitative social behaviour in 8 children with autism. This illustration shows the importance of imitation compared to the other positive behaviours displayed by low-functioning children with autism. The correlation between the occurences of imitative and non-imitative behaviours is positive and significant.

mute autistic children, diagnosed with the DSM-III-R (APA, 1980), took part in this experiment. They were all low-functioning with a CA between 6 to 15 years, and a non-verbal MA between 18 months and 42 months. Each autistic child met alone with an unacquainted experimenter in a rearranged room of their school, in which 10 very attractive paired toys had been placed. For the first three minutes, the experimenter sat motionless on a sofa, with a blank face. After a subsequent period of 3 minutes, during which the experimenter imitated the autistic child's gestures with the identical object, the adult returned to the same immobile position on the sofa. None of the children showed any persistent interest in the stranger during the first blank-face condition. On the other hand, during the second blank-face condition, all but one of the children came

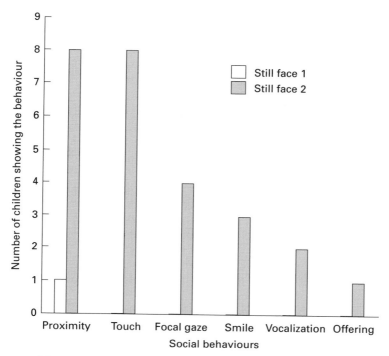

Figure 7.6. Effect of having been imitated on the social behaviour of 9 children with autism during the adult's still face 2. This illustration shows the sensitivity of children with autism to having been imitated: during the first still face posed by the unfamiliar adult, the children ignored the adult, but, after having been imitated, 8 out of 9 displayed positive social initiations toward the passive adult.

close to the adult and attempted to engage her in an interaction, touching her, some of them using eye-to-eye contact, others demanding caresses (see Figure 7.6). All these active behaviours are similar to those of 3-month-old babies when the mother starts to be still face (Gusella, Muir and Tronick, 1988; Murray and Trevarthen, 1985), before they become upset and finally withdrawn. However it is a highly unusual behaviour for autistic children who generally show more readiness to be recipients of interaction than to be initiators.

Turn taking and role shifting

Low-functioning children with autism are sensitive to being imitated and display some spontaneous gestural imitation in a social context. Are they able then to take turns or even to monitor the role shifting between imitator and imitatee?

Nadel and Pezé (1993) carried out 3 follow-up studies aimed at trying to teach turn taking to 2 boys and a girl. For these children with autism, they created a procedure which was later adapted to deaf–blind persons by Rivet (1994) and also, independently and successfully, to young children with congenital deafblindness by the European Working Group on Congenital Deafblindness and Communication (Daelman, Nafstad, Rodbroe, Souriau and Visser, 1996). In the case of children with autism, the procedure is more dynamic. There is no table to sit in front of and the child and the experimenters often stand up or run, or jump in a joyful way. First the experimenter imitates the child's gesture or posture with the identical object, while looking at him/her, then the experimenter faces the child while smiling and suggests a new gesture with the same or another object. If the child imitates the new gesture, the experimenter goes on a few seconds and then stops doing anything, except looking at the child while smiling, in order to let him/her switch from imitator to imitatee. If the child does not imitate, the experimenter turns to imitate again, and so on.

One of these follow-ups of a low functioning autistic child (DSM-III-R diagnosed) went on bimonthly during a year. Progressively, the child came to be an imitatee, stopping the experimenter's gesture and suggesting another, while taking control if his new activity was imitated (Nadel and Pezé, 1993). An important outcome was the appearance and progressive increase of spontaneous motor activity with objects, contrasting with the previous predominant passivity or stereotypic gestures. However, role switching was never totally mastered since there was no persistent attempt to be imitated if the experimenter did not immediately follow the child's suggestion. Furthermore, while the deaf-and-blind students were able to exploit their training to communicate with other deaf-and-blind persons, the child with autism did not progress in communicating with non-autistic familiar agemates. No offering, no showing and requesting gestures appeared during the training.

The absence of gestures inviting others to imitate with the identical object strikingly parallels the absence of joint attention gestures noted by Mundy, Sigman and Kasari (1993) and numerous other authors. This parallel reinforces our hypothesis of a close link between joint activity and imitative activity, with two identical objects taken as co-referents for a topic. From the 8 low-functioning autistic children meeting a non autistic familiar agemate, only one (F) was able to take turn in imitative sequences. Although they were sensitive to being imitated and although they were able to signal and develop attention to another by imitating, they did not show any attempt to co-ordinate the two facets of the imitative system in alternating the roles of imitatee and imitator, and hence they did not demonstrate capacities of referential and inferential communication via the use of an identical object. This underlines the developmental changes in communicative imitation, whose more advanced aspects are not available to all human populations.

A functional perspective

In this chapter, we traced the idea that, during the course of development, a behaviour can fulfil different functions, some of which may be transitory. Imitation is such a behaviour. We emphasised the two functions of imitation, its cognitive function and its communicative function, and demonstrated that both may be immediate or deferred. We underscored the transitory use of imitation as a means of communication. There are several reasons for studying this transitory function.

One reason is that immediate imitation is the first social behaviour available during the prelinguistic period for long-lasting exchanges with adults, and, later, with peers. It provides opportunities for the mastery of interpersonal timing by formatting turn taking and role taking between imitator and imitatee. It also sets the stage for referential communication, since imitation during long-lasting exchanges is supported by objects, and, especially, by identical objects. We have shown that converging attention on the same topic, the object, is easier when children both hold an exemplar of the topic. In this way, temporarily, but first in the developmental process, imitation fulfils a very important function: it prepares and supports the shift from primary to pragmatic communication. Once language is mastered, imitation is no longer useful as a pragmatic device, hence its decline.

Another reason is the state of the art in the field of autism. Examining the question of primary imitative deficits in autism, we concluded that the models as well as the findings are highly contradictory. Certainly, it will be helpful in the future to try to integrate in a comprehensive comparative framework a functional perspective that includes the transitory function. Just as adaptive behaviours go through change in young children, symptoms also change over the course of impaired development. Just as imitation is evolving as a mechanism in typical development, imitative capacities may change in children with autism. Just as it fulfils different adaptive goals in different contexts and at different levels within normal development, this may also be the case for children with autism. The confusing state of current knowledge concerning imitation in autism may be partly attributable to the different chronological ages of the children observed (imitative capacities evolve over time in children with autism as well), to their different mental ages (the cognitive function of imitation is highly linked to representational capacities), to the type of imitation studied (immediate or deferred) or to the various types of «autism» taken into account (Kanner's, Asperger's, Gilles de La Tourette's, autistic-like . . .). This by itself makes it difficult to draw a clear and convergent map. However, other biases may account in part for the contradictions mentioned above. These include the tools used to assess the imitative capacities, which differ from study to study: some are clinical scales, others are experimental measures; all are encompassed within a child–experimenter design, with no account of the different functions of imitation in different contexts.

We have begun the study of immediate imitation as a communicative device within a social context between children with autism and children with typical patterns of development. Other aspects of imitation are being investigated at this time by other researchers, including for example: cognitive exploration of a novel object through imitation, deferred imitative capacities, or praxis. The challenge for the future is to distinguish carefully types and functions in different contexts, and to compare only what is comparable–clinical assessments and experimental measures respectively in contexts where they are appropriate. Once this is accomplished, we will be able to rectify the present puzzling state of the art in comparative studies on imitation.

REFERENCES

American Psychiatric Association (1980). *Diagnostic and statistical manual of mental disorder.* 3rd edn revised. Washington DC: American Psychiatric Association.

Bakeman, R. and Adamson, L. B. (1984). Coordinating attention to people and objects in mother–infant and peer–infant interaction. *Child Development,* 55, 1278–89.

Bandura, A. (1971). *Psychological modelling conflicting theories.* Chicago: Aldine.

Baron-Cohen, S., Leslie, A. and Frith, U. (1985). Does the autistic child have a 'theory of mind'? *Cognition,* 21, 37–46.

Baron-Cohen, S., Cox, A., Baird, G., Swettenham, J., Nightingale, N., Morgan, K., Drew, A. and Charman, T. (1996). Screening for autism in a large population at 18 months of age: an investigation of the CHAT (Checklist for Autism in Toddlers). *British Journal of Psychiatry,* 168, 158–63.

Bronson, W. C. (1981). *Toddlers' behaviors with agemates: Issues of interaction, cognition and affect.* Norwood, NJ: Ablex.

Brown, J. (1996). Imitation, play and 'theory of mind' in autism: an observational and experimental study. Unpublished Ph.D.: University of St Andrews, Scotland.

Bruner, J. (1982). The organization of action and the nature of the adult–infant transaction. In E. Tronick (ed.), *Social interchange in infancy* (pp. 23–35). Baltimore: University Park Press.

Butterworth, G. and Jarrett, N. (1991). What minds have in common is space: Spatial mechanisms serving joint visual attention in infancy. *British Journal of Developmental Psychology*, 9, 55–72.

Camaioni, L. (1993). The development of intentional communication. In J. Nadel and L. Camaioni (eds.), *New perspectives in early communicative development* (pp. 82–96). London: Routledge.

Charman, T. and Baron-Cohen, S. (1994). Another look at imitation in autism. *Development and Psychopathology*, 6, 404–13.

Charman, T., Swettenham, J., Baron-Cohen, S., Cox, A., Baird, G. and Drew, A. (1997). Infants with autism: An investigation of empathy, pretend play, joint attention and imitation. *Developmental Psychology*, 33(5), 781–9.

Curcio, F. (1978). Sensorimotor functioning and communication in mute autistic children. *Journal of Autism and Childhood Schizophrenia*, 8, 281–92.

Daelman, M., Nafstad, A., Rodbroe, J., Souriau, J. and Visser, A. (1996). *Social interaction and the emergence of communication*. Text and video. Suresnes: Editions du CNEFEI.

Dawson, G. and Adams, A. (1984). Imitation and social responsiveness in autistic children. *Journal of Abnormal Child Psychology*, 12, 209–26.

Dawson, G. and Galpert, L. (1988). Mothers' use of imitative play for facilitating social responsiveness and toy play in young autistic children. Paper presented at the International Conference on Infant Studies, Washington.

DeMyer, M., Hingtgen, J. and Jackson, R. (1981). Infantile autism reviewed: A decade of research. *Schizophrenia Bulletin*, 7, 388–449.

Eckerman, C. (1993). Imitation and toddlers' achievement of co-ordinated action with others. In J. Nadel and L. Camaioni (eds.), *New perspectives in early communicative development* (pp. 116–38). London: Routledge.

Eckerman, C., Whatley, J. and Kutz, S. (1975). Growth of social play with peers during the second year of life. *Developmental Psychology*, 11, 42–9.

Eckerman, C. and Stein, M. (1990). How imitation begets imitation and toddlers' generation of games. *Developmental Psychology*, 26, 370–8.

Field, T. (1977). Effects of early separation, interactive deficits, and experimental manipulations on infant–mother face-to-face interaction. *Child Development*, 48, 763–71.

Fouts, G., Waldner, D. and Watson, M. (1976). Effects of being imitated on the behaviour of preschool children. *Child Development*, 47, 172–7.

Gómez, J.C., Sarria, E. and Tamarit, J. (1993). The comparative study of early communication and theories of mind: Ontogeny, phylogeny, and pathology. In S. Baron-Cohen, H. Tager-Flusberg and D. Cohen (eds.), *Understanding other minds: Perspectives from autism* (pp. 397–426). Oxford University Press.

Guérini, C. and Nadel, J. (1996). Topic sharing between young peers a microgenetic and developmental study. Poster presented at the European Research Conference: The Development of Sensory, Motor and Cognitive Abilities in Early Infancy: Antecedents of Language and the Symbolic Function, Barcelona, Spain, 10–15 April.

Gusella, J. L., Muir, D. and Tronick, E. Z. (1988). The effect of manipulating maternal behaviour during an interaction on three- and six-month olds' affect and attention. *Child Development*, 59, 1111–94.

Hammes, J. G. and Langdell, T. (1981). Precursors of symbol formation in childhood autism, *Journal of Autism and Developmental Disorders*, 11, 331–44.

Heimann, M. (1989). Neonatal imitation, gaze adversion, and mother–infant interaction. *Infant Behavior and Development*, 12, 495–505.

Jacobson, J. L. (1981). The role of inanimate objects in early peer interaction. *Child Development*, 52, 618–26.

Kugiumutzakis, G. (1993). Intersubjective vocal imitation in early mother–infant interaction. In J. Nadel and L. Camaioni (eds.), *New perspectives in early communicative development* (pp. 23–47). London: Routledge.

Maratos, O. (1973, April). The origin and development of imitation in the first sixth months of the life. Paper presented at the British Psychological Society Annual Meeting, Liverpool.

Meltzoff, A. (1988). Infant imitation and memory: Nine-month-olds in immediate and deferred tests. *Child Development*, 59, 217–25.

  (1995). Understanding the intention of others: Reenactment of intended acts by 18-month-old children. *Developmental Psychology*, 24, 470–6.

Meltzoff, A. and Moore, M. (1977). Imitation of facial and manual gestures by human neonates. *Science*, 198, 75–8.

  (1983a). Newborn infants imitate adult facial gestures. *Child Development*, 54, 702–9.

  (1983b). The origins of imitation in infancy: paradigm, phenomena and theories. In L. Lipsitt (ed.), *Advances in infancy research* (pp. 266–86). Norwood, NJ: Ablex.

Meltzoff, A. and Gopnik, A. (1993). The role of imitation in understanding persons and developing a theory of mind. In S. Baron-Cohen, H. Tager-Flusberg and D. Cohen (eds.), *Understanding other minds: Perspectives from autism* (pp. 335–66). Oxford University Press.

Mundy, P., Sigman, M. and Kasari, C. (1993). The theory of mind and joint attention in autism. In S. Baron-Cohen, H. Tager-Flusberg and D. Cohen (eds.), *Understanding other minds: Perspectives from autism* (pp. 181–203). Oxford University Press.

Murray, L. and Trevarthen, C. (1985). Emotional regulation of interaction between two-months-olds and their mothers. In T. M. Field and N. A. Fox (eds), *Social perception in infants* (pp. 177–97). Norwood, NJ: Ablex.

Nadel, J. (1986a). *Imitation et communication entre jeunes enfants*. Paris: Presses Universitaires de France.

  (1986b). Matching activities and the regulation of peer-toddler sustained interactions. In J. LeCamus and J. Cosnier (eds.), *Ethology and psychology* (pp. 55–67) Toulouse: Privat.

  (1994). The development of communication: Wallon's framework and influence. In A. Vyt, H. Bloch and M. Bornstein (eds.), *Early child development in the French tradition* (pp. 177–89). Hillsdale. NJ: Erlbaum.

  (1996). Early interpersonal timing and the perception of social contingencies. *Infant Behavior and Development*, 19, Special ICIS Issue, 202.

Nadel-Brulfert, J. and Baudonnière, P. M. (1982). The social function of reciprocal imitation in 2-year-old peers. *International Journal of Behavioral
Development*, 5, 95–109.

Nadel, J., Croué, S., Kervella, C., Mattlinger, M.-J., Canet, P., Hudelot, C.,
Lécuyer, C. and Martini, M. (submitted). Do children with autism have
ontological expectancies concerning human behaviour?

Nadel, J. and Fontaine, A. M. (1989). Communicating by imitation: a developmental and comparative approach to transitory social competence. In B.
Schneider at al. (eds.), *Social competence in developmental perspective* (pp.
131–44). Dordrecht: Kluwer.

Nadel, J. and Pezé, A. (1993). What makes immediate imitation communicative
in toddlers and autistic children? In J. Nadel and L. Camaioni (eds.), *New
perspectives in early communicative development* (pp. 139–56). London, NY:
Routledge.

Ohta, M. (1987). Cognitive disorders of infantile autism: A study employing the
WISC, spatial relationships, conceptualization and gesture imitations.
Journal of Autism and Developmental Disorders, 17, 45–62.

Papoušek, M. and Papoušek, H. (1977). Mothering and the cognitive head-start:
Psychobiological considerations. In H. R. Schaffer (ed.), *Studies in
mother–infant interaction* (pp. 63–85). New York: Academic Press.

(1989). Forms and functions of vocal matching in interactions between
mothers and their pre-canonical infants. *First Language*, 9, 137–58.

Pawlby, S. J. (1977). Imitative interactions. In H. R. Schaffer (ed.), *Studies in
mother–infant interactions* (pp. 203–24). New York: Academic Press.

Piaget, J. (1945). *La formation du symbole chez l'enfant*. Neuchatel/Paris:
Delachaux and Niestlé.

Prior, M. R. (1979). Cognitive abilities and disabilities in infantile autism: A
review. *Journal of Abnormal Child Psychology*, 7, 357–80.

Rivet, C. (1994). Communication imitative et double handicap sensoriel.
Université de Poitiers: Unpublished Manuscript.

Roberts, M., Wurtele, S., Boone, R., Metts, V. and Smith, V. (1981). Toward a
reconceptualization of reciprocal imitation phenomenon: two experiments.
Journal of Research in Personality, 15, 447–59.

Rogers, S. and Pennington, B. (1991). A theoretical approach to the deficits in
infantile autism. *Development and Psychopathology*, 3, 137–62.

Rogers, S. J., Bennetto, L., McEvoy, R. and Pennington, B. F. (1996). Imitation
and pantomime in high-functioning adolescents with autism spectrum disorders. *Child Development*, 67, 2060–73.

Ross, H., Lollis, S. and Elliott, C. (1982). Toddler-peer communication. In K.
Rubin and H. Ross (eds.), *Peer relationships and social skills in childhood* (pp.
73–98). NY: Springer-Verlag.

Rubenstein, J. and Howes, C. (1976). The effects of peer on toddler interaction
with mother and toys. *Child Development*, 47, 597–605.

Sigman, M. and Ungerer, J. A. (1984). Cognitive and language skills in autistic,
mentally retarded, and normal children. *Developmental Psychology*, 20,
293–302.

Stern, D. (1985). *The interpersonal world of the infant*. New York: Basic.

Thelen, M., Dollinger, S. and Roberts, M. (1975). On being imitated: its effects on attention and reciprocal imitation. *Journal of Personality and Social Psychology*, 31, 467–72.

Tiegerman, E. and Primavera, L. (1981). Object manipulation: an interactional strategy with autistic children. *Journal of Autism and Developmental Disorders*, 11, 427–38.

Tremblay-Leveau, H. and Nadel, J. (1996). Exclusion in triads: Can it serve 'meta-communicative' knowledge in 11- and 23-month-old children? *British Journal of Developmental Psychology*, 14, 145–58.

Trevarthen, C. (1977). Descriptive analyses of infant communicative behaviour. In H. R. Schaffer (ed.), *Studies in mother–infant interaction*. New York: Academic Press.

Užgiris, I. Č. (1976). Imitation with and without objects in infancy. Unpublished manuscript. Clark University.

(1981). Two functions of imitation during infancy. *International Journal of Behavioral Development*, 4, 1–12.

Užgiris, I. Č., Benson, J. B., Kruper, J. C. and Vasek, M. (1989). Contextual influences on imitative intentions between mothers and infants. In J. J. Lockman and N. C. Hazen (eds.), *Action in social context: perspectives on early development* (pp. 103–27). New York: Plenum Press.

Užgiris, I. Č., Broome, S. and Kruper, J. (1989b). Imitation in mother-child conversations: A focus on the mother. In G. E. Speidel and K. E. Nelson (eds.), *The many faces of imitation in language learning* (pp. 91–120). New York: Springer-Verlag.

Užgiris, I. and Hunt, J. (1975). *Assessment in infancy*. Urbana: University of Illinois Press.

(1987). *Infant performance and experience: New findings with the ordinal scales*. Urbana: University of Illinois Press.

Wallon, H. (1934). *Les origines du caractère chez l'enfant*. Paris: Presses Universitaires de France.

Wallon, H. (1942). *De l'acte à la pensée*. Paris: Flammarion.

Wing, L. (1976). *Early childhood autism*. Oxford: Pergamon.

Yando, R., Seitz, V. and Zigler, E. (1978). *Imitation: a developmental perspective*. Hillsdale, NJ: Erlbaum.

Zazzo, R. (1957). Le problème de l'imitation chez le nouveau-né. *Enfance*, 10, 135–42.

8   Neonatal imitation and imitation among children with autism and Down's syndrome

Mikael Heimann and Eva Ullstadius

This chapter rests on the assumption that infants have an inborn ability to imitate facial gestures. To us, this means that the newborn baby can be described as already knowing something about the body and that this 'knowledge' enables the baby in some unknown way to differentiate between the inside and the outside world (Heimann, 1997; Holmlund, 1995; Kugiumutzakis, 1993: Legerstee, 1991; and Meltzoff and Moore, 1992, 1994). A conclusion that, if completely substantiated, might have a strong impact on our theory building within developmental psychology as well as on the practice of psychology and our understanding of psychopathology.

As of today, the theory building needed as a consequence of our expanded knowledge of the capacity of the neonate has become a major concern for many researchers within the field of early infancy. Currently, there are several different coexisting approaches, for example: the theory of early infant intersubjectivity (Trevarthen, this volume; Trevarthen and Aitken, 1994), the theory of the virtual other (Bråten, 1988, 1994), and a dynamical systems approach (Thelen and Smith, 1994). It will probably still be some time before we have 'The New Theory' that explains the imitative capacity of the newborn child and its role in both normal and atypical development.

Thus, the basic motivation for this chapter is that a better understanding of links between imitation observed early and late in infancy will help us to a better understanding of both normal and pathological development. Some recent theoretical formulations (e.g., Rogers and Pennington, 1991) postulate that neonatal imitation is an important social competence, and that this ability is missing in children with autism, but not among children with Down's syndrome. According to Rogers and Pennington, neonatal imitation can be seen as an indication of an early co-ordination of self and other or a kind of body scheme. Such a body scheme is thought to be crucial for the development of social relatedness, an ability that is severely disturbed in autism. Thus, neonatal imitation becomes a prime candidate for an extremely early primary deficit in a developmental model of autism. However, to date, no observations exist on imitation in children with autism under a year old, although several studies on somewhat older subjects indicate that children with autism do indeed differ in the way they use imitation spontaneously and in how they can be motivated to use imitation (e.g., Heimann, Ullstadius, Dahlgren and Gillberg, 1992; Smith and Bryson, 1994). Furthermore, Nadel (this volume; Nadel and Pezé, 1993) has found that imitation as a means of communication might be a good predictor of social capacities for children with autism.

One way of enhancing our knowledge is through comparative studies on imitation among both typically developing infants and children with various developmental disorders. This is also the line of inquiry explored in this chapter: the first part presents longitudinal observations of imitation during the first year of life, part 2 describes a longitudinal study of imitation among 5 preschool children with autism and part 3 focuses on imitation in infants with Down's syndrome between 1 and 4 months old.

Part 1: Follow-up on typically developing infants

The problem that has puzzled researchers since neonatal imitation was first demonstrated experimentally is the underlying mechanism. How can an infant imitate movements made by others when the corresponding movements of his own body were known to him only tactually or kinaesthetically? It seemed obvious that the infant must possess some previously unknown mechanism in order to imitate. Meltzoff and Moore (1977, 1983) proposed a supramodal body schema that could map seen movements onto equivalent felt movements and Trevarthen (e.g. 1979, 1980, 1982) suggested that a template for a cerebral representation of persons must exist that makes it possible for the newborn to perceive, respond and relate directly to persons (primary intersubjectivity), even though the exact brain mechanism was still unknown. Furthermore, Goldman-Rakic (1985) and Vinter (1986) proposed that neonatal imitation is mediated primarily through subcortical processes, whereas imitation developing at later ages is based on cortical processes. This idea has also been supported more recently by Stein and Meredith (1993) whose research indicates that multimodal individual neurons and multisensory maps in subcortical areas (e.g., the superior colliculus) can provide a possible neuropsychological basis for neonatal imitation. Recently, Trevarthen (this volume; Trevarthen and Aitken, 1994) has proposed that a subcortical 'intrinsic motive system' exists, a system that enables the very young infant both to communicate and to imitate directly from birth. However, the exact mechanism is still unknown and no consensus exists regarding these complicated early interactions between the socio-emotional level (the baby with an adult) and the biological/cognitive inner processes taking place simultaneously.

Most investigators to date conclude that neonatal imitation is best understood at the interactional level as an early social capacity (e.g., Heimann, 1989; Holmlund, 1995; Kugiumutzakis, 1985; Maratos, 1982; Meltzoff and Moore, 1992, Trevarthen, 1982, 1996). According to Trevarthen neonatal imitation need not necessarily be accomplished by a comparison of seen and felt movements, but rather by some kind of 'image' of a movement to be made in response to a seen movement. Thus, the child is 'born capable of perceiving the bodies of others as like their own' (Trevarthen, 1996, p. 3). Bråten (1994) takes a step further and explicitly proposes that the infant mind has an innate dialogical structure consisting of self and a 'virtual' other. Newborns seek dialogic closure between self and 'virtual' other, but an actual other person is easily replaced into this pre-existent dyadic mind.

None of the existing theoretical positions make any specific prediction for the relationship between imitation at birth and imitation displayed later in development, although they more or less assume that neonatal imitation should have an effect on the overall socio-emotional develop-ment of the child (Holmlund, 1995; Meltzoff and Moore, 1994; Trevarthen, 1996). Thus, we still do not know if or how the neonate's ability to imitate affects psychological development beyond the infancy period. Observations to be presented here will, however, show that some associations can be observed between early and late imitation even if the relationships found so far must be considered fragile and very preliminary.

Imitation during the first month of life

We have found that children imitate both tongue protrusion and mouth opening at 3 days and at 3 weeks (Heimann, 1992, 1997; Heimann, Nelson and Schaller, 1989; Heimann and Schaller, 1985;) although the tendency to imitate is somewhat stronger for tongue protrusion. While two-thirds of the children imitated tongue protrusion during the first month, only about 45% responded with imitation to the mouth opening gesture. However, the observed imitation of mouth opening was in fact real, since we could detect several positive correlations between imitation at 3 days and at 3 weeks (range of $r = 0.49$ to 0.68) which related as much to mouth opening as to tongue protrusion. These correlations also high-light another aspect, that of early individual differences. According to our findings, children differ in their tendency to imitate as early as on day 3 post partum.

Imitation at birth and imitation at 3 months

Many researchers report that neonatal imitation of facial gestures disappears around 3 months of age (Abravanel and Sigafoos, 1984; Fontaine, 1984; Jacobson, 1979; Kugiumutzakis, 1985; Maratos, 1973) and Trevarthen (1980) described his observations of early imitation as 'magnetic', that is, fairly automatic but unpredictable, and in this sense not reflexive. In recordings of protoconversation in the second month Trevarthen (1982) rarely observed imitation. Instead it is the mother who imitates the baby. Around 5 months of age 'discretionary' imitation appears. The infant shows marked attention to the model and responds after a series of tentative attempts.

Our experiences from longitudinal studies of neonatal imitation are close to those of Trevarthen: It is increasingly difficult – but not impossible – to get an infant to imitate the facial gestures of tongue protrusion and mouth opening after 2 to 3 months, even for the mother (Heimann et al., 1989). Facial imitation is only rarely observed at 6 months according to preliminary observations made within our latest longitudinal study. It reappears shortly thereafter and is definitely back by 9 months. When imitating these expressions at 9 months, the baby's action is seemingly more voluntary and conscious, showing strong motor control and intent (and also self-conscious humour and playfulness). Usually one only sees a few strong responses that cannot be mistaken.

Our observations also seemed to indicate a general decline in facial imitation over the first 3 months (Heimann et al., 1989; Heimann, 1991); more infants imitated at 3 weeks than at 3 months. Further analyses did, however, reveal that the pattern was not so clear. A downward trend over the first 3 months is observed for tongue protrusion but not for mouth opening. Seventy per cent imitate tongue protrusion at 3 days, but only 30% at 3 months. In contrast, approximately half the group imitates mouth opening at all occasions.

Finally, an additional way of analysing our data does point towards a possible link between neonatal imitation and imitation at 3 months: high imitators at 3 days tended to be high imitators at 3 months as well (Heimann, in press). This finding must, however, be interpreted with extreme caution since (1) it is based on a relatively small sample, (2) it needs to be replicated and (3) to decide how to define a child as high or low in imitation this early in life is a rather delicate issue.

Imitation at birth and imitation at 12 months

To date, not a single published report has explicitly investigated whether and how experimentally elicited neonatal imitation (when the child is showing the first signs of primary intersubjectivity) is – in any way – related to imitation observed when the child has reached his or her first birthday (when the child is well into the world of secondary inter-subjectivity). The only attempt so far, is a follow-up carried out in Sweden as a continuation of our first longitudinal study. The results from this follow-up are described below, albeit briefly, since a more complete presentation is available elsewhere (Heimann, 1998).

An observation was added at 12 months for the children who had par-ticipated in the longitudinal study presented above (Heimann, 1991; Heimann et al., 1989). The imitation tasks used were chosen with the aim to cover a variety of domains: action with objects, social gestures, vocal tasks, facial imitation, verbal imitation and temperament. As suggested by Field, Goldstein, Vega-Lahr and Porter (1986) a broad range of tasks would increase the likelihood of finding a link in imitation over an extended time period, provided such a link really exists. Thus, we mod-elled 16 different imitation tasks as playfully as possible and succeeded in motivating 30 out of 32 parents to come back for this one-year follow-up.

Our results show that, at 12 months, the children imitated actions with objects and vocal tasks more often than they imitated facial gestures (e.g., tongue protrusion and mouth opening) or social gestures (e.g., eye blink-ing and sniffing on flower), but we failed to detect any significant correla-tion between imitation of facial gestures at birth and our measures of imitation at 12 months. This also held for observed correlations between imitation at birth and other domains of development (e.g., temperament or vocabulary) when the child was 1 year old. Thus, we found no support for any direct link between *neonatal imitation* and imitation at one year. But we did find some evidence for a link between *early infant imitation* and later imitation since significant correlations were detected between imita-tion at 3 months and imitation at 12 months. A child's tendency to imitate tongue protrusion at 3 months was positively associated with vocal imita-tion 9 months later ($r = 0.42$) as was imitation of mouth opening at 3 months and imitation of actions on objects at 12 months ($r = 0.38$). In sum, these findings do suggest that imitation at 3 months is in some way related to imitation at 12 months, although some caution is warranted. The obtained correlations only explain about 10% of the variance in imitation. Also needed, but still lacking, are replications confirming these observations.

Mother–infant interaction and early imitation

In an attempt to explore further the implications of the newborn infant's ability to imitate, we added a brief face-to-face interaction between the mothers and their 3-month-old children (Heimann, 1989). The first

2 minutes of this mother–infant dialogue were videotaped and sub-sequently analysed using categories adapted from the Infant Monadic Phases coding scheme (Tronick, Als and Brazelton, 1980). Our results show that a negative relationship exists between imitation and brief gaze aversion (the infant looks away for no more than 3 seconds). In other words, a child showing a high tendency to imitate early in life is less likely to display instances of brief gaze aversion while in a face-to-face interaction with the mother. To us, this finding indicates that there exists a link between imitation as an early ability and the rich and dynamic interactive flow taking place between the carer and the infant. Gaze aversion is closely tied to the amount of eye-to-eye contact between the mother and her child which, in turn, is often judged important for the emerging relationship (e.g., Field, 1977; Greenspan, 1982; Keller and Gauda, 1987). Neonatal imitation might be one important innate building block that both helps the infant to express his or her social competence (see Bråten, 1994) and to be an active partner in the co-regulative process already taking place between mother and child from the first day of life (see Fogel, 1993).

Imitation at 3 months and at 12 months: a special case?

We also found that brief gaze aversion at 3 months was negatively correlated with vocal imitation at 12 months ($r = -0.45$). Taken together with our other findings this suggests special links between imitation of tongue protrusion at 3 months, episodes of brief gaze aversion at 3 months and vocal imitation at 12 months. In short, our findings indicate the following:

(1) A negative correlation between imitation of tongue protrusion at 3 months and concurrently observed episodes of brief gaze aversion in a face-to-face situation.

(2) A negative correlation between brief gaze aversion at 3 months and vocal imitation at 12 months.

(3) A positive correlation between imitation of tongue protrusion at 3 months and vocal imitation at 12 months.

Stated in a more speculative manner, one might suspect that there is something special about the minority of children who actually displayed tongue protrusion at 3 months since only about one-third of our sample did imitate the gesture at this age. It might be the case that children imitating tongue protrusion at this age have in some way encountered a different developmental history during their first 3 months of life. Maybe these children have become more motivated to participate in social interactions and/or imitative-like games.

Part 2: Follow-up on children with autism

Deficient bodily imitation, often found in children with autism, is assumed to be caused by an impaired capacity to form or manipulate representations of movements of the self and others. Also, later developing problems of affect mirroring and sharing, and awareness of other's subjective states, might be traced to an original failure to represent the child's own and other people's bodies (e.g., Ohta, 1987; Rogers and Pennington, 1991; Smith, 1995). Meltzoff and Gopnik (1993) and Ritvo and Provence (1953) also refer to deficient imitation as fundamental for the emergence of childhood autism. Their ideas of the role of imitation in the development of self–other concepts are, however, opposed. While imitation, according to Ritvo and Provence, is central in the process of differentiation of the self from the non-self, it functions as mediator in a judgmental process of self–other equivalence, according to Meltzoff and Gopnik. Correspondences between one's own activities and those of others are recognised through imitation, and a foundation is laid to represent other's thoughts and feeling states, while deficiencies in imitation of others' actions contribute to failure to develop a theory of mind (Meltzoff and Gopnik, 1993).

Smith and Bryson (1994) object to Meltzoff and Gopnik's idea of the central imitation problem being to recognise the correspondences between the actions of self and others. Even if autistic children do not imitate themselves, they respond to being imitated by others (Dawson and Adams, 1984; Tiegerman and Primavera, 1984). Thus, Smith and Bryson (1994) suggest that more basic non-social deficits might underlie impaired imitation in autistic children, notably impaired perceptual organisation of movements, manifested in abnormal representation of actions.

According to Hobson (1993) imitation is of particular importance for the study of autism, since imitative exchanges might establish correspondences in attitude and action between people. Correspondences established by neonatal imitation and by responsiveness to being imitated, are, however, different from the more elaborated imitation by 1-year-old infants who can recognise other people's attitudes and actions. Children with autism probably show delays and limitations for both forms of imitation, and with large individual variations. Or, to paraphrase Baron-Cohen (1995), the processes involved might be considerably more complex than simply 'lack of neonatal imitative ability causes autism'.

Not only are there large differences in the theoretical frameworks used by researchers in the field, the imitation tasks used vary accordingly. From our perspective, that of neonatal facial imitation, so called 'body imitation' is of special interest. Body imitation may, however, be defined in a lot of different ways. From 'standing on one leg one minute' (DeMyer et al., 1972) or 'left hand's fingers against right hand's palm' (Bergès and Lézine, 1965) to learned gestures, like 'hand clapping' or 'waving good-bye'. Some of the pure body imitation tasks, especially those picked from the Bergès and Lézine (1965) scale, and other tasks used in neuropsychological examinations, require a great deal of instant body co-ordination. Failure to imitate such movements might reflect a co ordination as well as an imitation deficit.

Another group of tasks involves imitation of actions on objects. These tasks also vary from arbitrary object handling, like 'banging an object', to conventional object use in acts like 'drinking from a cup' or 'driving a nail into wood'. Furthermore, two additional types of tasks can be discerned: those constructed in order to study symbolic imitation and those aimed at imitation of emotional expressions. Almost all studies based on Piaget's theory have used the Užgiris–Hunt scale (e.g., Abrahamsen and Mitchell 1990; Charman and Baron-Cohen, 1994; Curcio 1978; Sigman and Ungerer, 1984). This scale is a special case, in that it follows Piaget's stages and the tasks are adapted to the individual child. Thus, all children within a study are not given identical tasks.

In sum, studies presented to date indicate that deficient body imitation and – probably – symbolic imitation are especially impaired among children with autism. Imitation of actions on objects seem to be less affected. However, a developmental and longitudinal approach is almost always lacking, and we are still far from a complete understanding of how imitation develops for children with autism and if their development should be viewed primarily as delayed or deviant.

Observation 1: Imitation in children with autism when 4 years old

In an attempt to explore imitation in autism from a more developmental perspective, we investigated the performance of a small group of children with autism on imitation tasks previously administered to neonates and 1-year-old children (see Heimann et al., 1992). Five children (one girl) with a median age of 54 months (range: 39–62 months), and whose mental age ranged from 25 to 51 months, participated. They were diagnosed according to the DSM-III-R (APA, 1987), and their diagnoses were confirmed by 2 independent child psychiatrists. In addition, 2 comparison groups were included: the first one consisted of 3 typically developing 4-year-olds (1 girl; chronological age: 45–48 months) while the second one consisted of 28 healthy 12-month-old infants from our follow-up study (see part 1, this chapter).

We observed and videotaped both the children with autism and the typically developing children during an hour-long home visit. First, the child was allowed a familiarisation period that was at least 5 minutes long. The next step was to give the child a chance to play freely with our toys, a phase that lasted 3 to 5 minutes. Finally, our imitation tasks were modelled for the child and this took between 17 and 36 minutes.

Two identical sets of toys were always used when modelling (one set for the child and one set for the experimenter) and each task was demonstrated twice, unless the child immediately produced a perfect imitation. Furthermore, tasks were only presented when the experimenter judged the child to be attentive, and verbal clues were never used (except for verbal messages needed in order to catch and keep the child's attention).

Fifteen different imitation tasks were presented to the children with autism, and to the 3 typically developing 4-year-olds, while the normal 1-year-olds only received 10 tasks (numbers 1–10 below). Our tasks can be briefly described as follows:

(a). *Action on objects.* 1) To take a small wooden block from the floor and then drop it; (2) to build a tower of two blocks; (3) to stir in a cup with a spoon; (4) to pretend to drink from a cup; and (5) to use a soft brush.

(b). *Vocal imitation.* (6) A hand puppet pretends to drink from a cup and says 'Aah!'; (7) the hand puppet drops a block and says 'Oy!'

(c). *Facial imitation.* (8) Tongue protrusion; (9) mouth opening; (10) sniffing a flower.

(d). *Motor imitation.* (11) Waving bye-bye; (12) yawn; (13) touch ear-knee-nose.

(e). *Object substitution.* (14) Using a cup as a hat; (15) using the brush as a cup.

Imitation was coded – from videotapes – as either complete (a score of 2), partial (a score of 1) or unsuccessful (score 0). Furthermore, imitation was only coded if the child responded within 10 seconds after the end of the presentation and if the response had not been displayed spontaneously during the initial free-play period.

Four of the children with autism did display imitation to some degree, while 1 child failed to imitate any of the acts. They responded with imitation to at least 1 of the tasks belonging to the group 'actions with objects'. In contrast, only 1 or 2 of the children with autism displayed imitation when tasks from the other 4 groups were modelled. More specifically, 2 children did imitate both vocal imitation tasks, 2 displayed some facial imitation, 2 imitated some of the object substitution tasks, but only 1 child imitated any of the motor imitation tasks. The motor imitation tasks were also most difficult to present, and we failed several times.

In conclusion, the level of imitation seems to vary as a function of the types of tasks presented. Object manipulation tasks were most often imitated, while motor and object substitution tasks displayed the lowest frequencies of observed imitation. Furthermore, we also noted variations in imitation among our 5 children with autism. Three of the children were responsible for a majority of the imitative responses observed. One of those 3 had an estimated mental age of only 33 months and also one of the lowest developmental quotients in our sample. Thus, imitation, as we observed it, is not *only* a function of the child's overall mental capacities.

None of the children with autism performed at the level of the normal 4-year-olds when we compared the children's overall imitation scores (0 = no imitation; 2 = complete imitation). The median score among the children with autism was 0.56 (range 0–1.0), while the median for the three 4-year-old children used for comparison was 1.2 (range 1.13–1.6). Similarly, the 28 healthy 1-year-old children in our second comparison group also displayed a higher tendency to imitate action on objects than the autism group (imitation score 0.80 versus 0.35). Overall, it was our clear impression that the children with autism imitated to a lesser degree than the normal one-year-olds.

Since we have been especially interested in facial imitation, it might be of interest to look a bit more closely on how the children performed when tongue protrusion or mouth opening were modelled. We managed to present these 2 gestures to 3 of our subjects, but just 1 (the only girl) responded with imitation. She very obviously imitated tongue protrusions, first showing her tongue to the experimenter and then turning directly towards the camcorder and protruding her tongue clearly a second time. There is thus no doubt that this girl imitated voluntarily, intentionally and playfully. This girl also showed awareness of self-and-other body knowledge, when she crawled up on the experimenter's lap and first touched her eyelashes (with mascara on) and then her own eyelashes.

Observation 2: Imitation in children with autism when 6 years old

Since autism is considered a developmental disorder, one would expect that children with autism would change in their tendency to imitate as they grow older (e.g., Rogers and Pennington, 1991). Thus, it becomes important to follow children with autism longitudinally and observe how imitation develops and how individual children keep their relative position over time (see Nadel, this volume).

A small first step towards a longitudinal approach was taken by us when we were given the possibility to carry out a follow-up 2 years after

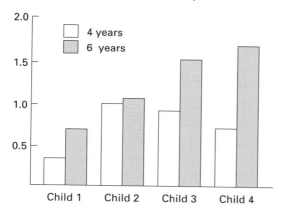

Figure 8.1. Average imitation scores for four children with autism at 4 and 6 years of age.

our original data collection. We were able to receive permission from the parents of 4 of our 5 children with autism. Thus, one severely retarded boy with autism (child 2 in Heimann et al., 1992) did not participate in this, previously unpublished, follow-up.

The 4 remaining children were once again observed in their homes using the same 15 imitation tasks as described earlier. All observations were videotaped and all imitation tasks were presented by a paediatric nurse (who was also an undergraduate student of psychology). The children were now between 63 and 88 months old (median age: 75 months) compared with 39 to 58 months (median: 48 months) at the time of the previous observation.

All children increased their imitative performance from 4 to 6 years (see Figure 8.1). The actual overall imitation scores ranged from 0.33 to 1.0 at 4 years and from 0.73 to 1.86 at 6 years. Moreover, the figure also reveals interesting changes in how the children keep their relative position over time. Child 1 has the lowest imitation score at both ages (score: 0.33 and 0.73) and child 3 (the girl) receives the second highest score both times (0.93 and 1.67). These two children had the two lowest developmental quotients (DQ) as measured by Griffiths Developmental Scales (Griffiths, 1954; Swedish standardisation: Alin-Åkerman and Nordberg, 1980) at the time of our 4-year observation (child 1: DQ = 65; child 2: DQ = 62). In contrast, the two children with developmental quotients within the normal range did change their relative positions. Child 2 (DQ = 106) slipped from the first position at 4 years to the third place at 6 years (score: 1.0 and 1.47) while child 4 (DQ = 86) made the opposite change: from position 3 to position 1 (score: 0.73 and 1.86).

In conclusion, all children did increase their tendency to imitate from 4 to 6 years of age, but only 2 kept their relative position over the same time period. Thus, we must be careful when evaluating a young child with autism showing no or little imitation since we have no way of knowing how this child will perform a couple of years later.

Part 3: Follow-up on children with Down's syndrome

Down's syndrome is a chromosomal aberration that most often is recognised (and diagnosed) at birth or shortly thereafter and children with this diagnosis typically end up being mildly to moderately retarded (Udwin and Dennis, 1995) although the discrepancy between a normal baby and a Down baby is less obvious during the first 6 to 9 months of life (Cicchetti and Beeghly, 1990).

Since children with Down's syndrome have been used as a comparison group in studies focusing on children with autism and, since the disorder is known early in life, one would expect that the early imitative capacity of these children had already been explored. However, to date no such report exists. Earlier reports on imitation in young children or infants with Down's syndrome have used a traditional Piagetian strategy (e.g., the Užgiris–Hunt scales) and this might explain why they have not included imitation of facial gestures like mouth opening or tongue protrusion (see Dunst, 1990). As far as is known to us, our own ongoing study in Sweden is the only exception. We have observed eight children with Down's syndrome as soon as possible after they have been diagnosed. The first results of this study have only recently been analysed and a brief summary is given here (Heimann, Ullstadius and Swerlander, 1998).

It was our main hypothesis that young infants with Down's syndrome, if able to imitate, would display a response pattern similar to that which we had observed earlier among typically developing infants. To be more specific, we expected to find the following pattern: (a) More imitation of tongue protrusion during the first 2 months of life than at 3 months, and (b) a more evenly distributed response pattern for mouth opening.

Eight children (one girl) with Down's syndrome participated in our study. Five children were successfully observed at 1 month (range: 25–52 days), 7 at 3 months (70–101 days old) and 7 at 4 months (97–143 days). All children were observed in a home setting, and both tongue protrusion and mouth opening were modelled using a procedure similar to Meltzoff and Moore (1983) and Heimann (1992).

Our results (see Table 8.1) show that all 5 children observed at 1 month imitated tongue protrusion. In other words, all of them displayed more tongue responses after modelling of tongue protrusion than when mouth opening was presented. In contrast, the result for mouth opening was not

Table 8.1. *Imitation of tongue protrusion and mouth opening in eight children with Down's syndrome as judged by each child's individual response oattern (from Heimann, Ullstadius and Swerlander, 1998)*

CHILD	Imitation at					
	1 month		3 months		4 months	
	TP	MO	TP	MO	TP	MO
A	YES	YES	–	YES	YES	–
B	YES	–	–	YES	–	YES
C	YES	YES	YES	YES	YES	–
D	YES	–	–	YES	–	YES
H	YES	YES	–	YES	n/a	n/a
E	n/a	n/a	–	YES	YES	–
F	n/a	n/a	–	–	–	–
G	n/a	n/a	n/a	n/a–	0	YES

Notes:

YES = Imitation. More target responses are observed after modelling of target gesture than after non-target gesture.

– = No imitation. More responses are observed after modelling of non-target gesture than after presentation of the target gesture.

n/a = Not applicable (no observations available).

as clear: judged individually, only 3 children imitated mouth opening at this age.

At 3 months, the pattern had changed. Now, only 1 child imitated tongue protrusion, but 6 imitated mouth opening. However, the response rates for both tongue protrusion and mouth opening increased as a response to seeing mouth opening being presented, and only 1 child imitated *both* gestures. Thus, it is uncertain if one can maintain the argument that the children actually imitate mouth opening at this age. Finally, at 4 months, we found that 3 children imitated tongue protrusion and 3 imitated mouth opening. None of the children at this age imitated both gestures.

Individual response patterns

Child A. This boy imitated both tongue protrusion and mouth opening at 1 month (see Table 8.1), mouth opening at 3 and tongue protrusion at 4 months.

Child B was born 4 weeks prematurely and his age at the first observation equals a gestational age of 40 weeks. He imitates tongue protrusion at 1 month and mouth opening at 3 and 4 months.

Child C. This boy imitates both gestures at 1 and 3 months but only tongue protrusion at 4 months. *Child D* imitates tongue protrusion at 1 month and mouth opening at 3 and 4 months. *Child E* imitates both gestures at 1 month but only mouth opening at 3 months.

Child F and *G* only participated in the 2 last observations. *Child F* imitates mouth opening at 3 months and tongue protrusion at 4 months, while *Child G* shows no instances of imitation to any of the gestures.

Finally we have the only girl in the sample, *Child H.* She entered the study relatively late and was only observed at 4 months when she successfully imitated mouth opening.

In sum, we are tempted to conclude that facial imitation is already present during the first month for children with Down's syndrome. Based on our observations, we suspect that even children with Down's syndrome would display neonatal imitation if observed directly after birth. As expected, the children's tendency to imitate diminished at 3 and 4 months.

Some tentative postulates

We have presented observations on imitation made among newborn infants, typically developing one-year-olds, infants with Down's syndrome and 4- to 6-year-old children with autism. Our findings might be tentatively summarised as follows:

(A) Neonatal imitation (NI)

(i)   Neonates do have the capacity to imitate.
(ii)   Some infants are more easily motivated to show imitation than others (possible individual differences).
(iii) Elicited neonatal imitation is related to the prototypical dialogue between the child and the mother (as observed through gaze aversion). NI is an innate social competence that is expressed, by the child, in a state of felt immediacy (see Bråten, 1994).
(iv)   NI is not directly linked to imitation at 1 year.
(v)   Imitation at 3 months and at 12 months are connected (at least for a subgroup of children).

(B) Children with autism

(i)   Clearly different development from typically developing children.
(ii)   Deficits especially in motor imitation, facial imitation and symbolic imitation.
(iii) The tendency and motivation to imitate might change dramatically

over time. A child displaying low imitation at 4 years might be much more easily lured into imitation games 2 years later.

(iv) Imitation during the neonatal period is affected only if the brain system responsible for primary intersubjectivity (Trevarthen, this volume, 1996; Trevarthen & Aitken, 1994) is affected.

Thus, we suspect that neonatal imitation is not a perfect divider between children developing autism and those who do not. It is our belief that some children with autism will not start to develop a deviant pattern for imitation until well into their first year of life (probably somewhere around 6 to 9 months of life, a period when intense changes are taking place on both the psychological and biological level of development).

(C) Children with Down's syndrome

(i)   Facial imitation is evident at 1 month of age. In other words, neo-natal imitation doees not require a 'normal' brain or nervous system.

(ii) Overall pattern shows similarities to previous observations on typ-ically developing infants.

(iii) Elicited imitation at 1 month probably reflects an innate social com-petence. A child with Down's syndrome can enter a prototypical mother–infant dialogue.

The threads of imitation research summarised above are not equally supported by our empirical observations. In short, we would claim that strong *or* relatively strong evidence exists for the neonate's ability to imitate (Ai), individual differences in imitation (Aii), imitation as an early social competence (Aiii), an imitation deficit among children with autism (Bi and Bii), and an early imitative competence among children with Down's syndrome (Ci). In contrast, only preliminary support can be found for links between imitation around birth and later in the first year (Aiv, Av and Biii), for an imitation deficit already at birth for children with autism (Biv), and for the importance of an imitative capacity among Down's syndrome children (Cii and Ciii).

ACKNOWLEDGMENTS

The research presented in this chapter has been supported by grants from the Bank of Sweden Tercentenary Foundation (no. 89/313), Stockholm, the Sven Jerring Foundation, Stockholm, the Claes Groschinky Foundation, Stockholm, Allmänna Barnhuset, Stockholm, and the Swedish First of May Flower Foundation, Göteborg, Sweden to Mikael Heimann. Support for writing this chapter has also been provided by the Centre for Advanced Study, the Norwegian Academy of Science and Letters, Oslo, Norway. Special thanks are due to Kristina Svärd for her invaluable help, as well as to all participating children and their families.

REFERENCES

Abrahamsen, E. P. and Mitchell, J. R. (1990). Communication and sensorimotor functioning in children with autism. *Journal of Autism and Developmental Disorders*, 20, 75–85.

Abravanel, E. and Sigafoos, A. D. (1984). Exploring the presence of imitation during early infancy. *Child Development*, 55, 381–92.

Alin-Åkerman, B. and Nordberg, L. (1980). *Griffiths utvecklingsskalor I och II*. Stockholm, Sweden: Psykologiförlaget (in Swedish).

American Psychiatric Association. (1987). *Diagnostic and statistical manual of mental disorders* (3rd edn revised). Washington, DC: American Psychiatric Association.

Baron-Cohen, S. (1995). *Mindblindness*. Cambridge, USA: MIT Press.

Bergès, J. and Lézine, I. (1965). The imitation of gestures. *Clinics in Developmental Medicine No 18*. (A. H. Parmelee Jr. trans.). London: W. Heinemann Medical Books.

Bråten, S. (1988). Dialogic mind: The infant and the adult in protoconversation. In M. E. Carvallo (ed.), *Nature, cognition, and system I* (pp. 187–205). Dordrecht, The Netherlands: Klüwer Academic Publishers.

   (1994). Self–other connections in the imitating infant and in the dyad: The companion space theorem. In S. Bråten (ed.), *Theory forum symposium pre-proceedings* (pp. 15–16). The Norwegian Academy of Science and Letters, Oslo.

Brown, J. and Whiten, A. (1994, July). Imitation, pretend play, theory of mind and social interaction in autism. Poster session at the International Conference on Infant Studies, Paris, France.

Charman, T. and Baron-Cohen, S. (1994). Another look at imitation in autism. *Development and Psychopathology*, 6, 403–13.

Cicchetti, D. and Beeghly, M. (1990). An organizational approach to the study of Down syndrome: contributions to an integrative theory of development. In D. Cicchetti and M. Beeghly (eds.), *Children with Down syndrome: A developmental perspective* (pp. 29–62). New York: Cambridge University Press.

Curcio, F. (1978). Sensorimotor functioning and communication in autistic children. *Journal of Autism and Childhood Schizophrenia*, 8, 281–92.

Dawson, G. and Adams, A. (1984). Imitation and social responsiveness in autistic children. *Journal of Abnormal Child Psychology*, 12, 209–26.

DeMyer, M. K., Alpern, G. D., Barton, S., DeMyer, W. E., Churchill, D. W., Hingtgen, J. N., Brysion, C. Q., Pontius, W. and Kimberlin, C. (1972). Imitation in autistic, early schizophrenic, and non-psychotic subnormal children. *Journal of Autism and Childhood Schizophrenia*, 2, 264–87.

Dunst, C. J. (1990). Sensorimotor development of infants with Down syndrome. In D. Cicchetti and M. Beeghly (eds.), *Children with Down syndrome: A developmental perspective*. New York: Cambridge University Press.

Field, T. M. (1977). Effects of early separation, interaction deficits and experimental manipulation on infant–mother face-to-face interaction. *Child Development*, 48, 763–71.

Field, T. M., Goldstein, S., Vega-Lahr, N. and Porter, K. (1986). Changes in imitative behavior during early infancy. *Infant Behavior and Development*, 9, 415–21.

Fogel, A. (1993). *Developing through relationships.* University of Chicago Press.

Fontaine, R. (1984). Imitative skills between birth and six months. *Infant Behavior and Development,* 7, 323–33.

Goldman-Rakic, P. S. (1985). Toward a neurobiology of cognitive development. In J. Meehler and R. Fox (eds.), *Neonate cognition: Beyond the blooming buzzing confusion* (pp. 285–306). Hillsdale, NJ: Erlbaum.

Greenspan, S. I. (1982). *Psychopathology and adaption in infancy and early childhood: Principles of clinical diagnosis and preventive intervention.* Clinical Infant Reports, no. 1. New York: International Universities Press.

Griffiths, R. (1954). *The abilities of babies.* University of London Press.

Heimann, M. (1989). Neonatal imitation, gaze aversion, and mother–infant interaction. *Infant Behavior and Development,* 12, 495–505.

(1991). Neonatal imitation: A social and biological phenomenon. In T. Archer and S. Hansen (eds.), *Behavioral biology: The neuroendocrine axis* (pp. 173–86). Hillsdale, NJ: Erlbaum.

(1992). *Neonatal imitation: Integrating findings from three Swedish studies.* Göteborg Psychological Reports, 22 (No. 4).

(1994). Possible implications of an early imitative capacity for the socio-emotional and cognitive development during the first year of life. In S. Bråten (ed.), *Theory forum symposium pre-proceedings* (pp. 19–20). The Norwegian Academy of Science and Letters, Oslo.

(1997). The never ending story of neonatal imitation. Poster presented at the 8th European Conference on Developmental Psychology, Rennes, France.

(1998). Imitation in neonates, older infants and in children with autism: Feedback to theory. In S. Bråten (ed.), *Intersubjective communication and emotion in ontogeny: A source Book.* Cambridge University Press.

(in press). Neonatal imitation – a fuzzy phenomenon or not? In F. Lacerda, C. V. Hofsten and M. Heimann (eds.), *Emerging cognitive abilities in early infancy.* Hillsdale, NJ: Erlbaum.

Heimann, M., Nelson, K. E. and Schaller, J. (1989). Neonatal imitation of tongue protrusion and mouth opening: Methodological aspects and evidence of early individual differences. *Scandinavian Journal of Psychology,* 90, 90–101.

Heimann, M. and Schaller, J. (1985). Imitative reactions among 14–21 days old infants. *Infant Mental Health Journal,* 6, 31–9.

Heimann, M., Ullstadius, E. and Swerlander, A. (1998). Imitation in eight young infants with Down syndrome. 1998 Paediatric Research, 44(5), 1–5.

Heimann, M., Ullstadius, E., Dahlgren, S-O. and Gillberg, C. (1992). Imitation in Autism: A preliminary research note. *Behavioral Neurology,* 5, 219–27.

Hobson, R. P. (1993). *Autism and the development of mind.* Hillsdale, NJ: Erlbaum.

Holmlund, C. (1995). Development of turntakings as a sensorimotor process in the first 3 months: A sequential analysis. In K. E. Nelson and Z. Réger (eds.), *Children's Language Vol. 8* (pp. 41–64). Hillsdale, NJ: Erlbaum.

Jacobson, S. W. (1979). Matching behavior in the young infant. *Child Development,* 50, 425–30.

Keller, H. and Gauda, G. (1987). Eye contact in the first month of life and its developmental consequences. In H. Rauh and H.-Ch. Steinhausen (eds.), *Psychobiology and early development* (pp. 129–43). Amsterdam: Elsevier.

Kugiumutzakis, J. (1985). The origin, development, and function of the early infant imitation. Unpublished doctoral dissertation, University of Uppsala, Sweden.

(1993). Intersubjective vocal imitation in early mother–infant interaction. In J. Nadel and L. Camaioni (eds.), *New perspectives in early communication development.* London: Routledge.

Legerstee, M. (1991). The role of person and object in eliciting early imitation. *Journal of Experimental Child Psychology*, 51, 423–33.

Maratos, O. (1973). The origin and development of imitation in the first six months of life. Paper presented at the Annual Meeting of the British Psychological Society, Liverpool, UK.

(1982). Trends in the development of imitation in early infancy. In T. G. Beaver (ed.), *Regressions in mental development: Basic phenomena and theories.* Hillsdale, NJ: Erlbaum.

Meltzoff, A. N. and Gopnik, A. (1993). The role of imitation in understanding persons and developing a theory of mind (pp. 335–66). In S. Baron-Cohen, H. Tager-Flusberg and D. J. Cohen (eds.), *Understanding other minds.* Oxford University Press.

Meltzoff, A. N. and Moore, M. K. (1977). Imitation of facial and manual gestures. *Science*, 198, 75–80.

(1983). Newborn infants imitate adult facial gestures. *Child Development*, 54, 702–9.

(1992). Early imitation within a functional framework: The importance of person identity, movement, and development. *Infant Behavior and Development*, 15, 479–505.

(1994). Imitation, memory, and the representation of persons. *Infant Behavior and Development*, 17, 83–99.

Nadel, J. and Pezé, A. (1993). What makes immediate imitation communicative in toddlers and autistic children? In J. Nadel and L. Camaioni (eds.), *New perspectives in early communication development.* London: Routledge.

Ohta, M. (1987). Cognitive disorders of infantile autism: A study employing the WISC, spatial relationship conceptualization, and gesture imitation. *Journal of Autism and Developmental Disorders*, 17, 45–62.

Ritvo, S. and Provence, S. (1953). Form perception and imitation in some autistic children: Diagnostic findings and their contextual interpretation. *The Psychoanalytical Study of the Child*, 8, 155–61.

Rogers, S. J. and Pennington, B. F. (1991). A theoretical approach to the deficits in infantile autism. *Development and Psychopathology*, 3(2), 137–62.

Sigman, M. and Ungerer, J. A. (1984). Cognitive and language skills in autistic, mentally retarded, and normal children. *Developmental Psychology*, 20, 293–302.

Smith, I. M. (1995, April). Imitation and gestural representation in autism. Poster session at the biennial meeting of the Society for Research in Child Development, Indianapolis, IN.

Smith, I. M. and Bryson, S. E. (1994). Imitation and action in autism: A critical review. *Psychological Bulletin*, 116(2), 259–73.

Stein, B. E. and Meredith, M. A. (1993). *The merging of the senses.* Cambridge, MA: MIT Press.

Thelen, E. and Smith, L. B. (1994). *A dynamic systems approach to the development of cognition and action.* Cambridge, MA: The MIT Press.

Tiegerman, E. and Primavera, L. (1984). Imitating the autistic child: Facilitating communicative gaze behavior. *Journal of Autism and Developmental Disorder,* 11, 427–38.

Trevarthen, C. (1979). Communication and cooperation in early infancy. A description of primary intersubjectivity. In M. Bullowa (ed.), *Before speech: The beginnings of human communication.* London: Cambridge University Press.

(1980). Neurological development and growth of psychological functions. In J. Sants (ed.), *Developmental psychology and society.* London: Macmillan.

(1982). Basic patterns of psychogenetic change in infancy. In T. G. Bever (ed.), *Regression in mental development. Basic phenomena and theories* (pp. 7–46). Hillsdale, NJ: Erlbaum.

(1993). The function of emotions in early infant communication and development. In J. Nadel and L. Camioni (eds.), *New perspectives in early communication development.* London: Routledge.

(1996, July). Innate intersubjectivity, cultural learning and getting advantage in human society: New support for Adam Smith's Other Theory. Paper presented at the conference on 'New Psychologies', Tarbert, Scotland.

Trevarthen, C. and Aitken, K. J. (1994). Brain development, infant communication, and empathy disorders: Intrinsic factors in child mental health. *Development and Psychopathology,* 6, 597–633.

Tronick, E., Als, H. and Brazelton, T. B. (1980). Monadic phases: A structural descriptive analysis of infant–mother face to face interaction. *Merrill-Palmer Quarterly,* 26(1), 3–24.

Udwin, O. and Dennis, J. (1995). Psychological and behavioral phenotypes in genetically determined syndromes: A review of research findings. In G. O'Brien and W. Yule (eds.), Behavioral phenotypes. *Clinics in Developmental Medicine, No. 138.* London: MacKeith Press.

Vinter, A. (1986). The role of movement in eliciting early imitations. *Child Development,* 57, 66–71.

Sally J. Rogers

Introduction

The past 5 years have seen a new wave of interest in imitation in the child development literature, with exciting new levels of theory building. Some of this interest is attributable to the provocative and stimulating programme of research on infant imitation coming from Meltzoff's laboratory (Meltzoff, 1990). Additionally, interest in imitation appears to be motivated from the explosion of work in the area of Theory of Mind. Stimulated by theory of minds research involving non-human primates (Premack and Woodruff, 1978) and the findings of autism-related deficits in theory of mind, the field has turned attention to questions concerning the origins of intersubjectivity and theory of mind. How does the infant and young child come to appreciate the internal, 'mental' life of the partner? How do children learn about others' inner intentions, desires and beliefs? How does the infant learn about the similarities of self and other? To answer these questions, researchers have turned to a re-examination of the earliest social processes, including imitation.

In 1985, Daniel Stern synthesised some new answers to these questions through his integration of the clinical and developmental literatures on infancy. In his important theoretical book, *The Interpersonal World of the Infant* (Stern, 1985), he suggested a model for how the infant comes to know the subjective experience of another person which was organised at four levels. The first level was built upon the very young infant's capacities in the areas of motor imitation and awareness of perceptual invariances and patterns. The second level was built upon the 3 to 9 month old's capacities for shared affect and awareness of co-ordinated internal affective states. The third level was built upon the 9–12-month-old infant's growing awareness of other minds as seen in joint attention, social referencing and awareness of intentionality. These infant accomplishments provided the groundwork for interpersonal development at the fourth level, involving mastery of social symbolic systems like speech and symbolic play, and further development in awareness of other's internal states, accomplished in the toddler and early preschool period.

The study of imitation and its role in social development has been stimulated by the approaches described in the literature on developmental psychopathology, in which information provided by the study of alternative developmental pathways and information provided by the study of typical developmental patterns are contrasted and compared in order to understand more deeply the nature of both (Cicchetti, 1989). In the case of imitation and its suggested importance to later interpersonal development, the study of disruptions in early imitative development may allow us to examine effects on higher-level social processes. Autism, with its associated deficits in motor imitation, provides the opportunity for such an examination.

Autism, first described by Kanner in 1943, is a severe disability involving deficits in social relationships, language, behaviour, and cognition (Kanner, 1943). Because autism devastatingly affects behaviours that are so fundamental to social functioning, there is an active search for developmental models that can (1) account for the various symptoms, (2) guide the search for underlying mechanisms and (3) lead to more effective treatments. In 1991, Rogers and Pennington (1991) suggested a developmental model which focused on the imitation deficit seen in persons with autism. After reviewing the autism literature, they suggested that motor imitation may be one of the primary deficits in autism, and they provided a model of the potential cascading effects on social development of a primary deficit in motor imitation from the beginnings of life. Built upon Meltzoff's findings concerning the preparedness of infants to imitate another's actions, and using Stern's (1985) theoretical model of interpersonal development, they hypothesised that a biological impairment in autism involved the capacity to co-ordinate self and other representations, preventing the infant with autism from developing the notion that 'the other is a template of the self'. This impairment directly affected motor imitation, contributing to the cascade effect suggested by Stern, resulting in specific symptoms in autism which are seen in the areas of affective, social and communicative development. This paper also suggested a possible neuropsychological mechanism for such a deficit that could involve prefrontal frontal–limbic brain systems, including the executive capacity for intentional motor movements. Rogers and Pennington thus highlighted two subcomponents of imitation that might underlie the imitative deficit in autism – self–other correspondence, and planning/sequencing/executing of intentional movements. The past 5 years have seen a renewed interest in the question of a primary imitation deficit in autism, and various models have been suggested that emphasised these or other sub-components.

This chapter will review the work on imitation in autism that has occurred since the publication of the Rogers and Pennington paper. It will discuss several recent theoretical approaches that have drawn from findings in autism to address the question of how infants develop awareness of self–other co-ordination. Finally, it will highlight the potential social deficits that could result from primary impairments in the ability to plan, sequence and execute intentional motor movements – praxis. A particular strength of the suggested model is its ability to account for the partial accomplishments (Haith, 1990) in the areas of imitation, emotion sharing and intersubjectivity that many persons with autism demonstrate.

A review of studies of imitation in autism

Autistic children's difficulty in imitating another person's actions was first described in the research literature by DeMyer and colleagues (DeMyer, Alpern, Barton, DeMyer, Churchill and Hingtgen, 1972). Since that time, a series of studies of imitation skills of autistic subjects has been published (see Meltzoff and Gopnik, 1993; Rogers and Pennington, 1991; and Smith and Bryson, 1994, for detailed reviews). These have varied considerably in the kinds of imitative behaviour studied, the means of eliciting the behaviour and the control groups used. The variation in the design of these studies appears to have led to some equivocal or inconsistent findings. What follows is a brief review of the most rigorously designed published experimental studies of imitation in autism; those which contrasted the performance of subjects with autism with the performance of mental age (MA) and chronological age (CA) matched comparison groups on experimental tests of imitation of body movements.

There are several reasons for these restrictions. The review is restricted to studies of body movements as opposed to imitation of emotional expressions, because the relationship between the two is not yet known. It is being restricted to experimental studies because, in an observational study or parent report, conditions for eliciting imitation may differ and motivation and attention effects are more of a possibility. The review is restricted to studies which have used both MA and CA matched control groups (which excludes studies using normally developing children matched only on MA) because of the problem of the co-occurrence of mental retardation in autism. There is evidence that imitation abilities are impaired to some extent in children with a variety of developmental disorders (Roy, Elliott, Dewey and Square-Storer, 1990). If imitation deficits co-occur with developmental deficits, then using the performance of typical children as a contrast to autism does not allow us to determine whether the imitation deficit in the children with autism is due to the more general developmental delay or retardation, or whether it is due specifically to autism. The only way to answer that question is to use a developmentally impaired control group.

The first group of studies to be reviewed examined children's imitations of hand movements. Unfortunately, few of these studies carefully controlled tasks in order to examine separately the effects of (1) actions involving objects versus those involving no objects; (2) familiar actions versus novel actions; (3) single movements versus sequential movements; (4) visually guided movements versus those out of the line of sight; and (5) meaningful versus non-meaningful movements. DeMyer and colleagues were the first to study empirically autistic children's difficulty in imitating another person's actions (DeMyer, Alpern, Barton, DeMyer, Churchill and Hingtgen, 1972). The authors compared 12 autistic and schizophrenic children, since diagnostic criteria were not well established at that time, with 12 mentally retarded controls. Tasks included a mixture of familiar and novel movements involving actions on objects as well as motor imitations. The autistic subjects were significantly poorer than controls on imitation of body movements, less deficient but still significantly poorer on imitations of actions on objects, and equivalent on non-imitated purposeful object acts; the last finding makes the alternative explanation of basic motor deficits unlikely. The authors use the example of dyspraxia from the adult neurological literature to argue that the imitation deficit in autism involves a deficit in praxis involving either (1) the inability to retain a visual representation of the model in memory or (2) the inability to make a cross-modal transfer from the visual representation held in memory to the motor output system.

Ohta (1987) studied simple body imitations unconfounded by objects in 16 non-retarded autistic subjects (with a mean age of 10 years) compared to 2 control groups, one consisting of 16 subjects matched on CA and Performance IQ, and the other a group of normal preschoolers. Ohta reported deficits in the autistic subjects in simple hand imitations (some meaningful and some not meaningful) compared to both control groups. Further, the imitation deficit was not related to IQ or MA, and the autistic subjects performed like the very youngest preschoolers (mean age 36 months) in the study. Ohta considered 2 subcomponents of motor imitation: (1) visual perceptual abilities and the perceptual cross-modal matching of one's own and other's bodies, and (2) praxic abilities involved in the motor utilisation system. Given the pattern of her findings, she suggested that the basis for the imitation deficit lay in the perceptual area, and involved a deficient representational capacity for body image, with 'praxic factors playing only a minor role' (p. 60).

In a study of sensorimotor intelligence in young autistic children, Sigman and Ungerer (1984) examined both motor and vocal imitation tasks in a group of 16 young autistic children compared to 16 MA matched children with mental retardation and 16 normal MA matched controls. Using the Užigiris–Hunt scales to examine the full range of sensorimotor skills, including motor and vocal imitation of both familiar and novel gestures, sounds and words, the authors found the only area of sensorimotor deficit in autism to be in imitation. Thus, this study demonstrated that the children with autism had basic sensorimotor cognitive development in line with control groups; the imitation deficit could not be explained by a deficit in general sensorimotor cognitive functioning or by deficits in the ability to hold visual representations in mind and use them to guide motor behaviour, as required by the object permanence, causal and spatial tasks.

A study by Hertzig and colleagues (Hertzig, Snow and Sherman, 1989) compared 18 lower functioning, verbal autistic subjects to both 14 IQ matched controls with mental retardation and 19 normal language matched preschoolers. Tasks involved 6 pictures of a model, 3 involving a meaningful action (eating, drinking, sleeping) and three involving an emotional display (happy, sad, angry), and the same portrayals of behaviours by a live model. The subjects were asked to match like pictures, select pictures based on descriptions of the content, imitate the pictures and the live model, enact the six movements when verbally directed, and match the pictures to an appropriate story line. While the subjects with autism had no trouble labelling or matching the action pictures, they were poorer than both control groups at imitating and enacting both affects and actions of a model, whether pictured or live. Furthermore, they had greater difficulty performing the emotional displays than the meaningful actions. In offering a potential explanation for their findings, the authors cite Hobson (1986) and suggest a specific impairment in integration of sensory information from various modalities, an hypothesis which seems related to Ohta's cross-modal perceptual explanation.

In addition to these studies of sensorimotor imitation, two studies of symbolic imitation, or pantomime tasks, involving IQ matched clinical comparison groups have been published. These are included in this review because pantomime can be understood as a kind of a deferred imitation (Rogers, Bennetto, McEvoy and Pennington, 1996), and because pantomime skills – like imitation – are considered to depend on intact praxic abilities (Kimura and Archibald, 1974). Hammes and

Langdell (1981) examined the performance on tasks of imitation of 8 children with autism and 8 with mental retardation, aged 9 years, with language levels of 4 years. One set of tasks involved imitation of common actions (serving tea, brushing teeth, eating soup) seen on a videotape, first with the real objects used in the tape, then with imaginary objects, and finally with counterconventional objects (a real object used in an inappropriate way, i.e. a shoe used as a cup). A second set of tasks involved immediate imitation of tool use with various levels of pantomime required. As DeMyer had earlier found, there was the least impairment in imitating real actions with real objects. Children with autism could imitate actions on real objects, both immediately and deferred in time, as well as controls. However, they could not imitate with imaginary objects, (i.e., pantomime), and when given counterconventional objects, the children with autism tended to use these in the way the object was intended to be used, rather than pantomiming the correct action with an incorrect object, as if the subject could not inhibit a well-practised response elicited by the object.

Bartak, Rutter and Cox (1975) examined the performance of 19 subjects with autism, mean age 7, mean V IQ 67, and 23 subjects with primary language impairments, mean age 8, V IQ 76 on a variety of measures of expressive production and receptive understanding of gestures which mimed common actions on objects. The authors report that the children with autism were far less able either to produce or to understand gestures used to pantomime actions than the comparison group.

The global nature of these studies does not allow for a more differentiated understanding of the nature of the imitation deficit in autism. Lack of precision in choice of tasks is seen in lack of control for: (1) symbolic or meaningful content to the movements (which is problematic because symbolic thought is related to the hypothesised metarepresentational deficit in autism, and is itself considered to be impaired in autism Baron-Cohen, 1988); (2) use of familiar or well-practised movements rather than novel movements, which is problematic because it may allow a subject to rely on automatic motor patterns rather than a more volitional or intentional execution of novel movements; and (3) actions involving objects, which may confound imitation with well-practised actions or with cause and effect schemas (Charman and Baron-Cohen, 1994; Sigman and Ungerer, 1984). Other variables that need to be examined, according to Smith and Bryson (1994) include the presence of visual feedback, the complexity of movements, bimanual versus unimanual co-ordination and intactness of body image.

Two studies have recently been carried out that have attempted to address these methodological issues. Rogers and colleagues (Rogers et al.,

1996) studied a group of 17 high-functioning adolescents with autism spectrum disorders and a clinical control group of 15 subjects matched on SES, CA, and verbal IQ. The experimental design manipulated both meaning, or symbolic content, and complexity (sequential versus single movements) for both face and hand imitation tasks, which were taken from the adult apraxia literature. Memory control tasks were matched to every experimental task. Motor capacity to perform the movements was examined, and discriminant tasks examined verbal short-term memory and visual motor ability.

There was a significant group effect on all imitation and pantomime tasks, with the group with autism performing more poorly on 6 of the 10 tasks administered, including both single and sequential movements, face and hand movements, and symbolic and non-symbolic movements. Interaction effects demonstrated that sequential movements were harder for subjects with autism than controls (providing some support for an executive function hypothesis) but that meaningful, or symbolic, movements were not more difficult for subjects with autism (disconfirming a symbolic hypothesis). In fact, on some tasks subjects with autism performed better on meaningful than on non-meaningful tasks. There was no evidence of any memory or motor deficits underlying the poor performance of subjects with autism. The findings were characterised as reflecting widespread deficits at the level of motor execution of movements on classic tasks of praxis. This study also appears to disconfirm Baron-Cohen's (1988) hypothesis, which suggested that autism-related difficulties on imitation and pantomime tasks were secondary to underlying symbolic deficits related to the primary metarepresentational deficit in autism. However, Smith and Bryson (1994) point out that the two views of the imitation deficit – the symbolic view and the praxic view – are not necessarily incompatible. They suggest that there is a deeper-level deficit – at the representational level – that affects both motor imitations and imitation of symbolic actions, and that a deeper-level deficit in the capacity to represent 'movement components of actions and their associated functional representations . . . could contribute to the development of higher level (social and cognitive) manifestations of autism' (p. 259).

Apparent non-replications

Two published studies of autistic subjects have not demonstrated imitation deficits. Morgan and colleagues (Morgan, Cutrer, Coplin and Rodriguez, 1989) studied imitation skills of 10 verbal autistic children compared to 10 language matched mentally retarded and 10 normal controls. Chronological age of the two clinical groups was 8 years, and receptive language levels of all 3 groups was 36 months. All subjects were administered the Dunst (1980) manual for the Užgiris–Hunt scales (1975). The tasks involved simple and complex gestures (i.e. patting the table, crumpling paper), and visible and invisible movements (i.e. pulling earlobes, hands over ears). The total score possible on the measure was 23. The mean score of both comparison groups was 23, and for the groupwith autism, 22.7. Thus, all three groups were at ceiling on the measure, which prevents one from extracting any information about their comparative performances. The measure used was thus inappropriate for the subjects. This does not constitute a non-replication. It is rather a study from which no conclusions can be drawn regarding comparative imitation performance of the subjects with autism due to methodological flaws involving the choice of the measure used.

The second apparent non-replication was reported by Charman and Baron-Cohen (1994). This study compared 20 subjects with autism, mean CA of 11 years, verbal MA of 46 months, non-verbal MA of 85 months, to a group of children with developmental delays, mean age 13 years, verbal MA of 37 months, non-verbal MA of 45 months. One set of measures used came from Meltzoff (1988), developed for infants under 18 months of age, consisting of a cause-and-effect action carried out on a simple object (i.e. pushing a button on a panel, pulling a dumb-bell apart). The authors also used four simple motor imitation items taken from the Užgiris–Hunt scales: clapping, pulling on ears, bending a finger, clapping hands over head. On the motor imitation tasks, which are our focus here, ceiling effects again prevent an interpretation of the findings. Out of a possible total of 4 points, the mean score for the group with autism was 3.9. (sd 0.5), and for the group with developmental disabilities the mean score was 3.8 (sd 0.7) resulting in severely limited ranges of variance. (The situation was similar for the object-related actions). Thus, this study is compromised by the same problems as in the Morgan et al. study: measures that are too simple for the subjects and thus lack discriminative capacity. As in the study above, this does not constitute a non-replication. All that these two studies can tell us is that at some point later on in development, in a demand situation, verbal autistic children and children with retardation can grossly imitate simple infant-type movements at degrees of accuracy similar to normally developing 1-year-old children. The fact that some level of skill may develop over time in an area does not rule imitation out as an area of primary deficit. Yet it does point out that the imitation deficit is not an all-or-nothing phenomenon. Theories that seek to account for the imitation deficit in autism will also have to account for the partial accomplishments (Haith, 1990) in imitation seen later in development.

Thus, every methodologically rigorous study so far published has found an autism-specific deficit in motor imitation. The hypothesis of a primary imitation deficit in autism has not yet been disconfirmed. Results from earlier work as well as recent, more refined work on imitation in autism support the hypothesis that the imitation deficit in autism is long-lasting and occurs even in mildly affected people. There is also evidence as to the specificity of the imitation deficit to autism in terms of its severity, given that most comparison groups have also had developmental disorders. Findings from the existing studies would appear to support the idea that the imitation deficit in autism fulfils 3 of the 4 criteria for a primary deficit: *universality* (that all persons with the disorder have the deficit), *specificity* (that the deficit is specific to the disorder) and *persistence* (that the deficit persists over time and can continue to affect development) (Pennington and Ozonoff, 1991). Given how early the imitation deficit appears in children with autism (Sigman and Ungerer, 1984), it may also fulfil the fourth criterion of *precedence* (that the deficit exists prior to the development of the symptoms which it is supposed to explain).

Explanations for the imitation deficit in autism

As the evidence for deficient imitation in autism has accumulated, several underlying deficits have been proposed to account for it. An arousal hypothesis, developed in the 1980s by Geraldine Dawson and restated recently by Smith and Bryson (1994), continues to influence the field. Dawson has considered the problem of imitation in autism in a variety of writings (Dawson and Lewy, 1989; Dawson, 1991) in which she suggests that infants with autism are easily overaroused and have a very narrow range of optimal stimulation. The relative novelty and inconsistency of social interactions become overly stimulating for the infant with autism, who withdraws from social interactions in order to maintain comfortable arousal levels. This social withdrawal results in a lack of attention to social partners and thus precludes the development of infant imitation, which affects the infant's emotional development, affect sharing and development of intersubjectivity, the cascade described by Stern. Certainly, attention to the model is a crucial component for motor imitation. There is empirical evidence of attentional difficulties in autism which supports Dawson's view (Dawson & Lewy, 1989) and thus it represents a testable alternative hypothesis regarding the faulty mechanisms behind the imitation deficit in autism.

Smith and Bryson (1994) suggest an information-processing hypothesis closely related to Dawson's. After reviewing the literature, they agreed with Rogers' and Pennington's conclusion that a motor imitation deficit appears to exist in autism, but they offer a different hypothesis. They suggest that the imitation deficit, rather than being primary, is secondary to more basic, non-social processing deficits, a view which is close to Dawson's. 'It appears to us that abnormalities in the cross-modal integration of experience, perhaps owing to an aberrant attentional system, provide one possible underlying mechanism for a tendency to form rigid and idiosyncratic representations of events and actions' (p. 268). They suggest that further study of non-social behaviour is necessary in order to explore this hypothesis.

Whiten and Brown have considered carefully the points raised in the Rogers and Pennington paper (Whiten and Brown, 1997). Based on the apparent non-replication studies, they suggest that the imitation deficit does not meet criteria for universality and persistence. Rather, they view the imitation deficit as quite impaired early in life but developing later (the issue of partial accomplishments), and they conclude by suggesting that it is not an inability to imitate which accounts for the imitation deficit in autism, but rather a lack of motivation or attentional processes that guide most other people into spontaneous imitation.

Whiten suggests an alternative hypothesis which has been popular over the years: that in elicited imitation paradigms, subjects with autism have difficulty with motivation. He further suggests that this problem is overcome with the Do-As-I-Do (DAID) method (Custance, Whiten and Bard, 1995) in which the subjects are systematically trained to produce imitative movements. While one cannot dismiss a motivational hypothesis, particularly in young, essentially non-verbal children with autism, there is also clinical information from the DAID method that implies that the lack of skilled imitation in children with autism reflects more than a motivational problem. Using the DAID method to teach imitation skills is, in fact, a crucial part of a variety of treatment programmes (i.e., Lovaas, 1981). Yet clinical experience shows us that using applied behaviour methods to teach the DAID rule to young children with autism can be a daunting task. It can take literally thousands of trials of training occurring over months and months before the rule is learned, even for children who are well motivated for rewards and who are learning other kinds of behaviourally taught skills (i.e., visual matching) rapidly. The difficulty that young children with autism have in learning how to imitate novel gestures suggests that more is involved than a motivational problem. Dawson also rules out a motivational explanation underlying children with autism's general failure to engage with other people, given the results of a study in which she demonstrated that autistic children's attention to and interactions with people could be enhanced by manipulating the partner's responses

(Dawson, 1991). Thus, while motivation is an important variable to consider, a motivational deficit alone does not appear to have sufficient explanatory power.

All of these theories share the idea that infant imitation is crucial to the developmental cascade into intersubjectivity so elegantly described by Stern in 1985. The theories vary in what they consider to be the cause of the imitation deficit. Imitation is a molar construct, and a careful analysis of the subcomponents of motor imitation implicate a whole sequence of molecular processes at work. The different points of emphasis described thus far represent different subcomponents of motor imitation: visual attention, cross-modal transfer, motor production, memory for and manipulation of representations, activation of a motor act (motivation or intentionality), representation of the body schema, formulation of a motor plan, holding the model or the plan in working memory and using it to guide movement, initiation and execution of the plan, monitoring and correcting the action in progress. Gonzalez-Rothi, Ochipa and Heilman (1991) have provided one such model in which they suggest both cognitive subcomponents and associated areas of brain function involved in producing motor imitations. While studies of imitation in autism have just begun to examine these subcomponent functions, this level of methodological rigour has been applied to other clinical populations, both adult and child (Dewey, 1993; Roy et al., 1990; Schwartz, Mayer, FitzpatrickDeSalme and Montgomery, 1993).

Thus, having established that a deficit in motor imitation exists in autism, efforts to understand its nature require that we shift levels of analysis to the subcomponents of imitation. One set of subcomponents involve *praxis*: the planning, execution and monitoring of the intentional motor action involved.

Is a praxis deficit a viable hypothesis in autism?

It has been suggested that the evolution of imitation depended on complex motor behaviour involving a sophisticated type of intentional, sequential motor planning known as praxis (Bruner, 1972; Donald, 1991). The term *praxis* refers to the capacity for consciously formulating and then executing an intentional motor plan in a particular context, a capacity not necessary for conditioned, automatic or reflexive movement patterns (Ayres, 1985). Imitation and pantomime tasks are considered classic tasks of praxis and deficits involving both face and hand imitations and pantomime are commonly found in neurologically impaired adults (De Renzi, Motti and Nichelli, 1980; Kimura and Archibald, 1974; Kolb and Milner, 1981; Mateer and Kimura, 1977). Such a deficit is labelled apraxia (or dyspraxia, a term used more commonly when referring to children) and refers to disorders of skilled movements not caused by specific motor abnormalities, dementia, or poor co-operation (Heilman, 1979).

In the 1980s, several investigators with backgrounds in neurology (DeMyer, Hingtgen and Jackson, 1981; Jones and Prior, 1985; Ohta, 1987) raised the possibility of an underlying neuromotor apraxia or dyspraxia to account for the imitation deficit in autism. DeMyer et al. (1981) and Jones and Prior (1985) suggested that a praxic deficit in autism was almost universal and interfered with the simple motor activities and social behaviour of everyday life, as well as interfering with non-verbal communication. Rogers et al. (1996) also suggested that the imitation and pantomime deficits seen in autism might reflect a praxis impairment severe enough to compromise social behaviour. Is there any evidence outside the imitation area that would implicate a problem in motor functions in autism, including those involved in praxis? Smith and Bryson (1994) provide a detailed review of the motor literature in autism, which suggests deficits involving intentional aspects of movement, lack of goal directedness in movements, stereotypies and difficulties with the execution of novel movements and perhaps movement sequences as well.

Early reports of children with autism described their preserved motor abilities, their good co-ordination and their graceful movements (Jones and Prior, 1985; Kanner, 1943). However, reports soon began to surface which noted abnormalities in postural control, motor skills and co-ordination, and the presence of dyspraxias (Colbert, Koegler and Markham, 1958; Damasio and Maurer, 1978; DeMyer, 1976; Jones and Prior, 1985; Ornitz, 1973; Wing, 1981).

A recent pilot study of postural control using a computerised method compared a very large international group of 91 children with autism to three comparison groups – normally developing younger children, children with cognitive impairments and adults with vestibular impairments (Kohen-Raz, Volkmar and Cohen, 1992). While the results must be considered tentative because the groups were not matched and there were other methodological constraints, the authors report three areas of striking abnormalities.

The children with autism showed a paradoxical response, in that their performance was more impaired on simpler than on more difficult postures, which involved occluding vision and giving them an unstable surface on which to stand, tasks on which their performance approached the level of the normal group. The low scores of the group with autism suggested that they were using more primitive, somatosensory postural control systems rather than the visually mediated vestibular control systems. They also demonstrated little improvement on the measures with age. Their performance showed little overlap with the group with cognitive impairments, and was quite different from that of the adults with vestibular abnormalities. Furthermore, the severity of their abnormalities on the postural measures was associated with the severity of their autism.

Given these findings, the authors suggest that the source of postural control problems in these subjects with autism was more likely to involve mesocortex or cerebellum than the brainstem or the vestibular postural control systems. The tendency of these subjects to use more primary postural control mechanisms corresponds to Damasio and Maurer's (1978) hypothesis of dysfunction in the mesial frontal lobes, basal ganglia and the neostriatum. The authors favoured hypotheses of cerebellar dysfunction, both because performance improved so markedly when visual sensory input was restricted, and because of the rigid and jerky quality of the subjects' postures.

A second area of motor research in autism has been undertaken to study a subgroup of autistic children, those with Asperger syndrome, who have been described as markedly clumsy. Clumsiness is a symptom which is considered to reflect problems with motor planning, a major component of praxis. This raises the question of discriminant validity of praxis problems in children with autism, because clumsiness is reported to be common in many childhood psychiatric disorders, including attention deficit disorder and developmental language disorders (Ghaziuddin, Butler, Tsai and Ghaziuddin, 1994). Similarly, Gillberg (1983) reported an association between perceptual and motor deficits and psychiatric disorders in a study of 141 7-year-old Swedish children. A significant methodological difficulty with both sets of descriptions is due to the reliance on clinical descriptions and impressions in both of these areas. Few researchers have actually used standardised tests of motor function to assess motor performance in children with autism spectrum disorders.

To try to explore the question using a more objective approach, Ghaziuddin and associates (Ghaziuddin et al., 1994) compared 9 children diagnosed as having Autistic Disorder with 11 children diagnosed as having Asperger syndrome on standardised tests of motor function. The groups were carefully selected to make sure that there was no diagnostic overlap between them, and that they were matched on chronological age (mean of 13 years), and verbal and performance IQ's (in the borderline to normal range). On the Bruininks–Osteresky test (1978) and looking at gross and fine motor skills separately, both groups performed significantly more poorly than the norms for their ages, but no group differences were found between the autistic and Asperger groups. The deficits in both groups were not due to the very poor functioning of a few subjects. Rather, their performance was universally poor. All 18 of the subjects scored far below the norms for their age. Furthermore, scores on the motor tests were independent of IQ. Thus, clumsiness was found to characterise virtually all of the subjects in these two high-functioning autism spectrum groups. However, Ghazziudin is careful to point out that clumsiness is a very vague term and that the origins of clumsiness could lie in a variety of deeper dysfunctions: including motor co-ordination, information processing, visual or spatial perception, sensory sensitivity. Thus, demonstrating the presence of motor dysfunction in both groups tells us little further about the source or the nature of those deficits.

A recent study by Manjiviona and Prior (1995) gave similar results using a different measurement of clumsiness. The majority of high-functioning children with autism and a similar group of children with Asperger's both showed significant levels of motor impairment in a variety of motor areas. Finally, Hughes (1996) has reported abnormalities in persons with autism in the execution of a set of very simple, sequential goal-directed movements involved in reaching to an object, grasping it and placing it on a target.

Thus, a significant body of evidence is accumulating that attests to motor difficulties in autism on non-imitative tasks which could play a role in the production of intentional, sequenced, co-ordinated movements needed to perform an imitation (Gonzalez-Rothi et al., 1991). However, as stated above, motor performance is only one aspect of a chain of sub-component behaviours involved in carrying out a motor imitation. As Smith and Bryson (1994) and Rogers et al. (1996) have indicated, we need a new generation of imitation studies in autism, focused less on molar questions and more on molecular questions involving the production of intentional actions, including imitated actions. The literature also suggests that praxic problems occur in children with a variety of disorders, raising the question whether the imitation deficit is specific to autism. However, given that most imitation studies of autism have used developmentally disabled control groups, the severity of the praxis deficit does seem to be specific to autism. A developmental dyspraxia control group would be important to add to autism studies. Studies designed to examine the subcomponents of imitation or praxis, using dyspraxic matched controls, will go a long way to providing the data needed to construct neuropsychological or neurophysiological models of the imitation deficit in autism. Existing neuropsychological models of praxis like that of Gonzalez-Rothi and colleagues (1991) should help us investigate the phenomenon with greater sophistication.

Development of self–other representations

However, we also need to maintain a focus on the larger question: how do closely co-ordinated representations of self and other typically develop, and how does this go so awry in autism? All theoretical approaches to the development of imitation in infancy are built upon the assumption of a set of self–other representations that the infant co-ordinates and that guides imitative behaviour. Theories differ in hypotheses concerning the origins of these representations. To what extent are these hard-wired, or innate, social abilities? Conversely, to what extent does the infant construct these self–other representations, and what are the key experiences for their construction? Does the infant learn about the other by generalising information already available about the self? Is the self the model for the other? Or the other a model for the self? Can the infant construct representations of self and other simultaneously? These are the main issues with which current theorists are grappling. And information from autism appears to be quite important in the construction of these answers.

However, any answers will have to account for the issue of partial accomplishments. Persons with autism do learn to imitate, perhaps inexactly, slowly, effortfully, but still they produce an imitation. The research on very young children with autism, which demonstrates deficits in joint attention, theory of mind, imitation and declarative gestures, belies the fact that many people with autism can demonstrate joint attention behaviour, imitation skills, fluent, abstract speech, symbolic play, empathy, even some accomplishments in theory of mind. For people with autism who do not have accompanying mental retardation, it is probably the rule rather than the exception that the main skills which mark the developmental cascade will eventually develop to some degree (i.e., Yirmiya, Sigman, Kasari and Mundy, 1992). The presence of partial accomplishments or delayed acquisitions of these skills in autism means that our theories cannot be all-or-nothing (Haith, 1990). Instead, we have to produce differentiated models of social and intersubjective development which can account for the partial accomplishments seen in autism while still addressing the core deficits in the disorder.

Let us now move to an examination of various approaches to the self–other problem. Several developmentalists have recently suggested models that could explain the infant's growing awareness of the other as a person and as a mind while incorporating findings from autism. We will consider the work of four main groups: Meltzoff and Gopnik, Tomasello and colleagues, Barresi and Moore, and Whiten and colleagues. Each of these groups is focused on interpersonal development in the first year of life and, specifically, on how the infant comes to know something of the inner life of the other. Each also emphasises the role of imitation in the process. They vary in the mechanisms they see as most important and how deficits in those mechanisms may account for the difficulties associated with autism.

Meltzoff and Gopnik (1993) suggest that development of an awareness of other minds is rooted in the notion that others are like the self. They ask the question, what gives infants this experience? And they suggest that the answer cannot be simply in innate perceptual preferences or in contingent social interactions, since neither of these experiences is specific enough to account for the awareness of self–other correspondence.

They propose that 'the infant's primordial "like me" experiences are based on their understanding of bodily movement patterns and postures' (p. 336), and that the infant's capacity for cross-modal matching between the proprioceptive information coming from their own movements and the visual information coming from the movements of the imitative partner give them this sense of fundamental relatedness between self and other. An important implication of this model is that the sense of correspondence of self and other is coming from an internal sense, the way it 'feels' to be in correspondence with another, a point also emphasised by Stern (1985).

Meltzoff and Gopnik go on to propose that shared emotions are a second bridge between the 'like-me' experience of bodies and the 'like-me' experience of minds. Citing research from emotion studies (Zajonc, Murphy and Inglehart, 1989), they suggest that infant's imitation of emotional facial expressions creates an internal feeling state in the infant that matches the partner's feeling state. This is an internal experience of sameness mirrored by the external sameness of facial expressions, an example of synchrony between self and others' internal and external states.

They go further to suggest that this internal mapping occurs not only for movements and emotions or feeling states, but also for motor intentions or plans, since carrying out a purposeful movement requires both an intention to act and the formulation of a motor plan. As the infant approaches the first birthday, development in the various intersubjective capacities affects imitation as well, allowing for a new level of understanding of other persons' intentions through imitation. This capacity for shared intentions regarding objects corresponds to shared emotions as seen in emotional referencing and shared attention as seen in joint attention behaviours. Thus, having a sense of internal correspondence between self and others' intentions is a midpoint on the way to a sense of correspondence of mental states of self and other, as seen in the development of a theory of mind. Even during the toddler and preschool period,

Meltzoff and Gopnik continue to see imitation as leading children to understanding others' intentions and others' mental states.

Thus, in this view, infants are never in a position of responding only to the external form of a movement, but rather have the sense of internal correspondences from the beginning; it may be that the capacity implies the absence of a mind–body dualism in infants (see also Meltzoff and Moore, this volume).

Meltzoff and Gopnik consider the issue of autism. Working from the hypothesis that children with autism are innately deficient in the capacity to imitate another's body movements (but without providing a deeper explanation for how this might come about), Meltzoff and Gopnik propose a model in which the primary imitation deficit blocks the child from developing the 'like-me' sense at the level of body correspondences, emotional correspondences or mind correspondences. The child with autism is unable to use imitation as a tool for construction of internal self–other correspondences at the level of affect or mind.

Another group of theorists who are working on these issues are Barresi and Moore (1996). They begin with the question that Meltzoff and Gopnik addressed: how do we come to know that self and other are similar? These authors focus on the cross-modal matching problem inherent in the construction of self–other similarity schemas. The infant has available two different kinds of sensory information: third-person information consisting largely of visual and auditory information from the partner, and first-person tactile, kinaesthetic, and proprioceptive information from the self, which must be co-ordinated. While Meltzoff and Gopnik suggest that this cross-modal or supramodal co-ordination is a capacity of normal infants from the time of birth, Barresi and Moore (1996) suggest that cross-modal knowledge of self–other similarities must be constructed by the infant. They suggest that imitative exchanges, in which partner and infant are matching each other's behaviour, are highly salient experiences for the construction of these first-person/third-person similarity schema.

While the young infant depends mostly on representations based on immediate experiences, the toddler becomes able to use mental representations to imagine self or other in various situations. This ability to imagine self and other as similar in various situations allows for the child to come to imagine self–other correspondences applying to mental and emotional events as well as physical events, and this allows the child to construct a theory of other minds.

The authors then suggest that the difficulty in autism of forming a theory of other minds is due to the inability to construct similarity schemas between first- and third-person information. Even when the child with autism becomes able to construct representations of self and other, the representations still are not co-ordinated as self–other correspondences. In their view, this is the core difficulty in autism – the co-ordination of self–other schemas at any level.

A third group addressing these issues involves Tomasello and his colleagues, who approach imitation from an evolutionary viewpoint (Tomasello, Kruger and Ratner, 1993a). They view imitation as a main vehicle for the transmission of species-specific behaviour: human socialisation and acculturation, a line of thinking first discussed by Baldwin (1906), and continued by Bruner (1972) and, more recently, Užgiris (1991), Donald (1991) and others. Tomasello's and colleagues' comparative work has examined imitation of novel actions on objects by human children, acculturated chimpanzees, and mother-reared chimpanzees (Tomasello, Savage-Rumbaugh and Kruger, 1993b). The authors' use of the term *imitation* is limited to object-oriented actions that replicate both the movements and the goal, or, to put it differently, the means and the ends, of the model. When imitation is defined in this way, numerous clear examples appear to come only from humans and from acculturated chimpanzees (Galef, 1989; Tomasello et al., 1993b, but compare with Custance et al., 1995). These findings suggest that imitation in its most sophisticated form may depend on both biologically and environmentally determined cognitive variables, and that typical human parenting interactions provide important tutorial functions in the development of complex imitation skills (Carpenter, Tomasello and Savage-Rambaugh, 1995).

Tomasello's (1995) definition of imitation is built upon the toddler's awareness of the intentional agency of persons. Thus, Tomasello focuses on a different aspect of imitation than Meltzoff and Gopnik, and highlights the toddler's intersubjective awareness of intentional agency, demonstrated not only through imitative learning, but also in joint attention, social referencing and the acquisition of symbolic communication. Imitative learning not only forms the starting-point for cultural learning, but is also its main vehicle until major new developments in social cognition (i.e., theory of mind) become part of the child's learning repertoire.

Tomasello uses examples from autism (Tomasello et al., 1993a) to illustrate the dependence of imitation on intersubjective understanding. He suggests that children with autism cannot acquire an awareness of others' intentionality, and thus do not develop the capacity for imitative learning. Nor can they progress into higher levels of social learning; he suggests that persons with autism are thus 'acultural'. He uses autism to illustrate the differences between imitation of behaviour without an understanding of the model's subjective state, which he describes as mimicry or emulation, and true imitation, which, by his definition, requires understanding of the model's intentional state. Thus, Tomasello conceptualises an autism-specific imitation deficit as secondary to an impairment in the understanding of intentionality (a formulation which also accounts for the joint attention and the social referencing deficit in autism).

Tomasello's answer to the question: 'How do we learn about self–other correspondence?' emphasises both early experiences of physical matchings (early infant imitation) and of synchronous and reciprocal exchanges (Tomasello, 1995). These complementary types of interactions give infants the experience of being both similar to, but different from, other people. The infant's development of differentiated means–end problem solving behaviour in the 9–12 month period gives infants the awareness of the self as an intentional agent. It also helps infants to see the means–end distinction in others' behaviour, leading to an awareness of the intentional agency of both self and others. This knowledge of intentionality becomes the foundation for the key behaviours in the 12–18 month period: imitation of novel actions on objects, social referencing, joint attention, and learning of symbolic communication.

Tomasello et al.'s (1993a) orientation to imitation, emphasising as it does the imitation of actions on objects and the child's awareness of intentionality, emphasises quite a different aspect of imitation from that of Meltzoff and Gopnik (1993). Examining imitation of physical movements in social exchanges, as do Meltzoff and Gopnik (1993) and Trevarthen (1993), highlights the richly affective interpersonal exchange which marks the majority of infant and toddler imitations. These are not so much disagreements as they are illustrations of the many-faceted nature of imitation.

Whiten (1996), the final theorist to be reviewed, has provided an important bridge between these approaches to imitation. He discriminates between the type of motor imitation described by Meltzoff and others – the motor matching of movements seen in infant–parent play and interactions – which he labels primary representations of imitation, from the more complex imitations of intentional actions and behaviours seen in toddlers and older children and adults described by Tomasello, which he labels secondary representations of imitation. He shares the view with Meltzoff and Gopnik (1993), Rogers and Pennington (1991), Tomasello (1995) and Dawson (1991), that early imitation leads the infant to a greater awareness of self–other correspondences via the developmental cascade. As infants develop intersubjective understanding of the internal life of the partner, and an appreciation for partners as intentional agents, as attentional beings and as separately affective beings, the toddler adds to his or her capacity for motor matching an ability to integrate the inner state of the model, which allows development of secondary representations of imitations. This provides the foundations for empathy, observational learning, pretending and dramatic play, and the kinds of perspective-taking abilities that are present in toddlers and young preschoolers, before a full theory of other minds, or complete metarepresentation, has developed. This grouping of joint attention, pretend play, empathy and imitation at the secondary level without needing to invoke an explanation requiring metarepresentation is supported by two sets of evidence: the cluster of deficits in autism; and the cluster of developments that occur between the toddler and preschool period.

Whiten goes on to say that, while in normal human development, primary imitation usually leads to greater awareness of self–other correspondences, it does not always do so. Both comparative work and studies of imitation in autism indicate that 'the imitative translation process can proceed without a necessary linkage to mindreading or secondary representation' p. 317 (Whiten, 1996). Thus, he suggests that persons with autism may eventually develop the primary level of imitation while still seeming unable to develop the secondary level, in which the co-ordination of intersubjective self and other is implied. Here is the first model to account for the partial accomplishment of imitation in autism in the face of severe problems in intersubjectivity. However, in turning to the question of why persons with autism tend not to imitate even when they have some capacities to do so, Whiten is less successful. He suggests that autistic people do not imitate naturally because they do not understand intersubjectively the meaning or purpose of the partner's movement.

The above theories demonstrate the importance assigned to imitation in the development of social cognition and self–other relations. They also underline the degree of knowledge of self–other correspondence that infants normally develop in the first year of life. Finally, they illustrate the importance that studies of imitation in autism have had on theory building. But how satisfying are these theories when applied to autism? Most of the theories present an all-or-none picture, in which the presence of partial accomplishments in the areas of imitation and joint attention are not easily integrated. Whiten (1996) and Tomasello et al. (1993a) allow for the possibility of partial accomplishments in imitation by presenting two-stage models. However, they portray the joint attention or intentionality deficit in autism as a barrier to further progress, and cannot thus account for partial accomplishments in these areas, nor can they account for continued imitation deficits in persons with autism who have at least partially mastered joint attention and other early intersubjective capacities.

Theoretical formulation

The findings continue to support the imitation deficit suggested by Rogers and Pennington (1991), as well as other theoretical models of autism with an imitation deficit at the social core. Hobson (1993) addresses the imitation deficit quite similarly to Rogers and Pennington, suggesting disturbances in (1) the 'hard-wiring' for imitation of others which interferes with the infant's learning of self–other correspondence and (2) abnormalities in imitation based on identification with another person. Meltzoff and Gopnik suggest a model of autism with an imitation deficit at the core of the impairment in intersubjectivity. However, none of these models deal with the issue of partial accomplishments in imitation.

What is needed is a model of development of intersubjective awareness that can account for the existence of imitative behaviour and joint attention behaviour in older, higher-functioning persons with autism, while still accounting for continuing difficulties in social relatedness, pragmatics and intersubjectivity. A possible answer may be found in the integration of the findings of an imitation deficit in autism with the fascinating area referred to as 'emotional contagion' (Hatfield, Cacioppo and Rapson, 1994). Emotional contagion is 'the tendency to automatically mimic and synchronize facial expressions, vocalizations, postures and movements with those of another person and consequently to converge emotionally' (p. 5). The behaviours involved in emotional contagion are seen as relatively automatic, unintentional, uncontrollable and largely inaccessible to awareness.

This automatic synchrony of movements allows for the transmission of emotions between the partners, and people's individual emotional experience is influenced continuously by the activity or feedback from this motor matching, including afferent feedback from their own emotional expressions, body postures and vocal tones. The synchronous body movement literally creates synchronous emotional experiences which are experienced as self–other co-ordinations. These would appear to be crucial for infant experiences of both external and internal self–other correspondences and establishment of primary intersubjectivity (Stern, 1985).

It is interesting to consider the concept of 'social relatedness' in light of the above. While abnormalities in relatedness are the *sine qua non* of autism, we have not gone very far in defining precisely what we mean by the term. Perhaps what is meant by relatedness is this kind of interpersonal synchrony – of bodies, voices, movements, expressions, and synchronized or complimentary feeling states. It is the interpersonal co-ordination that we feel, see and hear through the matching of our movements with our partners. While we may be unaware of this when it occurs normally, we may be quite sensitive to disruptions in it. Even mild disruptions in imitative abilities in our partners, as seen in problems with the timing, grading or inaccuracies of matching movements, could impede emotional synchrony, creating in the partner the feeling of a lack of interpersonal relatedness, the sense that something is 'off'.

The hypothesis being suggested is that a severe praxic deficit in an infant could markedly impair the physical co-ordinations that typically accompany social interactions. In so doing, it would interfere with the establishment and maintenance of emotional connectedness that is shared, unknowingly, between two people engaged in a typical social exchange. And it would interfere with the social cascade from primary to secondary intersubjectivity and on into shared attention, shared intention and ostensive communication.

Is this being offered as *the* primary deficit in autism? No. There are other conditions in which physical matching and co-ordination of infant and parent is severely impaired, as with an infant born with severe cerebral palsy, or an infant born blind. Blind infants do have some shared characteristics with autism early on, and difficulties with relatedness may mark the early months (Fraiberg, 1977). However, blind infants and their parents develop compensatory mechanisms, using voice, language and touch, through which emotions can be shared, connectedness experienced and intersubjective knowledge developed. Similarly, the movements of infants with severe cerebral palsy are not synchronous with their partners. Yet interpersonal relatedness can be established and emotional contagion experienced. In such an exchange, interpersonal synchronies and co-ordinations are established through eye contact, facial expressions, sounds, conversations: matching of the vitality affects (Stern, 1985) through whatever routes are available. In both examples, the non-impaired partner adapts by learning to ignore the non-coordinated aspects of movement and attending to those aspects that are synchronised. (Emde, Katz and Thorpe,1978 have illustrated a similar phenomenon nicely in their study of mothers' interpretations of the affective responses of their babies with Down's syndrome.) In both examples, the infants involved find other routes than imitative body movements for establishing and maintaining affective connections with the partner. Thus, a praxis deficit, while important, is not sufficient for explaining the intersubjective deficit in autism. We must look to the affective system as well, an area in which we need far more information than we now have.

In this way of thinking, the core deficit in autism continues to involve an inability to co-ordinate self and other representations, an inability to see the other as a template for the self (Rogers and Pennington, 1991). Given the weighting that all current theorists in this area are giving to the importance of early imitative experiences in developing self–other knowledge, understanding the nature of the imitation deficit in autism may take us closer to understanding the impaired intersubjective core of autism. New data will undoubtedly lead to new revisions. Given current findings of severe praxis problems even in very high-functioning and relatively social adolescents with autism, physical and resulting emotional synchronies in the construction of self–other correspondence representations can be weighted more heavily (as Meltzoff and Gopnik have also suggested). The hypothesis here is that the mechanisms that lead the normal infant into intersubjectivity involve imitative matchings and physical co-ordinations with the partner, with resulting emotional synchrony.

This leads to an elaboration of Rogers and Pennington's (1991) developmental model. The infant/young child with autism is unable to match the partner imitatively and reciprocally and consequently does not have ongoing, dependable experiences of emotional contagion. As development occurs, the degree of imitative ability that develops in autism varies from one person to the next. The child with autism may well learn some level of imitation, but the ongoing praxis problems prevent the synchronous, continuous matching of a partner through movements. The continuing problems in imitation involving timing, speed, grading and movements impede the establishment of emotional synchrony, and these two components lie behind the 'relatedness' deficit in autism. The capacity for emotional contagion and matching in autism varies across individuals. Moments of such relatedness can be created through carefully constructed interpersonal experiences (Dawson and Galpert, 1990; Rogers, 1991) and the potential for increased synchrony improves with development, as co-ordination of movements improves, assuming that the environment can provide continuing experiences of interpersonal matchings and assuming that the person with autism has not 'given up' on ever connecting with the social world.

The social cascade may occur, in partial, fragmented ways, for persons with autism. Partial improvements in imitation would lead to partial experiences of emotional contagion and moments of affective co-ordinations of self and other, which would in turn allow for partial development of intersubjective and intentional awareness, including some aspects of joint attention, empathy, symbolic play, language development. However, the physical synchrony of movements, voices, expressions, etc. continues to be impaired, even in high-functioning people. This results in continuing deficits in interpersonal relatedness, limiting the person with autism's access to internal states of the other through emotion contagion and synchrony, and preventing a full development of intersubjective knowledge and emotional attunements.

This disagrees with Whiten's suggestion that people with autism do not imitate others because they are unaware of the intentions behind the imitation. It may not be secondary representations of imitation that are affected in higher-functioning persons with autism, but rather the immediate, unaware, primary physical matchings that should occur easily, smoothly and consistently. When a person with autism sees the intention behind a movement, as in learning to open a container or operate a tool, and if they share the goal, they will attempt to imitate. The causal relations that link a motor action on a physical object to a visual–spatial outcome are demonstrated by people with autism, as has been demonstrated in studies of imitated actions on objects (DeMyer et al., 1972; Rogers et al., 1996). Some intentions appear to be understood, particularly those involving causal actions on the physical world and objects as mediators of those actions. Such intentions appear not to require the same kind or level of intersubjective knowledge of self and other as are involved in empathy or social referencing. However, in passing a familiar person on a street who waves at them, the person with autism does not have the fast, automatic matching of the physical move-ment available, and so social skills training tries to make conscious what most of us never have consciously to attend to: 'when someone that you know waves at you, it is important to wave back. If you don't, they will think you are ignoring them.' This hypothesis that a praxis deficit causes disruption in social co-ordination is not meant to exclude impairments in other aspects of early intersubjectivity. We agree with Hobson (1993) that parsing apart the intersubjective impairment into subcomponents may never explain autism as well as the focus on the child's 'limited experience of intersubjective engagement [and the constraints that that places on] their ability to develop an understanding of the nature of persons and *thereby* to evolve a range of supervenient cognitive, linguistic and social capacities. In this sense, abnormalities in the "intersubjective" domain would constitute an irreducible bedrock in the explanation of autism' (p. 13). The hypothesis suggests rather that the praxis deficit can continue to impair social relations across the lifespan in persons with autism, even when motor imitation skills have been learned. It also suggests that examination of interpersonal patterns during interactions between persons with autism and their social partners will reveal abnormalities at the level of synchronous and matching motor behaviours, including pos-tures, gestures, facial expressions, vocal quality. It provides a model of impaired social relations which can take into account partial accomplish-ments of a variety of intersubjective skills.

Questions that remain

Studies published since 1991 have not disconfirmed Rogers and Pennington's (1991) hypothesis that a primary deficit in motor imitation exists in persons with autism. The next generation of studies needs to examine the imitation deficit in far greater detail. The need to deconstruct imitation into its subcomponents has already been discussed. We also need to examine the hypothesised linkages between imitation and other social skills, such as use of gesture, empathy or joint attention. Donald (1991) has described an evolutionary model of human development that links mime, praxis, emotional expression, prosody and intentional communication (precisely the social abilities in which persons with autism are deficient) in a theoretical model of human social development. Nadel and Pezé (1993) and Dawson and Adams (1984) have reported relationships between imitation skills and other social skills in subjects with autism.

We also need to examine whether specific teaching of imitation skills to children with autism positively affects other kinds of social behaviour. It is interesting, in this regard, that the current treatments for very young children with autism that describe better outcomes (Dawson and Adams, 1984; McEachlin, Smith and Lovaas, 1993; Nadel and Pezé, 1993; Rogers and Lewis, 1989) and improved social and communicative behaviour (as well as improvements in symbolic play) all stress the development of motor imitation skills early in treatment. These findings also support our earlier directional hypotheses that better imitative abilities lead to better social functioning in other areas (Rogers and Pennington, 1991). However, far more work is needed to delineate the effects of imitation on social development.

The construct of emotional contagion seems extremely important in autism. Our information about emotional functioning in autism is currently inconsistent and contradictory. We need careful, programmatic work that will examine multiple facets of emotional experiences, knowledge and responses of persons with autism across development.

Finally, we need to explore more deeply the construct of 'relatedness'. Interpersonal synchrony is expressed in motor behaviour – movements, sounds, facial expressions, postures – the interpersonal 'dance' that we seemingly have from the earliest social encounters. As Meltzoff has suggested, and most of us have experienced in countless social encounters, joining a partner – whether infant or lover – in the dance of movements can quickly create a synchrony of affect and an experience of self–other convergence. It would not require the absence of imitative movements to disrupt this kind of social experience. A consistent disruption in the synchrony, timing and grading of these movements could be sufficient to halt the dance.

REFERENCES

Ayres, A. J. (1985). *Developmental Dyspraxia and Adult Onset Apraxia*. Torrance, CA: Sensor Integration International.

Baldwin, J. M. (1906). *Mental Development in the Child and the Race*, 3rd edn. New York: Augustus Kelly.

Baron-Cohen, S. (1988). Social and pragmatic deficits in autism: cognitive or affective? *Journal of Autism and Developmental Disorders*, 18, 379–402.

Barresi, J. and Moore, C. (1996). Intentional relations and social understanding. *Behavioral and Brain Sciences*, 19, 107–55.

Bartak, L., Rutter, M. and Cox, A. (1975). A comparative study of infantile autism and specific developmental receptive language disorder: I. The children. *British Journal of Psychiatry*, 126, 127–45.

Bruininks, R. (1978). *Bruininks–Osteresky test of motor proficiency*. Minnesota: American Guidance Service.

Bruner, J. S. (1972). Nature and uses of immaturity. *American Psychologist*, 27, 687–708.

Carpenter, M., Tomasello, M. and Savage-Rumbaugh, S. (1995). Joint attention and imitative learning in children, chimpanzees, and enculturated chimpanzees. *Social Development*, 4, 217–37.

Charman, T. and Baron-Cohen, S. (1994). Another look at imitation in autism. *Development and Psychopathology*, 6, 403–13.

Cicchetti, D. (1989). Developmental psychopathology: some thoughts on its evolution. *Development and Psychopathology*, 1, 1–4.

Colbert, E. G., Koegler, R. R. and Markham, C. H. (1958). Toe walking in childhood schizophrenia. *Journal of Pediatrics*, 53, 219–20.

Custance, D. M., Whiten, A. and Bard, K. (1995). Can young chimpanzees (*Pan troglodytes*) imitate arbitrary actions? Hayes and Hayes revisited. *Behavior*, 132, 837–59.

Damasio, A. R. and Maurer, R. G. (1978). A neurological model for childhood autism. *Archives of Neurology*, 35, 777–86.

Dawson, G. (1991). A psychobiological perspective on the early socio-emotional development of children with autism. In D. Cicchetti and S. L. Toth (eds.), *Rochester Symposium on Developmental Psychopathology, volume 3: Models and Integrations* (pp. 207–34). Hillsdale, NJ: Erlbaum.

Dawson, G. and Adams, A. (1984). Imitation and social responsiveness in autistic children. *Journal of Abnormal Child Psychology*, 12, 209–26.

Dawson, G. and Galpert, L. (1990). Mothers' use of imitative play for facilitating social responsiveness and toy play in young autistic children. *Development and Psychopathology*, 2, 151–62.

Dawson, G. and Lewy, A. (1989). Arousal, attention, and the socio-emotional impairments of individuals with autism. In G. Dawson (ed.), *Autism: Nature, Diagnosis, and Treatment* (pp. 49–74). New York: Guilford Press.

De Renzi, E., Motti, F. and Nichelli, P. (1980). Imitating gestures: A quantitative approach to ideomotor apraxia. *Archives Neurological*, 37, 6–10.

DeMyer, M. K. (1976). Motor, perceptual, and intellectual disabilities of autistic children. In L. Wing (ed.), *Early Childhood Autism* (pp. 169–93). Oxford: Pergamon Press.

DeMyer, M. K., Alpern, G. D., Barton, S., DeMeyer, W., Churchill, D. W., Hingtgen, J. N., Bryson, C. Q., Pontius, W. and Kimberlin, C. (1972). Imitation in autistic, early schizophrenic, and nonpsychotic subnormal children. *Journal of Autism and Childhood Schizophrenia*, 2, 264–87.

DeMyer, M. K., Hingtgen, J. N. and Jackson, R. K. (1981). Infantile autism reviewed: A decade of research. *Schizophrenia Bulletin*, 7, 388–451.

Dewey, D. (1993). Error analysis of limb and orofacial praxis in children with developmental motor deficits. *Brain and Cognition*, 23, 203–21.

Donald, M. (1991). *Origins of the Modern Mind*, Cambridge, MA: Harvard University Press.

Dunst, C. J. (1980). *A clinical and educational manual for use with the Užgiris and Hunt scales of infant psychological development*. Baltimore: University Park Press.

Emde, R. N., Katz, E. L. and Thorpe, J. K. (1978). Emotional expression in infancy: II. Early deviations in Down's syndrome. In M. Lewis and L. A. Rosenblum (eds.), *The Development of Affect*, New York: Plenum Press.

Fraiberg, S. (1977). *Insights from the blind: Comparative studies of blind and sighted infants*. New York: New American Library.

Galef, B. F. (1989). Imitation in animals. In T. Zentall and B. F. Galef (eds.), *Comparative Social Learning*, Hillsdale, NJ: Erlbaum.

Ghaziuddin, M., Butler, E., Tsai, L. and Ghaziuddin, N. (1994). Is clumsiness a marker for Asperger syndrome? *Journal of Intellectual Disability Research*, 38, 519–27.

Gillberg, C. (1983). Perceptual, motor, and attentional deficits in Swedish primary school children: Some child psychiatric aspects. *Journal of Child Psychology and Psychiatry*, 24, 377–403.

Gonzalez-Rothi, L. J., Ochipa, C. and Heilman, K. M. (1991). A cognitive neuro-psychological model of limb praxis. *Cognitive Neuropsychology*, 8, 443–58.

Haith, M. M. (1990). Progress in the understanding of sensory and perceptual processes in early infancy. *Merrill-Palmer Quarterly*, 36, 1–26.

Hammes, J. G. W. and Langdell, T. (1981). Precursors of symbol formation and childhood autism. *Journal of Autism and Developmental Disorders*, 11, 331–46.

Hatfield, E., Cacioppo, J. T. and Rapson, R. L. (1994). *Emotional Contagion*, New York: Cambridge University Press.

Heilman, K. M. (1979). Apraxia. In K. M. Heilman and E. Valenstein (eds.), *Clinical Neuropsychology* (pp. 159–85). New York: Oxford University Press.

Hertzig, M. E., Snow, M. E. and Sherman, M. (1989). Affect and cognition in autism. *Journal of the American Academy of Child and Adolescent Psychiatry*, 28, 195–9.

Hobson, R. P. (1986). The autistic child's appraisal of expressions of emotion. *Journal of Child Psychology and Psychiatry*, 27, 321–42.

(1993). *Autism and the development of mind*. Hillsdale, NJ: Erlbaum.

Hughes, C. (1996). Planning problems in autism at the level of motor control. *Journal of Autism and Developmental Disorders*, 26, 99–109.

Jones, V. and Prior, M. (1985). Motor imitation abilities and neurological signs in autistic children. *Journal of Autism and Developmental Disorders*, 15, 37–46.

Kanner, L. (1943). Autistic disturbances of affective contact. *Nervous Child*, 2, 217–50.

Kimura, D. and Archibald, Y. (1974). Motor functions of the left hemisphere. *Brain*, 97, 337–50.

Kohen-Raz, R., Volkmar, F. R. and Cohen, D. J. (1992). Postural control in children with autism. *Journal of Autism and Developmental Disorders*, 22, 419–32.

Kolb, B. and Milner, B. (1981). Performance of complex arm and facial movements after focal brain lesions. *Neuropsychologia*, 19, 505–14.

Lovaas, O. I. (1981). *Teaching Developmentally Disabled Children: The Me Book*, Baltimore: University Park Press.

Manjiviona, J. and Prior, M. (1995). Comparison of Asperger syndrome and High-functioning autistic children on a test of motor impairment. *Journal of Autism and Developmental Disorders*, 25, 23–40.

Mateer, C. and Kimura, D. (1977). Impairment of nonverbal oral movements in apraxia. *Brain and Language*, 4, 262–76.

McEachlin, J. J., Smith, T. and Lovaas, O. I. (1993). Long-term outcome for children with autism who received early intensive behavioral treatment. *American Journal on Mental Retardation*, 97, 359–72.

Meltzoff, A. (1988). Infant imitation after a 1-week delay: Long-term memory for novel acts and multiple stimuli. *Developmental Psychology*, 24, 470–6.

Meltzoff, A. N. (1990). Foundations for developing a concept of self: The role of imitation in relating self to other and the value of social mirroring, social modeling, and self-practice in infancy. In D. Cicchetti (ed.), *The Self in Transition* (pp. 139–64). University of Chicago Press.

Meltzoff, A. and Gopnik, A. (1993). The role of imitation in understanding persons and developing a theory of mind. In S. Baron-Cohen, H. Tager-Flusberg and D. J. Cohen (eds.), *Understanding Other Minds* (pp. 335–66). Oxford: Oxford University Press.

Morgan, S. B., Cutrer, P. S., Coplin, J. W. and Rodriguez, J. R. (1989). Do autistic children differ from retarded and normal children in Piagetian sensorimotor functioning? *Journal of Child Psychology and Psychiatry*, 30, 857–64.

Nadel, J. and Pezé, A. (1993). What makes immediate imitation communicative in toddlers and autistic children? In J. Nadel and L. Camaioni (eds.), *New Perspectives in Early Communication Development* (pp. 139–56). London: Routledge.

Ohta, M. (1987). Cognitive disorders of infantile autism: A study employing the WISC, spatial relationships, conceptualization, and gestural imitation. *Journal of Autism and Developmental Disorders*, 17, 45–62.

Ornitz, E. M. (1973). Childhood autism: A review of the clinical and experimental literature. *California Medicine*, 118, 21–47.

Pennington, B. F. and Ozonoff, S. (1991). A neuroscientific perspective on continuity and discontinuity in developmental psychopathology. In D. Cicchetti and S. L. Toth (eds.), *Rochester Symposium on Developmental Psychopathology, V.3: Models and Integrations*. Rochester, NY: University of Rochester Press.

Premack, D. and Woodruff, G. (1978). Does the chimpanzee have a theory of mind? *Behavioral and Brain Sciences*, 4, 515–26.

Rogers, S. J. (1991). A psychotherapeutic approach for young children with pervasive developmental disorders. *Comprehensive Mental Health Care*, 1, 91–108.

Rogers, S. J., Bennetto, L., McEvoy, R. and Pennington, B. F. (1996). Imitation and pantomime in high functioning adolescents with autism spectrum disorders. *Child Development*, 67, 2060–73.

Rogers, S. J. and Lewis, H. (1989). An effective day treatment model for young children with pervasive developmental disorders. *Journal of the American Academy of Child and Adolescent Psychiatry*, 28, 207–14.

Rogers, S. J. and Pennington, B. F. (1991). A theoretical approach to the deficits in infantile autism. *Development and Psychopathology*, 3, 137–62.

Roy, E. A., Elliott, D., Dewey, D. and Square-Storer, P. (1990). Impairments to praxis and sequencing in adult and developmental disorders. In C. Bard, M. Fleury and L. Hay (eds.), *Development of Eye-hand Coordination Across the Life Span* (pp. 358–84). Columbia, SC: University of South Carolina Press.

Schwartz, M. F., Mayer, N. H., FitzpatrickDeSalme, E. J. and Montgomery, M. W. (1993). Cognitive theory and the study of everyday action disorders after brain damage. *Journal of Head Trauma Rehabilitation*, 8, 59–72.

Sigman, M. and Ungerer, J. (1984). Cognitive and language skills in autistic, mentally retarded, and normal children. *Developmental Psychology*, 20, 293–302.

Smith, I. M. (1995). Imitation and gestural representation in autism. Poster presentation at the Society for Research in Child Development Biennial Conference. Indianapolis, Indiana.

Smith, I. M. and Bryson, S. E. (1994). Imitation and action in autism: A critical review. *Psychological Bulletin*, 116(2), 259–73.

Stern, D. N. (1985). *The Interpersonal World of the Human Infant*. New York: Basic Books.

Tomasello, M. (1995). Joint attention as social cognition. In C. Moore and P. Dunham (eds.), *Joint attention: Its origins and role in development*. Hillsdale, NJ: Erlbaum.

Tomasello, M., Kruger, A. C. and Ratner, H. H. (1993a). Cultural learning. *Behavioral and Brain Sciences*, 16, 495–552.

Tomasello, M., Savage-Rumbaugh, S. and Kruger, A.C. (1993b). Imitative learning of actions on objects by children, chimpanzees, and enculturated chimpanzees. *Child Development*, 64, 1688–705.

Trevarthen, C. (1993). The function of emotions in early infant communication and development. In J. Nadel and L. Camaioni (eds.), *New Perspectives in Early Communicative Development* (pp. 48–81). New York: Routledge.

Užgiris, I. (1991). The social context of infant imitation. In M. Lewis and S. Feinman (eds.), *Social Influences and Socialization in Infancy* (pp. 215–51). New York: Plenum Press.

Užgiris, I. Č. and Hunt, J. McV. (1975). *Assessment in Infancy*. Urbana: University of Illinois Press.

Whiten, A. (1996). Imitation, pretence, and mindreading: secondary representation in comparative primatology and developmental psychology? In A. E.

Russon, K. A. Bard and S. T. Parker (eds.), *Reaching Into Thought: The Minds of the Great Apes* (pp. 300–24). Cambridge University Press.

Whiten, A. and Brown, J. (1997). Imitation and the reading of other minds: perspectives from the study of autism, normal children, and non-human primates. In S. Bråten (ed.), *Intersubjective communication and emotion* in *Ontogeny: A Sourcebook*, Cambridge University Press.

Wing, L. (1981). Asperger's syndrome: A clinical account. *Psychological Medicine*, 11, 115–29.

Yirmiya, N., Sigman, M., Kasari, C. and Mundy, P. (1992). Empathy and cognition in high-functioning children with autism. *Child Development*, 63, 150–60.

Zajonc, R. B., Murphy, S. T. and Inglehart, M. (1989). Feeling and facial efference: Implications of the vascular theory of emotion. *Psychological Review*, 96, 395–416.

Index

288   Index